MW00604957

Women and Public Life in Early Meiji Japan

Michigan Monograph Series in Japanese Studies
Number 71
Center for Japanese Studies
The University of Michigan

Women and Public Life in Early Meiji Japan:
The Development of the Feminist Movement

MARA PATESSIO

Center for Japanese Studies
The University of Michigan
Ann Arbor   2011

Copyright © 2011 by The Regents of the University of Michigan

All rights reserved.

Published by the Center for Japanese Studies,
The University of Michigan
1007 E. Huron St.
Ann Arbor, MI 48104-1690

Library of Congress Cataloging-in-Publication Data

Patessio, Mara, 1975–
    Women and public life in early Meiji Japan : the development of the feminist movement /
Mara Patessio.
    p. cm. — (Michigan monograph series in Japanese studies ; no. 71)
    Includes bibliographical references and index.
    ISBN 978-1-929280-66-7 (hbk. : alk. paper) — ISBN 978-1-929280-67-4
(pbk. : alk. paper)
    1. Women—Japan—History—19th century.   2. Women—Japan—History—
20th century.   3. Feminism—Japan—History—19th century.   4. Feminism—
Japan—History—20th century.   5. Japan—History—1868–   I. Title.   II. Series.

HQ1762.P38 2011
305.48'8956009034—dc22

                                                        2010050270

This book was set in Times New Roman.
Kanji was set in Hiragino Mincho Pro.

This publication meets the ANSI/NISO Standards for Permanence of Paper for
Publications and Documents in Libraries and Archives (Z39.48–1992).

Printed in the United States of America

Contents

Acknowledgments   vii

1 Early Meiji Women and the Public Sphere   1

2 Female Students and Teachers
   in Private and Public Schools   33

3 Foreign Women Missionaries
   and Their Japanese Female Charges   71

4 Women's Groups and Their Activities   107

5 Women's Political Participation   141

6 Conclusions and a Step Forward   173

Bibliography   195

Index   223

Acknowledgments

A number of individuals have helped me with this project in various ways over the past ten years. My PhD would not have been finished without the generous support, help, and direction of my supervisor, Professor Peter Kornicki. Now that I am a teacher myself, I better appreciate the amount of time and help he devoted to my research. I hope with this book I have not let him down.

Discussions with Dr. Francesca Orsini, Dr. Susan Daruvala, Dr. Mark Morris, Dr. Chiara Ghidini, Dr. Anya Andreeva, Dr. Anna Boermel, Dr. Darren Aoki, Dr. Sean Bready, Dr. Tracey Gannon, Dr. Gaye Rowley, and Dr. Barak Kushner stimulated new ideas. I am really grateful to them for the time and meals they shared with me.

While a PhD student, the generous support of the Japan Foundation Endowment Committee enabled me to do research in Japan. My research in Japan would not have been so successful without the help and generosity of all the archivists and librarians of the various schools opened for girls during the Meiji period that I visited, as well as the archivists at Tokyo University's Meiji Shinbun Zasshi Bunko, who always helped me locate hard to find Meiji period articles. Their time and expertise have been invaluable. In Cambridge, the Japanese studies librarian, Mr. Noboru Koyama, as well as Mrs. Kazumi Cunnison, always found the time to answer my questions. To them I am most grateful.

After completing my PhD, I went to Japan with a postdoctoral scholarship from the Japan Society for the Promotion of Science and collaborated with Professor Ogawa Mariko for a year. Her help in obtaining the scholarship was crucial for the development of my project. While there I was able to participate in the activities of Ochanomizu University's Gender Study Center, and I want to thank Professor Tachi Kaoru, Professor Ito Ruri, soon to be Dr. Hasegawa Kazumi, and all the graduate students for allowing me to become a member of their group. Meeting Cynthia Enloe, who was a visiting professor at the center, was like being catapulted into a new world.

Although at that point Cambridge seemed to be a closed chapter in my life, Professor Peter Kornicki, not having done enough for me already, was granted funding from the Leverhulme Trust for a collaborative project, and I found myself in Cambridge for two additional years. Part of that time was spent doing research in

Acknowledgments

Japan, and I want to thank in particular Mr. Kawao Toyoshi, director of Takinogawa Gakuen, for opening its doors to me.

While in Cambridge I was fortunate enough to meet Dr. Naoko Shimazu, who not only gave me a temporary lectureship at Birkbeck, University of London, but also became a precious supporter and friend. Her suggestions and discussions have been extremely important for my career's development, and I hope to be able to count on her friendship and support in the coming years as well.

My colleagues at the University of Manchester, where I work now, and especially Professor Ian Reader and Mr. Jonathan Bunt, have been extremely positive toward my work and have allowed me to bring it to a conclusion. After working with Professor Kornicki, I thought it would be impossible to find such a congenial environment in which to work, but I was wrong. Further financial support by the Japan Foundation Endowment Committee allowed me to bring this project to a close.

The two anonymous readers of my manuscript made many important suggestions that strengthened my theories and the way in which I presented them. Susan Meehan kindly consented to go through this work and helped me with its style. Janet Opdyke, my copyeditor, and Bruce Willoughby, executive editor of the Michigan Monograph Series in Japanese Studies, gave the manuscript its final push. Thank you.

Some of the arguments developed in the following chapters were first attempted in the articles "Western Women Missionaries and Their Japanese Female Charges, 1880–1890," *Women's History Review* 16.2 (2007): 59–77 (journal website: http://www.informaworld.com); "The Creation of Public Spaces by Women in the Early Meiji Period and the Tōkyō Fujin Kyōfūkai," *The International Journal of Asian Studies*, 3.2 (2006): 155–82 (published by Cambridge University Press); and "Women's Participation in the Popular Rights Movement (Jiyū Minken Undō) during the Early Meiji Period," *U.S.-Japan Women's Journal* 27 (2004): 3–26 (© Josai International Center for the Promotion of Arts and Sciences, Josai University).

To my family and to Andrew words fail me.

1

Early Meiji Women and the Public Sphere

Beyond the wall on one side of our school was a rough path leading past several small villages, with ricefields and patches of clover scattered between. One day, when a teacher was taking a group of us girls for a walk, we came upon a dry ricefield dotted with wild flowers. We were gathering them with merry chattering and laughter when two village farmers passed by, walking slowly and watching us curiously. "What is the world coming to," said one, "when workable-age young misses waste time wandering about through bushes and wild grass?" "They are grasshoppers trying to climb the mountain," the other replied, "but the sun will scorch them with scorn. There can be only pity for the young man who takes one of those for his bride." . . . We walked on homeward. Just as we reached our gate in the hedge wall one of the girls, who had been rather quiet, turned to me. "Nevertheless," she said, defiantly, "the grasshoppers *are* climbing the mountain into the sunlight."[1]

In recent years, an ever-increasing amount of scholarship has been published in English on Japanese women. On the one hand, the Edo period (1603–1867) has long been regarded as an age of female oppression, but recent publications show that this was not always the case.[2] On the other hand, the activities and opinions of Taishō (1912–26) and Shōwa (1926–89) women, as opposed to women of earlier periods, are easier to investigate as the number of published articles written by

---

1. Etsu Sugimoto, *A Daughter of the Samurai* (North Clarendon: Tuttle, 1990), 143–44.
2. See, for example, Martha Tocco, "Norms and Texts for Women's Education in Tokugawa Japan," in *Women and Confucian Cultures in Premodern China, Korea, and Japan,* edited by Dorothy Ko, Jahyun Kim Haboush, and Joan Piggott, 193–218 (Berkeley: University of California Press, 2003); and P. F. Kornicki, Mara Patessio, and G. G. Rowley, eds., *The Female as Subject: Reading and Writing in Early Modern Japan,* Michigan Monograph Series in Japanese Studies, no. 70 (Ann Arbor: Center for Japanese Studies, University of Michigan, 2010).

women increased significantly from the 1910s onward, and a great deal has been written on their lifestyles, occupations, writings, and the discourses they initiated. They are represented as extremely vocal in their demands for social and political rights and in expressing their opinions.[3]

Scholars have focused less on late-nineteenth-century women. Late-nineteenth-century books containing the words *women, girls,* or *married women* in their titles were mostly written by men who were concerned with the reform of the condition of women and with women's roles in society, making it harder to gain an accurate picture of what women themselves thought.[4] Most of the early Meiji (1868–90) women who contributed to the print media submitted their articles to periodicals owned by men who probably edited and filtered them, and they often did not sign their articles or used pen names, partly in fear of being accused of overstepping social boundaries.

Consequently, it is more difficult to evaluate early Meiji women's opinions on contemporary Japanese society and their participation in public activities and the developing print culture. Nevertheless, if the early twentieth century showed a steep rise in Japanese women's public activities, the question of how this was made possible is still unanswered. Were Taishō women able to cunningly negotiate public spaces within "male society" from which to launch their activities or had such spaces already been formed in previous decades and therefore their appropriation by Taishō women was not an issue?

The existing Japanese and English scholarship on early Meiji women only partially answers this question. Sharon Sievers has shown how 1880s "women" became a topic of debate among male intellectuals and how some individual women managed to take part in these debates. Rebecca Copeland has studied women involved in literary production who expanded the boundaries of acceptable female public behavior. Sharon Nolte and Sally Hastings and Patricia Tsurumi have described the ways in which "Meiji women" were objects of government legislation and exploitation.[5]

---

3. Vera Mackie, *Feminism in Modern Japan: Citizenship, Embodiment, and Sexuality* (Cambridge: Cambridge University Press, 2003); and *Creating Socialist Women in Japan: Gender, Labour, and Activism, 1900–1937* (Cambridge: Cambridge University Press, 1997). See also Tomida Hiroko and Gordon Daniels, *Japanese Women: Emerging from Subservience, 1868–1945* (Folkestone: Global Oriental, 2005); and Jan Bardsley, *The Bluestockings of Japan: New Woman Essays and Fiction from Seito, 1911–1916,* Michigan Monograph Series in Japanese Studies, no. 60 (Ann Arbor: Center for Japanese Studies, University of Michigan, 2007).

4. For example, see Kakita Junrō, ed., *Fujin oyobi kasei* (Women and household management) (Min'yūsha, 1888); and Yoshizumi Junzō, ed., *Onna kyōkun yomeiri dōgu* (A dowry of moral lessons for brides-to-be) (Osaka: Satō Shingi, 1880). I would like to thank Thomas Harper for suggesting the translation of this last book title.

5. Sharon Sievers, *Flowers in Salt: The Beginnings of Feminist Consciousness in Modern Japan* (Stanford: Stanford University Press, 1983); Rebecca Copeland, *Lost Leaves: Women Writers of Meiji Japan* (Honolulu: University of Hawai'i Press, 2000); Sharon Nolte and Sally Hastings. "The

If the history of Japanese women is analyzed diachronically, Meiji women tend to be represented as powerless, for they did not have nor did they attain the social and political rights enjoyed by some Meiji men. Tokuza, for example, writes that "The Meiji period thus altered, reinforced, and exploited the continued subjugation of women; the Japanese women's movement began in earnest only after that period ended."[6] In *Japanese Women: Emerging from Subservience, 1868–1945*, Tomida and Daniels have argued that "Even after the Meiji Restoration in 1868, women's status was not significantly improved, except for the availability of expanded higher education and marginally broadened job prospects. Many pieces of the new legislation, including the Meiji Constitution of 1889 and the Meiji Civil Code of 1898, were introduced, but they hardly provided women with any legal, political and social security."[7]

Works on early Meiji women often concentrate on individual women, girls' schools, or women's activities in a particular environment.[8] There were many remarkable women living and working during the early Meiji period, but the danger of focusing on a limited number of them is that these individuals are then considered to have been the only women who were active in public spaces. The first aim of this work, then, is to demonstrate that the individual remarkable women we know of were but representatives of larger social and political women's movements.

To be sure, some studies have adopted a perspective more revealing of social change by presenting the history of nursing and medicine, missionaries' work in Japan, or Meiji schools and the girls studying in them.[9] Books on local women's histories and collections of Meiji newspaper articles afford access to women's

Meiji State's Policy toward Women, 1890–1910," in *Recreating Japanese Women, 1600–1945*, edited by Gail Lee Bernstein, 151–74 (Berkeley: University of California Press, 1991); and Patricia Tsurumi, *Factory Girls: Women in the Thread Mills of Meiji Japan* (Princeton: Princeton University Press, 1990).

6. Akiko Tokuza, *The Rise of the Feminist Movement in Japan* (Tokyo: Keio University Press, 1999), 48. Hirota also writes that the Japanese women's movement and women's active participation in public society date from the late Meiji period when women first developed an awareness of their sex as something in which to take pride, broke out of the framework of *ryōsai kenbo* (good wives, wise mothers), and tried to reduce the constraints placed on women. Masaki Hirota, "Notes on the 'Process of Creating Women' in the Meiji Period," in *Gender and Japanese History*, edited by Wakita Haruko, Anne Bouchy, and Ueno Chizuko, vol. 2, 197–219 (Osaka: Osaka University Press, 1999), 214.

7. Tomida and Daniels, *Japanese Women*, 1–2.

8. See, for example, Barbara Rose, *Tsuda Umeko and Women's Education in Japan* (New Haven: Yale University Press, 1992); and Elizabeth Eder, *Constructing Opportunity: American Women Educators in Early Meiji Japan* (Lanham, Md.: Lexington Books, 2003).

9. See, for example, Kameyama Michiko, *Onnatachi no yakusoku: M. T. Tsuru to nihon saisho no kangofu gakkō* (A promise made among women: M. T. True and the first school for female nurses in Japan) (Kyoto: Jinbun shoin, 1990); Kohiyama Rui, *America fujin senkyōshi* (American women missionaries) (Tokyo daigaku shuppankai, 1992); Aoyama Nao, *Yasui Tetsu to Tokyo joshi daigaku* (Yasui Tetsu and Tokyo Women's University) (Keio tsūshin, 1982); and idem., *Meiji jogakkō no kenkyū* (A study of Meiji *jogakkō*) (Keio tsūshin, 1970).

3

activities at the regional and national levels, so it is no longer possible to argue that early Meiji women, as a category, were excluded from public activities during the 1880s.[10] Nevertheless, these works do not in themselves form a composite picture of the ways in which women were active within a particular environment *and* across borders. They do not show, for example, the ways in which women activists were linked to girl students or how the actions of one group of women impacted the lives of another. Missing is a historical analysis demonstrating how early Meiji women's groups and their activities were interconnected and why these links were significant. To redress this omission is the second aim of my work.

This book concentrates on a short period, roughly the first twenty years of the Meiji period (the entire period lasted from 1868 to 1912), years in which Japanese institutions underwent far-reaching changes partially motivated by North American and European models. I decided to concentrate on a short period in order to introduce a significant number of individuals and groups that were active in the capital and elsewhere. I present the links these women established with each other, and I do so in order to re-present them as participants in the formation of new ideas and cultural identities, in dialogues with the authorities, and in the search for social and political empowerment. Finally, I argue that by understanding their roles in early Meiji public society we can gain a better and more accurate picture of the period as a whole.

This work does not present a national map of all feminist activities in the early Meiji period for we lack the necessary primary material to complete such a project while, as Kornicki has argued, regional differences in early Meiji Japan were still very marked.[11] I concentrate mainly on Tokyo and other major cities for it was there that schools for girls were opened, girl students could meet women missionaries, numerous *enzetsukai* (public speech meetings) were organized, it was easier to access published material, and women could find supporters for their cause. When some of these conditions were met in other regions, for example when missionaries sent their former students to open or work in girls' schools in the provinces, it was likely that more women's activities developed in those areas as well. On the other hand, it was in certain provinces, such as Kochi and Okayama, that male political groups supported women's political activities, and so in those areas we find many

10. Aoki Mitsuko and Mitsuda Kyōko, eds., *Minkenki Okayama joseishi kankei shiryō* (Historical records related to the history of women in Okayama during the Minken period), vol. 4 of *Okayama minken undōshi kankei shiryōshū* (Collection of historical records related to the history of the Okayama Minken movement) (Okayama: Okayama Minken undō hyakunen kinen gyōji jikkō iinkai, 1982).
11. P. F. Kornicki, "Women, Education, and Literacy," in *The Female as Subject: Reading and Writing in Early Modern Japan*, edited by P. F. Kornicki, Mara Patessio, and G. G. Rowley, Michigan Monograph Series in Japanese Studies, no. 70 (Ann Arbor: Center for Japanese Studies, University of Michigan, 2010), 7–37.

examples of such activities. The information and analysis presented here form a picture of the patterns women employed in order to find supporters for their causes and public spaces in which to voice them, and of the ways in which the seeds for the formation of a feminist movement were sown.

A Prosopographical Approach

Given the problems inherent in relying on widely dispersed primary sources, and in any attempted representation of women's past experience, a partly prosopographical approach to the questions addressed in this book seems the most suitable course. Stone has defined prosopography as the "investigation of the common background characteristics of a group of actors in history by means of a collective study of their lives. The method employed is to establish a universe to be studied, and then to ask a set of uniform questions—about birth and death, marriage and family, social origins and inherited economic position" in order to establish the social and economic roots of political action or to examine and account for social structure and mobility.[12] In other words, by looking at the details in individuals' lives (level of education, nature of employment, marital status, and so on) it is possible to deduce how society changes over time and how those changes are brought about.

Since a large part of the primary material investigated here relates to the experiences and activities of individual women, any study of women as a category has to generate a collective picture from the mass of individual cases, but here a systematic examination of the individual cases as espoused by Stone and other demographers is out of the question given the patchy nature of the available sources. For example, even when we have some biographical details about the girls and women who wrote articles for the print media or participated in women's groups, their lives often remain obscure, and when analyzing how girl students tried to use the education obtained at school to better their social position, only the lives of a few of them are traceable. I have tried to preserve the individuality of each woman presented, for behind the "common background" of Japanese women as a category lie individual differences that highlight the horizon of possibilities available to them, but since this has not always been possible due to the lack of systematic information, the answers given to some questions have to be tentative. This is also why I decided to keep the presentation of statistics about girls' literacy and school attendance to a minimum. Tachi writes that the percentage of girls attending primary schools

12. Lawrence Stone, *The Past and the Present* (London: Routledge, 1981), 45–46. *Prosopography*, a term employed especially in classical studies, has also been defined as "collective biography" by historians of the modern period. I would like to thank Dr. Anna Beerens for introducing me to the concept of prosopography.

during the Meiji period was 15 percent in 1873, 28 percent in 1887, and finally 90 percent in 1903. In the various kōtō jogakkō, which offered secondary education for girls, there were 286 students in 1882, 2,363 in 1887, and 12,000 in 1900.[13] However, these statistics and data become almost meaningless when we are faced with girls who were enrolled at school but attended sporadically, attended courses in more than one school, or did not finish their course of study—all of which were common at that time.

Nevertheless, the prosopographical analysis of the data concerning these individuals can tell us a great deal not only about the links they formed with like-minded women and men, and the patterns they established in order to express their opinions and bring forth their criticism of society and women's place in it, but also about the period in which they lived, the institutions of which they were a part, and the general mentality of their times. A large number of the women presented here grew up or began their education in the Edo period. Some were married to men who supported their ambitions or, having converted to Christianity, left their wives relatively free to pursue activities organized by missionaries. Others had a family but became teachers and participated in women's groups as a means of increasing their knowledge. Finally, many girls and women started traveling within Japan to obtain an education or take up employment as teachers in government or missionary schools and formed networks of women that were not connected to each other through family relations or proximity but through common interests.[14] These were exceptional women, but they show us what was possible and thinkable during the early Meiji period.

Social class, economic background, and education almost always played a decisive part in both women's and men's lives, but exclusion and class segregation were not universal. Much of this book deals with middle- and upper-middle-class women who could afford to be educated and had free time that could be used to organize or participate in women's meetings, to find information about Western women's lives, and to read widely. However, some schools and political groups organized public speech meetings in which poorer women were active as well, while

13. Tachi Kaoru, "Ryōsai kenbo" (Good wives, wise mothers), in Kōza joseigaku (Lectures on women's studies), vol. 1, Onna no imeji (Images of women), edited by Joseigaku kenkyūkai, 184–209 (Keisō shobō, 1984), 188. Boys' attendance at the elementary level was higher. The rate was 39.9 percent in 1873, 67.2 percent in 1883, and 98.8 percent in 1911. Murakami Toshiaki and Sakata Yoshio, eds., Kyōiku, dōtoku hen (On education and morals), vol. 3 of Meiji bunka shi (A cultural history of the Meiji period), edited by Kaikoku hyakunen kinen bunka jigyōkai (Yōyōsha, 1955), 248, cited in Mikiso Hane, Peasants, Rebels, Women, and Outcastes: The Underside of Modern Japan (Lanham, Md.: Rowman and Littlefield, 2003), 322, n. 42.

14. Hatoyama Haruko, for example, wrote that the first time she left home was to study in Tokyo. Hatoyama Haruko, Waga jijoden (Telling my life) (Nihon tosho Center, [1929] 1997), 50.

a number of poor girls came into contact with women missionaries and their education. Although the activities of middle-class women were and are more visible, and they created networks that are easier to trace, their discourses also reached other groups of women of whom, unfortunately, we do not yet know enough.

It is also a prosopographical collection of biographies that reveals how, even though marriage was a stepping-stone in the lives of early Meiji women, some were able to postpone theirs for a while because they were spending more years at school, or how others could participate in women's groups or write about women's issues after divorcing their husbands or because they had jobs to support themselves. I am not implying that most divorced women automatically became activists, and divorce was certainly not new for Japanese women, but the novelty lies in how they used the possibilities they had in the Meiji period to change the direction of their lives.

A prosopographical approach is also important when we want to look at the audience individual women addressed and the links they established with other women. We know a great deal about the ways in which the thoughts of some early Meiji women were shaped and what kind of ideas they espoused in public, but they turn out not to have been the only ones who contributed to new movements and the spread of women's discourses. Although some opened up new paths for the next generation, other girls sought higher education in Japan or abroad or launched powerful criticisms of society from within their schools and the women's groups. Women's groups that were founded in relatively small towns might not have reached an interregional audience and might not have lasted as long as larger and better-known national organizations did, but their existence did not go unnoticed in those areas because of press coverage for even relatively small towns boasted their own newspapers. This does not mean that women could freely participate in women's activities organized in their areas, nor that all women's groups were feminist groups, but there is evidence of women who became conscious of social debates through the media and decided that they, too, wanted to take part, or of women who read of groups formed in some distant part of the country and decided to launch one themselves, or again of women who became social activists, enthused by those they heard speaking.

Early Meiji Women and Public Spaces

Early Meiji women's first struggle was to gain access to public spaces where they could discuss their ideas and formulate their demands. As Peiss has argued in another context, it was not that Japanese women had not been involved in production, barter, and exchange in public spaces before; both Edo and Meiji women had been and indeed were visible in public spaces, whether as farmers, teachers, factory workers, or market vendors.[15]

Early Meiji women were not the first to participate in political activities either. Peasant protests and riots were a part of political life during the Edo period and continued to be so throughout the Meiji period and beyond. Walthall has uncovered the stories of Edo peasant women who challenged conventional restrictions on what they were supposed to know about politics and managed to obtain greater access to public spaces and bring their demands to the authorities. These Edo peasant women were reported as having stated that they had to speak up because there were no men on their side and in order to maintain the patrilineal family. Walthall has argued that signatures added by Edo women to petitions drafted by villagers meant that when they were heads of households their right and duty to participate in village affairs were recognized and that women had begun to join men in confrontations with the authorities.[16] Walthall's study of Matsuo Taseko 松尾多勢子 (1811–94), the wife of a village head who in 1862 went to Kyoto and took part in the movement to "revere the Emperor and expel the barbarians," also unravels the history of an Edo woman who circumvented social conventions of female behavior and extended her sphere of action to the public and political sphere. Walthall argues that this was possible because Matsuo was in her fifties and had already fulfilled the expectations Edo society entertained in regard to women; before going to Kyoto she married and had children, helped her family's financial situation by breeding silkworms, and finally became a widow. She was an educated woman whose social position had allowed her time to study and to travel.[17] Some Edo women were indeed groping for a public role and were engaging in activities beyond the realm of the private. However, the social worlds in which these women moved were almost entirely male and their activities were not critical of patriarchal institutions. As Walthall explains, Matsuo Taseko joined the Hirata school of *kokugaku* (national learning), which did not favor female students, and then in Kyoto she met male scholars, male activists, and male students. Edo women's lack of female companions or associates does not diminish the importance of such individuals within Japanese women's history, nor does it diminish the exceptional public role they played, but it marks a critical distinction between Edo and early Meiji women.

---

15. Kathy Peiss, "Going Public: Women in Nineteenth-Century Cultural History," *American Literary History* 3.4 (1991): 823.

16. Anne Walthall, "Devoted Wives/Unruly Women: Invisible Presence in the History of Japanese Social Protest," *Signs* 20.1 (1994): 106–36; "Edo Riots," in *Edo and Paris: Urban Life and the State in the Early Modern Era*, edited by James L. McClain, John M. Merriman, and Ugawa Kaoru, 407–28 (Ithaca: Cornell University Press, 1994).

17. Anne Walthall, *The Weak Body of a Useless Woman: Matsuo Taseko and the Meiji Restoration* (Chicago: University of Chicago Press, 1998). Other women traveled to Kyoto on political business during the Edo period. Shiba Keiko, *Kinsei onna tabi nikki* (Early modern women's travel diaries) (Yoshikawa kōbunkan, 1997).

The early Meiji women presented here also participated in political activities, joining forces with men, challenging conventional norms, and bringing their demands to the authorities. As with Edo women, the cases presented in this work reveal educated women acting in, and reflecting on, political issues of which they considered themselves a part, but, in contrast to Edo women, they also helped shape the image of a society in which women were able to establish networks with other like-minded women and were active organizers of new gendered public spaces in which they could discuss political issues, thereby forming the basis of a women's movement.

During the 1870s, articles about women appeared in magazines and newspapers that were either not written for a female audience or, being published by men for a female public, distorted women's views and goals through a journalistic prism. By the early 1880s, instead, Japanese women were obtaining up-to-date information about women's social and political activities that were being organized in different areas and reported in the print media and started writing their own articles on those topics in the same media, which were now giving them space. As a matter of fact, a large part of the primary sources I use here comes from the periodical press. Compared to the Edo period, early Meiji women became more prominent in public by writing about their activities in periodicals and books.

The public spaces early Meiji women accessed helped them to form and discuss their opinions and to publicize their own visions of their imagined community and their own ideas about nationalistic Japanese women, both concepts that I discuss below. These women made some male intellectuals nervous when they engaged in public activities together, showing that there were forces at work that opposed government directives and legislation and that had to be taken seriously. They challenged the authorities through the public use of their reasoning, and the interesting point is not just how they structured their reasoning but also how the authorities tried to find answers to their requests that would not disturb the status quo, producing new forms of subordination in order to maintain the existing social order.

How did women manage to form new female spaces from which to challenge existing social norms and legislation? This is another question that is fundamental to my research, and in order to answer it I employ the concept of "public sphere," expanding and reconceptualizing it to include Japanese women as well.

Jürgen Habermas has argued that the public sphere was formed by groups of private people who used discussion as a medium through which to deliberate about common concerns, thus participating in public activities.[18] Such activities, and the spaces in which they were organized, were distinct from "the state" and

---

18. Jürgen Habermas, *The Structural Transformation of the Public Sphere: An Inquiry into a Category of Bourgeois Society* (Cambridge, Mass.: MIT Press, 1991), esp. 25–27.

often critical of its ideology. They were also separated from the state economy, or, in Fraser's words, the official economy, since those spaces were not set up to sell, buy, or exchange goods but in order to facilitate dialogue with other groups or the authorities and to publicize new topics in the public arena.[19] Although Habermas has applied his theorization of the "public sphere" exclusively to European realities during the seventeenth and eighteenth centuries, in the past few years numerous fruitful applications of his basic interpretive framework to analyze different realities and periods have been proposed.[20]

In the case of early Meiji women, the theoretical definition Habermas developed creates an imagined sphere in which female communities could be formed, shaped, and defined. I use it heuristically to provide a framework for comprehending the disparate activities and discourses engaged in public by women. Thus, the term *public sphere* is employed here to define the totality of the individual public spaces available to Japanese men and women, whereas I intend the terms *public space* or *public spaces* to indicate individual spaces within the more overarching public sphere. Once we understand the public sphere as the site where different groups living in different areas expressed different ideas through various mediums, forming numerous public spaces that were at times separate and at times linked, it is easier to see how these (unrelated) actors were actually working within the same public sphere and thus were able to become an important social and political force.

Early Meiji women themselves, also because of the substantial rise in the number of women participating in the expanding print culture, considered their activities to be interventions in the public, open, shared, and growing Meiji public sphere. For example, the president of the Tokyo fujin kyōfūkai 東京婦人矯風会, a group I discuss in chapter 4 that was formed during the mid-1880s with the aim of reforming Japanese society, urged women "to assist their husbands in the home and to help men in the world," for it was their responsibility to "work in public and private life (*naigai kōshi*)."[21] If we neglect these women's involvement in the formation of the early Meiji public sphere and consider their work as separate from main-

19. Nancy Fraser, "Rethinking the Public Sphere: A Contribution to the Critique of Actually Existing Democracy," in *Habermas and the Public Sphere*, edited by Craig Calhoun, 109–42 (Cambridge, Mass.: MIT Press, 1999), 111.

20. Orsini has applied it to the Hindu public sphere during the 1920s and 1930s. Francesca Orsini, *The Hindi Public Sphere, 1920–1940: Language and Literature in the Age of Nationalism* (Oxford: Oxford University Press, 2002). Chalmers has applied it to the formation of a Nepali public sphere. Rhoderick Chalmers, "'We Nepalis': Language, Literature, and the Formation of a Nepali Public Sphere in India, 1914–1940," PhD diss., School of Oriental and African Studies, 2003. And Eger and her colleagues have applied it to women in eighteenth-century England. Elizabeth Eger, Charlotte Grant, Cliona O Gallchoir, and Penny Warburton, eds., *Women, Writing, and the Public Sphere, 1700–1830* (Cambridge: Cambridge University Press, 2006). As for Japanese women, Mackie has dealt with women's participation in public activities, especially during the twentieth century, in her *Feminism in Modern Japan* and *Creating Socialist Women*.

21. *Jogaku zasshi*, no. 70, 06.08.1887, 192, also published in *Chōya shinbun*, no. 4148, 06.08.1887, 3.

stream society and the development of new Meiji institutions and ideas, it becomes impossible to grasp the full development of Meiji civil society.

How are we to define *civil society* in relation to the early Meiji period? Habermas has been widely criticized for not having included *women* in his discussion of European public societies, but his definition of *civil society* nicely fits my purpose.[22] He has argued that civil society can be understood as comprising those "spontaneously emergent associations, organizations, and movements that, attuned to how societal problems resonate in the private life spheres, distill and transmit such reactions in amplified form to the public sphere." "Moving in from this outermost periphery," Habermas continues, "such issues force their way into newspapers and interested associations, clubs, professional organizations, academies, and universities. They find forums, citizen initiatives, and other platforms before they can catalyze the growth of social movements and new subcultures. The latter can in turn dramatize contributions, presenting them so effectively that the mass media take up the matter."[23] What is the difference, then, between society and civil society? Kim writes that it lies "not so much in class differences as in the public consciousness and organizational capacity of the latter's constituents."[24] Following this definition, I argue that what early Meiji women did was to organize associations through which to define new topics of public debate and to influence the ones already circulating. These associations, which often were quite small to start with, were publicized in magazines and newspapers, and the topics they debated were criticized and publicized as well, reaching a wider audience. The growing power of such voices meant that women's criticism and demands for change were sometimes transformed into national movements to be reckoned with and dealt with by the government and intellectuals.

Public Rights, Public Opinion, and Public Discussion (Discourses)

The word *public* can be found in the early Meiji period in relation to political rights. The Newspaper Regulation of 1887, for example, used the term *kōken* (citizenship, political rights), which literally means "public rights," whereas *kōmin*,

---

22. For a criticism of Habermas's exclusion of women, see Nancy Fraser, *Unruly Practices: Power, Discourse, and Gender in Contemporary Social Theory* (Minneapolis: University of Minnesota Press, 1989); "Politics, Culture, and the Public Sphere: Toward a Postmodern Conception," in *Social Postmodernism: Beyond Identity Politics*, edited by Linda Nicholson and Steven Seidman, 287–314 (Cambridge: Cambridge University Press, 1995); and "Rethinking the Public Sphere." See also Johanna Meehan, ed., *Feminists Read Habermas: Gendering the Subject of Discourse* (London: Routledge, 1995).
23. Jürgen Habermas, *Between Facts and Norms: Contributions to a Discourse Theory of Law and Democracy* (Oxford: Polity Press, 1996), 367, 381. See also Frank J. Schwartz and Susan J. Pharr, eds., *The State of Civil Society in Japan* (Cambridge: Cambridge University Press, 2003).
24. Kyu Hyun Kim, *The Age of Visions and Arguments: Parliamentarianism and the National Public Sphere in Early Meiji Japan* (Cambridge, Mass.: Harvard University Press, 2007), 6.

"public people," were those who held political rights.[25] Who had political rights? Not women. We will see in chapter 5 that at the beginning of the Meiji period some women managed for a limited period to vote in local assemblies, but that was rectified very quickly, thus making them an anomaly rather than the result of a conscious decision on the part of the central government to extend citizenship to women. Contrary to Habermas, who has argued—and has repeatedly been proved mistaken—that women did not have any part in political life, we also know that there were women who explicitly demanded the right to vote during the early Meiji period, although their requests were rejected by the government. In fact, even male citizenship was limited, for Japanese men had to be the head of a household and possess a certain amount of wealth before they were able to assume an active political role.[26]

Meiji men and women were not seen "as possessing inherent natural rights, but as enjoying only the benefits conferred on them by a benign sovereign in return for their loyalty and obedience," and, as Mackie has argued, the gendered nature of their subjecthood was clear.[27] This is especially evident in the Civil Code promulgated in 1898 (discussed in chapter 4), which made explicit women's dependence on the patriarchal family, the basis of the *kazoku-kokka* (family-state). Some public figures, such as Sasaki Toyoju and Ueki Emori (discussed in chapters 4 and 5), had during the 1880s written about *jinmin*, the Japanese "people," but the Meiji Constitution, promulgated in 1889, spoke instead of "subjects," *shinmin*.[28] Although some of the women discussed in this work had hoped to obtain more social and property rights, the Civil Code shattered their hopes.

Mackie has argued that it is nevertheless helpful to consider the concept of citizenship when analyzing the ways in which women acted in early Meiji society. Citizenship is understood "in the context of the legal and institutional structures

25. The Shinbunshi jōrei 新聞紙条例 (Newspaper Regulation) and its revisions are reprinted in Matsumoto Sannosuke and Yamamuro Shinichi, *Genron to media* (Debate and the media), vol. 11 of *Nihon kindai shisō taikei* (Collection on modern Japanese thought) (Iwanami shoten, 1990), 410–25. See Kim, *The Age of Visions*, 203, for *kōmin*. *Public* and *private* were not terms invented during the Meiji period; they existed before and were used in ways that differed from Meiji usage. On the ways in which the meanings of *public* and *private* changed during the long Edo period, see Tetsuo Najita, *Visions of Virtue in Tokugawa Japan: The Kaitokudō Merchant Academy of Osaka* (Chicago: University of Chicago Press, 1987), chap. 6; Kim, *The Age of Visions*, 48–57; and Germaine A. Hoston, "Civil Society and the Public Sphere in the Construction of Modernity in Japanese Political Thought," paper presented at the annual meeting of the American Political Science Association, Washington, D.C., 2005.

26. In 1890 the Japanese electorate of 450,000 comprised only 1.1 percent of the population. Carol Gluck, *Japan's Modern Myths: Ideology in the Late Meiji Period* (Princeton: Princeton University Press, 1985), 67.

27. Tessa Morris-Suzuki, *Re-inventing Japan: Time, Space, Nation* (London: M. E. Sharpe, 1998), 188; Mackie, *Feminism in Modern Japan*, 24.

28. Morris-Suzuki, *Re-inventing Japan*, 188; Sotozaki Mitsuhiro, *Ueki Emori to onnatachi* (Ueki Emori and women) (Domesu, 1976), 183–84.

which determine who has the legal right to participate in the political systems of voting and elected governments." Rights are matched by duties such as individuals' liability for taxation and the performance of military service. Following this definition, the majority of the Japanese people were subjects not citizens. However, as Mackie points out, individuals can behave as citizens even when they are not considered so by the state, and so the term *citizenship* implies the possibility of participating in public discourse on issues over which individuals or groups have common concerns.[29] In this work, I argue that this is precisely what early Meiji women did. The term *public opinion* (*kōron* or *yoron*) was used during the period under consideration in government documents and by intellectuals in relation to the debates over which form the Meiji government should take.[30] Although these documents were concerned with upper-middle-class *male* public opinion, the early Meiji women presented here had opinions about circulating discourses as well and sought—successfully—to make them public. Their goal was to influence public opinion by participating in public discussions about topics which concerned them.

For the majority of the women introduced here, rather than the right to vote or be elected, it was the right to listen to political debates and be informed about national or international matters that was important. They were interested in obtaining a political education. They argued that women had to first obtain more education, property rights, employment opportunities, and rights within the family. They tried to influence male political decisions from outside electoral channels by asking for new laws regulating prostitution, divorce, higher education, and property rights among others. They thought that women's suffrage would not solve more pressing problems in women's lives. In a sense, then, political rights were the ultimate goal for early Meiji women, a goal they deemed unattainable but one that was taken up by successive generations of feminists.

If, for early Meiji women, *public* meant "active citizenship," if not "political rights," what, then, was considered private? First, I intend this term to define what women thought but did not make public. It is a fact that the primary material used here was published in one form or another having passed through at least some sort of personal censorship. Thus, I cannot argue that what women wrote or stated was exactly what they thought, "in private," when they did not need to justify their opinions to anyone. Second, I use this term to define the ways in which the Meiji state

---

29. Mackie, *Feminism in Modern Japan*, 4–5.
30. Lu has translated some of these documents. See, for example, "Memorial on the Establishment of a Representative Assembly" (Minken giin setsuritsu kenpaku 民権議院設立建白), written in 1874, but also earlier ones such as "Document on the Form of Government" (Seitaisho 政体書, 1868). David J. Lu, *Japan: A Documentary History—the Late Tokugawa Period to the Present* (London: M. E. Sharpe, 1997), 327–29, 308–9. The originals are reprinted in Ōkubo Toshiaki, ed., *Kindaishi shiryō* (Sources on modern history) (Yoshikawa Kōbunkan, 1965), 51, 145. See also Gluck, *Japan's Modern Myths*, 50.

and some intellectuals tried to limit women's social participation to the "private sphere.] For example, Sakatani Shiroshi 阪谷素 (1822–81), a member of the male group Meirokusha 明六社 (Meiji Six Society), argued that "Women are weak; men strong. The husband deals with the outside world while the wife manages domestic matters. . . . [I]t would be well to speak of preserving the spheres of men and women (*danjo shubun*) or the harmonious bodies of husband and wife."[31] The same was stated by Tsuda Mamichi 津田真道 (1829–1903), another Meirokusha member, who wrote, "There is a distinction between the spheres of the husband outside [the home] and the wife inside [the home], and husband and wife will mutually respect each other's sphere once they honor this distinction."[32] The women presented here did not accept this solution. As Afsaneh Najmabadi has shown in the case of Iran, when women started to acquire a different position and value in society—as mothers rather than merely wombs, as managers of their households in their husbands' stead, and as educated wives who could be of help to their husbands—the idea of the family, too, was reenvisaged and no longer linked to other kin groups but to the national community. Because of this reconfiguration, motherhood assumed new meanings; mothers were nurturers and educators of their children and by extension of their country. As a consequence, "The new home to whose management they now began to lay a claim was no longer their conjugal household but the national home, Iran."[33] A similar situation can be detected in early Meiji Japan as well, with women being empowered to think that their education, the education they were to give to their children, the support they were offering to their male relatives, and their employment were important for the development of their nation. Given this new understanding of women's worth and work for the development of a powerful nation, it became easier for them to start making claims over social customs and political matters that they thought needed to be reformed because they were deleterious to their nation. They supported the argument that a shift in women's position in the family was merely the first step toward a more general social change. For the early Meiji women introduced here, then, the family and the "private" lives of its individuals became issues to be discussed in public. Some scholars and intel-

31. Sakatani Shiroshi, "On Concubines," *Meiroku zasshi*, issue 32, March 1875, translated in William Braisted, *Meiroku Zasshi: Journal of the Japanese Enlightenment* (Cambridge, Mass.: Harvard University Press, 1976), 394–95, 400 n. 18.

32. Tsuda Mamichi, "The Distinction between Husbands and Wives," *Meiroku zasshi*, issue 22, December 1874, translated in Braisted, *Meiroku Zasshi*, 277–78.

33. Afsaneh Najmabadi, "Crafting an Educated Housewife in Iran," in *Remaking Women: Feminism and Modernity in the Middle East*, edited by Lila Abu-Lughod, 91–125 (Princeton: Princeton University Press, 1998), 101–3, 114. At the end of the eighteenth century, Mary Wollstonecraft conceived a similar theory on the place of European women in society and the home. See Sylvana Tomaselli, "The Most Public Sphere of All: The Family," in *Women, Writing, and the Public Sphere, 1700–1830,* edited by Elizabeth Eger, Charlotte Grant, Cliona O Gallchoir, and Penny Warburton, 239–56 (Cambridge: Cambridge University Press, 2006), 241.

lectuals used the term *private* to refer to those discourses that they did not want to become public, as in the case of the existence of prostitutes in Meiji society. The Meiji educator Fukuzawa Yukichi 福沢諭吉 (1835–1901), for example, had stated that Japanese people should not discuss the presence of concubines and prostitutes in men's lives, for that was a private business that should not be brought to public attention.[34] The women presented here held a different opinion on the subject and started discussing such topics in public, criticizing the discrepancy between men's public and private behavior. The home as it was organized, the way in which women understood it, and what women wanted to do outside of it are all underlying themes of late-nineteenth-century Japan and are also what links all the individual women and women's groups active in the public sphere, including those that are not presented in this work, since none of them could have discussed female roles without redefining their role within their family and nation. Furthermore, in the next chapters I show how, thanks to the articles published in newspapers and women's magazines, early Meiji women started to obtain information about women's activities in Europe and North America and wrote articles introducing the names of Western women who had already achieved public recognition. By showing that Western women did not belong only to the "private sphere," they presented more examples to support their argument that the dichotomy between home/women and external world/men was illusory. By taking female education as a starting point from which to change women's position within the home and in society, they also linked discourses on family, marriage, and women's education to those on government, laws, and politics.

Finally, feminist scholarship on nationalism has challenged "traditional assumptions, based on public-private dichotomies, about both the form and the location of politics."[35] In this work, particularly in chapters 4 and 5, I consider those topics related to the "private lives" of Meiji men and women to have been political, for they began to be used in order to affect government decisions and social behavior. During the early Meiji period, then, both *public* and *private* were terms that had a distinctive political flair.

---

34. He wrote, "In the West, the number of prostitutes is very large and their business prospers, but the decorative techniques used are very thorough, and nothing is revealed to the public eyes. . . . Prostitution, because it is a secret matter in all civilized nations of the world, must be concealed from public view in Japan, too. . . . To conclude, in order to lead our young generation in the right direction concerning their moral attitude, and to keep them from confusion, first of all, that nonchalant attitude of the older generation must be stamped out. Then an effective warning must be given to the morally corrupt men. If they are unable to cooperate, at least allow them be moderate in their behavior and carry out a policy of secrecy." "On Morality," translated in Kiyooka Eiichi, *Fukuzawa Yukichi on Japanese Women: Selected Works* (Tokyo: University of Tokyo Press, 1988), 90, 92, 96.

35. Sita Ranchod-Nilsson and Mary Ann Tetreault, *Women, States, and Nationalism: At Home in the Nation?* (London: Routledge, 2000), 4.

To conclude this section and before proceeding further, given that in the previous pages I have used the term *discourse*, a term I employ throughout this work, it is important to explain what I mean by it. The concept of discourse has been used across the social sciences, and scholars have defined it according to the academic disciplines in which they work.[36] I follow Sara Mills, who has argued that discourses do not occur in isolation but as dialogues, and thus they are also in opposition to other "groups of utterances."[37] In the early Meiji case, new discourses were initiated by women, and some were in opposition to the nationalist ideology or to those already in circulation. In each chapter I deal with the topics of such discourses, whether they defined women's needs for more education, different kinds of employment, or the right to participate in political activities. Scholars have also highlighted the way in which some social groups, because of exclusion based on race, gender, and property, find it difficult to participate in circulating discourses.[38] In the case of Meiji Japan, Gluck has argued that *minkan no yoron* (public opinion of the people) was not a "populist phrase but a reference to the elite who were not in government" such as members of opposition parties, intellectuals, journalists, or local notables.[39] I present the discourses upper-middle-class women introduced in the early Meiji public sphere on issues that they considered to be of common concern, although, for the major part, they included and touched on the needs of their class alone. Discourses have also been intended to "accomplish a rationalization of public opinion and will formation."[40] The women introduced here participated in or started new discourses because they wanted to inform other men and women but also because they wanted to educate those who were supporting competing discourses or were simply refraining from participating in discourses over, for example, the composition of the family. Through the spread of such discourses in public spaces all over Japan, their ultimate goal was that of changing Japanese people's mentality and the state's laws. Finally, as Foucault has posited, "What is the status of the individuals who—alone—have the right, sanctioned by law or tradition, juridically defined or spontaneously accepted, to proffer such a discourse?"[41] What sort of women, during the early Meiji period, were allowed to join or initiate public discourses?

Given that I focus specifically on female spaces that were created in order to help women formulate their own identity and engage public authorities in debates

---

36. For a general overview of this concept and its uses in various disciplines, see David R. Howarth, *Discourse* (Buckingham: Open University Press, 2000).
37. Sara Mills, *Discourse* (London: Routledge, 1997), 10.
38. Fraser, "Rethinking the Public Sphere."
39. Gluck, *Japan's Modern Myths*, 50.
40. Simone Chambers, "Discourse and Democratic Practices," in *The Cambridge Companion to Habermas*, edited by Stephen K. White, 233–59 (Cambridge: Cambridge University Press, 1995), 235.
41. Michel Foucault, *The Archaeology of Knowledge* (London: Routledge, 2003), 55.

to challenge hegemonic discourses, it is useful to proceed with a discussion of Japanese realities and social changes during the Meiji period and then move toward a definition of the groups of early Meiji women that I consider in this work.

The Early Meiji Period

One of the conditions for a critical discussion of public issues in Meiji Japan was the presence and development of the print market. During the Edo period, an active publishing industry had printed books for men and women, and, as Berry has argued, this availability created the notion of a public and a domain of public knowledge.[42] By the end of the nineteenth century, this reading public had notably expanded and could access a larger domain from which to acquire its knowledge.[43] Besides the books already in circulation or written during the early Meiji period, it also became possible for educated men and women to buy translations of Western books, or the foreign-language books themselves, in bookstores opened in Tokyo and other major cities.[44] Foreign nonfiction works were also used in boys' and girls' schools and associations and were shared among girl students, as we will see in the next chapters. Furthermore, with the development of newspapers, which did

42. Mary Elizabeth Berry, "Public Life in Authoritarian Japan," *Daedalus* 127.3 (1998): 152. On the development of commercial printing and the print market during the Edo period, see Peter Kornicki, *The Book in Japan: A Cultural History from the Beginnings to the Nineteenth Century* (Leiden: Brill, 1998). See also Mary Elizabeth Berry, *Japan in Print: Information and Nation in the Early Modern Period* (Berkeley: University of California Press, 2006). For a study of the circulation of manuscripts in Edo, see Peter Kornicki, "Manuscript, Not Print: Scribal Culture in the Edo Period," *Journal of Japanese Studies* 32.1 (2006): 23–52. On women as readers and writers during the Edo period, see Peter Kornicki, "Unsuitable Books for Women? Genji monogatari and Ise monogatari in Late Seventeenth-Century Japan," *Monumenta Nipponica* 60.2 (2005): 147–93; and Kornicki, Patessio, and Rowley, *The Female as Subject*. For an analysis of the Edo public sphere, see Kim, *The Age of Visions*, chap. 1. He argues that teahouses, shops, and theaters were among some of the public spaces available during the Edo period where popular culture could be consumed.

43. It is difficult to compose meaningful statistics on the number of books circulating during the Edo and Meiji periods for they should include reprints and newly published books and manuscripts and consider regional variety. A general idea of the number and contents of books published during the Edo period can be obtained by looking at the *Kokusho sōmokuroku* (Catalog of national books), 9 vols. (Iwanami Shoten, 1989–91), a catalog of books published before 1867. On its usefulness for a better understanding of publishing during the Edo period, see Henry D. Smith, "The History of the Book in Edo and Paris," in *Edo and Paris: Urban Life and the State in the Early Modern Era*, edited by James L. McClain, John M. Merriman, and Ugawa Kaoru, 332–52 (Ithaca: Cornell University Press, 1994). By comparison, the *Kokuritsu kokkai toshokan zōsho mokuroku* catalogs Meiji publications. Kokuritsu Kokkai Toshokan Toshobu, ed., *Kokuritsu kokkai toshokan zōsho mokuroku: Meiji-ki* (Catalog of the collection of Meiji period books in the National Diet Library), 8 vols. (Kokuritsu kokkai toshokan, 1994–95).

44. For the number of foreign novels translated into Japanese, see Jonathan Zwicker, *Practices of the Sentimental Imagination: Melodrama, the Novel, and the Social Imaginary in Nineteenth-Century Japan* (Cambridge, Mass.: Harvard University Press, 2006), 150.

17

not exist during the Edo period and by the late 1880s were published even in small towns, it was easier to access information about local or national events and developments.[45] The same was true for magazines, which during this period began to be defined according to the gender of their readership. Women and girls could purchase, lend, and borrow magazines and publish their opinions or responses to circulating discourses in them.

With the publication of magazines and newspapers in every region and the emergence of new arenas of debate; with the new transportation system, which enabled news, goods, and people to move to distant areas more quickly; and with the search for a national and simpler language that began to be used in textbooks and newspapers throughout Japan, early Meiji intellectuals and men from the upper classes started to create alternative spaces, separate from the government, in which to debate the future of their nation, addressing the state's public discourses and policies. "Male" magazines and journals and numerous societies therefore became platforms that favored the emergence of a public and public discussion.

The Japanese public that emerged from such public discussions was in fact made up of many publics since, at least during the first twenty years of the Meiji period, those who were debating in a society or newspaper in, for example, Kochi were not necessarily known to those engaging in the same activities in Kanagawa. Furthermore, although during the very first years of the Meiji period it was difficult for the central government to control each and every activity organized—allowing for a certain freedom of expression—such public spaces were by no means free; with the introduction of censorship, which came into force in the early 1870s, the state clearly defined who could talk about which matters in public.[46]

During the Edo period, books on the history of Japan such as the *Dai Nihonshi* 大日本史 (The Great History of Japan) had encouraged Japanese people to imagine themselves as sharing a common past and identity, but from the beginning of the Meiji period such identity, and the construction of a national character, began to be reinforced and forced on the population.[47] As Fujitani has poignantly shown,

45. During the Edo period, other forms of visual and nonvisual media were used to spread information quickly and widely. These included satirical and polemical prints, graffiti, and even poetic forms. See Kim, *The Age of Visions*, 36–47, 93–94 for newspaper circulation data.
46. The Newspaper Regulation of 1871 legislated that newspapers should enlighten people and no topic regarding military and government affairs could be discussed. It was revised in 1873 and 1875, when it began to impose punitive measures on newspapers, owners, editors, and journalists who did not comply, and it became even stricter during the 1880s. The regulation and its revisions are reprinted in Matsumoto and Yamamuro, *Genron to media*, 410–25. See also Kim, *The Age of Visions*, 90; and Jay Rubin, *Injurious to Public Morals: Writers and the Meiji State* (Seattle: University of Washington Press, 1984).
47. On the project and importance of the *Dai Nihonshi*, which was started in the 1650s by order of Tokugawa Mitsukuni, lord of Mito domain, see Masahide Bitō, "Thought and Religion,

the 1870s and 1880s were decades in which symbols of national identity, such as representations of the emperor and the empress, school textbooks, the elimination of regional barriers, the introduction of the postal system, stamps, banks and banknotes, and songs sung in public schools, were implemented, expanded, and reinvented.[48] Girls and boys were supposed to frequent government schools that did not differentiate according to social class, and the authorities' official line was that education was to be the same for all. The abolition of territorial divisions and class distinctions was a clear effort made by the state to "unite" its people and territory, and this national identity was to be forged against the presence in Japan of communities of foreigners. As a consequence, beginning in the 1870s, and especially during the 1880s, through the publication of books, newspapers, and magazines (what Anderson has termed "print capitalism"), such an imagined "modern and progressive" community was starting to take shape.[49] New publications and public activities supported the creation of new public spaces, which were supported in their emergence by the expanding public sphere, but they also facilitated the growth of a mainstream national identity. Thus, if we understand the "nation" as an imagined community socially and politically integrated through a large-scale, identity-forming, collective discourse, then it is clear that during the first twenty years of the Meiji period state policies were geared toward the formation of "the most basic of collective political identities."[50]

The formation of new institutions, the emergence of public spaces, and the striving for "modernization" were closely linked to the state policy of rethinking and redefining gender relations in order to improve upon the characteristics of Edo society.[51] As we will see in the next chapter, already during the last decades of the Edo period intellectuals and local authorities had started to reevaluate the importance of women's education and position in society, but it was with the new centralized government that this project became widely discussed and was put into practice.

1550–1700," in *The Cambridge History of Japan,* edited by John Whitney Hall, vol. 4, 373–424 (Cambridge: Cambridge University Press, 1991), 408–12.

48. Fujitani Takashi, *Splendid Monarchy: Power and Pageantry in Modern Japan* (Berkeley: University of California Press, 1996).

49. Benedict Anderson, *Imagined Communities: Reflections on the Origins and Spread of Nationalism* (London: Verso, 1991), 43–44.

50. Craig Calhoun, *Critical Social Theory: Culture, History, and the Challenge of Difference* (Oxford: Blackwell, 1995), 272–73.

51. A similar process can be identified in England in the late eighteenth and nineteenth centuries. See Gary Kelly, "Bluestocking Feminism," in *Women, Writing, and the Public Sphere, 1700–1830,* edited by Elizabeth Eger, Charlotte Grant, Cliona O Gallchoir, and Penny Warburton, 163–80 (Cambridge: Cambridge University Press, 2006).

Feminism and Nationalism

The nationalist vision espoused by the Meiji government could succeed only if women and men were to live according to prescribed roles. The early Meiji nationalist project required women to participate in national processes in various ways. First, since one of the ways a civilized country was supposedly recognizable was by the level of education its women could achieve, Japanese women's education and position in society became paradigms intended to prove to the "enlightened" West that Japan had reason to be welcomed into the "modern" international community.[52] Second, as Tsurumi's study of girls working in the mills has shown, early Meiji women were to participate in their country's economic advancement, their labor being necessary for the survival of their families and the formation of a strong Japan.[53] Finally, women were supposed to be the biological reproducers of the Japanese nation and the transmitters of Japanese culture to their children.

Scholars have pointed out that in every culture "the home" and "the family" comprised a fundamental site from which nationalists launched their modernization projects. As Shakry states in the Egyptian case, "[M]otherhood was fundamental to the constitution of national identity and entailed the formation of a series of discursive practices that demarcated women as both a 'locus of the country's backwardness' and a sphere of transformation to be reconstituted and raised up onto the plane of enlightened rationality." As such, it figured centrally in modernizing discourse and "was essential to the nationalist project."[54] The meanings given by various Japanese individuals and groups to the concept of "motherhood" played on different levels. On the one hand, nationalistic ambitions helped women gain an education and a public position, for women could argue that their education and participation in women's meetings would help them become more knowledgeable and therefore better teachers for their children. On the other hand, in chapters 2 and 4 we will see how some Meiji intellectuals were defining women's social and educational roles for "the public good," in this way promoting women's conformity to the national mission rather than their personal freedom. By stating that only through education could women become good companions for their husbands and valuable teachers for their sons, many were proposing an image of women as part

---

52. In her introduction to a collection of articles published in 1886, Inoue Nao (discussed in chapter 2) makes precisely this point. The ideas that the status of women was inseparably tied to the status of a nation and the condition of women needed to be improved if a country wanted to advance were to be found in various modern nations, especially when they were subjected to Western imperialism. See, for example, Najmabadi, "Crafting an Educated Housewife in Iran," 101.

53. Patricia Tsurumi, *Factory Girls*.

54. Omnia Shakry, "Schooled Mothers and Structured Play: Child Rearing in Turn-of-the-Century Egypt," in *Remaking Women: Feminism and Modernity in the Middle East*, edited by Lila Abu-Lughod, 126–70 (Princeton: Princeton University Press, 1998), 126–27.

of society only within the home and only in subordination to men. These moves encouraged women to support the nationalist project as mothers and wives, but they also represent an acknowledgment of the potential of women's ideas and an attempt to incorporate burgeoning competing discourses and identities within the already circulating ideology on the formation of a strong Japanese nation.

This "incorporation" of women into the "nationalistic project" was by no means a straightforward matter. Yuval-Davis and Anthias remind us that while women are "acted upon as members of collectivities, institutions or groupings" they are also incorporated at various levels within civil society and the economy, and so the state cannot achieve absolute control over them.[55] In the case of Meiji Japan, the state's influence on, and regulation of, women's and men's lives was far from absolute. This was so because, although this "new" and "progressive" identity was supposed to encompass the whole "Japanese people," it included only those men and women who had the means or interest to be part of an informed public and obtain access to such public spaces, thus coming to understand what the representation of their nation, and the meaning of their own lives within their nation and in a new era, was supposed to be. It is likely that the majority of the men and women belonging to the poorer classes, who were not going to school, were not using banks or stamps, and did not travel extensively, were not influenced by all the national symbols and fetishes mentioned above. As Gluck states, "Some subjects faded from view by the time they reached the village, where silkworms were likely to take precedence over *kokutai* [national polity] as a topic of lively interest."[56] Furthermore, although such identity formation became a goal for the new government from the very beginning of the Meiji period, for example through the various educational ordinances and the conscription system of the 1870s, it was only by the late 1880s that the state's intervention in citizens' lives became stronger thanks to, among other things, the promulgation of the Constitution (1889), the Imperial rescript on education (1890), and the opening of the Diet (1890). As Kim has argued, "Despite its astonishing success in transforming Japan into a centralized nation-state in such a short period, the Meiji state in 1880 still remained a coalition government, torn by factional politics and intrabureaucratic struggles."[57] As a consequence, although during the 1880s the Meiji authorities were clearly defining who could speak about what in public, the public that made up such a community was not so compact or integrated. As Gluck put it, "If ideology proposes, or imagines, a relation between men and their world, it is fair to say that the dominant ideology in imperial Japan imagined

---

55. Yuval-Davis, Nira, and Flora Anthias, "Introduction," in *Woman-Nation-State,* edited by Nira Yuval-Davis and Flora Anthias, 1–15 (New York: Macmillan, 1989), 6.
56. Gluck, *Japan's Modern Myths,* 13.
57. Kim, *The Age of Visions,* 23.

a nation that was more unified and a society that was more stable than those who lived within them knew to be the case."[58] Voices that opposed government policy and legislation could find public spaces in which to be heard, as in the case of the *minken undō* (a political movement for "popular rights" discussed in chapter 5). It was only by the 1890s that the state's intervention in people's private and public lives became stronger. For these reasons, and although concerted efforts by women activists cannot be identified in great numbers before the 1880s, I focus my research on the 1870s and 1880s in order to understand the ways in which women came to realize their potential and act in public spaces, how they became involved in different spaces within civil society, and how they escaped absolute control by the state during the 1880s.

Neither Anderson nor Habermas has taken women into consideration in his analysis and definition of *nationalism*, but if nationalism is the sum of national collectivity and imagined identity, what were early Meiji women imagining? How were they defining their own vision of nationalism and national identity? The women presented here proposed their vision of civic nationalism during the 1880s, which Ignatieff has defined as the need to "reconcile their right to shape their own lives with the need to belong to a community."[59] They went to school, did not repudiate their roles as mothers and wives, and took care of the house and the household economy. However, they also worked to change their position by arguing that their roles as mothers and wives did not imply that they had to accept exclusion from certain jobs and could not be refused social and political rights just because they were women.

This definition of what early Meiji women wanted brings me to another definition, that of *feminism*. What kind of feminism were early Meiji women espousing and, more to the point, how did they come to attain it? Badran writes that feminism is the "awareness of constraints placed upon women because of their gender and attempts to remove these constraints and to evolve a more equitable gender system involving new roles for women and new relations between women and men."[60] If we understand *feminism* to mean the awareness of constraints placed on women, then a "feminist movement" implies a concerted active demand for a more equitable system. Japanese women's resistance to widely supported discourses on women's position in society and their expression of different aspirations were already to be found during the Edo period, but it was only during the early Meiji that they started to organize themselves and publicly demand a more equitable gender system.

58. Gluck, *Japan's Modern Myths*, 39.
59. Michael Ignatieff, *Blood and Belonging: Journeys into the New Nationalism* (London: Vintage, 1994), 3.
60. Margot Badran, *Feminists, Islam, and Nation: Gender and the Making of Modern Egypt* (Princeton: Princeton University Press, 1995), 19–20.

Who was a feminist in Meiji Japan? I understand as feminists those (mostly female) individuals who perceived women's social and political position to have been restricted compared to that of the men of the same social class because they were women and who wanted to change this state of affairs. There were various ways in which these individuals and groups of women tried to change society's understanding of women's worth. Some argued that male and female "natural" rights and duties were different but complementary and that women should be allowed to fully use their qualities because by doing so their country would benefit. Others, especially when influenced by Christianity, argued that women embodied qualities that allowed them to see deleterious social customs and therefore had the duty to criticize them. Japan, they firmly stated, would attain the level of the more enlightened countries only through the changes they advocated. Others argued that men and women were different only because women's intellectual development had been hampered, and so it was necessary to give them more education, employment opportunities, and other social rights so that they could occupy the position that was lawfully due to them and become accomplished human beings.

(Transgressing) Gender Boundaries

In her study of British women in the public eye, Gonda wonders if the "public sphere" had to be always considered a "stage," and therefore improper for women in general, or if it was a place only for improper women.[61] Copeland, too, describes how Meiji women writers had to carefully remain within the boundaries of female respectability when proposing their fictional writings. They could not state that they were writing because they liked the creative act and had to mask their desires with nationalistic remarks or present themselves as good daughters, the image that society required of them.[62] What was considered suitable for an early Meiji woman? What was deemed degrading or outside a woman's sphere? When did a girl student cease to be a student and become instead a problem for her family and society?

Women getting out of their homes and gathering in associations or working in a public environment had to justify their public position by defending their activities as something that did not stem from economic or personal interests but from the desire to work for their country. The criticism Meiji women aroused shows how "proper" women were welcomed in "the Meiji public sphere" when they complied with social expectations and worked for the state-defined public good. Thus,

---

61. Caroline Gonda, "Misses, Murderesses, and Magdalens: Women in the Public Eye," in *Women, Writing, and the Public Sphere, 1700–1830,* edited by Elizabeth Eger, Charlotte Grant, Cliona O Gallchoir, and Penny Warburton, 53–71 (Cambridge: Cambridge University Press, 2006).

62. Rebecca Copeland, *Lost Leaves: Women Writers of Meiji Japan* (Honolulu: University of Hawai'i Press, 2000).

Yamakawa Sutematsu 山川捨松 and Tsuda Umeko 津田梅子, women exerting themselves for the education of the daughters of noble families, were active in a proper space because they were furthering women's advancement in fields that were considered necessary by Japanese society.[63] On the other hand, Kusunose Kita 楠瀬喜多 (1836–1920), who petitioned the local government for the right to vote in local elections, was addressed in the following terms: "The demon mother Kusunose Kita of Karabito-chō has recently set aside her pride. She has taken the tonsure, changed her attire to black and vigorously fingers her rosary beads."[64] And she was not the only one, for women speakers at public meetings, girl students demanding a university education and expressing their opinions in the print media, and women in medicine were defined as women occupying improper spaces since they were working outside the boundaries imposed on them. These women—consciously or not—sought to deflect criticism by adopting nationalist discourses to support their arguments and stated that only through their participation and involvement in society could Japan reach the level of the Western nations.

How did some of them manage to define their ideal position in society, discuss such ideas in public spaces, and confront the authorities when their treatment did not seem right?

What Groups of Early Meiji Women?

Women and men do not form unitary categories, and differences in social class shape their lives along with the possibility of changing them. Furthermore, in

63. Yamakawa Sutematsu, who was known as "the flower of the Rokumeikan," married Ōyama Iwao, the minister of war, with a wedding reception at the Rokumeikan, entertaining eight hundred Japanese and two hundred Western guests. She became famous for her knowledge of the "Western way." Kuno Akiko, *Unexpected Destinations: The Poignant Story of Japan's First Vassar Graduate* (Kodansha International, 1993), 152, 154. The Rokumeikan was built to entertain important Western guests and diplomats so that they would form a positive image of Japan and be more willing to revise the unequal treaties then in place. There women who knew Western ways of socializing could project the image Japanese authorities wanted Western men to have and could put into practice what they had learned at school. Ōyama was often sent abroad for long periods, and Yamakawa became an example, with Tsuda Umeko and other such women, of an upper-class woman busy with charity and educational work. She was the first to propose the idea of a charity bazaar, as she had seen them in North America, although she knew that it might meet with objections since it would be the first time ladies of high society would *sell things*. Letter from Yamakawa Sutematsu to Adeline Lanman, reprinted in Barbara Rose, *Tsuda Umeko and Women's Education in Japan*, 64–65. The bazaar was organized by the Fujin jizenkai 婦人慈善会 (Women's Charity Association) at the Rokumeikan in order to raise funds for the opening of a school for nurses (see chapter 3); it lasted three days, and the staggering sum of 7,500 yen was raised. Kuno, *Unexpected Destinations*, 162–63. On Tsuda, see Rose, *Tsuda Umeko*.

64. *Doyō shinbun*, 01.05.1883, translated in Marnie Anderson, "A Woman's Place: Gender, Politics, and the State in Meiji Japan," PhD. diss., Ann Arbor, University of Michigan, 2005, 45–46.

most cultures and historical periods the participation or presence in public spaces of different groups of women is not regarded in the same way by society and the state. Some groups of Edo and Meiji women were indeed seen and worked in public whereas others were supposed to stay at home and, at most, occupy themselves with domestic work or the education of their children. As a general rule, maidservants, farm wives, unpaid female workers in family enterprises, or female laborers, namely, those women belonging to social groups that needed women's labor in order to survive, were not limited in their activities and were seen working with their male family members. When, however, the women in question were of the former samurai class and were seeking paid employment, the situation was different.

Other women belonged to categories that had previously existed but had somehow become problematic during the Meiji period, and their very public presence became contentious. On the one hand, girl students and women teachers had existed during the Edo period, but their "modern" images, education, and attitudes were remarked upon and criticized in the Meiji papers. On the other hand, prostitution and prostitutes became topics of concern for some, mainly when their presence in public spaces produced negative international publicity for Japan.

Class was a divider in other ways as well. Early Meiji women were linked to their "old regimes' societies and institutions" and did not want to or could not evade them and oppose their class's interest.[65] Those who spoke in favor of men's or women's rights were flagging rights for a minority of the Japanese people; social class determined who had access to which public spaces, while it was mainly a male-gendered sphere, since there were no women in societies like the scholarly Meirokusha let alone the government. No Japanese woman during the 1880s could graduate from a Japanese university, but it was upper-middle-class girls that were helped by missionaries to study in North American universities, not poor ones.

In the case of women from the aristocracy and upper-rank former samurai, Alice Bacon (whose family had given hospitality to Yamakawa Sutematsu when she went to America with the Iwakura mission and who was later employed at Kazoku jogakkō, the most elite girls' school of the period) held that her English evenings were

> one of the few festivities that the poor girls are allowed to go to, as their rank is too high to permit them to enjoy themselves like common folks. The girls of the highest rank are not, as a rule, permitted even to enter

---

65. Kelly has shown how in the European case those who were part of "bluestocking feminism" came from gentry or upper-middle-class families and "had a large stake in their class' material interests, even though they all experienced the subordination and exploitation of women that helped sustain those interests." Kelly, "Bluestocking Feminism," 168.

the houses of the samurai class, but because we are their teachers they can come to us, although they could not go anywhere else.[66]

Bacon's opinion of upper-class Japanese women's position might have been biased by her North American education and upbringing, but it is nevertheless clear that when, during the 1870s but especially during the 1880s, Japanese women belonging to the upper classes were present in public at state occasions, for example, at the Rokumeikan, they were there "as functions rather than as persons, their individuality subsumed in rank," as Caroline Gonda has argued in the case of British women.[67] They participated in social life by attending balls, parties, dinners, and events such as bazaars to promote their families' and nation's interests rather than expressing their interests as individual beings, and it is only from the 1890s that some such women purposely left those environments to work for women's education and well-being, as in the case of Tsuda Umeko and Ishii Fudeko 石井筆子.

On the other hand, women of the poorer classes had never been expected to remain at home, nor was it a simple task to make them send their children to school since child labor was often necessary for their families' survival. For them, we have seen, nationalist discourses, the differentiation between private and public life, and the formation of the Japanese modern nation had less, if not little, significance, although it did have an impact on their lives in economic terms. The girls in the silk-reeling and cotton-spinning mills were in a similar situation, as they were considered a vital source of income for their families and crucial to the economic growth and prosperity of their country. As Tsurumi has shown, girls of the former samurai class were initially given a place in the factories, but as time passed factories became places where poor families could send their daughters in order to have fewer mouths to feed and to bring home some extra income. The plight of these girls indeed demands attention for the light it sheds on systems of exploitation. They participated in two mill strikes in 1886 and 1889, itself evidence of organization, consciousness, and discourse, but they were unable to establish links with other women's groups. Conversely, I did not come across upper-middle-class women discussing the condition of girls working in the mills before the 1890s nor any evidence that the women presented here were aware of their fate. One can only

---

66. Alice Mabel Bacon, *A Japanese Interior* (London: Gay and Bird, 1893), 23. On the Iwakura Mission see Kume Kunitake, *The Iwakura Embassy, 1871–1873: A True Account of the Ambassador Extraordinary and Plenipotentiary's Journey of Observation through the United States of America and Europe*, 5 vols. (Princeton: Princeton University Press, 2002).

67. Gonda, "Misses, Murderesses, and Magdalens," 66. For these young women and their mothers, the Rokumeikan was the first public space in which they were seen with their fathers and husbands and in which they had an important role to play.

speculate as to why this happened; what is clear is that the needs and aspirations of the two groups of women were different.

The early Meiji women that I define as feminists and discuss in this work tried to obtain better rights for themselves rather than for all Japanese women. There were a few exceptions, and I introduce some examples of upper-middle-class women who did help women of other classes. The fact that the majority wanted better rights for themselves, however, is not surprising, nor does it detract from early Meiji women's accomplishments, as historically feminism was not born out of the need of *all* women to associate and demand better treatment but as a result of a small number of women who looked at their own situation and only later extended their support to other and weaker groups of women.

Thus, what I define as "women's entrance into the public sphere" or "women's use of public spaces" refers to women from former samurai and wealthy merchants' and farmers' families who could afford to educate their female members and saw that there was something to be gained from their wives' and daughters' education. This also set the boundaries within which they worked for women's emancipation since the issues they addressed were meaningful only to their class. Until much later, however, theirs remained the most challenging and vocal group in Japanese modern history.

The Ryōsai Kenbo *Ideology*

Upper-middle-class women became the focus of the *ryōsai kenbo* (good wives, wise mothers) ideology, a term that seems to have been coined by Nakamura Masanao 中村正直 (1832–91) during the early 1870s when he was the principal of Tokyo joshi shihan gakkō, the first normal school for girls opened by the Meiji government. Nakamura had studied in England and become convinced of the fact that educating women was a necessary step for the progress of a nation; he had already implemented this ideology in his Dōjinsha 同人社 academy, where some girls studied from 1877 on, but it was during his years as principal of Tokyo joshi shihan gakkō that he further developed his theories on women's education.[68] For Nakamura, *ryōsai kenbo* signified educated and knowledgeable women who could become good companions for their husbands, good teachers for their children, and good workers, all important goals in the creation of a strong and powerful nation. He argued that didactic tracts such as *Onna daigaku* 女大学 (Greater Learning for Women), the Edo period text

---

68. At Dōjinsha translations of books written by John Stuart Mill and Herbert Spencer were used. Ogawa Sumie, *Nakamura Masanao no kyōiku shisō* (The educational philosophy of Nakamura Masanao) (Tochigi: Ogawa Sumie, 2004), 332–33. Information regarding Nakamura's life was reported in *Jogaku zasshi*, no. 269, 13.06.1891, 14; and no. 270, 20.06.1891, 1–5.

purporting to outline the knowledge women ought to have (or rather *not* have), did not offer the knowledge Meiji women needed since women were supposed to teach their children moral and religious lessons before they went to school and therefore had to be educated themselves.[69] Hastings writes that William Smith Clark (1826–86), who was teaching at the Sapporto Agricultural College in 1876, told his male students to be ambitious, but she did not find proof of educators asking Japanese girls to be ambitious.[70] Yamakawa Kikue, for one, remembers that when girls complained that they did not understand what Nakamura taught them he would scold them, stating that if boys of those girls' age could understand problems and theories then they should as well.[71] Boys in Meiji educational environments were explicitly told to be ambitious and work hard, and the history of the Meiji period has been represented in part as a period in which young men were able to use that ambition to improve their worth and, as a consequence, help their country "reach" the level of the Western nations. Girls who came into contact with Nakamura were also told that they could use their education to improve their lives and society. During the 1880s women used the *ryōsai kenbo ideology* as a platform to help organize themselves and participate in public activities. In response to the perceived threat that women's presence in public society posed to the status quo, by the late 1880s the term was reconceptualized and came more and more to designate an education for women based on feminine qualities and duties centered around the home, a dimension that was not preponderant when Nakamura Masanao originally coined it.[72]

---

69. Yamakawa Kikue, *Onna nidai no ki* (Two generations of women) (Heibonsha, 1972), 27–34; idem., *Nihon fujin undō shōshi* (A short history of the Japanese women's movement) (Daiwa shobo, 1981), 43; Nakamura Masanao, "Creating Good Mothers," *Meiroku zasshi,* issue 33, March 1875, translated in Braisted, *Meiroku Zasshi,* 401. On the *Onna daigaku,* see Kornicki, Patessio, and Rowley, *The Female as Subject.* For a discussion of how Kishida Toshiko interpreted the *Onna daigaku,* see Noriko Sugano, "Kishida Toshiko and the Career of a Public-Speaking Woman in Meiji Japan," in *The Female as Subject: Reading and Writing in Early Modern Japan,* edited by P. F. Kornicki, Mara Patessio, and G. G. Rowley, Michigan Monograph Series in Japanese Studies, no. 70 (Ann Arbor: Center for Japanese Studies, University of Michigan, 2010), 171–89.
70. Sally A. Hastings, "Hatoyama Haruko: Ambitious Woman," in *The Human Tradition in Modern Japan,* edited by Anne Walthall, 81–98 (Wilmington: Scholarly Resources, 2002), 81–82.
71. Yamakawa, *Onna nidai,* 33.
72. On the ways in which this term was used and manipulated during the nineteenth and twentieth centuries, see Koyama Shizuko, *Ryōsai kenbo to iu kihan* (The "good wife, wise mother" standard) (Keisō shobō, 1991); and Tachi, "Ryōsai kenbo." On the way in which Iwamoto Yoshiharu and Mori Arinori understood it, see Katano Masako, "Ryōsai kenbo shugi no genryū" (The origins of the *ryōsai kenbo* policy), in *Onnatachi no kindai* (The modern period for women), edited by Kindai joseishi kenkyūkai, 32–57 (Kashiwa shobō, 1978). In English, Uno looks at how the term was used in post–World War II Japanese society. Kathleen S. Uno, "The Death of 'Good Wife, Wise Mother'?" in *Postwar Japan as History,* edited by Andrew Gordon, 293–322 (Berkeley: University of California Press, 1993).

The *ryōsai kenbo* ideology was also used to support women's participation in *fujinkai* (ladies' associations) as a way to learn new and "modern" methods of taking care of their duties and families. Membership in these associations was not limited to married women; in fact, men and unmarried young women also participated in their activities or became members. The emphasis was on women's "modern" ways of associating rather than merely on their background and position in life. Whereas it had hitherto been difficult to find groups of men and women sharing the same physical spaces and engaging in fruitful relationships outside private houses or the pleasure quarters, those years witnessed the emergence of new female social spaces in which the (future) mother and wife was supposed to be the active participant and influential men were invited to deliver speeches. Books and magazines devoted to household economics, child rearing, letter writing, literature, and the arts began to be published for this "new" audience and were discussed in the groups. These media, and the new position of women, redefined women's roles within the family. The *shufu*, the "housewife," was now also supposed to "enter information into the family account books, interact with the servants, and maintain the family fortune, in addition to making objects of daily use," making the new meaning given to *shufu* closely linked to the new roles given to women, who had to become mistresses of the household and managers of domestic affairs.[73]

Cott has pointed out that domesticity and domestic discourse could be used by various ideologues to define the boundaries of feminine propriety.[74] The men and women participating in the groups covered in this work embraced the basic ideology of *ryōsai kenbo*. However, the additional meanings they invested in this term were varied. Consequently, this basic ideology was supported by the men and women who lobbied for more education for women, by those who wanted women to devote their lives entirely and exclusively to their families, but also by those who wanted women to be active in the reformation of public morality. Conservative as well as progressive ideas about women's roles in Meiji society were born out of, and developed around, the *ryōsai kenbo* ideology and were supported and discussed in various groups.

Finally, Habermas has also failed to acknowledge the impact of religion, an important factor influencing the formation of the Meiji public sphere. Religion can be considered a "compelling base for the development of national identity, because it provides an interpretation of the meaning of life and death, values, beliefs, traditions

---

73. Kazumi Ishii and Nerida Jarkey, "The Housewife Is Born: The Establishment of the Notion and Identity of the *Shufu* in Modern Japan," *Japanese Studies* 22.1 (2002): 36.
74. Nancy Cott, *The Bonds of Womanhood: "Woman's Sphere" in New England, 1780–1835* (New Haven: Yale University Press, 1977), esp. chap. 2, "Domesticity."

and rituals which can create communal experience and collective identity," but what happens when a foreign religion is imported?[75] It is difficult to unravel the layers of meaning in the writings missionaries and Japanese girl students left behind since nationalistic beliefs played a vital role on both sides, while missionaries' writings pose epistemological problems because they are heavily coated with a layer of religious and gendered convictions. However, my study of missionaries' schools in Japan shows how Christianity, a Victorian understanding of womanhood, and the *ryōsai kenbo* ideal supported a new assertion of women's potential power within the home and a new confidence outside it, and I present additional examples of girls active in ways that were sometimes in opposition to the state's ideology regarding women's position in society.

Gendered Words

The way in which early Meiji women were able to create their own, if limited, spaces within the public sphere becomes clearer when we look at the language they used in their writings. Many new terms were coined in relation *to* Japanese women in those years. Thus, while there was no gendered name for things and spaces pertaining to the male world, when girls or women became part of the school system, founded associations, or wrote novels their gender had to be made clear by using the words *jo* (female) in the case of *jogakkō* (girls' schools), *joryū sakka* (women writers), and *joken* (women's rights) and *fu* (married woman, lady) in *fujinkai*, thus segregating them (the terms and the women) to a woman's sphere.[76]

Discourses, in other words, could not have been generated without having the words to describe them, and women, too, started to use their own words in parallel, if not in opposition, to the terms used by the government to describe everything that had to do with their sex. *Freedom* and *independence* were newly coined words that had quite unfamiliar meanings for all Japanese citizens, and it is important to note that women used them, too. At the same time, early Meiji women started to use words such as *fujin shakai* (women's world), *aidokusha* (my faithful readers), and *shimai* (sisters).

Cott has suggested that the American feminist movement of the nineteenth century grew out of the separation of spheres and took its distinctive shape and interests *from* that separation. For her, although the idea of a "women's sphere" was not necessarily protofeminist, domesticity and feminism were linked by "women's

---

75. See Linda Racioppi and Katherine O'Sullivan See, "Engendering Nation and National Identity," in *Women, States, and Nationalism: At Home in the Nation?* edited by Sita Ranchod-Nilsson and Mary Ann Tetreault, 18–34 (London: Routledge, 2000), 23.

76. On *joryū sakka*, the only group that I do not analyze here, see Copeland, *Lost Leaves*; and Rebecca Copeland and Melek Ortabasi, eds., *The Modern Murasaki: Writing by Women of Meiji Japan* (New York: Columbia University Press, 2006).

perception of 'womanhood' as an all-sufficient definition and of sisterhood implicit in it." That *consciousness*, Cott has argued, was a necessary precondition for feminism, even though in opening up certain avenues to women because of their sex it excluded others.[77] The Meiji government was trying to define the woman's sphere, but some of the women who were the target of this policy developed their own definitions and culture, acknowledging that their world was different from that of men and that they were starting to form their own ideological spaces in Japanese society. If the separation of male and female spheres of behavior and activism was an ideology imposed *on* women by the government and some intellectuals, part of this same ideology was also used *by* women.

Final Remarks

For Meiji women, finding a place for themselves was not just a matter of getting out of their houses and speaking in public. It implied the possibility of articulating topics of common concern through a common language and of finding an audience. In spite of the fact that in the mid-1880s women's goals were limited and defined by their social class, group, or region, without public spaces in which to debate and extend those debates to the wider population what women accomplished in these years would have taken many more decades to develop.

Through the publicity they obtained and created as a result of their activities, early Meiji women arrived at a definition of their own world, *fujin shakai*, which was characterized by the willingness to support the development of their nation through the full use of their abilities without renouncing what they considered to be their rights.

Just as Colley writes of Britain, "At one and the same time, separate sexual spheres were being increasingly prescribed in theory, yet increasingly broken through in practice," it will become clear that the promulgation in 1880 and 1890, respectively, of the Ordinance on Public Assembly and the Law on Assembly and Political Associations, which limited women's participation in political activities, far from being proof of women's limitations, were signs that early Meiji women had indeed created for themselves the possibility of speaking and acting in Japanese society.[78] To be sure, these measures prove that women's efforts were neither strong nor concerted enough to reach their goals and that they partially failed through lack

---

77. Cott, *The Bonds of Womanhood*, 197–205.
78. Linda Colley, *Britons: Forging the Nation, 1707–1837* (London: Vintage, 1996), 263. Lerner argued that it was no accident that in North America "the slogan 'woman's place is in the home' took on a certain aggressiveness and shrillness precisely at the time when increasing numbers of poorer women *left* their homes to become factory workers." Gerda Lerner, "The Lady and the Mill Girl: Changes in the Status of Women in the Age of Jackson," *Midcontinent American Studies Journal* 10.1 (1969): 12.

of venues, money, education, and social power and cohesion. However, if there had been no significant numbers of women attending meetings, delivering speeches, and asking for political and property rights, more education, more freedom of thought, and greater participation in public society there would have been no need for these laws.

Finally, the Meiji period has been described as the age in which more democratic forms of government were envisioned, the print media truly developed, associations were founded to allow enlightened men to discuss matters of interest to Japan and educate their fellow men, and men could come face-to-face with the "West" as a place to explore if not necessarily learn from.[79] In this book I draw attention to the roles and activities women played in the development of Meiji society. With two chapters on public, private, and missionary girls' schools, the topics they taught, the friendships the students formed, and the ways in which girls wanted to use such education; with two chapters on women's organizations, Japanese women's encounters with Western women and their theories on womanhood, and Japanese women's struggles to obtain property, legal, and political rights; with articles taken from contemporary newspapers and magazines detailing the number and types of public speeches women organized and took part in and the books and articles they published; it will be clear that women's activities and thoughts were not corollary to or by-products of those of men and that we need to look carefully at women's participation in social and cultural life if we want to understand the development of Meij society.

79. Most recently, see Kim, *The Age of Visions.*

2

Female Students and Teachers in Private and Public Schools

> In the process of educating girls and women, we must put across the idea of serving and helping their country. The models for women are a mother nurturing her child; a mother teaching her child; her son coming of age and being conscripted to go to war and leaving his mother with a good-bye; a son fighting bravely on the battlefield; and a mother receiving a telegram informing of her son's death in the war.[1]

This passage, written by Mori Arinori 森有礼 (1847–89) in 1887 when he was minister of education, reflects the gendered nationalistic ideology of late-nineteenth-century Japan in which men were supposed to contribute to the formation of a strong and powerful country by serving their nation in times of peace and war. Mori believed that male subjects could deliver the desired results only if women, too, lived according to well-defined codes of behavior, and therefore the Meiji school system was aimed at educating women to be *ryōsai kenbo* (good wives, wise mothers).

The products of this education system, however, also included women who asked for female higher education and developed gendered criticisms of Japanese society. Their opinions were not only the result of personal ambitions but also of external influences such as the education they received at school and from their families. There is therefore a clear need to consider how these women responded to the authorities' educational goals rather than just what they were supposed to derive from such education.

1. Morosawa Yōko, ed., *Dokyumento onna no hyakunen* (One hundred years of documents on women), vol. 2, *Onna to kyōiku* (Women and education) (Heibonsha, 1978), 24, translated in Kimi Hara, "Challenges to Education for Girls and Women in Modern Japan: Past and Present," in *Japanese Women: New Feminist Perspectives on the Past, Present, and Future*, edited by Fujimura-Fanselow Kumiko and Kameda Atsuko, 93–106 (New York: Feminist Press, 1995), 96.

Given the scattered nature of the primary sources available, and given that the percentage of girls attending schools was much lower than that of boys, a pattern that would not change until the early twentieth century, in this chapter I can only present relatively sparse information about what girls and young women themselves thought of, and wanted from, their schooling. My purpose, however, is not to show how a *quantitative* difference in the number of girls receiving an education helped them rethink the aims of such education, although numbers certainly played a part in such development, but how a *qualitative* difference in education and educational environments enabled some of them to debate female education and its uses.

Education for girls did have antecedents, so before examining the impact of the educational reforms started during the early Meiji period and of the institutions that were created for that purpose it is important to survey what had been possible before.

The Late Edo Period

As a general rule, female education in the Edo period suited the needs of the different classes.[2] Girls of samurai families were taught weaving, sewing, reading, writing, and domestic skills at home by their female relatives or private tutors. Their lives were expected to revolve around their households, and their roles in life consisted of giving birth to sons. Although examples of samurai women who defied gendered expectations and obtained a male education—for example, in Chinese learning—have come to light, this does not mean that they were able to forfeit their duties, as they often pursued their educational ambitions later in life, *after* having fulfilled their roles. On the other hand, girls of lower-rank samurai families, whose lives were more similar to those of merchants and commoners, were less restricted in their movements and could attend *terakoya*, local schools that taught basic reading and writing; *ohariya*, schools that taught needlework and other female chores; and in some cases *shijuku*, private schools or classes where subjects such as Japanese, Chinese, and Western studies were taught to students who had already obtained a certain degree of education. However, lower-rank samurai girls had less free time, and their educational goals were not so much intellectual or artistic development as the acquisition of practical numeracy and literacy in order to contribute to their families' occupations.[3]

2. Walthall also points out that the kind of literacy men and women acquired during the Edo period was largely a matter of chance, depending on the books and teachers the students could access. Anne Walthall, "Women and Literacy from Edo to Meiji," in *The Female as Subject: Reading and Writing in Early Modern Japan*, edited by P. F. Kornicki, Mara Patessio, and G. G. Rowley, Michigan Monograph Series in Japanese Studies, no. 70 (Ann Arbor: Center for Japanese Studies, University of Michigan, 2010), 215–35.

3. The number of girls in these "schools" was much higher in Edo (Tokyo) and the other major cities than in the provincial towns, where it appears that a large percentage of *terakoya* taught boys and

Advocates of a less home-centered female education started to appear during the late Edo period, and in the 1850s more schools for samurai girls were opened to replace home schooling. In 1837 Okumura Kisaburō 奥村熹三郎, a bakufu retainer, published *Reasons for the Establishment of Jogakkō* (girls' schools). He argued that it was necessary to remedy the state of extravagance and moral degeneracy among women in Edo, and since mothers had clearly failed in this task, girls should be sent to schools where women teachers would educate them in traditional values. He was not addressing girls of wealthy families alone, though, for he considered that education could turn "even" girls of the commoner class into good mothers.[4] In *Outline of Education for Warriors* (1856), the samurai intellectual Yoshida Shōin 吉田松陰 (1830–59) argued that it was necessary to open *jogakkō* and that teachers should be selected from among middle-aged widows of samurai families. There *bushi* (samurai) girls would study writing, reading, moral textbooks, and womanly skills, and dormitory accommodations would be provided for those far away from home. He also argued that state-funded education for all would produce a land of educated men and women.[5] That these aims were being partly fulfilled is clear from the many examples of private classes conducted by samurai (and sometimes commoner) women who could earn a living using their skills.[6] In any case, during the Edo period the ultimate goal of female education was for girls to become wives, procreators, and workers.

---

girls in the same buildings, although many had separate spaces and textbooks for the two sexes. See Kanbe Yasumitsu, *Meiji shoki Tokyo no jogakkō* (Girls' schools in Tokyo during the early Meiji period) (Unknown publisher, 1964), 1–7, 1 n. 10. See also Umihara Tōru, *Kinsei no gakkō to kyōiku* (Early modern schools and education) (Kyoto: Shibunkaku, 1988), 266–76.

4. *Jogakkō hokki no shui* 女学校発起之趣意. See Murakami Tadashi, "Kinsei Zōjōji ryō ni okeru 'Jogakkō hokki no shuisho' ni tsuite" (On the "Reasons for the establishment of *jogakkō*" in the land belonging to the Zōjōji temple in the early modern period), *Hōsei shigaku* 30 (1978): 16–31; and Seki Tamiko, *Edo kōki no joseitachi* (Women of the late Edo period) (Aki shobō, 1980), 105–114, both cited in Lola Okazaki-Ward, "Women and Their Education in the Tokugawa Period of Japan," MPhil thesis, University of Sheffield, 1993, 90–92.

5. *Bukyō zensho kōroku* 武教全書講録, cited in Okazaki-Ward, "Women and Their Education," 91–93; Inoue Hisao, "A Historical Sketch of the Development of the Modern Educational System for Women in Japan," *Education in Japan: Journal for Overseas* 6 (1971): 17. The original is reprinted in Matsumoto Sannosuke, ed., *Yoshida Shōin* (Yoshida Shōin), vol. 31 of *Nihon no meicho* (Japanese famous authors) (Chūō kōronsha, 1973), 137–89, esp. 179–84.

6. Many such examples are noted in Haga Noboru, Ichibangase Yasuko, Nakajima Kuni, and Soda Kōichi, eds., *Nihon josei jinmei jiten* (Biographical dictionary of Japanese women) (Nihon tosho Center, 1993). There were two kinds of women teachers during the late Edo period, those who worked in *terakoya* and those who taught in *shijuku*. Both female teachers and students were rare in *shijuku*, especially outside Edo, while the teachings offered in Edo period *terakoya* were often to be found in early Meiji period *kajuku* (another kind of private school often located at the home of the teacher). Sugano Noriko, "Terakoya to onna shishō" (Terakoya and women teachers), in *Kyōiku to shisō* (Education and ideology), vol. 8 of *Nihon joseishi ronshū* (Collection of essays on Japanese women's history), edited by Sōgō joseishi kenkyūkai, 140–58 (Yoshikawa kōbunkan, 1998).

Upper-Middle-Class Female Education
during the Early Meiji Period

Although comprehensive school attendance statistics of the late Edo and early Meiji periods cannot be ascertained due to the lack of substantial hard data and the unreliability of that which is available, and although fewer girls attended *terakoya* and *shijuku* during the Edo period than in the early Meiji period, it is nevertheless arguable that the ratio of women "obtaining an education" during the end of the Edo period was not much lower than that of the early Meiji period.[7] If so, why was there so much criticism directed at girls' education during the early Meiji period?

First and foremost, it was the content of female education that came under scrutiny. In 1871 Kuroda Kiyotaka 黒田清隆 (1840–1900), deputy minister of the Development Bureau in Hakodate (Hokkaido), argued that education was a tool that could transform people and make Japan prosper. Education was transmitted in the Western world in the first place by mothers, so in Japan it was necessary to teach girls who would then become good wives and mothers. In 1871 the Iwakura mission arrived in North America with five girls, as recommended by Kuroda. These girls were supposed to receive an education that would benefit Japan on their return and would serve as a sign of Japan's willingness to transform itself into a "modern and civilized" power. In 1872 Kuroda also supported the opening of a girls' school, the Kaitakushi jogakkō 開拓使女学校, which aimed at educating girls who would remain in Hokkaido in an endeavor to help with its development.[8]

Thus, for Japan to achieve the level of "development" of Western countries it was necessary to educate Japanese men *and* women. In the various *jokunsho* 女訓書 (conduct books) and *ōraimono* 往来物 (works for popular education) published during the Edo period there is little or no mention of women as educators of their children, and children were often raised by someone other than the mother.[9] It was not until the late years of the Edo period, and especially during the Meiji period, that motherhood was invested with this new task, the Japanese people being

---

7. Umihara Tōru, *Kinsei no gakkō to kyōiku*, 266–73, offers some data for the late Edo and early Meiji periods.

8. On the Iwakura mission and its journey to North American and Europe, see Kume Kunitake, *The Iwakura Embassy, 1871–1873: A True Account of the Ambassador Extraordinary and Plenipotentiary's Journey of Observation through the United States of America and Europe*, 5 vols. (Princeton: Princeton University Press, 2002). The Kaitakushi jogakkō was set up in Tokyo. It employed Japanese and foreign teachers, and the majority of the students were granted government scholarships. It was then moved to Sapporo and renamed Sapporo jogakkō. Kanbe, *Meiji shoki*, 26–28.

9. For an analysis of such books, see Saitō Junkichi, "Edo jidai no kazoku kyōiku" (Home education during the Edo period), *Nihon shigaku kyōiku kenkyūsho kiyō* 21.1, 22.1, 23.1 (1986–88): 349–80, 419–54, 443–75.

influenced by ideas from abroad. For instance, the educator Nakamura Masanao, who had gone to England as a student, noted that English children could answer difficult questions because their mothers were well educated.[10]

David Murray of Rutgers University, who in 1873 became an adviser to the Japanese Ministry of Education, replying in 1872 to Mori Arinori's questions about the North American school system, wrote:

> Female education is equally important with male education. . . . She must receive that culture which will make her the acceptable and equal companion of man. The comfort and happiness of home depend largely upon her, and it is the part of wisdom to give her the means of making it refined and cultivated. The care and supervision of children naturally fall into her hands during their most impressible years, and the guardians of the future men and women of a nation ought, in common prudence, to be well educated.[11]

The topic of Western women's education was taken up even in novels. In Yokogawa Shūtō's 横河秋濤 *Passage to Enlightenment*, published in 1874, Kaika Bunmei (Mr. Enlightenment Civilization), one of the characters, states that women in the provinces were working in the fields and helping their families, whereas women in the cities were putting on makeup, plucking their eyebrows, dressing up, and enjoying life. Since their daughters learned only to play music or dance, if they were sent to Western countries they would become a nuisance to the people there. Girls in those countries attended school from the age of six or seven and obtained the same education as boys. Japanese girls, without a similar education, and without even knowing the first book of the *Onna daigaku*, would not be able to befriend them.[12]

---

10. Yamakawa Kikue, *Onna nidai no ki* (Two generations of women) (Heibonsha, 1972), 28–31. Among the members of the group Meirokusha, Mitsukuri Shūhei 箕作秋坪 (1825–86) thought that to achieve a strong and powerful country parents had to recognize the training of their children as their responsibility; those children would do the same with their children, and this would become common practice. Mitsukuri Shūhei, "On Education," *Meiroku zasshi*, no. 8, May 1874, translated in William Braisted, *Meiroku Zasshi: Journal of the Japanese Enlightenment* (Cambridge, Mass.: Harvard University Press, 1976), 106–8. Fukuzawa Yukichi held a similar opinion. Japan could "attain civilization" only if men and women obtained an education. If women remained ignorant, he argued, they would not be able to improve their condition or teach their children, and as a consequence Japan would not progress. Fukuzawa Yukichi, "Nippon fujin ron" (On Japanese Women) translated in Kiyooka Eiichi, ed. and trans., *Fukuzawa Yukichi on Japanese Women: Selected Works* (Tokyo: University of Tokyo Press, 1988), 6–69.

11. Arinori Mori, ed., *Education in Japan: A Series of Letters Addressed by Prominent Americans to Arinori Mori* (New York: D. Appleton Century, 1873), 87–108, quoted in Herbert Passin, *Society and Education in Japan* (New York: Columbia University Press, 1982), 222–23.

12. Yokogawa Shūtō, *Kaika no iriguchi* (Passage to enlightenment) (Osaka: Matsumura bungaidō, 1874), vol. 4, 3–4.

Not only the education of women and their children but also the merits of prenatal "education" for the development of the mental and physical strength of the child were discussed, and such an "education" could be provided only by strong, healthy, morally abiding, and educated women.[13] This belief was used to justify the need for new schools; in 1876 the Okayama prefectural government promulgated the "Rules of Women's Vocational School," which was established soon thereafter. It stated, "A woman is the mother of education. A person's character, whether he becomes good or bad, talented or silly, is dependent on the education of his mother. Education starts from the womb throughout the growing years under the care of a mother."[14] It is not surprising, then, to find that soon after the Meiji period began new publications started to appear for an educated male and female readership, such as the magazine *How to Raise Children*, published as early as 1877, and this philosophy continued to be propagated throughout the Meiji period.[15]

Many Japanese women quickly accepted this new educational ideology. Kozaki (Iwamura) Chiyoko 小崎千代子 (1863–1939), for example, later a member of the Fujin kyōfūkai and the wife of the Christian Kozaki Hiromichi 小崎弘道 (1856–1938), was convinced that Japan would not progress if girls did not receive an education that was different from that imparted during the Edo period since education was a necessary step toward the well-being of her nation. Girls were expected to become mothers and raise their children, but how could they raise the next generation if they themselves had no education?[16]

The new educational goal of raising mothers who could become teachers for their children as espoused by the government and some intellectuals was not without critics, who thought that women did not have the mental ability required to learn, that the new education proposed was pointless for their roles as wives and procreators, or that women would become conceited if they were given more than

13. Nakamura Masanao, "Creating Good Mothers," *Meiroku zasshi*, no. 33, March 1875, translated in Braisted, *Meiroku Zasshi*, 401–4.
14. Takahashi Educational Institution Volunteer Centre, *Fukunishi Shigeko and Her Life: Never Ending Challenges and Dedication to Women's Education and Women in Development (WID)—the Junsei Spirit* (Takahashi: Okayama gakuen, 2001), 11. I could only find the English version of the text.
15. *Kosodate no sōshi*, 子育の草子, in Kindai josei bunkashi kenkyūkai, ed., *Fujin zasshi no yoake* (The dawn of women's magazines) (Ōzorasha, 1989), 9. To give one more example, in the *Reasons for the Opening of San'yō eiwa jogakkō* (*San'yō eiwa jogakkō setsuritsu shushi* 山陽英和女学校設立趣旨 written in 1886, the year in which this school was opened in Okayama) the authors declared that "whether a child becomes a virtuous man or a villain, an intelligent man or a fool, depends on the education given by the mother. Even in the West they say that 'A person's life is decided by his seventh year of age'." Document preserved, uncataloged, in the archive of San'yō gakuen daigaku, Okayama.
16. Nakajima Masukichi, ed., *Meien no gakusei jidai* (Famous ladies' school days) (Yomiuri shinbunsha, 1907), 182–87.

a basic education. Others argued that girls were overstepping social boundaries and bringing to public attention different, more controversial characteristics of women's education by wearing *hakama* (trouserlike kimonos worn by men, which allowed women more freedom of movement), showing a confidence that did not befit women, and reading literature that was not deemed proper for a female audience. Here lies a major difference between Edo and Meiji period education for young women, one that helps explain why there was so much critical discussion of women's education during the early Meiji period. During the Edo period, girls who were able to obtain an education in subjects that were deemed suitable only for men gained recognition for their achievements within their locality or social circle at best. When they participated in social or political activities, as in the case of Matsuo Taseko, most of them did so without gendering their actions or formally criticizing the place they had in society, and when they obtained prominent positions, for example, by becoming physicians, their names were often known only in their area or region.[17] Such isolation meant that they could be more easily controlled and that it was more difficult for them to become troublemakers. During the early Meiji period, on the other hand, girls' education became of public use. It was linked to national development and strength through the creation of girls' schools, it was paraded at the Western balls organized in the capital for a foreign audience, and it was discussed in the print media and male and female associations. However, it was also represented in public by girls who were defiant of social mores. These were what I call "dangerous women" not only because they demanded greater educational rights, advocating new social systems or models of womanhood, but especially because they were featured in magazines and newspapers, attracting an audience.

Finally, although Okumura Kisaburō seems to have been the first to use the word *jogakkō* (girls' school) in 1837 in the work discussed above, it was not until the Meiji period that this word came to be widely used to indicate the gendered aspect of such schools, defining private, public, and missionary education for girls. It did not signify the same level of education throughout the Meiji period or throughout the country, and during the early Meiji period it was often used to refer to elementary schools. The students at these schools were known as *jogakusei*, a term that distinguished "female students" from male "students." From the beginning of the Meiji period government documents and journal articles referred to *joshi kyōiku*, "female education," but I found little or no mention of *danshi kyōiku*, "male

---

17. Anne Walthall, *The Weak Body of a Useless Woman: Matsuo Taseko and the Meiji Restoration* (Chicago: University of Chicago Press, 1998). On women physicians, see Mara Patessio and Mariko Ogawa, "To Become a Woman Doctor in Early Meiji Japan (1868–1890): Women's Struggles and Ambitions," *Historia Scientiarum* 15.2 (2005): 159–76.

education." Such new words helped to create a sense of separate spheres and were used not only in the context of the school system but also in relation to all other jobs and activities women were allowed to perform; thus words like *jokyōshi,* "women teachers," *joi,* "women doctors," and *fujinkai,* "ladies' associations," came into widespread use. Although this policy of gender differentiation defined the distinctive place Meiji authorities were assigning to girls and women, it also indirectly helped some of them recognize the government's gendered practices and shape and address their criticism accordingly.

The First Steps

During the Edo period there had existed a network of schools where boys could learn Chinese, Japanese, and Western studies. However, the regional and class disparities in Edo period female and male education meant that when the Ministry of Education issued the *Gakusei* 学制 (Fundamental Code of Education) in 1872, the proposed revolution was supposed to have a profound impact on people's lives. Under its provisions, the subjects taught at the elementary level were no longer to differ according to the social class of the students. Moreover, stating that "there shall be, in the future, no community with an illiterate family, or a family with an illiterate person," the newly organized system aimed to abolish, at least nominally, educational inequalities, openly decreeing that education was for everybody, women included.[18] This educational reform was eventually to provide Japan with an educated population, but the creation of a national school system, together with the formation of a national language, was also perceived as a way to eliminate regional disparities and differences and generate a national level of common knowledge.

The education system changed slowly, in spite of the ambitious *Gakusei,* and even after the establishment of the Ministry of Education (Monbushō) in 1871, private schools did not vanish and many were opened by women.[19] "Private schools,"

18. Translated in Passin, *Society and Education,* 209–11. The Japanese version is reprinted in Monbushō, ed., *Gakusei hyakunenshi* (History of the educational system during the past one hundred years) (Gyōsei, 1972), vol. 2, 11.

19. There were at least 24 private schools in Tokyo, where in 1871 girls could study subjects such as Chinese learning, painting, literature, and arithmetic. See Kanbe, *Meiji shoki,* 5–6, for descriptions of each school, and also 34–6. Although it is not clear how long they stayed open, according to Monbushō statistics for 1873, of 492 private schools offering an elementary education that year, 73 were founded by *shizoku* (former samurai) women. Mitsui Reiko, *Gendai fujin undōshi nenpyō* (Timeline of the contemporary women's movement) (San'ichi shobō, 1963), 3. For additional examples of private schools opened by women during the early Meiji period, see Tokyo-to, *Tokyo no joshi kyōiku* (Female education in Tokyo) (Tokyo-to, 1961), 29–30. Given that not all the schools that accepted girls were called *jogakkō,* as Miwada Masako's 三輪田真佐子 Meirin gakusha 明倫学舎, opened in 1880 in Ehime prefecture, shows, it is difficult to evaluate the extent and content of early Meiji private female education. Miwada Masako, *Miwada Masako:*

which, at least at the beginning of the Meiji period, were often nothing more than "private classes," were not merely remnants of Edo period education but were starting to fulfill some of the objectives of the *Gakusei* by offering girls and boys new educational opportunities, for example, by teaching English.[20] One famous private school for girls in Tokyo was Ueda jogakkō 上田女学校, also known as Mannenbashi jogakkō, opened in 1872 in Tsukiji by Ueda Shun 上田畯 who, as a supporter of female education, sent his daughter, Ueda Sadako 上田悌子, to America with the Iwakura mission. Yamakawa Chise 山川千世 (1857–1947), the mother of the socialist and feminist Yamakawa Kikue 山川菊栄 (1890–1980) and the daughter of a Mito Confucian scholar, studied there from 1872 with nine other students who were mainly from upper-class families. Kikue wrote that one day Julia Carrothers, a Presbyterian missionary, showed the students a terrestrial globe, indicated the position of Japan, and explained the movements of the earth. Chise was deeply impressed and told her parents what she had learned at school.[21]

The plan of the Monbushō was to supplant private schools with its own, but in order to do so it first needed to train teachers. In 1872, teacher training schools were opened throughout Japan, making it possible to obtain a certificate that allowed women and men to teach at the elementary level after a few months' training.[22] In December 1871 the Monbushō issued the "Regulations for the Opening of Girls' Schools," according to which girls between eight and fifteen years old who could afford it would study in *jogakkō* five hours a day, and in 1872 it opened the Takebashi jogakkō, which later became Tokyo jogakkō.[23] There girls were taught Japanese classics, mathematics, physics, chemistry, manual arts, history, home economics, geography, gymnastics, and English for six years by six Japanese teachers and one foreigner, Margaret Clark Griffis (1838–1913). Among the textbooks used were two best sellers: Nakamura Masanao's translation of Samuel Smiles's *Self Help*, *Saigoku risshihen* 西国立志篇 (Tales of Successful Men in Western Countries), which had been published in 1871; and Fukuzawa Yukichi's *Gakumon no susume* 学問のす〉め

Oshiegusa/hoka (Miwada Masako: *Oshiegusa* and other writings) (Nihon tosho Center, 2005); and Margaret Mehl, "Women Educators and the Confucian Tradition in Meiji Japan (1868–1912): Miwada Masako and Atomi Kakei," *Women's History Review* 10.4 (2001): 579–602.

20. *Chōya shinbun* (no. 1379, 05.04.1878, 4) told its readers that an English woman teacher residing in Tsukiji was looking for students; she taught English and penmanship among other subjects.

21. Yamakawa, *Onna nidai no ki*, 16–17. On Chise, see also Martha Tocco, "Norms and Texts for Women's Education in Tokugawa Japan," in *Women and Confucian Cultures in Premodern China, Korea, and Japan*, edited by Dorothy Ko, Jahyun Kim Haboush, and Joan Piggott, 193–218 (Berkeley: University of California Press, 2003).

22. Karasawa Tomitarō, *Joshi gakusei no rekishi* (A history of female students) (Mokujisha, 1979), 28.

23. *Jogakkō nyūmon no kokoroe* 女学校入門之心得, *Nichiyō shinbun*, no. 3, January 1872, 4–5, also reprinted in Tokyo joshi kōtō shihan gakkō, ed., *Tokyo joshi kōtō shihan gakkō rokujūnenshi* (Sixty years of the Tokyo women's higher normal school) (Daiichi shobō, 1981), 48.

(An Encouragement of Learning, 1876).[24] In its first year, Tokyo jogakkō had 38 students, increasing to 78 the next year, and the school was intended as an example to be replicated in other prefectures as well.[25] The school's aim was to educate wealthy girls, and one such student was Hatoyama Haruko 鳩山春子 (1861–1938), the daughter of a government officer, who could afford to go to school in *jinrikisha* and owned a copy of Hepburn's Japanese-English dictionary, which was worth eleven yen and considered a "luxury item." Her father had decided to send her there, but Hatoyama recalled that she was concentrating more on enjoying her studies than on the meaning of her education for her nation's development.[26]

Another step the Monbushō took was the opening of Tokyo joshi shihan gakkō (Tokyo Women's Normal School, now Ochanomizu University), which became a model for similar schools in various provinces. It was established in 1874 and opened in 1875, and the empress donated five thousand yen to it, giving the imperial seal of approval to female higher education.[27] If in the case of Tokyo jogakkō girls were supposed to obtain an education before getting married, those graduating from a normal school—most of whom, at least at the beginning, came from *shizoku* (former samurai) families—were educated explicitly to become teachers. However, it was common practice for girls to be withdrawn before the end of their course. Once the school opened, 193 girls applied and 74 were chosen, but only 15 graduated in February 1879 and 18 in July.[28] Finding suitable women teachers in

---

24. Tokyo joshi kōtō shihan gakkō, *Tokyo joshi*, 49. Griffis, who was teaching English, initially earned a monthly stipend of 50 yen, which became 110 by 1873 and 150 in 1874. Usui Chizuko, "Meiji kaikaki ni okeru Margaret Griffis no yakuwari" (The role of Margaret Griffis during the "civilization and enlightenment" period in the Meiji era), in *Za Yatoi: Oyatoi gaikokujin no sōgōteki kenkyū* (The yatoi: A comprehensive study of foreign employees in Japan), edited by Shimada Tadashi, 130–50 (Shibunkaku, 1987), 131.

25. Tokyo joshi kōtō shihan gakkō, *Tokyo joshi*, 26. In 1875 the government decided to make Tokyo jogakkō a school for higher studies, and therefore the rules changed. Girls were supposed to be between fourteen and seventeen years of age and to have received an elementary education. The course of study was four and a half hours of lessons each day over six years. Although in 1876 there were 152 students, the school was closed in 1877, apparently due to lack of funding. Students who wanted to continue their education were sent to Tokyo joshi shihan gakkō. Tokyo joshi kōtō shihan gakkō, *Tokyo joshi*, 49; Monbushō, ed., *Gakusei hachijūnenshi* (History of the educational system during the past eighty years) (Ōkurashō insatsukyoku, 1954), 152.

26. Hatoyama Haruko, *Waga jijoden* (Telling my life) (Nihon tosho Center, [1929] 1997), 52–58. Hatoyama worked for a few years at her alma mater, founded the school Kyōritsu joshi shokugyō gakkō 共立女子職業学校 (now Kyōritsu joshi daigaku) in 1886, and was an active member of the Aikoku fujinkai. Karasawa, *Joshi gakusei*, 21. In English, see Sally A. Hastings, "Hatoyama Haruko: Ambitious Woman," in *The Human Tradition in Modern Japan*, edited by Anne Walthall, 81–98 (Wilmington: Scholarly Resources, 2002).

27. Tokyo joshi kōtō shihan gakkō, *Tokyo joshi*, 23.

28. The course of study was five years, and students had to be between fourteen and twenty years old to apply. Most of the applicants were from Tokyo, and many girls from the provinces saw tables and chairs there for the first time and had difficulty eating the meat served in the dining hall. After receiving their diplomas, female graduates were required to teach for five years, and male

the early years of the school's existence also proved to be problematic. Yamakawa writes that one teacher, a certain Ōta, realizing how limited her knowledge was, decided to resign and become a student herself, graduating with the second class. Although she did not do so, Toyoda Fuyuko 豊田芙雄子 (1845–1941) from Mito domain also felt that she should resign and become a student.[29]

Girls had a hard time completing their courses for various reasons. Illness of family members often meant that they had to withdraw from school or renounce the possibility of furthering their education once they graduated. Ōshima (Ibuka 井深) Hanako 大島花子 (b. 1864), for example, a girl from a samurai family, wrote that her mother, whose education had been exceptional for the Edo period, was not satisfied with private schooling for her girls. Ōshima was sent to a government school after the Meiji Restoration (even though her mother was afraid that contact with children of other social classes would make her "rude"), but by the age of thirteen she had to leave to take care of her ill mother and the household.[30] Many parents were against the idea of educating their daughters. Yamawaki Fusako 山脇房子 (1867–1935) from Matsue, Shimane prefecture, later the director of Kōtō joshi jisshū gakkō 高等女子實修学校, recalled that her mother did not value female education. Yamawaki nevertheless entered an elementary school when she was twelve and helped her mother with the household chores from the age of fourteen, and when a *joshi shihan gakkō* was opened in Matsue she was able to persuade her father to send her there. The school was closed one year before her graduation, and Yamawaki was convinced that one reason for its closure was that locals were criticizing its very existence, for they thought that a woman who received "too much" education would become *namaiki*, "conceited." The school authorities felt sorry for the thirty students and awarded them the graduation certificate nevertheless.[31]

---

graduates for ten, but they could be sent anywhere for the first three years in the case of male teachers and two in the case of females. Ochanomizu joshi daigaku hyakunenshi kankō iinkai, ed., *Ochanomizu joshi daigaku hyakunenshi* (One hundred years of Ochanomizu Women's University) (Ochanomizu joshi daigaku, 1984), 40–43, 56; Karasawa Tomitarō, *Kyōshi no rekishi: kyōshi no seikatsu to rinri* (A history of teachers: Their lifestyle and ethics) (Sōbunsha, 1955), 108. In 1876 a kindergarten was attached to the school. Tokyo joshi kōtō shihan gakkō, *Tokyo joshi*, 37. According to Fukaya and Fukaya, 593 girls were studying in *shihan gakkō* in 1886 and 889 in 1894. Fukaya Masashi and Fukaya Kazuko, *Jokyōshi mondai no kenkyū: shokugyō shikō to katei shikō* (A study of women teachers: The conflict between employment and family) (Nagoya: Reimei shobō, 1971), 257.

29. Yamakawa, *Onna nidai no ki*, 39–40.

30. She recalled that she could study and read newspapers at night but during the day she had no time for herself. Hana Ibuka, paper preserved in the Archive of Mount Holyoke College and Special Collections.

31. Interview in Nakajima, *Meien no gakusei jidai*, 98. Asada Mikako, a student of the missionary Joshi gakuin, also recalled that in her hometown female education meant elementary schooling since, it was believed, with anything more than that girls would become *namaiki*. Tamura Hikari, ed., *Joshi gakuin hachijūnenshi* (Eighty years of Joshi gakuin) (Joshi gakuin, 1951), 112.

Some parents were ashamed of their daughters' thirst for learning, as the following case shows.

> I apologize from the bottom of my heart to all my esteemed ancestors for having raised a daughter who wanted to study at a women's normal school [Chiba joshi shihan gakkō]. . . . We held a family meeting to discuss the matter, and it was eventually decided by my father-in-law that it would be best to enroll her in the school rather than oppose a prefectural ordinance which had established the school for all qualified applicants. Thus, we let her go. However, so as not to bring shame to the honor of our family name, our daughter was enrolled under her mother's family name.[32]

A debate that took place in Tokushima prefecture tells us why people were resistant to the idea of female teachers. Those who were in favor of this kind of occupation for women stated that their patient disposition made them suitable for teaching children, they could be paid lower wages, and they could occupy positions that would allow men, who had hitherto been the teachers, to work in business or industry. Others argued that women were weak and could not be given the responsibility of educating young children, who instead needed active and capable teachers, while their jobs would clash with their natural occupations as mothers and wives.[33] Finally, the story of Kawachiyama Tora 河内山寅 (1855–1930) from Nagano prefecture suggests that women teachers were a surprising novelty in some areas since when she started working in an elementary school in 1877 her students said that she had become a teacher *even though* she was a woman.[34]

Although not all the young women who attended normal schools became teachers, the fact that their numbers rose steadily tells us that teaching was a desirable profession that enabled women to have an income that was the fruit of their "respectable" and "enlightened" work. In some cases, education changed women's lot and allowed them to earn a living, which in turn helped spur the drive for women's education.[35] Women teachers progressed quickly, in terms of both numbers and

---

32. Karasawa, *Kyōshi no rekishi*, 110, translated in Elizabeth Knipe Mouer, "Women in Teaching," in *Women in Changing Japan*, edited by Joyce Lebra, Joy Paulson, and Elizabeth Powers, 157–90 (Stanford: Stanford University Press, 1976), 162. I was not able to see the book Karasawa used as a source for this information.

33. *Kyōiku jiron*, 25.04.1888, reported in Kido Wakao, *Fujin kyōshi no hyakunen* (One hundred years of women teachers) (Meiji tosho shuppan, 1968), 22–23, and translated in Mouer, "Women in Teaching," 163.

34. Reported in Karasawa, *Kyōshi no rekishi*, 110. See also her reminiscences in *Kyōiku jiron*, no. 796, 25.05.1907, 18–20.

35. Whereas in 1873 there were 411 women teachers, by 1878 there were 1,965. Fukaya and Fukaya, *Jokyōshi mondai*, 248. Yajima Kajiko (chapter 3), who in 1873 was working in an elementary school in Tokyo, earned five yen a month. For Fukuda Hideko (aka Kageyama Hideko, chapter 5),

level of responsibility, as they often became directors of schools or dormitories. Take the example of Matsumoto Ogie 松本荻江 (1851–99), from Chichibu, whose father, Matsumoto Man'nen 松本万年, opened a medical practice and a private school where Ogino Ginko, the first woman officially recognized as doctor during the Meiji period, studied. Ogie married at nineteen but was sent home when her child died, allegedly because her husband's family accused her of being responsible for his death since she spent her days reading. She studied Chinese classics with her father, and when the Tokyo joshi shihan gakkō opened in 1875, she started teaching there at a monthly salary of fifteen yen, eventually becoming the head teacher of the Akita prefecture joshi shihan gakkō in 1885.[36]

For some girls becoming a teacher was a dream held since childhood, but others had different reasons to aspire to such a profession. Inokuchi Aguri 井口あぐり (1870–1931), from Akita prefecture, had been inspired by watching her father, who worked at the teachers' training school in her hometown. However, she recalled that for her sister becoming a teacher chiefly meant being able to study in an urban center, and she was not the only one thinking that way. Out of the 1,876 girl students living in Tokyo and frequenting private, public, and missionary schools in 1890, the majority came from Tokyo, but 100 came from Shizuoka prefecture, 50 from Nagano prefecture, 56 from Tochigi prefecture, 77 from Chiba prefecture, 59 from Gunma prefecture, 41 from Kagoshima prefecture, and 70 from Saitama prefecture.[37] By 1890 similar schools had been opened closer to these girls' homes, but they still chose to study in Tokyo.

Girls' Visibility

Since it was not easy to find students who could afford to pay the school fees or spend many years at school, the Tokyo joshi shihan gakkō also offered scholarships, and Hatoyama Haruko, who entered in 1877 and graduated in 1881, obtained a scholarship of four yen and fifty sen a month.[38] However, the number of students

---

being a teacher with a three-yen salary meant that she was financially independent and could reject marriage proposals. Kido, *Fujin kyōshi*, 16–17; Chieko Irie Mulhern, ed., *Heroic with Grace: Legendary Women of Japan* (London: M. E. Sharpe, 1991), 218. Fukuda discusses her teaching job in her autobiography, reprinted in Murata Shizuko and Ōki Motoko, eds., *Fukuda Hideko shū* (Collection of documents by and about Fukuda Hideko) (Fuji shuppan, 1998), 14. Hane has translated a part of Fukuda's autobiography in which she describes such a marriage proposal. Mikiso Hane, *Reflections on the Way to the Gallows: Rebel Women in Prewar Japan* (Berkeley: University of California Press, 1988), 35.

36. Nirazuka Ichisaburō, *Saitama no onnatachi: Rekishi no naka no 24 nin* (Women of Saitama: Twenty-four case studies) (Urawa: Sakitama shuppankai, 1979), 181–7.

37. For Inokuchi's memoirs see the interview in Nakajima, *Meien no gakusei jidai*, 1–2; for the data on Tokyo see *Jogaku zasshi*, no. 202, 01.03.1890, 18.

38. Hatoyama, *Waga jijoden*, 68.

applying to study there was not as high as expected, and the government could not offer a substantial number of scholarships, which, in any case, seem to have gone to girls whose families were already wealthy. As a solution, many such schools were closed and *joshibu* (girls' sections) were attached to male schools in an attempt to save funds. Tokushima joshi shihan gakkō, for example, having opened at the end of 1878, closed in 1880, and instead a jogakkō was attached to Tokushima chūgakkō (a male middle school).

Given that enrollment figures at the *jogakkō* attached to Tokushima chūgakkō were not as high as the local authorities had hoped, the Joshi shōgeikai 女子奨芸会, a temporary display of the works of the students of the *jogakkō* and the neighboring elementary school, was organized as a way to recruit students. The exhibition was considered a success and was repeated in successive years.[39] These exhibitions served to draw attention to girls' education and its products, thus publicizing girls' schools. Kornicki has argued that Japan participated in international exhibitions in order to search for export markets and to improve its international status and image but it also established domestic exhibitions as public spaces in which culture could be shown and promoted.[40] Girl students were becoming a group whose works were to be displayed in such exhibitions, for they were students of the new system set up in order for Japan to reach *bunmei kaika* (civilization and enlightenment) but also because they were the first groups of girl students ever to be seen in public places and therefore a curiosity.

Female students' and teachers' attitudes and appearance quickly became objects of discussion. The earliest public speech meetings organized by women I have come across were held in 1876 at Tokyo joshi shihan gakkō. The first speech was on female education and attracted about 350 people. The speakers included the social activist Sasaki Toyoju 佐々城豊寿 (1853–1901), then a student of the school, and the educators Toyoda Fuyuko and Tanahashi Ayako 棚橋絢子 (1839–1939). The last speech was made by Nakamura Masanao, the school's director.[41] The second public meeting was held in April 1878, and two girls, Kobayashi Eiko 小林

39. Tokushima-ken kyōikukai, ed., *Tokushima-ken kyōiku enkakushi* (A history of Tokushima prefecture's educational system) (Tokushima: Tokushima-ken kyōikukai, 1959), 799–801. Girls' works were becoming a regular feature at public exhibitions. *San'yō shinpō* (no. 6, 14.01.1879, 2) advertized that "the female students of the training school in our prefecture [Okayama] presented their products at the exhibition opened this year." Reprinted in Aoki Mitsuko and Mitsuda Kyōko, eds., *Minkenki Okayama joseishi kankei shiryō* (Historical records related to the history of women in Okayama during the Minken period), vol. 4 of *Okayama minken undōshi kankei shiryōshū* (Collection of historical records related to the history of the Okayama Minken movement) (Okayama: Okayama minken undō hyakunen kinen gyōji jikkō iinkai, 1982), 18.

40. Peter Kornicki, "Public Display and Changing Values: Early Meiji Exhibitions and Their Precursors," *Monumenta Nipponica* 49.2 (1994): 167–96.

41. *Tōkyō nichinichi shinbun*, no. 1485, 15.11.1876, 2.

栄子 and Sakata Shizuko 佐方鎮子, gave speeches.[42] The *Kōeki mondō shinbun* reported that Kobayashi and Sakata looked bold and presumptuous, had butterfly coiffures, and walked in an unfeminine way, striding along three feet at a time.[43]

A number of similar descriptions had appeared much earlier than 1878. In 1872, for example, *Shinbun zasshi* reported that girl students, wearing male *hakama*, "come and go with Western books"; if this custom were to spread, the paper warned, the true nature of female education would be lost.[44] Atomi Kakei 跡見花渓 (1840–1926), who founded Atomi jogakkō in 1875, wrote that around 1870, when the only *jogakkō* in Tokyo was Takebashi jogakkō, girl students behaved in a conceited manner; they had "their hair cut and wore thin sashes like men; they did not wrap their books in a furoshiki cloth, but clasped them under their armpits, and then there were some who deliberately strutted along wearing long, striped haori jackets."[45] *Chōya shinbun* reported in 1875 that a group of (male?) teachers from a *jogakkō* had gone to a teahouse with seven or eight girls wearing *hakama*. They had called for some geishas and after partying for a few hours left the teahouse. This made clear the virtues of what was called "parity of rights" between the sexes, for in a period of civilization it was a good thing that men *and* women could enjoy the company of geishas.[46] Girls overstepping social boundaries could create further

---

42. Tomita Hitoshi, ed., *Jiten kindai nihon no senkusha* (A dictionary of pioneers in modern Japan) (Nichigai Associates, 1995), 268.

43. Reprinted in Miyatake Gaikotsu, *Meiji enzetsushi* (A history of speaking in public during the Meiji period) (Yūgensha, 1926), 38.

44. *Shinbun zasshi*, no. 35, 02.1872, 7. At the beginning of the Meiji period, female students and teachers at Tokyo jogakkō and Tokyo joshi shikan gakkō used *hakama* as the official school uniform, but in 1883 the government prohibited them from wearing it. Honda Masuko, *Jogakusei no keifu: saishiki sareru Meiji* (A genealogy of girl students: a vivid representation of the Meiji period) (Seidosha, 1990), 68–72, 79–88. On page 71 there are two photographs showing girl students at Tokyo joshi shikan gakkō during the late 1870s and the ways in which their uniforms had changed. See also Ochanomizu joshi daigaku hyakunenshi kankō iinkai, *Ochanomizu joshi daigaku*, 48–49. As with many other aspects of girls' education, what was decided and implemented in Tokyo was not necessarily followed in other areas, and so it cannot be assumed that "girls' uniforms" were the same everywhere. For example, during the Rokumeikan period girls from Tokyo joshi shikan gakkō and Kazoku jogakkō wore Western clothes, especially when they participated in the balls organized at the Rokumeikan, but that did not necessarily apply to students in provincial schools. It was only by the late 1890s that a new "female *hakama*," the *ebicha hakama* (maroon *hakama*), began to be used at Kazoku jogakkō and then became *the* girl students' uniform. Honda, *Jogakusei no keifu*, 79–88.

45. Mehl, "Women Educators," 588. The original interview was published in Nakajima, *Meien no gakusei jidai*, 87. Atomi opened her school in Tokyo and taught Japanese, Chinese classics, painting, poetry, arithmetic, sewing, Japanese music, tea ceremony, flower arranging, and physical education to the daughters of the upper classes, including the writer Miyake Kaho 三宅花圃 (1868–1943), who studied there soon after it opened. Haga et al., *Nihon josei jinmei jiten*; Rebecca Copeland, *Lost Leaves: Women Writers of Meiji Japan* (Honolulu: University of Hawai'i Press, 2000), 57. In 1890 she had 136 students, of which 61 were from Tokyo. *Jogaku zasshi*, no. 202, 01.03.1890, 18.

46. *Chōya shinbun*, no. 494, 10.04.1875, 1.

trouble. Another newspaper reported that girls wearing male *hakama* were a disturbing sight and parents had to pay attention to their daughters' behavior since otherwise they would think that it was good to imitate men and perhaps might go so far as to urinate like them.[47] Similar articles were published throughout the Meiji period. In 1885 the *Tokyo Yokohama mainichi shinbun* stated that as soon as girls learned how to read a little they lost their feminine virtues, walked along with bare arms, and frequented cheap shops where they rivaled the male students, sitting immodestly and ordering meat and sake out loud.[48]

Peiss has argued that,

> unconventional cross-gender behavior represented women's assault on the public realm. Thus women's entrance into the public sphere was tracked not only by their explicit grasping for political power and economic independence but through a number of symbolic acts, such as smoking, wearing bloomers or comfortable dress, and riding bicycles.[49]

Female education and girls' behavior became a matter of public debate from the beginning of the Meiji period, not only among the educated but also in the media since *jogakusei* were starting to become a visible presence in public society. For some, girls' masculine clothes and the way they walked, cut their hair, carried their books, talked, and presented themselves in public spaces were signs that they were losing their femininity.[50] They were seen as appropriating men's prerogatives, and if such behavior were to become widespread, then female education would become a danger to Japan's progress, rather than having a beneficial effect on it.

On the other hand, newspapers also provided girls living in the provinces with information about the various schools set up in the major cities, helping them decide which one to attend. Hani Motoko 羽仁もと子 (1873–1957), for example, recalled that *Chōya shinbun*, the newspaper her grandfather read, carried reports about the schools in Tokyo, and by reading them granddaughter and grandfather were able to choose the one most suitable for her.[51] Noguchi Yūka 野口幽香 (1866–1950),

---

47. *Yūbin hōchi shinbun*, no. 239, 15.01.1874, 2.
48. The article was reprinted in Inoue Nao, ed., *Nihon fujin sanron* (Collection of theories on Japanese women) (Privately published, 1886), 45–61, and translated by Marnie Anderson in "A Woman's Place: Gender, Politics, and the State in Meiji Japan," PhD diss., Ann Arbor, University of Michigan, 2005, 102.
49. Kathy Peiss, "Going Public: Women in Nineteenth-Century Cultural History," *American Literary History* 3.4 (1991): 818.
50. On female students' use of male language during the Meiji period, see Momoko Nakamura, "Discursive Construction of the Ideology of 'Women's Language': 'Schoolgirl Language' in the Meiji Period (1868–1912)," *Shizen Ningen Shakai* 36 (2004): 43–80.
51. Hani Motoko, *Hansei o kataru* (Telling my life so far) (Fujin no tomosha, 1928), 44. See also her story in Nakajima, *Meien no gakusei jidai*, 90–6.

from a lower-rank *shizoku* family in Bizen Okayama, stated that her parents were afraid to let her go to Tokyo to study because for them it seemed as far away as North America, so it is clear that many girls would have remained at home had their families not learned more about the suitability of the schools they were considering for their daughters also through newspaper advertisements.[52] Whereas newspapers offered sparse information, *Iratsume* 以良都女, *Jogaku zasshi*, and other magazines for women constantly published news about private, public, and missionary schools, their curricula, their goals, how much they cost, where they were located, and the number of students enrolled there, so that even people living far from these places could find the best options available.[53]

Changes in Government Policies and Their Impact on Female Education

Yoshioka Yayoi 吉岡弥生 (1871–1959), founder of the Tokyo Women's Medical School, Tokyo joi gakkō 東京女医学校 (1900), wrote extensively about the problems associated with compulsory education for girls in the 1870s. Her father was a doctor in a small town in Shizuoka prefecture where there were two or three *terakoya*, but when the *Gakusei* was promulgated an elementary school was opened in her area. The villagers did not have the financial resources to erect a school building or pay for a teacher, and therefore a temple was used as a school. However, many of the villagers were farmers who did not understand the value of education and kept their children at home. When Yoshioka entered the school in 1876, there were about fifty students but only one other girl, who quit soon after.[54]

The Meiji government decided that the *Gakusei* was not producing the expected results because of a lack of the textbooks, trained teachers, and financial resources necessary to implement it effectively throughout the country; in 1879, therefore, the *Kyōiku rei* 教育令 (Education Ordinance) was promulgated, and in 1880 the level

---

52. Kanzaki Kiyoshi, *Gendai fujin den* (Biographies of contemporary women) (Chūō kōronsha, 1940), 47. Noguchi, who was studying at Tokyo joshi shihan gakkō in 1885, wrote that once musicians from the Imperial Household Ministry had come there to play. Since many of the students came from rural areas, they were not able to take part in the dances, whereas students at Tokyo kōtō jogakkō, who mostly belonged to the upper classes, were enjoying themselves dancing with their male teachers. This was, she continued, the way to teach girls how relations between men and women were supposed to be conducted in the new era. Aoyama Nao, *Yasui Tetsu to Tokyo joshi daigaku* (Yasui Tetsu and Tokyo Women's University) (Keiō tsūshin, 1982), 27–28.

53. A table with the information published in *Jogaku zasshi* from 1889 onward is given in Ōhama Tetsuya, ed., *Joshi gakuin no rekishi* (The history of Joshi gakuin) (Joshi gakuin, 1985), 202–3. Such news was reported from 1885, the year in which the journal commenced publication. On *Iratsume*, see Yamada Yūsaku, *"Iratsume" kaidai, sōmokuji, sakuin* (*Iratsume*: Introduction, table of contents, index) (Fuji Shuppan, 1983).

54. Yoshioka Yayoi, *Yoshioka Yayoi den* (Yoshioka Yayoi's biography) (Nihon tosho Center, [1967] 1998), 41–43.

of compulsory schooling was lowered to three years. This was not the only reason for the change in educational policy. In the same year, the *Kyōgaku taishi* 教学大旨 (Great Principles of Education) was issued. It stated that since the beginning of the Meiji period Japan had concentrated on gaining "new knowledge" from around the world, but because of this the Japanese people were losing their traditional customs and virtues. It was therefore necessary to teach Japanese children Confucian values such as filial piety, loyalty, humanity, and justice.[55] Soon thereafter all sorts of regulations on educational matters were published to make sure that, among other things, teachers would know how to successfully prepare elementary lessons with a strong emphasis on values such as obedience to superiors, discipline, and love for the nation and emperor.[56] Also in 1879 Nakamura Masanao resigned from his position as principal of Tokyo joshi shihan gakkō. His successor, Fukuba Bisei 福羽美静 (1832–1907), a fervent nationalist, supported a more controlled environment, and Nakamura Masanao's translation of Smiles's *Self Help* and Fukuzawa Yukichi's *Gakumon no susume* were taken off the textbook list. In addition, girls had to change their school attire from the "masculine" *hakama* to a more feminine uniform.[57]

The *Kyōiku rei* also legislated that girls and boys were to receive a separate education, and in some cases this had negative repercussions. Yoshioka Yayoi, for example, recalled that because of the new set of regulations the school she was attending closed down. Another school opened far from her home, and, although she went there with seven or eight girls, they all dropped out before the end of the course.[58] It is difficult, however, to grasp the full effects of separate education, for even after 1879 this separation was not always implemented. This happened in private schools such as Miwada Masako's Meirin gakusha but also in government and prefectural schools, and it was due to the fact that the number of girls obtaining an education as prescribed by the government was small and *chūgakkō* were better organized and more evenly distributed than *jogakkō*.

Coeducation was not easy. Hani Motoko wrote that when she was in the fifth grade at elementary school, since there were only five or six girls, they were moved

---

55. Midori Wakakuwa, "The Gender System of the Imperial State," *U.S.-Japan Women's Journal* 20–21 (2001): 41–43; Carol Gluck, *Japan's Modern Myths: Ideology in the Late Meiji Period* (Princeton: Princeton University Press, 1985), 105–111.

56. For example, the *Shogakkō kyōsoku kōryō* 小学校教則綱領 (Essential principles of elementary education, 1881) defined the structure of elementary education (three years for compulsory courses, three for middle, and two for advanced), the content and aims of the subjects taught, the number of days and hours per week students were supposed to attend school, and so on. See also *Shogakkō kyōin kokoroe* 小学校教員心得 (Guidelines for elementary school teachers, 1881), in *Gakusei hachijūnenshi* (History of the educational system during the past eighty years), edited by Monbushō (Ōkurashō insatsukyoku, 1954), 763, 844. On the scholars who shaped these educational policies, see Gluck, *Japan's Modern Myths*, 107–9.

57. Tokyo joshi kōtō shihan gakkō, *Tokyo joshi*, 41; Yamakawa, *Onna nidai no ki*, 58.

58. Yoshioka, *Yoshioka Yayoi*, 45–49, 69.

to the boys' school where the boys gave them nicknames (Hani's was "dumpling").[59] Ebina Miyako 海老名みや子, the daughter of Yokoi Shōnan 横井小楠, also recalled that the wife of Captain Leroy Janes, the American teacher at the school for boys in Hosogawakō, Kumamoto prefecture, had obtained permission to teach some girls, and Ebina was one of them. They left when she could not teach anymore, but Ebina and Yuasa (Tokutomi) Hatsuko 湯浅初子 studied with the boys, though not in the same class. Some of the boys (among them Ebina Danjō 海老名弾正, who would marry Miyako) complained about their presence, and Janes had to scold them and tell them that women were human beings and that the boys themselves had been raised by their mothers.[60]

If the *Kyōiku rei* was a clear statement of the government's gendered practices, it also shows that girls were becoming a category perceived to be at risk of being influenced by new ideas. Furthermore, during the following decade *jogakkō* proved to be the first and one of the most important places in which girls became *a group*, a *community*, especially when they lived together in boarding schools. This communal spirit influenced the way some looked at their lives and their place in society. Even when they attended private, public, or missionary schools that offered an old-fashioned image of women and laid down strict regulations governing female education, the girls were nevertheless exposed to activities, associations, and ideas that often either originated or were promoted in schools and departed from school policy. These influences were as important to them as the teachings they received.

Female education did not always succeed in molding minds as the government wanted, and women who went to government schools, married, or followed their families' wishes developed independent viewpoints. This was the case with Kimura Eiko 木村栄子 (aka Kimura Akebono 木村曙, 1872–90), who attended Tokyo kōtō jogakkō from 1884 to 1888. This school was attached to Tokyo joshi shihan gakkō in 1882 "with the object of giving girls a general education of high grade, having for its principal aim the inculcation of moral and ethical principles and the sending forth of accomplished young women of good character."[61]

---

59. Hani, *Hansei o kataru*, 14.
60. Nakajima, *Meien no gakusei jidai*, 73–74; Yuasa Kōzō, ed., *Yuasa Hatsuko* (Yuasa Tasuke, 1936), 45–46. On Janes, see Fred George Notehelfer, *American Samurai: Captain L. L. Janes and Japan* (Princeton: Princeton University Press, 1985).
61. Its course of study lasted five years (divided into three years for the lower and two for the upper level), and girls with an elementary diploma could enter. They were required to study, among other subjects, moral education, etiquette, household economy, child rearing, sewing, and handicrafts. Nihon joshi daigaku joshi kyōiku kenkyūsho, ed., *Meiji no joshi kyōiku* (Women's education in the Meiji period) (Kokudosha, 1967), 23–30; Hisako Shibukawa, "An Education for Making Good Wives and Wise Mothers," *Education in Japan: Journal for Overseas* 6 (1971): 51–52. Similar schools were opened in other prefectures. Monbushō, *Gakusei hachijūnenshi*, 153–54. The statement reported in the text was written by the educator Naruse Jinzō 成瀬仁蔵 (1858–1919). See Okuma Shigenobu, comp., *Fifty Years of New Japan*, translated by Marcus B. Huish (London: Smith, Elder, 1909), vol. 2, 213.

Kimura Akebono was the daughter of a businessman who had chosen her a husband, then convinced her to divorce him, and finally employed her in one of his restaurants. Kimura wrote a novel, *Mirror of Womanhood* (*Fujo no kagami*, 婦女の鑑), which was published in installments in the supplement to *Yomiuri shinbun* beginning in January 1889 and in which one of the characters is a Japanese girl who goes to study at Newnham College, Cambridge, works in a spinning mill in North America, goes back to Japan, opens a factory to employ poor girls and teach them a trade, and attaches a nursery to the factory to take care of the workers' children. Although Kimura attended one of the most strictly controlled schools and had to follow her father's wishes in the choices she made throughout her life, she was able to express through her writing a longing for travel and her perception of the need for jobs for women who had to support themselves or help their families.[62] It is worth remembering that *Fujo kagami* was also the title of the ethics text compiled in 1887 by the Confucian Nishimura Shigeki 西村茂樹. Wakakuwa states that the task was given to Nishimura by the empress herself, who wanted the text to be distributed to the students of the Peeresses' school (Kazoku jogakkō) first and later to each girls' school.[63] By the late 1880s, then, there were different mirrors in which women could reflect themselves.

How did girls such as Kimura find the means to voice their opinions and ambitions? This happened first of all because girl students and women teachers had begun to form an imagined community. The accuracy of Meiji period educational data cannot be taken at face value, but the numbers of private, missionary, and government girls' schools opened during the 1870s and 1880s, together with the fact that many did not close, show that there was indeed a demand for such schools. Table 1, which was probably compiled using information included in the various reports of the Ministry of Education, gives us at least a tentative idea of the numbers involved.[64]

Second, looking at the table one might argue that the low number of girls completing their courses meant that female schooling was not successful. In reality, it was common for girls to attend different schools and move from missionary to government schools and vice versa. If it was more difficult in this situation to obtain a "proper" education, some girls nevertheless took advantage of the opportunities offered to them, as the examples of girls whose educational careers we can trace show. Sakurai Chika 櫻井ちか (1855–1928) was born in Tokyo and at eighteen married Sakurai Akinori 櫻井昭悳. She learned English at Saitō Saneaki's

---

62. A short account of her life appeared in *Yomiuri shinbun*, no. 5270, 11.03.1892, 3. See also Yukiko Tanaka, *Women Writers of Meiji and Taishō Japan* (Jefferson: McFarland, 2000), 28–32.

63. For a discussion of this book's contents, see Wakakuwa, "The Gender System," 30–9. Wakamatsu Shizuko wrote that the empress assiduously patronized women's education and had ordered "the lives of one hundred celebrated women" to be "compiled into book form to be read by women all over the Empire." Iwamoto Yoshiharu, ed., *In Memory of Mrs. Kashi Iwamoto with a Collection of Her English Writings* (Jogaku zasshisha, 1896), 21.

64. *Jogaku zasshi*, supplement to no. 46, 05.01.1888.

TABLE 1

Female teachers and students in Japanese schools.

	1881	1882	1883	1884
Female teachers	3,112	3,343	4,446	5,010
Girl students	750,630	931,178	1,032,391	1,025,994
Girls who completed the course	18,417	26,928	36,915	ca. 46,735
Overall number of schools for boys and girls at all levels	30,887	30,662	31,792	ca. 31,362

斎藤實堯 Hōeisha 芳英社, attending classes in the morning and teaching the poorer students in the afternoon.[65] When she came across the sentence "Our Father smiles upon me" and asked why *Father* was capitalized, the teacher sent her to a church in Tsukiji where she met Julia Carrothers. In 1874 she was baptized. She entered the missionary Kyōritsu jogakkō 共立女学校 in Yokohama, and in 1876 she opened Sakurai jogakkō. In 1878 she opened a school for poor people together with other persons linked to missionary work, and in 1879 a private kindergarten was attached to Sakurai. Sakurai employed one foreign and four Japanese women teachers, one being Asai Saku 浅井作 (b. 1843) and another Nagamine Teiko 長嶺貞子 (1862–1931), who started working there as soon as she graduated from Tokyo joshi shihan gakkō in 1881. They both became active participants in the Fujin kyōfūkai. In 1881 Akinori found a job in Hakodate, and so the school passed into the hands of the Presbyterian mission. Chika worked as a teacher at Hakodate joshi shihan gakkō, helped her husband with his missionary work, and later took a position at Osaka jogakuin.[66] Asai, on the other hand, opened the Chōei jojuku 長栄女塾, a

65. The Hōeisha (also called Hōei jojuku) was opened in Kanda in 1871. The teachers were Saitō's twenty-one-year-old wife Tsune and the wife of Horace Wilson, a teacher of English at Daigaku nankō 大学南校. Tokyo-to, *Tokyo no joshi kyōiku*, 31–32.

66. Ōhama, *Joshi gakuin*, 69–120; Tokyo-to, *Tokyo no joshi kyōiku*, 51–62; Sakurai Junji, ed., *Sakurai Chika shōden: Sakurai jojuku no rekishi* (A short biography of Sakurai Chika: History of the Sakurai private school for women) (Sagamihara: Sakurai Junji, 1976). In 1881 Sakurai had 60 students, and the monthly salaries of both Nagamine and Asai were ten yen. Inoue Yuriko, *Chikara o ataemase: Honda Yōitsu fujin Teiko no shōgai* (Give me strength! The life of Teiko, Honda Yōitsu's wife) (Aoyama gakuin, 2004), 45–46. By 1887 the daily attendance was 240 and 50 young girls were attending the kindergarten. There were plenty of girls who were studying half a day and working as teaching assistants during the other half. Letter from Mrs. True, *Records of U.S. Presbyterian Missions,* vol. 6, 3/5, 44–163, December 6, 1887, Archive of the U.S. Presbyterian Missions, Yokohama Kaikō Shiryōkan, Yokohama. In 1888 Nagamine married Honda Yōitsu 本多庸一 (1848–1912), the first Japanese principal of Aoyama gakuin after it changed its name from Tokyo eiwa gakkō to Aoyama gakuin in 1894. Inoue, *Chikara o ataemase*.

preparatory school for girls who wanted to become teachers, in 1883 and subsequently taught at Baika jogakkō in Osaka.[67]

Another interesting case is that of Inokuchi Aguri, who graduated from Akita prefecture's shihan gakkō, helped in an elementary school, and entered the female department of the jinjō shihan gakkō there around 1887. The course of study was four years, but she left after two because she had been chosen, together with Mogi Chieko 茂木ちえ子, from the same prefecture, to attend the *joshibu* of the Tokyo kōtō shihan gakkō. In 1899 Inokuchi was sent by the Ministry of Education to North America to study physical education, and in 1900 she attended the Boston Normal School of Gymnastics.[68]

As a last example, we have seen that Ebina Miya, after completing the elementary course, entered the male school that was opened in Kumamoto. In 1877, at the age of fifteen, Ebina went to Tokyo, but since the Takebashi jogakkō had closed her brother, Yokoi Tokio 横井時雄, decided that she should go to the missionary Aoyama jogakuin. When he moved to the missionary-supported Dōshisha in Kyoto, she went there as well. The directors of the school, first Niijima Jō 新島襄 (1843–90) and then Yamamoto Kakuma 山本覚馬 (1828–92), had set up a small but functioning class with a few girl students, the Kyoto Home, then Dōshisha jogakkō, where she studied with Yamamoto Mineko 山本峰子, the director's daughter.[69]

By changing cities, schools, teachers, and classmates in this way, girls established a circle of acquaintances that was not related to their families or the areas in which they were raised, experienced different realities, and formed their own networks and communities. In many cases, the friendships formed at school were strengthened through participation in activities outside the schools while the networks these girls formed could be exploited when information regarding women's activities was to be circulated.

---

67. *Jogaku zasshi*, no. 79, 08.10.1887, 166.

68. Interview in Nakajima, *Meien no gakusei jidai*, 1–4; Haga et al., *Nihon josei.*

69. Interview in Nakajima, *Meien no gakusei jidai*, 74–76. See also Matsuura Masayasu, *Dōshisha romansu* (Dōshisha romance) (Keiseisha shoten, 1918), 61. In 1875 Niijima Jō became engaged to Yamamoto's sister, Yamamoto Yaeko 山本八重. Yaeko was dismissed from her teaching job at the Kyoto prefectural girls' school because she was going to marry a Christian and it was feared that she would convert her students to Christianity. Niijima described her in a letter as "not a beauty, but a person whose acts are beautiful. And that is enough for me." In 1883 Dōshisha jogakkō's advertisement stated that there were schools for girls in each prefecture and girls were supposed to acquire as much enlightened education as boys. This was a cause for celebration, but young women who had obtained an education were vaunting their learning and no longer listening to their superiors. Seeing this, some had begun arguing that it would be best not to educate girls at all. Dōshisha jogakkō would take great care in teaching its students modesty, kindness, and loyalty. Students would be taught general subjects at a high standard in Japanese, English literature by two Western ladies, and all the feminine arts and chores. Niijima was the head of the school, but when this statement was made the names of five Japanese female teachers were also included. Gendaigo de yomu Niijima Jō henshū iinkai, ed., *Gendaigo de yomu Niijima Jō* (Reading the writings of Niijima Jō in contemporary Japanese) (Maruzen, 2000), 128–29, 164–65.

Educational Possibilities Abroad

It was not only the increasing visibility of female students and teachers that encouraged other girls to voice their opinions. Young women who studied abroad also personified the expanding horizons of female education in the Meiji period. We know that five girls were taken to North America with the Iwakura mission to be educated and become symbols of national progress. Two of them, Yamakawa Sutematsu and Tsuda Umeko, worked for the education of upper-class girls, but other, lesser-known girls also crossed the ocean to pursue their studies. A table published in *Jogaku zasshi* reported that while no girl studied outside Japan at government expense, 9 had gone to North America, 1 to Russia, 3 to China, and 4 to England to continue their education with private funds.[70] *Jogaku zasshi* also described Newnham College, Cambridge, detailing its location and setting, and reported that it had 120 students, whereas Dr. Okami Keiko 岡見京子 (b. 1859) became the first Japanese woman to obtain a degree in medicine in North America in 1889.[71]

Okami was the only Japanese woman I know of to have studied medicine in North America during this period, but other women went there for different reasons. Kōga Fuji 甲賀ふじ (1857–1937) studied and worked at the missionary school Kobe eiwa jogakkō and was baptized while there. She left for Boston around 1886 and for three years studied to become a kindergarten teacher. Once back in Japan, she worked at schools in Kobe and at the kindergarten annexed to Hiroshima eiwa jogakkō.[72] The story of Katō (Takeda) Kinko 加藤錦子 (1861–1913) is similar. She was born into a samurai family in Edo and studied with Nakamura Masanao and the wife of George Cochran, a Canadian Methodist missionary. She entered Tokyo jogakkō in 1872, and when that closed she moved to Tokyo joshi shihan gakkō, graduating in 1880. In 1877 she started teaching English and mathematics at her father's private school, and from 1880 on she worked at the kindergarten attached to Tokyo joshi shihan gakkō. She enrolled in the Salem Normal School (now Salem State College) in September 1886, completed the two-year program, and moved on to Wellesley College for a year, where she concentrated on kindergarten studies. In 1890 she was given a job at Tokyo joshi kōtō shihan gakkō, a school founded to train teachers for *chūgakkō*.[73] While

70. Their identities remain unclear. *Jogaku zasshi*, supplement to no. 46, 05.01.1888.
71. *Jogaku zasshi*, no. 95, 04.02.1888, 22; Yoji Nagatoya, "Dr. Keiko Okami: Japan's First Female Medical Student Who Studied Abroad," *Journal of the American Medical Women's Association* 15.12 (1960): 1175–77; Patessio and Ogawa, "To Become a Woman Doctor."
72. See the entry in Haga et al., *Nihon josei*; and Kobe jogakuin, ed., *Kobe jogakuin hyakunenshi: Kakuron* (One hundred years of Kobe jogakuin: A detailed discussion) (Kobe: Kobe jogakuin, 1981), 206.
73. Kanbe, *Meiji shoki*, 45. News of her studies abroad was reported in *Jogaku zasshi*, no. 13, 25.01.1886, 22; and no. 169, 06.07.1889, 28; and *Tokyo fujin kyōfū zasshi*, no. 13, 20.04.1889, 12. In *Dai nihon fujin kyōikukai zasshi*, no. 22, 13.12.1890, 19–28, there is a lengthy article on her life in North America in which she relates various curiosities about American and Japanese life and customs.

there she published *Joshi eigo yomihon* 女子英語読本, the only textbook I came across written by a woman for girls studying English.[74]

In *Yomiuri shinbun* we also read that Fukuoka Teruko 福岡照子, after studying English at the missionary Shinsakae jogakkō 新栄女学校 and becoming a teacher, planned to leave for North America to undertake higher studies there. Her goal was to use her education in order to improve the condition of women at home.[75] We can gain some idea of what she meant by "reforming the condition of women" by looking at the book she published in 1888, *Joshi dokuritsu enzetsu hikki* 女子独立演説筆記 (Transcription of the Public Speech on Women's Independence), which I discuss in detail in chapter 4. Fukuoka argued that women's advancement would bring social advancement. Japanese women had to support their husbands and take care of the housework and children, but they also had to work outside their homes, and she cited examples of Western women who helped their husbands in the political and educational fields. She supported the expansion of women's social relations, writings, and public speeches and considered that, like Western women, Japanese women had to ask for the right to a higher education.

As a final example, in 1890 *Jogaku zasshi* reported that Tsukamoto Fujiko 塚本ふじ子 (1870–1927) was studying at Wilson College, Matsue Tazuko 松江たず子 was at Wellesley, Miyagawa Toshiko was at Mount Holyoke, Watanabe Tsuneko was at Carleton college, and Masuda Tsuru 増田つる was to go to Wellesley; indeed, this was an impressive achievement for them all.[76]

Japanese girls traveled to Europe as well. Seventeen-year-old Ikuta Minoru, 生田みのる, from Yamaguchi prefecture, was reported to be going to France for five years to continue her education.[77] Toyoda Fuyuko 豊田芙雄子 (1845–1941), whose father, Kuwabara Nobutake 桑原信毅, had married Fujita Yukiko 藤田雪子, sister of the well-known Confucian scholar Fujita Tōko 藤田東湖 (1806–55), was the wife of Toyoda Kotarō 豊田小太郎, son of Toyoda Tenko 豊田天功. She was born into an influential family that produced many famous scholars but became a widow at the age of twenty-two when her husband was killed in Kyoto. She opened a *shijuku* for girls as a means of supporting herself but was then asked to teach at Tokyo joshi shihan gakkō, and in 1879 she was called to Kagoshima to help open the second government kindergarten attached to the local *joshi shihan gakkō* (the first opened in Tokyo in 1876). In 1886 we find her name among the founders of Kyōritsu joshi shokugyō gakkō in Tokyo, a school opened to teach women subjects useful in finding suitable occupations, together with Hatoyama Haruko and

74. Takeda Kinko. *Joshi eigo yomihon* (English reader for women), 4 vols. (Kinkōdō, 1902).
75. *Yomiuri shinbun*, no. 3966, 30.03.1888, 2.
76. *Jogaku zasshi*, no. 227, 23.08.1890, 20.
77. *Tokyo fujin kyōfū zasshi*, no. 11, 16.02.1889, 10.

Matsumoto Ogie.[78] In 1887 she left for Rome as the private teacher of the wife of the Japanese ambassador to Italy, and because of her expertise in educational matters she was also commissioned by the Ministry of Education to conduct a survey of women's education in Europe. Once back home, she published articles on her findings in Europe and other educational matters and opened her own private school where she put into practice her theories on female education.[79]

Compared to the five young girls who left Japan with the Iwakura mission, the women described above had already obtained an education before leaving their country and left because they wanted to continue their studies. Once back in Japan, most of them were able to put their experiences to work in furthering women's education and drew media attention for doing so. More generally, *Jogaku zasshi* published information on female education in other countries, and Japanese girls, at least in the major cities, were able to interact with foreigners and observe confident Western women who had left their countries in order to teach in Japan. Examples of filial women were all over the media, but there was also exciting news about other models of womanhood, and these might explain why, during the same years, Kimura Akebono decided to include in her novel the character of a young woman being educated abroad.

Male Support

Girls started expressing their opinions and voicing their demands for higher education during the second half of the 1880s also because of the support they received from male intellectuals. Discussions regarding the suitability of female education continued throughout the Meiji period, and plenty of men disapproved of it. For example, it was reported that at a meeting of the Dai nihon fujin kyōikukai 大日本婦人教育会 (Great Japan Women's Education Society, the membership included *educated* women such as Shimoda Utako 下田歌子 [1854–1936], Katō Kinko, Nagai Tsune, and Ishii Fudeko) Katō Hiroyuki, soon to be president of Tokyo Imperial University, had stated that as the female mind was weaker than the male it was deleterious to apply the same standards to male and female higher education. To give Japanese women, who had just started attending school, the same education women received in the West would be detrimental to their bodies; it was best to give Japanese women a simple and general education.[80] Nevertheless, an increasing

---

78. Kyōritsu joshi gakuen, ed., *Kyōritsu joshi gakuen hyakunenshi* (One hundred years of Kyōritsu joshi gakuen) (Kyōritsu joshi gakuen, 1986), 2–4.
79. News of her trip was reported in *Tokyo nichinichi shinbun*, no. 5465, 14.01.1890, 2; and *Fukuoka nichinichi shinbun*, no. 3815, 19.01.1890, 3. She published articles in *Dai nihon fujin kyōikukai zasshi*, no. 15, 12.04.1890, 30–38; and no. 78, 11.01.1896, 25–28. Material regarding her life is preserved at Ibaragi kenritsu rekishikan in Mito.
80. *Jogaku zasshi*, no. 156, 6.04.1889, 9–11.

number of supporters of female education and employment lent their voices to the women's cause. In response to Katō's remarks, *Jogaku zasshi* argued that it was normal for people to aspire to higher goals, while with experience and through education people learned what was true and expanded their knowledge. "As far as their circumstances allow for it," the article continued, "it is normal for men and women to aspire to a better education, and we should encourage this." This did not mean that men and women should obtain the *same* education but that both sexes should attempt to acquire the best possible education for themselves as women and men. "To say that if women obtain higher education they will become weak in their bodies is a foolish theory," the article declared, "for it is not only women's bodies that are weakened by too much higher education, but also men's." Furthermore, women had to obtain higher education if they were to become educated mothers and wives. As a consequence, the magazine observed, it would be better to stop arguing whether higher education was good or bad for women and start discussing what subjects women should study. The first students of Kaisei gakkō 開成学校 (founded in 1873 and later renamed Tokyo Imperial University), the article concluded, were considered very knowledgeable at the time, but such knowledge was obtained by contemporary second-year students at Meiji jogakkō.[81]

One of the most interesting cases of a woman who benefited from male support is that of Ogino Ginko 荻野吟子 (1851–1913). Born in Saitama prefecture, Ogino's life changed drastically when she divorced two years after her marriage as a result of her husband infecting her with a venereal disease. She spent two years in a hospital being treated by men and decided to become a doctor as she wanted to give women the option of being treated by other women. In 1873, after a successful recovery and despite receiving no support from her family, she enrolled in Tokyo joshi shihan gakkō.[82]

Ogino won the support of one of her teachers at Tokyo joshi shihan gakkō, who, knowing that she wanted to become a doctor, helped her enroll in a private medical school. After attending medical school, male students were supposed to take a medical exam that would allow them to open a practice. Although there was no specific rule prohibiting them from taking this examination, given the lack of

81. Ibid. 13. Meiji jogakkō was founded in 1885 by Kimura Kumaji 木村熊二 (b. 1845). The educator Tsuda Umeko, the political activist Tomii Tora 富井於兎 (aka Tomii Oto or Otora, 1865–85), and Kimura's wife, Kimura Tōko 木村鐙子, were among the teachers.

82. During Ogino's time there, Mori Arinori signed a prematrimonial contract and exchanged marriage vows with his bride, Hirose Tsuneko 広瀬つね子, before the governor of Tokyo and with Fukuzawa Yukichi as a witness. However, according to Yoshioka Yayoi, Mori had previously promised to marry another woman. She was a schoolmate of Ogino, and apparently Ogino visited Mori and complained about his behavior. After her visit, Mori decided to pay the woman's school fees until her graduation. Whether Mori took this decision because of Ogino's protest is unclear, but if the episode really happened, this was no small step for a young woman. Nihon joshi hensan iinkai, ed., *Nihon joshi* (History of Japanese women doctors) (Nihon joikai, 1991), 59–60. The original source is not identified.

precedent, women were not allowed to sit for it. Ogino managed to break this rule and qualified as a doctor in 1885. Ogino's acquaintances and male connections, along with her strong will and considerable desire to pursue her dreams, were the reasons why she managed to succeed in her ambition to become a doctor. Furthermore, although she was the first woman to be recognized as a doctor by the new government, others were demanding the same right during those years, showing how, though exceptional, Ogino was but one manifestation of a female community beginning to feel empowered.[83]

One intellectual who helped Ogino in her medical practice was Iwamoto Yoshiharu 巖本善治 (b. 1863), the most prominent promoter and supporter of female education, employment, and achievements, as can be seen from all the articles he published in *Jogaku zasshi*, the magazine he edited, and the innumerable books he advertised on these topics in it. Iwamoto studied with Nakamura Masanao at Dōjinsha beginning in 1876, and when the school closed he moved to Tsuda Sen's Gakunōsha nōgakkō 学農社農学校, graduating in 1884. He was influenced and baptized by Kimura Kumaji (who had studied in North America in the 1870s) and then became Meiji jogakkō's administrator. Interestingly, whereas statements presenting the reasons for the founding of girls' schools sent to the central or local governments for approval normally contained an opening sentence explaining why girls' education was important for the creation of good mothers and nationalistic subjects, Meiji jogakkō's statement did not emphasize the moral and nationalistic meaning of female education but simply said that the school was to teach girls various subjects.[84]

Yoshioka Yayoi wrote that *Jogaku zasshi* was inundated with novels, translations, and articles on women's education, the problem of prostitution, social reform, and new knowledge and ideas, and for young women it constituted a light in the darkness.[85] Hani Motoko, on the other hand, reported that she took the entrance examination for Tokyo joshi kōtō shihan gakkō at the end of the 1880s with two friends but failed because she had not studied, being distracted by the new environment and society in which she was living. The solution was to enroll in Meiji jogakkō, a Christian school that did not limit students' freedom and did not require them, as tended to be the case with missionary schools, to go to church on Sunday. Money was a problem for Hani, but Iwamoto gave her a job at *Jogaku zasshi*, where she supplied *furigana* (phonetic renderings printed next to characters as a reading aid) for the texts to be published and could pay for her maintenance in that way.[86]

83. See Patessio and Ogawa, "To Become a Woman Doctor."
84. Meiji jogakkō's course of study lasted five years; students between fourteen and thirty years of age could apply, but they were expected to possess an elementary education. Tokyo-to, *Tokyo no joshi kyōiku*, 163–66. In 1890 the school had 224 students, of which 61 were from Tokyo. *Jogaku zasshi*, no. 202, 01.03.1890, 18.
85. Yoshioka, *Yoshioka Yayoi*, 72.
86. Hani, *Hansei o kataru*, 49–50; Nakajima, *Meien no gakusei jidai*, 93–94.

Iwamoto married the writer Wakamatsu Shizuko 若松賤子 (1872–95) and supported her career, hired Ogino Ginko in his school, and published all kinds of articles in *Jogaku zasshi* on the various jobs women could find in North America, Europe, and even Russia. According to Iwamoto, Japanese women had been left behind in the educational and employment fields because of discrimination; they were indeed weaker mentally and physically, but this did not mean that with the right training they could not become accomplished human beings. He argued that traditional social customs, such as despising women as "lower creatures," should be reformed. As women were supposed to take care of their children's physical, moral, and intellectual well-being, to help and support their husbands, and some-times also to find paid employment, an education based merely on learning how to perform household chores was not enough.

Jogaku zasshi periodically published the names of those who graduated from girls' schools, and articles written in it by girls were signed either with their names and that of the school they attended or, for example, as "student of Ferris jogakkō." Although some men, such as Sakuma Shōzan 佐久間象山 (1811–64), who had stated that "it is unseemly for a woman to show off her literacy and knowledge of books by taking part in conversations, no matter how well informed and well-read she may be," criticized women who expressed themselves in public, *Jogaku zasshi* not only allowed them to do just that but also encouraged them to take part in debates on all sorts of topics affecting women in Japan.[87] The girls who read these issues found other, like-minded students in their pages. It was in this way, and through the circulation of magazines such as *Jogaku zasshi*, that a community for *jogakkō* and *jogakusei* was formed. This community was not interested "only" in educational matters, for we will see in chapters 4 and 5 that girl students participated in female associations and other public activities. Thus, it is not surprising that the govern-ment was particularly interested in monitoring girls' movements and behavior, for they were an important force within the various women's movements.

Women's Voices

Some women did not explicitly fight for the right to an education but did what they could to obtain it, as in the case of Murakami Komao 村上駒尾, the wife of Abe Isoo 阿部磯雄, later a member of the Social People's Party and, among other things, a supporter of Ishii Jūji's 石井十次 (1865–1914) Okayama orphanage. She was born in Fukuoka prefecture and lost both parents in her teens, and as she had to take care of the household and her siblings she could not afford the time and

---

87. Sakuma Shōzan, *Jokun* (Moral text for women), in *Nihon kyōiku bunko* (Collection of books on education in Japan), vol. 5, *Jokunhen* (Moral texts for women), edited by Kurokawa Mamichi (Dōbunkan 1910), 732, translated in Okazaki-Ward, "Women and Their Education," 88.

money to obtain an elementary education. She tried to teach herself at first, but subsequently attended an evening course at the missionary school Baika jogakkō in Osaka. As the school's financial situation was precarious, the students decided to help through their services and by donating money.[88]

Others were more ambitious and tried to change existing regulations. *Jogaku zasshi* reported that, although in Germany and North America women could obtain higher and university education, two Japanese girls were refused entrance into Tokyo Imperial University's medical and science departments.[89] The girls who applied to the university might have been Hisaeko 久重子 and Hideko 秀子, the daughters of doctor Kimura Seikō 木村井光 from Nara. Hideko entered the private medical school Tōa igakkō 東亜医学校 in Tokyo in 1880 and passed all the examinations. In 1884 she sent a letter to the government asking for permission to take the final medical examination, and in 1885 the two sisters also sent a petition asking to be allowed to take the preliminary examination for Tokyo Imperial University, but their requests were turned down. Hisaeko died, and Hideko, according to the sources, was admitted to the university in 1886 as a medical student on an irregular course, becoming the first woman, as far as I can ascertain, to be allowed to attend university lectures in Japan.[90] She then worked at Tokyo joshi senmon gakkō, opened by Kimura Matsuko 木村松子, where German medical studies, midwifery, English, and economy for the first year, plus psychology, astronomy, and moral philosophy for students in their second year were taught. She also wrote a book on how girls should behave in the presence of different people, from men to people of different ages, which was published in 1888.[91]

Other young women asked for higher education during the same period, indicating that a movement demanding educational opportunities was forming, and these were far from isolated cases. *Jogaku zasshi* reported that, although the Kimura sisters were the first, Inoue Nao 井上直, compiler of *Nihon fujin sanron* (1886); Kōsaka Torako 香坂とら子, who graduated from Kobe jogakkō and was working at Shōei jogakkō 頌榮女学校 in Tokyo; Togawako Shikako 戸川小鹿子, who also graduated from Kobe jogakkō and was a teacher at Meiji jogakkō; and others had expressed the same desire for higher education for women. In Fukuoka

88. Interview in Nakajima, *Meien no gakusei jidai*, 127–28. I would like to thank Dr. Masako Gavin for the information regarding Murakami's name, which was not included in Nakajima's book.

89. *Jogaku zasshi*, no. 28, 05.07.1886, 261 (the news was reported from *Chōya shinbun*, 22.06.1886). Articles published throughout the Meiji period made note of foreign female students who enrolled at foreign universities. For example, see *Kyōiku jiron*, no. 148, 25.05.1889, 26–27, for North American girl students.

90. *Jogaku zasshi*, no. 37, 05.10.1886, 140; *Kijo no tomo*, no. 6, 20.11.1887, 258.

91. *Jogaku zasshi*, no. 47, 15.01.1887, 138. Tokyo-to, *Tokyo no joshi kyōiku*, 120–24, states that the aim of the school was to educate women in Chinese, English, and German so that they could teach these languages at the highest level. When the school opened there were six Japanese teachers and one German. Kimura Hideko, *Kōsairon* (On interpersonal relations) (Seibundō, 1888).

prefecture, eighteen girls had sent a petition to the president of the prefectural assembly asking for the expansion of women's education as a way to improve society.[92] Dr. Mariana Holbrook (chapter 3) wrote that at the end of the 1880s two graduates of Kobe jogakuin had applied for admission to Tokyo Imperial University. "They were refused—not unwisely, it seems to us—because they were women. I was told by one of them that if they were successful other 14 would follow, but now they are studying alone."[93] Who were the two young women who applied? And who were the fourteen who were ready to follow? Were they from Kobe jogakuin? Were they trying to find ways to organize themselves and help push their requests forward? What were they "studying alone"? The information and signatures we have for the young women who were attempting to obtain higher education are visible representations of a desire that ran deeper into Japanese society and was shared by others who might not have had the resolve to make their demands public but were ready to follow in the footsteps of those who did.

As a final example, a student from Kyōritsu jogakkō wrote an article in *Jogaku zasshi* entitled "Progress of Woman." She held that,

> even in that nation which is known throughout the world as the land of liberty, when a woman first wished to become a physician or a lawyer, there was much fighting on that subject, not of the sword, but of the pen. . . . And as the signs of the time are tending more favorably towards the better condition of women, let us not boast of this privilege, but with modesty and meekness which are characteristics of the sex endeavor to direct all our efforts toward the ever-increasing ennoblement of the human race.[94]

As Cott has argued, a suitable education for American women would "preserve the family as an agency of moral instruction, facilitate male entrepreneurship, and generalize frugality and economic discipline. Without threatening male dominance, it would make women more capable adjuncts of their husbands and families." Additional arguments were necessary, however, when young women started asking for higher educational opportunities, for there was no perceived need for "women's participation in the advancement of knowledge."[95] Many Japanese women supported the government's call for female education on the basis of the "fukoku kyōhei" 富国強兵 (wealthy country and strong army) ideology they

92. *Jogaku zasshi*, no. 42, 25.11.1886, 39; no. 43, 05.12.1886, 62–63. The magazine reported the girls' names.
93. Charlotte B. DeForest, *History of Kobe College, 1875–1950* (Chicago: Kobe College Corporation, 1950), 30.
94. *Jogaku zasshi*, no. 41, 15.11.1886, 15 (original in English).
95. Nancy Cott, *The Bonds of Womanhood: "Woman's Sphere" in New England, 1780–1835* (New Haven: Yale University Press, 1977), 104–5.

believed in, but "fukoku kyōhei" also became a flag to be waved by women looking for ways to advance their requests, particularly during a period of rising nationalist feelings such as the late 1880s. See, for example, the preface to *Nihon fujin sanron* 日本婦人纂論 (Collection of Theories on Japanese Women), a book edited by Inoue Nao that contains four essays on female education and women's position in society, one being Fukuzawa Yukichi's "Nihon fujinron" (On Japanese Women). I could not find any details about her life, but she was one of the three women mentioned above who asked for higher education whose names were published in *Jogaku zasshi*, while her volume was also prefaced with Nakamura Masanao's signature as a stamp of approval. In its introduction, Inoue argued that "it is not an exaggeration to say that the female half of the Japanese population is treated like slaves by men. This is because the women of our country depend entirely on their husbands, and only few find employment outside their homes." The low status of women was a direct consequence of old Confucian customs such as *danson johi*, despising women and revering men. The question of women's position in society was, then, related to the issue of national development, for Inoue argued that "Education is the basis of a strong country, but the spread of education is also based on the development of home education. In order to reach that goal, the most important task now is to develop female education, for women are the basis of national education." She concluded her introduction by stating that those countries that treated women like farm animals were barbaric, whereas those that gave men and women equal value were civilized and praised by the rest of the world. Giving women rights, she reasoned, would benefit the country as a whole.[96]

The stress in most of these statements was on feminine qualities, but these women argued that women could also contribute to society in professions that were just starting to be available to them and that requests for female educational advancement were not based on selfish ambitions but on the willingness to contribute to the advancement of their country. Even if girls knew they could not obtain higher education in Japan, or better jobs, they began to realize that it was a question of asking for what they wanted and finding the right words, supporters, and forums in which to do so rather than submitting to the status quo. This is one of the major differences between Edo and Meiji women. There were women during the Edo period who wanted to further their education. What Meiji girls had was the possibility of making their voices heard through their petitions and articles reporting their activities. The result might have been the same—no higher education for both groups of women—but the latter could at least console themselves by thinking that there were other women in their position. Furthermore, whatever all these women really thought, it is clear that the "*ryōsai kenbo* ideal" was not just an ideology imposed on women by more or less conservative scholars. It was also a tool that could be

96. Inoue, *Nihon fujin sanron*, preface.

used by women to obtain an education, and while obtaining it they were also forging the arguments with which to ask for a higher or university education.

Finally, by understanding that their problems and goals were the same as those of women of different nationalities, these individuals started to acknowledge that theirs was an international struggle. In 1886 *Jogaku zasshi* published an article reporting on a speech given by Mary Leavitt (who had arrived in Japan to promote the Woman's Christian Temperance Union), entitled "To My Japanese Sisters," in which she argued that while some people thought higher education would cause women to lose their virtue or that their health would suffer if they studied for "too long," actually women who were allowed to attend universities, professional schools, or schools of a similar level received general admiration and were in good health. She quoted a young woman who had recently graduated from a university in North America who said that, compared to male students, her schoolmates were doing well in their studies, exercised every day in the fresh air, studied the right number of hours, slept well, and did not drink alcohol or smoke. When women were allowed to develop their minds and obtain a good education they were also able to find employment. Teaching was a good profession, but in North America many women were becoming doctors and some were becoming lawyers.[97]

Education was helping young American women to develop their abilities and was not seen as contrary to women's nature. In fact, educated women would become useful members of society by taking up jobs in which their services would be appreciated. If this was true for American women, it was also possible for Japanese women. In this way, and through women's magazines such as *Jogaku zasshi*, the question of women's education was internationalized from a female perspective.

The End of the Early Meiji Period:
Criticism from Intellectuals and the Media

In 1888 Miyake Kaho published the novel *Yabu no uguisu* 薮の鶯 (Warbler in the Grove), in which she depicted the life of *jogakusei* and wrote that during that period scholars were signaling the negative effects of knowledge on women, as a little education, they argued, instilled in them a desire to become teachers and not marry or have children, tendencies regarded as unpatriotic.[98] By this time, schools for girls were no longer a rarity, and a growing number of parents and husbands were sending their daughters and wives to them or were allowing and helping them to become doctors, nurses, or teachers; to go abroad to further their education; or to organize

97. *Jogaku zasshi*, no. 37, 05.10.1886, 131–32. The first part was printed in no. 36, 25.09.1886, 111–12.
98. See Copeland, *Lost Leaves*; and Rebecca Copeland, trans., "Warbler in the Grove," in *The Modern Murasaki: Writing by Women of Meiji Japan*, edited by Rebecca Copeland and Melek Ortabasi, 80–125 (New York: Columbia University Press, 2006).

women's groups. Thus, by the end of the 1880s debates about higher education for women were less pointed as female education was a reality. Nevertheless, and precisely for this reason, new articles were published on the physical problems higher education would create for women and on scandals among girl students.

During these years, theories on the physical limitations of women that would hinder them from obtaining higher education were widespread in North America and Europe, and similar ideas were to be found in Japan. In an article entitled "On the Physiological Suitability or Unsuitability of Coeducation for Girls and Boys," the writer explained that since female and male bodies were different it was natural for their education to be different. If girl students devoted themselves to their studies, they would become weak in mind and body. Those who graduated from schools or obtained higher education were good students, but when they married they were unable to have children since they had used up all their energy in their studies, and it was impossible not to call them crippled mothers.[99]

Other public means of discrediting female education were soon to be found. *Yomiuri shinbun* followed soon after with a series of articles against girls' schools and girl students that often took up the entire page and made various accusations concerning girl students' behavior and morality. These were quickly taken up by other newspapers as well, and the debate that followed included missionaries, intellectuals, government authorities, and supporters of female education from Osaka to Hokkaido.[100]

To inflame the situation even more—it is not clear whether this was the spark that started the whole scandal—the *Japan Gazette* reported that an article in the Tokyo kōtō jogakkō magazine (*Kuni no motoi*), "advising the sort of gentlemen educated ladies should marry," had appeared.

> By the outside public this was somewhat warmly commented on, and caused some, not unreasonably, to liken the school to a matrimonial agency. . . . The publication of the article was warmly censured by the Department of Education and the author's connection with the school severed.[101]

99. "Danjo kyōgaku ron no kahi wa seirijō yori kore o ronsubeshi," in *Kyōiku jiron*, no. 121, 25.08.1888, 9–11. This point was repeated by Miyake Kaho in *Yabu no uguisu*, in which one of her characters stated, "If women push themselves to such extremes in their studies, as Shinako does, they weaken their mental health and, as a result, will produce weak children." Copeland, "Warbler in the Grove," 100.
100. *Yomiuri shinbun*, 21 (no. 4338, 1), 22 (no. 4339, 1), 29 (no. 4345, 3), 30 (no. 4346, 1), all published in June 1889; 20 (no. 4551, 3), 21 (no. 4552, 3), 22 (no. 4553, 3), 23 (no. 4554, 3), 24 (no. 4555, 3), 26 (no. 4557, 3), 28 (no. 4559, 3), all published in February 1890; and no. 4561, 02.03.1890, 1. Iwamoto Yoshiharu asked to be shown the names of the girls and schools the newspaper was criticizing, but his requests were denied. *Jogaku zasshi*, no. 202, 01.03.1890, 27–28; no. 203, 08.03.1890, 25–27; and no. 204, 15.03.1890, inside front cover.
101. *The Japan Gazette*, 17.06.1889, 2.

What had happened? Mr. Nose, headteacher of Tokyo kōtō jogakkō, had published an article in *Kuni no motoi* 国乃もとい (Foundation of the Country), arguing that educated young women should not marry journalists, doctors, politicians, merchants, or military men. By marrying doctors women would be at risk of contracting diseases and their daily lives would be interrupted by urgent calls. If they married farmers they would live away from the cities, making it difficult for them to continue their studies and meet new people. Japanese journalists were not like the respectable North American ones, and among them were men who hated educated women. The "ideal husband," as he put it, was a person who had studied abroad, somebody who published books or owned properties or an intellectual.[102]

Soon after this was published, an article appeared in the English-language *Japan Weekly Mail* commenting that the only thing girls could be considered guilty of was knowing about Nose's ideas, whereas Alice Bacon wrote that because of these rumors

> the scandal was in the mouths of all Tokyo. When the school gates [of Kōtō jogakkō] were opened in the morning, scurrilous placards were found posted upon them, and as the girls went to school they were insulted by school-boys and students on the street, and all this because stories which had no foundation, except that one of the teachers had once delivered before the girls a rather foolish and ill-advised lecture on the choice of husbands, in which he had viewed marriage from the somewhat sentimental standpoint of Europe and America, instead of taking the purely business view of it common in Japan. . . . That this was intended for an attack not simply on the one school, but on female education in general, seems likely from the fact that these same low papers are now busying themselves with some of the more important missionary schools for girls, though as yet they have done them no harm.[103]

The debate extended beyond the capital and was used to oppose female education in general; for example, it was suggested that all students frequenting normal schools or other institutions that trained women teachers should marry as soon as they graduated and that the Monbushō should hire only married teachers (as if that was going to stop extramarital liaisons!).[104] Enomoto Takeaki 榎本武揚, then minister of education, was reported to have argued that Mori Arinori, the previous minister of education, had worked hard for women's rights and against *danson johi*.

---

102. *Kuni no motoi*, no. 3, 01.06.1889, 1–8. The news was reported in *Shinonome shinbun*, supplement to no. 427, 16.06.1889, 1.
103. *Japan Weekly Mail*, no. 25, 22.06.1889, 17, signed by Isabella G. Prince; Alice Mabel Bacon, *A Japanese Interior* (London: Gay and Bird, 1893), 221–22.
104. *Dōyō shinbun*, no. 2256, 22.05.1890, 2.

If anybody had helped the expansion of women's education and the development of women's society, it was Mori. However, it was necessary to reform women's education again by teaching girls simple subjects such as penmanship, Western and Japanese sewing, and arithmetic and giving them easy readings from which they would learn moral values. Rather than intellectual training, they should be taught moral education, so that they would not be "impertinent" anymore, while it was also necessary to find an alternative to male teachers for female students.[105]

Bacon was right in pointing out that the attacks were critical of women's education in general and not of one school in particular. However, Tokyo kōtō jogakkō was supposed to be the model for female education and was certainly not offering an overtly progressive education. How could it be, then, that papers were attacking a government institution? And why were all these problems only now emerging given that female students and teachers had existed prior to the Meiji period and girl students were accepting their status as filial daughters and selfless wives?

To be sure, so-called excessive westernization, which had been pursued in the first place by the government, was now coming under attack. Girls and women at the Rokumeikan had enjoyed Western dances and English conversation while publicly supporting their fathers, husbands, and nation, but when westernization began to come under scrutiny the authorities attacked the girls and women who participated in the Rokumeikan balls since not only had the Rokumeikan become an improper place for women but also the women going there began to be criticized for improper behavior. Even Ōyama (Yamakawa) Sutematsu seems to have ceased going to the balls when a rumor started that she was divorcing her husband.[106] Similar attacks were waged against mission schools, their girl students, and English classes. For example, in *Kyōiku jiron* it was explained that the aim of Tokyo kōtō jogakkō had hitherto been that of teaching the necessary subjects to women of the upper classes, who had to fulfill public positions. However, that was going to be changed and virtuous subjects useful for women to become mothers and wives would be the focus of the education offered while English would be dropped from the curriculum. In addition, there was the hope that this reform would be adopted by similar schools all over the country.[107] Western women's lifestyles were also criticized. It was argued that European women were behaving immorally, in North

---

105. *Shinonome shinbun*, no. 429, 19.06.1889, 1. The only article I found suggesting that these scandals were exaggerated was in *Hokkaido mainichi shinbun*, no. 586, 28.06.1889, 3. The head of the school, the article reported, called a meeting of the students where he stated that Nose's article only expressed his own opinion and not that of the school, trying in this way to limit the damage done to the reputation of the school. It also stated that girls' schools should hire married male teachers and directors of schools should be older men.

106. Kuno Akiko, *Unexpected Destinations: The Poignant Story of Japan's First Vassar Graduate* (Kodansha International, 1993), 166–67.

107. *Kyōiku jiron*, no.125, 05.10.1888, 32–33.

America there were hospitals where women could give birth to children without fathers, and therefore avoid abortion, and in France there were even places where women could leave their children if they did not want them. If Japan were to follow the Western model of education, girls would become like their Western counterparts, and this, the argument ran, could only be avoided by teaching them sound moral virtues.[108]

By the late 1880s a change in attitude was becoming visible. The rapid rush to modernize and adopt Western values and institutions had started to slow down in the mid-1880s and was reversed in the late 1880s as a period of reaffirmation of Japanese values and customs set in. At one point, a westernized female education was seen as highly desirable in furthering Japan's modernization, but then it became dangerous, as the government and a segment of society feared Japan was becoming too westernized and the Japanese were losing their unique character; hence there was a need to roll back overt westernization.

The reaction against excessive westernization, however, cannot alone explain the outrage against girls' education and behavior for, after all, Tokyo kōtō jogakkō was a government institution and one in which the daughters of the richer classes were studying. There is, therefore, the need to go deeper if we want to explain, on the one hand, such widespread Japanese fears and, on the other, the defense of girls' education espoused by some Western women.

Conclusions

The extent of female education and its importance were highly debated topics in Europe and North America during the nineteenth century, and this debate also reached Japan, in particular because Japanese authorities were convinced that female education was one of the factors linked to national progress. On the other hand, much research on the early Meiji period deals with the difficulties former samurai had in finding new positions within Meiji society, while young men who had the financial resources to be educated in the new disciplines gained social prestige and economic rewards even when they came from nonsamurai backgrounds.[109] Early Meiji women, too, tried to maintain their social status while their samurai heritage was being erased by the government. They went to school to obtain an education that in most cases was used to marry them off to better families, they became teachers to help their families financially, or they participated in *fujinkai*

---

108. *Yomiuri shinbun*, no. 4331, 13.06.1889, 1. Similar "information" was recorded in diaries kept by members of the Iwakura mission, where it was noted that pregnant prostitutes and unmarried women could go to a certain hospital in New York and give birth to children who would be raised there. Kume, *The Iwakura Embassy*, vol. 1, 373.

109. See Kenneth B. Pyle, *The New Generation in Meiji Japan* (Stanford: Stanford University Press, 1969); and Gluck, *Japan's Modern Myths*.

in order to learn more about "proper" or "modern" behavior and taste while simultaneously supporting the ideal of "good wives, wise mothers" proposed by the government. The education received by the majority of the girls who enrolled in the schools opened by the Meiji government was similar to the education Edo period girls had acquired. It had well-defined uses and often practical purposes, and it was tailored to allow girls little freedom of thought. Many Meiji girls even failed to complete their course of study.

The girls presented here, however, were far from comprising a homogeneous category; acceptance and support of the government line was true of some, but others had a different agenda. This was the first time large numbers of girls from different areas studied together, forming a distinct group in society. Girls' schools were set up in the cities, where it was easier to find magazines published for a female public and leaflets advertising speech meetings organized by women and where women's activities in general were much publicized. Girl students were supposed to learn subjects designed for the international advancement of their country and were treated as objects of scrutiny in newspapers, exhibitions, and prints. In the process, however, some of them managed to become part of an active group of public speakers, presenting their opinions on the society they were observing, while the fact that magazines were allowing so many to publish those opinions meant that their experiences, ideas, and dreams could be increasingly shared with like-minded persons.

The new educational ideology of the Meiji school system taught girls that their education was patriotic and that they should be proud of teaching the next generation. These new environments helped them define their role within Meiji society and ask for more education also on the basis that they were doing so for their country. Those who made careers for themselves, who asked for more rights outside their homes, who wanted to be financially independent and have a say in public discourses concerning women's matters were not strictly following social expectations and were presenting a different model of womanhood.

The new education system transformed "girl students" into a category, *jogakusei*, but the social changes affecting Japanese society also made it a category "at risk"; by the late 1880s some of them had become visible in society and had embraced discourses that differed greatly from those of the government and supported the expansion of the woman's sphere. They were criticized because women were not considered to have the mental ability for higher education but also because they were a new group threatening the validity of their government's policies. By stretching the boundaries of their private and public lives, they were becoming "degenerate girls."

For the first time in Japanese history significant numbers of girl students and women teachers were able to contribute to the public discourse on female education and women's position in society. For example, although petitions to government authorities were certainly not a novelty in Japan, they were so when sent by *jogakusei* who were expressing their desire to obtain more education.[110] Thus, the passage by Mori Arinori quoted in the epigraph that opens this chapter should also be considered an expression of his concern about female public activities and demands rather than merely a statement of the government's aim to impose on women a fixed set of acceptable behaviors and thoughts.

110. Roberts, who has studied the use of petitions in the Edo period, writes that no petition seems to have been written by a woman in his area of research. Luke Roberts, "The Petition Box in Eighteenth-Century Tosa," *Journal of Japanese Studies* 20.2 (1994): 423–58.

3

Foreign Women Missionaries
and Their Japanese Female Charges

> The domesticating intent of the 'mission of sisterhood' requires the rupturing of the very image it relies on for its coherence: the "angel in the house" gives way to the agencies and effects of, first, the working wife and then, more subversive still, the highly trained presence of the "lady missionary."[1]

Together with the government and private individuals, missionaries, too, established schools for girls during the early Meiji period, and many of the teachers and head teachers in these institutions were women missionaries. Missionaries' presence in Japanese society was not readily accepted, and therefore girls were publicly criticized not only because they were studying in girls' schools but also because they were studying with Westerners. On the other hand, many of the women who tried to challenge Japanese society also turned to Western women, and their perceived power or freedom, to support their requests. Whereas some read about them in the papers or met them at women's meetings, the girls attending missionary schools could obtain knowledge about Western women's ideas and lifestyles firsthand through their interaction with women missionaries. Women missionaries did support Japanese women's active participation in public society, and were also among the first to found schools for nurses in Japan, so their work is important from the point of view of occupational opportunities as well.

Some of the material written by girls who studied at missionary schools is of questionable value as evidence of their impressions of Western women. As it was written in their adult years and for publication in school histories, it was tinged with

1. Jane Haggis, "'Good Wives and Mothers' or 'Dedicated Workers'? Contradictions of Domesticity in the 'Mission of Sisterhood,' Travancore, South India," in *Maternities and Modernities: Colonial and Postcolonial Experiences in Asia and the Pacific*, edited by Kalpana Ram and Margaret Jolly, 81–113 (Cambridge: Cambridge University Press, 1998), 89.

romanticism and inevitably spoke highly and happily about their time as students there. Furthermore, school histories do not normally record the number of girls who gave up their studies or any problems missionaries encountered. While missionaries' letters and reports show how many times girls failed, they say almost nothing about the fate of the hundreds of girls who frequented their schools only for a while, about those who did not like their teachings, or about the quarrels that inevitably must have arisen among students or with the teachers. Thus, information about those who left school and why remains elusive.[2]

Nevertheless, there still remains an abundant amount of primary material describing in a positive way girls' encounters with women missionaries that cannot be dismissed, and by using that material I present in this chapter a picture that adds to our understanding of girls' educational and employment opportunities during the Meiji period.

Missionaries' Work

Missionary denominations in Japan offered informal classes for boys and girls as an alternative to proselytization, which was banned until 1873, when Japanese authorities decided that proscribing Christianity was harming their relations with Western countries.[3] When these classes were not sufficient to meet the demand anymore, they opened schools where children could learn subjects taught in the West, and among these children there were many girls.

Missionary organizations began their work by sending male missionaries to Japan who were often accompanied by their wives. These women were supposed

2. In 1878 the Presbyterian Belle Marsh wrote about Japanese women, "Don't tell anybody this. We would never dare to let it be known at home. We write home thrilling accounts of the work of our beloved Bible women, etc; but we have to tell them just where and when to go, exactly what to say, and impress upon them that we are not going to be fooled." Richard Poate Stebbins, ed., *The Japan Experience: The Missionary Letters of Belle Marsh Poate and Thomas Pratt Poate, 1876–1892* (New York: Peter Lang, 1992), 59.

3. The British Church Mission Society was in Nagasaki in 1869; Osaka in 1873; Tokyo and Hakodate in 1874; Tokushima, Fukuoka, and Matsue in 1888; and Hiroshima and Sapporo in 1892. Archive of the Church Mission Society (hereafter CMS), Special Collections Department, University of Birmingham. The American Board of Commissioners for Foreign Missions (ABCFM) commenced its activities in Japan in 1869, and the British Society for the Propagation of the Gospel arrived in 1873. On male missionary activities in Japan, see A. Hamish Ion, *The Cross and the Rising Sun: The Canadian Protestant Missionary Movement in the Japanese Empire, 1872–1931* (Waterloo, Ont.: Wilfrid Laurier University Press, 1990); Koizumi Takashi, *Nakamura Keiu to kirisutokyō* (Nakamura Keiu and Christianity) (Hokuju shuppan, 1991); Ōe Mitsuru, *Senkyōshi Uiriamuzu no dendō to shōgai: Bakumatsu Meiji beikoku seikōkai no kiseki* (The life and work of the missionary Williams: The American Episcopal Church during the Bakumatsu and Meiji periods) (Tōsui shobō, 2000); and Watanabe Masao and Enomoto Emiko, trans., *Kai to jūjika. Shinkaronja senkyōshi J. T. Gyurikku no shōgai* (The shellfish and the cross: The life of J. T. Gulick, evolutionist and missionary man) (Yūshōdō Shuppan, 1988).

to re-create a family atmosphere for their husbands in a faraway country, but they also helped spread the gospel. One such example is that of Clara Hepburn, the wife of Dr. J. C. Hepburn (1815–1911), who arrived in Japan in 1859 as a member of the Presbyterian Church. Clara took care of the house, the children, and the Japanese helpers, but she also established the Hepburn Juku, a class for boys and girls.[4]

Soon, however, those organizations allowed unmarried women to sail to Japan; Mary Kidder (b. 1834), the first single woman of the American Reformed Church sent to Japan, wrote in 1869 that the board had decided to try "the experiment of sending the first unmarried lady missionary to Japan." Kidder took over the Hepburn Juku and transformed it into the Ferris Seminary (then Ferris jogakuin フェリス女学院), where Wakamatsu Shizuko and Sasaki Toyoju studied and the political activist Kishida Toshiko 岸田俊子 (1863–1901) taught for a brief period.[5] This "experiment" was a success, and many others joined, financed by the many women's boards and groups that supported women's missionary activities.[6] And there was no shortage of women volunteers: the treasurer of the Church Mission Society (CMS) complained, "It is said that [we] . . . ought not to send out ladies by themselves into the Mission-field, but the managers of the missionary societies know very well that it is not a question of sending out ladies; it is the keeping of ladies back more often than not."[7] Given that, according to the 1851 English census, 42 percent of the female population between the ages of twenty and forty was unmarried and one-third of the six million women in Britain were self-supporting, it is clear that missionary work was appealing as one of the jobs open to middle-class women.[8]

---

4. Ferris jogakuin hyakunenshi henshū iinkai, ed., *Ferris jogakuin hyakunenshi* (One hundred years of Ferris jogakuin) (Yokohama: Ferris jogakuin, 1970), 18–19.

5. Ferris jogakuin, ed., *Kidaa shokanshū* (Collection of Kidder's letters) (Kyōbunkan, 1975), 25; Ferris jogakuin hyakunenshi henshū iinkai, *Ferris jogakuin*, 32–33. The number of students was quite small when Kidder took the educational work of the girls in her hands, whereas boys were asked to find another school. Ferris jogakuin hyakunenshi henshū iinkai, *Ferris jogakuin*, 27–28.

6. For example, members of the order Soeurs de l'Enfant-Jesus arrived in 1872, and members of the Soeurs de l'Enfant-Jesus de Chauffailles arrived in 1877, having been asked to help the priests of the Paris Foreign Mission Society in their work there. Ann Harrington, "The First Women Religious in Japan: Mother Saint Mathilde Raclot and the French Connection," *The Catholic Historical Review* 87.4 (2001): 603–23. The Woman's Union Missionary Society of America for Heathen Lands (WUMS) was founded in 1860 and opened the American Mission Home in Yokohama in 1871. The (British) Society for Promoting Female Education in China, India and the East (subsequently renamed the Society for Promoting Female Education in the East and also known as the Female Education Society, or FES) started recruiting women for the mission field in 1834. It was founded largely by missionary wives and other women who supported women's work for women in "heathen lands." Archive of the Society for Promoting Female Education in China, India and the East, Special Collections Department, University of Birmingham.

7. Judith Rowbotham, "'Soldiers of Christ'? Images of Female Missionaries in Late Nineteenth-Century Britain—Issues of Heroism and Martyrdom," *Gender and History* 12.1 (2000): 99.

8. Mary Poovey, *Uneven Developments: The Ideological Work of Gender in Mid-Victorian England* (Chicago: University of Chicago Press, 1988), 4.

However, for nineteenth-century North American and European missions, spreading Christianity by sending out women was not a straightforward decision, especially when the women were single. Male missionaries not only feared that it would be difficult to guarantee women's physical and mental safety among "heathen" people but also worried that they might marry and therefore be lost to the missionary effort. In 1872, Dr. J. C. Hepburn sent home the first of many letters warning of the dangers of single women and women's work in the mission field. He argued that married women enabled men to carry on with their jobs and sometimes opened small classes, whereas single women, who were useful for teaching young children, managing orphan asylums, and nursing the sick, should live together since the worst choice was that of sending unmarried women *alone*. He wrote that it was a waste of money

> to send out a young unmarried woman, who is not likely to know much either of herself, the world, or the work she is going for. The best thing such as one can do, is to get married as [speedily?] as possible as they generally do, and if they do not marry a missionary they are lost to the work of missions. . . . try and be careful to send *experienced* women, and if they are not very *handsome* don't let it trouble you.[9]

However, the idea that unmarried women could be less trustworthy and faithful to the missionary effort seems to have been more of a male fear than a reality. Jane Haggis, who has investigated the selection process for those young women who wanted to go abroad and participate in the spread of Christianity, writes that the Ladies' Committee of the London Missionary Society was specifically looking for candidates who were between twenty-one and twenty-eight years old, the marrying age for middle-class British women. She also suggests that missionary work did require women of high educational standing.[10]

Educated women were indeed willing to answer the missionaries' call. To give just a few examples, Katherine Tristram (b. 1858), a member of the Female Education Society, was the daughter of the canon of Durham, had been educated at Cheltenham Ladies' College, and in 1882 was appointed a mathematical lecturer at Westfield College, London. She became the headmistress of Bishop Poole Girls' School in Osaka in 1890 (now Poole gakuin daigaku プール学院大学).[11] Martha J.

9. Archive of the U.S. Presbyterian Missions, Records of U.S. Presbyterian Missions, Yokohama Kaikō Shiryōkan, Yokohama, vol. 2, 4/5, 87–99, August 21, 1872. See also vol. 4, 5/15, 73–87, October 12, 1878.

10. Jane Haggis, "'A Heart That Has Felt the Love of God and Longs for Others to Know It': Conventions of Gender, Tensions of Self, and Constructions of Difference in Offering to Be a Lady Missionary," *Women's History Review* 7.2 (1998): 174.

11. The school was founded in 1879 and initially named Eisei jogakkō. See the entry for Katherine Alice Salvin Tristram in the *Oxford Dictionary of National Biography: From the Earliest Times*

Cartmell (b. 1845), the first missionary of the Woman's Missionary Society of the Canadian Methodist Church of Canada (WMS-CM) sent to Japan, had been the headmistress of Hamilton public girls' school.[12] Finally, in 1874 Miss Dora Schoonmaker (1851–1934) of the American Methodist Episcopal Mission opened Joshi shōgakkō, which later became Aoyama jogakuin 青山女学院, even nowadays one of the most prestigious schools in Tokyo. Schoonmaker was the first principal of the school, and during the first years of its existence all principals and superintendents were women, mostly single.[13]

Sending women missionaries around the world meant giving them the task of spreading North American and European Victorian ideals of womanhood. Missionaries agreed that in Japan "The people no longer regarded Christianity with the horror and aversion of former years . . . the nature of Christianity being naturally identified by the Japanese with the character and lives of those who had come to bear it to them."[14] Expanding on this idea, Julia Carrothers wrote, "As fathers see their daughters learning and becoming good, wise women; as the educated young men seek wives among the girls who have been taught in the schools, and intelligent women have the care and training of children, and boys no longer despise their mothers, and husbands learn to trust their wives—the family relations will all be changed, and the power of pure womanhood will be felt in the land."[15]

Women missionaries told Japanese women that their duty was to become good Christian mothers and wives. However, they also showed them that women's work was as important as men's, that women's dependence on their husbands was not necessarily the rule, and that women could have a rewarding life outside of their homes by working for the good of society while their household chores did not

to the Year 2000, edited by H. C. G. Matthew and Brian Harrison (Oxford: Oxford University Press, 2004).

12. Ion, The Cross and the Rising Sun, 30.

13. Aoyama sayurikai, ed., Aoyama jogakuin shi (History of Aoyama jogakuin) (Aoyama sayurikai, 1973), 19. Schoonmaker opened the school with the help of the scholar Tsuda Sen. The very first students were Tsuda's wife, daughter, two sons, and a friend of his wife. Aoyama gakuin, ed., Aoyama gakuin kyūjūnenshi (Ninety years of Aoyama gakuin) (Aoyama gakuin, 1965), 90–91. From the start, the school was expensive, and in 1877 students paid three yen a month to attend. Kanbe Yasumitsu, "Meiji shoki Tokyo ni okeru shiritsu gakkō no keiei" (The development of private schools in Tokyo during the early Meiji period), Shigaku kenshū 13 (1961): 135. In 1878 it was renamed Kaigan jogakkō 海岸女学校 and in 1895 Aoyama jogakuin. In 1886, Kaigan jogakkō had ninety-five students of which eighty-five were boarders. Jogaku zasshi, no. 27, 25.06.1886, last page.

14. Proceedings of the General Conference of the Protestant Missionaries of Japan, Osaka, vol. 1 (Yokohama: R. Meikle John, 1883), 40. In India, too, Christian converts thought that "Change would come gradually through direct contact with European women. Hindu women must 'see with their eyes' the superiority which education imparts to female recipients." David W. Savage, "Missionaries and the Development of a Colonial Ideology of Female Education in India," Gender and History 9.2 (1997): 213.

15. Julia Carrothers, The Sunrise Kingdom; or, Life and Scenes in Japan, and Woman's Work for Woman There (Philadelphia: Presbyterian Board of Publication, 1879), 263.

necessarily have to take precedence over more important tasks such as learning. Eliza Talcott, one of the founders of Kobe jogakuin 神戸女学院, wrote that it was thanks to her freedom from household chores that her time could be fully used to study and teach. In order to continue her work, she wanted to hire a woman who could "free [her] to some extent from the distracting thoughts of 'what shall we eat?'"[16] Ebina Miyako also recalled an episode that occurred when she was studying at Dōshisha jogakkō 同志社女学校 in Kyoto. It was her turn to cook, and she had been entrusted with the task of preparing a meat dish, but she had forgotten about it, having instead focused her attention on her English lesson, and the dinner was completely burned. The other girls were speechless, but her teacher, Miss Alice Starkweather, told her that it was nothing to worry about as it had happened because she was absorbed in her studies, which was a good thing.[17] Some women missionaries embodied the image of strong-willed, educated, and independent individuals who were finding gratification in their work. Such fulfillment, or perhaps we should call it independence, was derived from actively working for the education of other women.[18]

16. Kobe jogakuin (initially called Kobe Home and then renamed Kobe eiwa jogakkō) was opened in 1873 with twenty girls age eight or older. The first class graduated in 1882. Charlotte B. DeForest, *History of Kobe College, 1875–1950* (Chicago: Kobe College Corporation, 1950), 2–3. Talcott arrived in Japan with Julia Dudley in 1873 as a member of the American Board of Commissioners for Foreign Missions.

17. Matsuura Masayasu, *Dōshisha romansu* (Dōshisha romance) (Keiseisha shoten, 1918), 82. Miss Starkweather started teaching in the girls' department of Dōshisha in 1876. During the first year of its existence, the school was called Kyoto Home, Kyoto Girls' School, or Starkweather's School. Sakamoto Kiyone, "Dōshisha jogakkō shodai fujin senkyōshi A. J. Starkweather no kutō" (The struggle of the woman missionary A. J. Starkweather in the early days of Dōshisha jogakkō), in *Rainichi America senkyōshi. American bo-do- senkyōshi shokan no kenkyū 1869–1890* (American missionaries in Japan: A study of the correspondence of the American Board, 1869–1890), edited by Dōshisha daigaku jinbun kagaku kenkyūsho, 303–26 (Kyoto: Gendai shiryō shuppan, 1999), 303–4.

18. In 1887, Miss Eliza Spencer (1855–1933, then Ms. Large), who was working at Tōyō eiwa jogakkō, wrote, "No one but those of us who are here can realize the joy and strength that come to our own hearts through these conversions. God has indeed been good, and has permitted us to see much *fruit*. What we should do if we did not feel the Master near in all our daily worries and trials, I do not know." Tōyō eiwa jogakuin shiryōshitsu iinkai, ed., *Tōyō eiwa jogakuin shiryōshū* (Sources on Tōyō eiwa jogakuin) (Tōyō eiwa jogakuin shiryōshitsu iinkai 1985), vol. 2, 20. Miss Kate Youngman (1841–1910), who was teaching at B-rokuban jogakkō, stated, "It had been promised to my aunt I would go back home after five years. I am sad at the idea of not seeing her anymore but God is showing me I have to stay here. I can and have given up my *all* for Jesus and he has returned me a hundred fold." Records of U.S. Presbyterian Missions, vol. 4, 6/15, 88–107. Such independence had also to be protected from interfering powers. When in January 1882 Alice Starkweather learned that the committee of the Woman's Board of Missions in Boston was thinking of handing over to the Japanese authorities the girls' department at Dōshisha, which she had helped found, she wrote to Dr. Clark, the secretary of the board, asking, "[Is] the missionary object . . . to see how little 'foreign money' shall be credited to Japan? Or how surely and deeply the true Word of God shall be planted here to *grow* with deep roots like the cedars of Lebanon *at whatever cost*"? Sakamoto Kiyone, "Beikoku dendōkai senkyōshi bunsho: A. J. Starkweather

Women Missionaries and East Asian Women

Missionaries had to keep close links with the mission boards and the Christian readership at home in order to recruit more workers and obtain contributions, and their letters were published in missionary journals that provided their readership with reports on their fieldwork. Such letters often emphasized the perceived superiority of Christian and Western societies, and that of the readership itself, while justifying women's presence and work abroad.

Women missionaries went to Asia regarding themselves as the only ones in a position to teach true "womanhood," especially when they were faced with Chinese women's foot binding, Indian women's suttee, or Japanese concubines.[19] As Padma Anagol points out, overseas opportunities provided a space for the surplus of white women but also empowered them through collaboration in the ideological work of the empire.[20] Minna Tapson, a CMS missionary, expressly tells us in the following letter that it was the Christianity brought by women like herself that was awakening Japanese women, who were "unaccustomed to take any independent line for themselves, have adhered far more generally to the creed in which they were brought up, and very often, one sees them waking up to *think* for the first time, when they are brought under the influence of Christianity."[21] Women missionaries

---

shokan (4)" (The documents of the missionaries of the American Board of Commissioners for Foreign Missions: The correspondence of A. J. Starkweather, part 4), in *Sōgō bunka kenkyūsho kiyō*, vol. 10, 69–96 (Kyoto: Dōshisha joshi daigaku, 1993), 77.

19. One missionary wrote about Indian women, "Two wives of one man; the one pleasant and unloved; the other very forbidding. A poor little child, with a head in a state that is half-sickening to look at!" quoted in Rowbotham, "Soldiers of Christ?" 97. The Chinese woman, instead, "is not desired at birth, is subject to father, husband, and son, and is denied the privileges of education. To destroy girl babies at birth was formerly exceedingly common. . . . Girls are simply sold as bondmaids to relieve poverty; and a wife may legally be sold or rented by her husband to another man for a fixed period. The binding of the feet is but an outward and visible sign of the crippled lives and energies of one-half of the Chinese people." Helen Barrett Montgomery, *Western Women in Eastern Lands* (New York: Macmillan, 1910), 48. The Japanese wife was not doing much better. She was "often superseded by a younger or more favored rival, to whom she must become subordinate, [and] passes her idle, profitless life with those silent yearnings for sympathy and affection which are born in every woman's heart. The daughter, especially if handsome, must set aside her own free choice and be wedded as the father wills; perhaps to one whom she hates, or, worse still, be bartered away for unhallowed gain." Archive of Yokohama kyōritsu gakuen, Records of the Woman's Union Missionary Society of America for Heathen Lands, WUMS Annual Report, 1876, 72. These reports were produced also to describe men's lives. One missionary wrote that a Japanese father had killed his son because he had found him stealing and then waited for the authority to sentence him. Tōyō eiwa jogakuin shiryōshitsu iinkai, *Tōyō eiwa jogakuin shiryōshū*, vol. 1 (1984), 6.

20. Padma Anagol, "Indian Christian Women and Indigenous Feminism, c.1850–c.1920," in *Gender and Imperialism*, edited by Clare Midgley, 79–103 (Manchester: Manchester University Press, 1998), 81.

21. Minna Tapson, "Recollections of Japan," *Cheltenham Ladies' College Magazine*, Spring 1895, 134.

could not baptize, were working under the rules dictated by boards normally controlled by male missionaries, and were not supposed to take on dangerous work but rather to complement men's work. However, since it was almost impossible for men to enter Asian and Middle Eastern homes, women missionaries felt empowered by a task that only they could accomplish among Asian women, who were the focal point in every family and could lure Christian male converts back into paganism and train "another generation of idol-worshippers in their homes."[22] Of course, if this "approach" could help them define their position and worth within the missionary world, it also alienated those Japanese men and women who did not think they needed to be saved.

Missionary Education

Nevertheless, compared to other situations, missionaries came to see Japanese women of all classes as having potential because some of those women started to visit them and show interest.[23] "Statistics of Missions and Missionary Work in Japan for the Year 1887" lists 25 different missions belonging to the various denominations that were present in Japan, with a total of 128 married and 20 unmarried male missionaries and 103 unmarried females. In 1886 the figures had been, respectively, 111, 17, and 85. If we accept these figures as correct and include married women, the effort put into women's work by the various mission boards is evident. From the same document we also know that there were 29 girls' schools with boarders in 1887 (as opposed to 12 boys' schools) with 1,716 students in 1886 and 2,707 in 1887.[24]

Although to begin with missionaries were willing to take on every girl who asked to be taught, as the number of girl students rose during the second-half of the 1880s these same schools started to be distinguished according to the social class of the girls studying there. The girls' department of Seiritsu gakusha 成立学舎 in Tokyo, for example, taught girls whose fathers were government officials or military officers or were working in commerce and industry.[25] Among the students at Tōyō

---

22. H. L. Platt, *The Story of the Years: A History of the Woman's Missionary Society of the Methodist Church, Canada, from 1881 to 1906* (Canada: Woman's Missionary Society, 1909), vol. 2, 7, makes this point in the case of Japanese women.
23. For example, during the first decades of their work in Bengal, missionaries had become disillusioned with upper-caste girls' education and opened boarding schools for poor girls, who, they thought, would listen to their teachings more effectively. M. A. Laird, *Missionaries and Education in Bengal, 1793–1837* (Oxford: Clarendon Press, 1972), 137–40.
24. In 1887, most missionaries were living in Yokohama, Tokyo, Kobe, Sendai, Nemuro, Osaka, Kanazawa, Hiroshima, Sapporo, Nagasaki, Kumamoto, Nagoya, and Shizuoka, Archive of the CMS, G2/J/O 1888/64B.
25. Ōhama Tetsuya, ed., *Joshi gakuin no rekishi* (The history of Joshi gakuin) (Joshi gakuin, 1985), 206.

eiwa jogakkō 東洋英和女学校, opened in Tokyo in 1884 by the Woman's Missionary Society of the Methodist Church of Canada, were the daughters of counts, viscounts, and naval and military officers but also many from the middle class.[26] The evangelization of the poorer classes is less well documented. It was pursued through home visits, evening meetings, Sunday schools, and Bible classes, but, although these were efforts that took up a lot of missionaries' time, I have not found substantial material written by poor women describing their encounter with Christianity. Missionaries did their best to establish scholarships for poor students, which were normally financed by Western patrons and through appeals published in their journals, but these were few.[27] Those students who won a scholarship were usually required to work for a couple of years for the missions, but they often worked for longer periods, either because they converted or because it was a good opportunity. Others had the possibility of joining a mission school as a teacher-pupil and supporting themselves in that way, although this possibility was exceptional.[28] Missionaries also opened schools for mixed-race children and orphans. During the 1870s many children were born in Yokohama to Japanese mothers and Western fathers, and missionaries started to worry about their future. The Woman's Union Missionary Society of America for Heathen Lands announced in 1871 that "The object of the proposed Mission is to gather into a suitable home and school

26. The school accommodated 2 pupils at its opening. In 1887 there were 127 boarders, 100 day students, and a teaching staff of 8 to 10 Japanese. Every graduate and 50 percent of the students seem to have embraced Christianity. Platt, *The Story of the Years*, vol. 2, 10–14; Tokyo-to, *Tokyo no joshi kyōiku* (Female education in Tokyo) (Tokyo-to, 1961), 88–95.

27. One exception was Kwassui jogakkō, founded in 1879 in Nagasaki. The school was doing particularly well in 1887, for there were 130 students enrolled, of which 124 were still attending by the time the academic year ended in June 1887. Of the 56 students who were granted a scholarship, 38 were entirely supported. The school was successful in teaching girls an occupation, for 30 were in the Industrial Department, knitting and crocheting infants' clothing, underwear, dresses, coats, and so on. Missionary schools were also places where new members for the Fujin kyōfūkai could be recruited, and Kwassui was one such example, for a local group was organized by the girls in the school. Minutes of the fourth session of the Woman's Conference of the Methodist Episcopal Church in Japan, 1887, 33–34, Archive of Aoyama gakuin, Tokyo.

28. By 1880 Methodist Protestants were supporting seventeen girls in Yokohama where forty dollars was enough to maintain a girl for one year. John Krummel, "Methodist Protestant Beginnings in Japan, Part 1: The Development of the Methodist Protestant Foreign Missions." *Ronshū*, no. 13 (Aoyama gakuin daigaku, 1972), 6. Protestant missionaries offering scholarships took girls on trial for three months, and if they proved capable their parents signed a contract promising that they would remain in the school a certain number of years as pupils and two additional years as helpers. *Proceedings,* 161. Tōyō eiwa jogakkō's fees were waived in some cases, but the students were then required to work for the missionaries for two years as teachers, interpreters, or Bible women. Tōyō eiwa jogakuin shiryōshitsu iinkai, *Tōyō eiwa jogakuin shiryōshū*, vol. 1, 18; Platt, *The Story of the Years*, vol. 2, 12. The Presbyterian missionaries working at Joshi gakuin helped open Joshi dokuritsu gakkō 女子独立学校, where students who could not afford to pay for their education worked in the school while studying. Tokyo-to, *Tokyo no joshi kyōiku*, 151.

the outcast daughters of Japanese women, who, born to degradation, are growing up neglected vagrants, and a curse to the land."[29] For this reason, in August 1871 Mary Pruyn, Louise Pierson (1832–99), and Julia Crosby (1833–1918) opened the American mission home (America fujin kyōjusho 亜米利加婦人教授所) in Yokohama where girls in particular were taught to be Bible women, persons who traveled, especially inland, to spread the faith. In 1872, because of the growing number of students, the school moved and was renamed Nihon fujo eigakkō 日本婦女英学校, becoming Kyōritsu jogakkō 共立女学校 in 1875.[30] As a final example, in 1873 French Catholic sisters reported that their girls' school in Yokohama housed fifteen European boarders and thirty-six orphans. They also opened a school and orphanage in Tokyo, and in both cases their establishments were filled to capacity.[31]

Japanese Reactions to Missionary Education

Many intellectuals and government authorities who valued Western customs and knowledge helped the missionaries with their work. This holds true for women's work as well, as can be seen in the case of Miss Mary Kidder, who wrote in 1871 from Yokohama, "The governor of Tosa [Kochi] sent last week to know if I would go there to teach the girls. The messenger told me that Tosa has already sent to America for three ladies to come and teach them." However, since it would be some time before those women arrived, they wanted her as soon as possible.[32] Local governments or patrons who were willing to spend money on girls' education often paid for the school buildings and monthly expenses.[33] Cases of Japanese living in neighboring communities who helped missionaries when typhoons and fires de-

---

29. Records of WUMS, Annual Report, 1871, 27, Archive of Yokohama kyōritsu gakuen, Yokohama. Founded in New York in 1860 by Mrs. Sarah Doremus and supported by women from various churches, WUMS was intended as a vehicle for sending single women as missionaries to women in Asia.

30. Yokohama kyōritsu gakuen, *Yokohama kyōritsu gakuen hyakunijūnen no ayumi* (One hundred and twenty years of Yokohama kyōritsu gakuen) (Yokohama: Yokohama kyōritsu gakuen, 1991), esp. 54–59.

31. By 1877, there were eighty girls under the care of the sisters, twenty boys, and fifty children, some living in the surrounding areas with families who agreed to take care of them. Mother Saint Mathilde wrote about a poor mother who had asked her to take three of her daughters who would otherwise be sold into prostitution. She agreed on the condition that these girls would stay with the sisters until the age of twenty and would be allowed to become Catholics. Harrington, "The First Women Religious," 615–16.

32. "Kidaa joshi dendō kyoku ate kōshiki shokan" (The official correspondence of the missionary Ms. Kidder), unpublished material, Ferris jogakuin daigaku, 20.

33. The governor of Shizuoka prefecture, whose daughter was studying at Tōyō eiwa jogakkō, helped with the founding of Shizuoka eiwa jogakkō in 1887, which opened with twenty-three students, followed in 1889 by Yamanashi eiwa jogakkō in Kōfu, where in 1891 there were thirty-one students, twenty-eight boarders, and nineteen Christians. The buildings of both schools were provided and furnished by Japanese supporters. Ion, *The Cross and the Rising Sun*, 121–23. In 1872 Ōe Taku 大江卓, the governor of Kanagawa prefecture, supplied materials and offered a building

stroyed part of their buildings, explaining that missionaries were doing good for the children of "their country," are also traceable.[34] Furthermore, Scheiner has argued that former samurai accepted Christianity more easily when the new religion was seen as a supplement to bushido, the samurai philosophy, and when missionaries appeared to dedicate themselves to Christianity *and* Japan. They believed, he continues, that Christian principles could help in the formation of a strong country.[35] Nakamura Masanao, who was baptized in 1874, was one such example. In 1871 he addressed a memorial to the emperor, stating that Christianity was the spirit and essence of Western civilization and attempts to adopt Western things without it would not lead to a good result. Around the same time he helped find students for the American mission home.[36] Tamura Naoomi 田村直臣 (1858–1935), a Christian leader, recalled how he had converted to Christianity because he was convinced that Japan should adopt it as one of the strong points of Western civilization so as to be able to compete with other nations.[37] On the other hand, Fukuzawa Yukichi, a staunch promoter of education in general, supported missionaries' activities because of his interest in their schooling system. When Alice Hoar (1845–1922) wrote to her board in February 1876, she announced that Fukuzawa had offered the use of part of his house, inside the campus of Keiō gijuku 慶応義塾, so she could teach a few girls. In her next letter, written in June 1876, she stated that she had eight pupils and one of them was Fukuzawa's niece.[38]

Many of the young women frequenting these schools came from the upper middle classes. They were obtaining an education similar to that imparted in government schools while living in a Western environment that was considered a necessary part of a good upbringing for girls who would later become the wives of influential

---

for Kidder's school. Ōe's wife was among the students. Ferris jogakuin hyakunenshi henshū iinkai, *Ferris jogakuin*, 32–33. Similarly, Miss Eliza Talcott and Miss Julia Dudley opened the Kobe Home for girls in 1873 with the help of Viscount Kuki Takayoshi 九鬼隆義 and other Japanese supporters. The school had thirty-nine students of which seventeen were self-supporting. It became Kobe jogakuin in 1894. DeForest, *History of Kobe College*, 4–6.

34. Harrington, "The First Women Religious," 620.

35. Irwin Scheiner, *Christian Converts and Social Protest in Meiji Japan* (Berkeley: University of California Press, 1970), esp. chap. 2; "Christian Samurai and Samurai Values," in *Modern Japanese Leadership*, edited by B. S. Silberman and H. D. Harootunian, 171–94 (Tucson: University of Arizona Press, 1996).

36. Earl Kinmonth, "Nakamura Keiu and Samuel Smiles: A Victorian Confucian and a Confucian Victorian," in *Meiji Japan: Political, Economic, and Social History, 1868–1912*, edited by Peter Kornicki, vol. 2, 280–302 (London: Routledge, 1998), 286; *Jogaku zasshi*, no. 270, 20.06.1891, 1.

37. Tamura Naoomi, *Shinkō gojūnenshi* (Fifty years of faith) (Keiseisha, 1924), 24, cited in Emily Anderson, "Tamura Naoomi's *The Japanese Bride*: Christianity, Nationalism, and Family in Meiji Japan," *Japanese Journal of Religious Studies* 34.1 (2007): 208.

38. Archive of the Ladies' Association for the Promotion of Female Education in India and other Heathen Countries, Rhodes House Library, Oxford (hereafter LAPFE), CWW 238, 64–66, 224–27. Their collaboration seems to have lasted a little more than a year. Shirai Takako, *Fukuzawa Yukichi to senkyōshitachi* (Fukuzawa Yukichi and foreign missionaries) (Miraisha, 1999), 138–39.

persons and therefore had to master both ways of living. In a letter to two women on their appointment at Eisei jogakkō 永生女学校 in Osaka, the board stated that their efforts were to be of "educational character, the instruction given being comprehensive in its nature, not exclusively religious, though all conducted in a religious tone, and being also not special but general, intended to fit the pupils not for particular vocations but generally for life in the high circles of Japanese society."[39] The writer Miyake Kaho remembered that when she was fifteen her mother told her that even girls had to learn English, and she was therefore enrolled in Sakurai jogakkō. The fact that she was not the only student reporting such reasons for enrolling in missionary schools tells us that this was not an uncommon situation.[40]

A final example of the interest Japanese authorities had in Western education, and of the way in which missionaries sought to profit from it, is summarized in an article published in a missionary journal. Professors at Tokyo university, wanting to educate upper-class women, "who share continually in the life which the enterprise of their husbands and fathers has so wonderfully developed," had proposed the foundation of an institute, the Tokyo jogakukan 東京女学館 (Tokyo Institute for the Women's Learning, opened in September 1888), and contacted Edward Bickersteth, missionary bishop of the Church of England, to hire Christian women as teachers and managers. Residence and board were to be provided by the Japanese. The institute was to function as a club, a lecture theater, and a high school where courses in housekeeping, nursing the sick, dress, deportment, literature, cooking, and ethics were to be offered. Importance was given to the association of these ladies with Western women, and they were to listen to lectures, play outdoor sports, and attend evening gatherings.[41] Supporters of this institute were much more interested in etiquette and social relations with Western ladies than in Christianity, but it was nevertheless considered a good deal for both sides.

39. "Instructions to Miss Tristram and Miss Tapson proceeding to the Japan Mission, October 1888," Archive of CMS, minutes of Committee of Correspondence, G2/J/L2.

40. Kanzaki Kiyoshi, *Gendai fujin den* (Biographies of contemporary women) (Chūō kōronsha, 1940), 86. Satō Tetsuko 佐藤哲子 noted that when she was studying at the normal school for girls in Kyoto around 1884 everything that was based on Western teachings was much acclaimed and so she went to Ferris jogakkō to learn English. Yamamoto Hideteru, ed., *Ferris waei jogakkō rokujūnenshi* (Sixty years of Ferris waei jogakkō) (Yokohama: Ferris waei jogakkō dōsōkai, 1931), 61.

41. *Grain of Mustard Seed or, Woman's Work in Foreign Parts*, January 1 and February 1, 1887. Periodical published by the Ladies Association for the Promotion of Female Education among the Heathen, in the Missions of the "Society for the Propagation of the Gospel." The Western women employed were not allowed to teach Christianity. Natori, 1984. They were Mrs. Caroline Kirkes (56 years old); Miss Susan Barnett (23) and Miss Flora Bristowe (23), who had studied at Cambridge University; Miss Ellen MacRae (43); Miss Alice Parker (27), who had studied at London University and was the principal of a girls' school; Miss Frances Dunkley (28), a graduate of London University; and Mrs. Joanna MacLeod (57), a graduate of the London Royal Academy of Music. Tokyo-to, *Tokyo no joshi kyōiku*, 118–20. Information about this collaboration was reported in *Tokyo nichinichi shinbun*, no. 4551, 14.01.1887, 2.

As a general rule, missionaries did not force their students to convert, so the "Christian" part of their children's education was not always considered important—or dangerous—by the parents. According to Sugimoto Etsuko 杉本鉞子 (1873–1950), who was sent to a mission school, Western teachers were seen as the transmitters of the language and manners of North America while the fact that they were *Christian* teachers was not considered at all.[42]

However, having come into contact with Western people and their values, some Japanese slowly became interested in Christianity as well. The Kumamoto band, a group of young boys from Kumamoto who gathered around Captain Leroy Janes, went against their families' wishes and asked him to teach them about his religion.[43] The education provided could also open up the possibility of teaching in governmental, missionary, and private schools, which was an important factor for young middle-class Japanese women who did not necessarily have to marry at the end of their courses or who wanted to find "respectable" employment.

Japanese relations with missionaries were not always positive. The same Fukuzawa Yukichi was dissatisfied with the results of his collaboration with women missionaries, and his support was short-lived; Shidachi Taki 志立たき (b. 1876), one of his daughters, recalled that, although her older sisters were sent to school, she was educated at home, for Fukuzawa had lost confidence in the education system for girls while his wife had never believed in female education.[44] Furthermore, since the very idea of girls' education was still not accepted by many, those who were opposed to it were even less in favor of a foreign education, the benefits of which were not yet proven. Mitani Tamiko 三谷民子 (1873–1945), who graduated from Joshi gakuin 女子学院 in 1891 and later became its headmistress, wrote that during her first days at Sakurai

> I was determined also not to confess my home sick feelings, because it was by my wish and decision that I was allowed to come to the school and I was afraid to be taken out of the school at any such mention, for the family, especially, my grand-mother was very much opposed to girls' education and that at a Christian school—the Christian part was not

42. Etsu Sugimoto, *A Daughter of the Samurai* (North Clarendon: Tuttle, 1990), 145. At school she particularly enjoyed the Old Testament, writing, "The figurative language was something like Japanese; the old heroes had the same virtues and the same weaknesses of our ancient samurai; the patriarchal form of government was like ours, and the family system based upon it pictured so plainly our own homes that the meaning of many questioned passages was far less puzzling to me than were the explanations of the foreign teachers." Ibid., 130.

43. See Fred George Notehelfer, *American Samurai: Captain L. L. Janes and Japan* (Princeton: Princeton University Press, 1985).

44. "Chichi no joshi kyōiku wa okashii" (Dad's education for women is strange). The title of the journal where this interview was published is not legible. A copy is preserved in the archive of Yokohama kyōritsu gakuen.

very much thought of by the parents either and of course not by the child [Tamiko] herself.[45]

Missionaries were confronted with other serious problems. Julia Carrothers stated:

> We sent once in the fall for O Chiye san's father to come and talk about his daughter's baptism. He said that he had no objection himself, but in his department the ya-cu-nins [*yakunin*, "officials"] were obliged to send the names of any who received baptism to the central government, and his own daughter's name might cost him his office and means of support; but he promised to give his consent within three months.[46]

Buddhist priests also opposed missionaries' presence in Japan. One woman missionary wrote that of all the children frequenting her school the girls had disappeared after Buddhist priests visited their homes to criticize missionaries' work while another wrote that one of her girls' parents had removed her from school and promised her nice clothes if she went to the temple.[47] Girls, too, if not directly

---

45. Tamura Naoomi and Asada Mikako, eds., *Joshi gakuin gojūnenshi* (Fifty years of Joshi gakuin) (Joshi gakuin dōsōkai, 1928), 46 (original in English). She worked at Takada jogakkō in Niigata prefecture, was a member of the Fujin kyōfūkai, and studied at Northfield University in Massachusetts in 1900 and at Oxford University in 1907. Mitani Tamiko henshū iinkai, ed., *Mitani Tamiko: Shōgai, omoide, iboku* (Mitani Tamiko: Her life, memories, and writings) (Jogakuin dōsōkai, 1991). Joshi gakuin, which is still open, has a long and complicated history. A-rokuban jogakkō (also called Carrothers jogakkō) was opened in 1870 by Julia Carrothers in the Tsukiji settlement. It closed in 1876, and Carrothers moved with some of her students to Hara Taneaki's 原胤召 Hara jogakkō in Ginza. The other students went to B-rokuban jogakkō, also known as the Graham Seminary, which was opened in 1874 by the Presbyterian Kate Youngman and Mary Parke (Mrs. Thompson). When Hara jogakkō closed in 1880, the students moved to B-rokuban, which was renamed Shinsakae jogakkō in 1876 when the school was relocated to Shinsakae. Watase Masakatsu, ed. *Watase Torajirōden* (The biography of Watase Torajirō) (Watase Dōzoku, 1934), 20–21. Around 1883, Shinsakae was attended by thirty-five students, mostly boarders, and some daughters and wives of well-to-do families. Tamura, *Joshi gakuin hachijūnenshi*, 66–68. In 1886, there were eighty-two students. *Jogaku zasshi*, no. 27, 25.06.1886, last page. Kishida Toshiko taught Chinese classics there in 1887, and her presence was valued by both the students and her colleagues, but since Nakajima Nobuyuki 中島信行, her husband, was moving to Yokohama, she was considering the possibility of leaving the job. If so, the students and staff would be greatly saddened. *Jogaku zasshi*, no. 92, 14.01.1888, 24. Yokoi Tamako 横井玉子 (1855–1902), the wife of Yokoi Tokiharu 横井時治 and a relative of Yokoi Shōnan 横井小楠, also worked there and in 1900 cofounded the Joshi Bijutsu gakkō, a school that taught art, now Joshi bijutsu daigaku 女子美術大学. Joshi bijutsu daigaku, ed, *Joshi bijutsu daigaku hachijūnenshi* (Eighty years of Joshi bijutsu daigaku) (Joshi bijutsu daigaku, 1980). Sakurai jogakkō and Shinsakae jogakkō merged in 1890, becoming Joshi gakuin.

46. Carrothers, *The Sunrise Kingdom*, 234–35.

47. Letters dated February 18, 1878 from Mrs. Wright in Tokyo (document CWW173, page 108–111) and August 22, 1878 from Alice Hoar in Tokyo (document CWW173, pages 305–9). LAPFE Archive.

opposed to the missionaries, did not always value their teachings, and some were expelled from school because they were found stealing, laughing at prayer, talking against Christians, and teasing younger students. Others lost interest in Christianity when they realized that they would not be hired to teach in missionary schools to the point of selling their Bibles to secondhand bookshops.[48]

Others were concerned that proper young ladies were becoming women who did not conform to Japanese feminine standards because of the teachings they received. Missionary schools, it was feared, could transform girls into the semblance of Western ladies by teaching them English while keeping them housed in Western-style dormitories and wearing Western-style clothes. Kobe jogakuin was even accused of educating concubines for "unprincipled" foreigners, and it was held that its students were starting "to walk like men" and in church did not keep their eyes cast down as they should.[49]

On the other hand, precisely because of the publicity the government and intellectuals devoted to the strategy of building a new and "modern" Japan, and the importance attached to Western education, some segments of the population naturally came to think that learning English would be enough; Alice Starkweather, who was teaching in the girls' department of Dōshisha, recalled that "this same young man was planning the course of study and wanted it to be 'only English', [and] when it was suggested that *all* girls might not have the time or be able to pursue a thorough English course, he said with considerable force, 'Well then, they can never be suitable companions for *us!*'"[50]

Missionaries' efforts were thus not producing the kind of results they hoped for. Dr. J. C. Hepburn argued that in some schools "The girls are mostly from poor families, and by living in such comforts are often unfitted for their native homes, some marry heathen husbands, some Christians, some become helpers as Bible readers—but of the vast majority I am not able to speak."[51] Furthermore, during the late 1880s opposition to the missionaries' work began to grow in conjunction with the rise of nationalistic feelings. As criticism of Westernization and Christianity

---

48. Sakamoto, "Beikoku dendōkai senkyōshi bunsho," 82, 88; Minutes of the Tenth Session of the Woman's Conference of the Methodist Episcopal Church in Japan, 1893, 41, Archives of Aoyama gakuin.
49. DeForest, *History of Kobe College*, 9.
50. Sakamoto, "Beikoku dendōkai senkyōshi bunsho," 89. Miss Linda Smith of the Woman's Foreign Missionary Society of the Methodist Episcopal Church (WFMS) also reported that work was not particularly satisfactory among day students in Fukuoka, for many were from families of officials and attended missionary classes solely to learn English. Minutes of the sixth session of the Woman's Conference of the Methodist Episcopal Church in Japan, 1889, 59, Archive of Aoyama gakuin.
51. Records of U.S. Presbyterian Missions, vol. 4, 9/15, 147–166, May 7, 1880.

grew, people spoke out against those women who were either attending missionary schools or were linked to their churches and made it even more difficult for girls to further their education.[52]

Japanese Girls and the Missionary Environment

For girls living in the major cities it was not difficult to meet missionaries and find out more about their culture, as missionaries took part in many public activities in order to spread their faith. Hani Motoko, for one, recalled that once one of her classmates invited her to church, where she met Japanese people who seemed good at English, some women dressed in Western clothes, and also foreigners who were fluent in Japanese and were nice to her even though it was the first time they met.[53] Missionaries were asked to participate in various women's meetings; in 1889 a certain Miss Carter gave a speech at a Dai nihon fujin kyōikukai meeting that was published in the group's magazine. She was reported to have argued that people should educate themselves in order to be able to help others; drawing, music, and sewing were all skills that women should learn in order to enrich themselves and enable them to do good in society. Her father had taught her that strong people should help the weak, and that was one of the reasons why she decided to participate in missionary work. When people asked her why she had not married, she answered that she had set her heart on helping people, so that idea had never entered her thoughts.[54]

Missionaries' influence on girls' education was stronger in their schools, where they could teach them Western knowledge, customs, and values. Their teachings were imparted, as Isabelle Leete wrote, to raise Christian wives and mothers or "modest breadwinners" who would use their wisdom and knowledge in their work.[55] Mrs. Louise Pierson argued that Japanese women

> have graced the imperial court, obtained victories upon the battle field, and have given their own mental tone to the prevailing literature of the period. . . . Thus mathematics, discipline, knowledge of foreign lan-

52. See Gluck, *Japan's Modern Myths*, 133; and Inoue Kennosuke, *Tōyō eiwa jogakuin shichijūnenshi* (Records of Tōyō eiwa jogakuin during the past seventy years) (Tōyō eiwa jogakuin, 1954), 3–4. The number of girl students in missionary schools decreased during the late 1880s and early 1890s also because there were more government schools. Osaka jogakuinshi kenkyū iinkai, ed., *Osaka jogakuinshi kenkyū* (History of Osaka jogakuin) (Osaka: Osaka jogakuin, 1984), 3.
53. She was baptized shortly thereafter. Hani Motoko, *Hansei o kataru* (Telling my life so far) (Fujin no tomosha, 1928), 48–49.
54. Miss Carter, "On Female Education," *Dai nihon fujin kyōikukai zasshi*, no. 4, 20.04.1889, 21–33 (in Japanese).
55. Letter dated August 26, 1887. She also wrote, "No, not for an instant, would I decry education for women, but I would put a school in every centre of missionary effort." Records of U.S. Presbyterian Missions, vol. 6, 2/5, 25–43.

guages expands and liberalizes; science opens new avenues, leading to the great central temple of eternal truth. And this is the *summum bonum* of education, induction into the eternal verities of God.

This education could be achieved only in missionary schools through the use of English, Pierson continued, since English was the key to literary resources such as poetry and prose. Japanese schools were deficient in this respect and lacking in Christian instruction, thus failing to "accomplish the highest object of Education."[56]

The first and most important tool for forming accomplished women was obviously the Bible, and in teaching the Bible missionaries took examples from the everyday lives of people in Western countries. Leete, in the letter cited above, wrote, "Christianity cannot be poured, it must be instilled by precepts and examples and we must know and love our girls, and be known and loved by them." Some women missionaries must have been successful in this task, for Tanioka Teiko 谷岡貞子, who graduated from Joshi gakuin in 1906, wrote that Miss Milliken "knew the Bible and tried to live it," so women missionaries' words were not empty.[57]

Obviously, not all the girls, especially when very young, understood the message missionaries wanted to convey or took their teachings seriously. Tsuneko (Yamada) Gauntlett (1873–1953) was the daughter of a samurai family from Aichi prefecture who graduated from Joshi gakuin in 1890, married the British George Edward Gauntlett in 1898, taught in various schools in Japan, and was involved in the activities of the Fujin kyōfūkai throughout her life. She tells us about her "encounter" with Christianity while at Sakurai jogakkō. "When Mr. Sakurai, the pock-marked, black-bearded, fierce-looking ex-sea-captain, stood up and gave us young girls, or rather tiny tots, some lengthy exhortation, we used to wonder if God who spoke to Elisha or Moses looked like him." Girls went to church every Sunday, but many would have preferred doing something else instead.

> Many of us spent half the sermon hours in a great struggle to keep the sand-man from our eyes. I once was made to sit on the very front seat near the organ. I thought I was listening to the wonderful story of

56. *Proceedings*, 213–16. A similar statement was made by Miss Russell (WFMS), who wrote that in her educational work in Nagasaki her "reading, history, arithmetic, and algebra classes are all in English, the language of civilization, the language of progress. We look for result not only in the acquisition of a knowledge of these subjects, but in the waking up of powers that would forever lie dormant under the mental enervation that seems to be induced by the continued study of Chinese; but the teaching of these branches is indirectly religious work and we may look for early results in the practical work of every-day life, in the students' steadily broadening views on all subjects, in their more logical thinking, in the more symmetrical development of their intellectual powers." Minutes of the Third Session of the Woman's Conference of the Methodist Episcopal Church in Japan, 1886, 25, Archives of Aoyama gakuin.
57. Letter dated August 26, 1887. Records of U.S. Presbyterian Missions, vol. 6, 2/5, 25–43. Tamura Hikari, ed., *Joshi gakuin hachijūnenshi* (Eighty years of Joshi gakuin) (Joshi gakuin, 1951), 149.

"Daniel in the lion's den," when suddenly I found myself flat on the floor with a big bump on my forehead, evidently making an untimely collision with the organ in front.[58]

Others were startled by the differences between Japanese and Western cultures. For example, Mitani Tamiko (of Joshi gakuin) wrote:

> The first supper with so many other girls was a trial for the new girl, for I was the only child of the family then. . . . Still to watch those foreign ladies garbed in red and pink (in Japan it is only babies who can wear those colors for out-side garments), use chopsticks and eat rice and pickles and more than that, to see them laugh and talk like ordinary people and Tami Mitani sitting and eating with them was like a fairy tale and those interesting things were enough to keep back my ready rising tears.[59]

Relationships between the girls and the missionaries could be difficult at first because of the language barrier and also because the girls were sometimes very young. However, before long women missionaries often came to take on the roles of mothers and grandmothers. Nobejiri Yasuko 野邊地里安子 wrote that when she entered Shinsakae jogakkō in 1883 as a boarder she was the youngest girl, and the director called her "baby" and treated her as a grandmother would. Tamura Eiko (of Sakurai jogakkō) and Ebina Miyako and Yuasa Hatsuko (of Dōshisha jogakkō) reported that teachers and students behaved like parents and children.[60]

Some students were positively impressed by the Bible and Christian teachings since the new religion did not differentiate between men and women and taught that both could be saved and converted. For Sano Umeko 佐野梅子 (b. 1868), a girl who attended Joshi gakuin around 1887 despite the fact that her parents did not value girls' education, lectures about the Bible were like water for the thirsty and food for the hungry. She was convinced that if one believed in Christianity it was possible to reform society and the ways in which people behaved.[61] Hayashi Utako 林歌子

---

58. Tamura and Asada, *Joshi gakuin*, 58–59 (original in English). On Tsuneko and George Gauntlett, see Saiko Gauntlett, "Edward Gauntlett (1868–1956), English Teacher, Explorer and Missionary," in *Britain and Japan: Biographical Portraits*, edited by Hugh Cortazzi, vol. 6, 299–306 (Folkestone: Global Oriental, 2007). During the 1920s Tsuneko became involved in the movement for women's suffrage and created a women's peace association. See Manako Ogawa, "The 'White Ribbon League of Nations' Meets Japan: The Trans-Pacific Activism of the Woman's Christian Temperance Union, 1906–1930," *Diplomatic History* 31.1 (2007): 21–50.

59. Tamura and Asada, *Joshi gakuin*, 45 (original in English).

60. Ibid., 17. Ōhama, *Joshi gakuin no rekishi*, 285; Matsuura, *Dōshisha romansu*, 90.

61. Tamura and Asada, *Joshi gakuin*, 11–12. Sano recalled that she had to leave school for a period of time because her father was ill and she was ordered to go home to Okayama prefecture. Remembering the missionaries' teachings, she prayed for her father, and when he recovered she at-

(of Rikkyō jogakkō 立教女学校), later the founder and director of the Osaka fujin kyōfūkai, recalled that it was a revelation when she heard a missionary stating that Christ was the ruler of all creatures and that for God humans were all brothers and sisters.[62] Ōe Sumi 大江スミ (of Tōyō eiwa jogakkō), who did not have the same financial means as the other girls but realized that the teachers treated everybody in the same way, thought that if there was a God that loved everybody so much one had to believe in him. As she listened to the teacher's words, she recalled, the world assumed a different meaning for her, and hope sprang in her for the first time.[63]

Missionaries were helped in their work by girls who had graduated from their schools and whom they relied on and trusted. The friendship between Mitani Tamiko and Miss Milliken was based on trust, sharing opinions, and reading together. Mitani herself wrote of the many pleasant days passed studying and reading with Milliken.[64] Ōshima (Ibuka) Hanako, who graduated from Kobe jogakuin in 1889, wrote that one summer Miss Emily Brown, a teacher there, helped her in her work and that "Her few days' visit with me was a very precious one in my memory, and her sweet and noble words by the Lake Biwa quite late in the evening shall never be forgotten in my life."[65]

These girls had decided that education was important and had discovered that religion could help them, and other people, to improve society. Education, according to Mori Arinori, was supposed to form good wives and proud mothers for their soldier sons, but here we have examples of girls who wanted to be the subjects and not the objects of their education and thought that their society could be changed for the better.

Girl students at missionary schools met girls from different areas of Japan and were taught by women from other countries, who often became their friends and, in part, role models. Asada Mikako 淺田みか子 tells us her story. In 1886 in

---

tributed it to God's intervention and asked her family for permission to be baptized. Tamura and Asada, *Joshi gakuin*, 12–16.

62. Kanzaki, *Gendai fujin den*, 17.

63. She was born in Nagasaki Prefecture in 1875 and moved to Tokyo with her family, joining Tōyō Eiwa in 1889. Ōe taught in schools in Okinawa prefecture and left for England in 1902, where she studied with a government scholarship until 1906. Ōhama, *Ōe Sumi sensei*, 67–78.

64. Mitani Tamiko henshū iinkai, *Mitani Tamiko*, for example 227.

65. In addition she wrote, "My social life in the Kobe school was a blessed one to me, having every good influence around me. Miss Searle's noble and sublime character was reflecting upon us, Miss Brown's motherly love and consecration were an example to us day after day. I often thought of what excuse I could make for my being worthless. Fortunately I had intimate friends among the poorest girls in the school, so that I could exercise my sympathy all the time. Not only had I a chance to help them, but also I had an excellent opportunity to learn what consecration means from them. After I had been ill with typhoid fever I could realize more that I was not my own, and wanted Him to use me instead of doing my own will." Hana Ibuka, personal memoirs, 12 (original in English), Archive of Mount Holyoke College and Special Collections, South Hadley, Massachusetts.

her hometown there was no education available for girls beyond elementary, and, although she wanted to continue her studies, her father was of the opinion that educated women were "impertinent." She was finally able to enter Sakurai jogakkō, where she saw foreigners for the first time. Yajima Kajiko, one of her teachers there, granted her permission to attend lessons in shorthand at Meiji jogakkō with another girl. She later became the coeditor of her school's (Joshi gakuin) history in which her recollections were published. In it she argued that at the time of its publication girl students were saying that they wanted to become good wives and mothers but when she was a student those words were a disgrace. She said things such as, "In the future I want to become independent and open a jogakkō" or "I want to become a scholar" but never "I want to become a wife."[66] She was certainly exaggerating when claiming that in her school there was no instruction about how to become a good wife, but her story is even more telling because of this. She was a student at a Christian school and was receiving a Christian education based on the concept of the "Christian home." She prayed every day before lessons, in the evenings, during Sunday services, and probably at other times as well, and yet not only did she not want to become a *good* wife, but she did not want to become a wife at all. How did she come to develop such a conviction? Was she the only one?

In this context it is important to recognize the role of dormitories and boarding facilities. Eating, living, studying, and playing together was a new reality for girls, one that often created a feeling of sisterhood among them and enabled them to widen their world beyond that of siblings or other relatives. Hayashi Sadako 林貞子 (of Ferris jogakkō) wrote that the students loved their school and would think "we are doing this for our school" or "we cannot do this because it is not good for our school."[67] This girl was proud of her education, and in talking of "her school" she considered herself part of a group, acknowledging her presence, as well as that of her school, in public society. Tsuneko Gauntlett wrote about living together with other girls; for her, it was a way of creating a communal "female spirit" outside the home and of sharing and discussing similar interests with Japanese and Western women. Tamura Eiko was of the same opinion, remembering that, more than a school, hers resembled a big family.[68]

On a lighter note, Sugimoto Etsuko recalled that while she was studying in a missionary school in the capital "a wave of excitement over love stories struck Tokyo. All the schoolgirls were wildly interested. When translations were to be had we passed them from hand to hand through the school."[69] Ōe Sumi recalled how her two sisters, who had attended a *jogakkō*, forgot the English learned there

66. Tamura and Asada, *Joshi gakuin*, 85–88.
67. Yamamoto, *Ferris waei*, 93.
68. Tsune Gauntlett. *Shichijūshichinen no omohide* (Memories of my seventy-seven years) (Ōzorasha, [1949] 1989), 22, 35; Tamura, *Joshi gakuin hachijūnenshi*, 84.
69. Sugimoto, *A Daughter of the Samurai*, 131.

as soon as they graduated, but that did not happen to Ōe, and it was thanks to the way in which her teachers at Tōyō eiwa had taught her that she was still able to converse with foreigners many years later. She also recalled that girls at her school once decided to start a group called the King's Daughters; they sold their needlework and held a meeting to decide what to do with the money earned. They concluded that they would begin a class for poor students.[70] Mitani Tamiko remembered how their teacher once assigned them a composition and that her topic was "twilight."

> But my twilight could go no further than "the sun went down and birds stopped their singing." It was the same way with "Tears" and others and we had come to the last night before we were due to hand in our compositions. We four girls looked at each other and decided to stay up and finish them.[71]

Many spoke about the best day of the week, when they were allowed to go to their teachers' or friends' rooms and spend time talking and eating snacks together.[72] We also find some impressions of their graduation day. These ceremonies were a new feature of Meiji schools, and, like today's, they defined the end of a period of study but also celebrated the achievements of those girls who managed to complete the course. Hayashi Sadako wrote that since during the ceremony girls read papers they had written in English and Japanese and sang songs and played instruments, it was considered an important day that needed a lot of preparation.[73] Their studies, and the environment in which they lived, helped these girls develop a taste for organizing meetings, discussing various topics, undertaking collective activities, deciding how to spend money earned through such activities, and pursuing new interests. These "new kinds of learning" proved to be extremely important for the women I introduce in the next two chapters, many of whom had studied or worked with missionaries and acquired abilities that nobody had taught them before.

Living with missionaries also meant being able to obtain literature otherwise almost inaccessible, and it is likely that such literature supported discussions on Japanese women's education between the Japanese girls and the missionaries. Tamura Eiko wrote that before magazines such as *Jogaku zasshi* were published she could only read old novels, but then she was able to read books that had been difficult to find such as a translation of *Christy's Old Organ* by Amy Catherine

---

70. Ōhama, *Ōe Sumi sensei*, 36–37; Kanzaki, *Gendai fujin den*, 207. Similar meetings were held in various missionary schools, and sometimes general meetings were also organized. Yamamoto, *Ferris waei*, 65.

71. Tamura and Asada, *Joshi gakuin*, 50 (original in English).

72. See, for example, Nobejiri Yasuko, in Tamura and Asada, *Joshi gakuin*, 22.

73. Yamamoto, *Ferris waei*, 94.

Deck (Mrs. O. F. Walton, 1849–1939) and Mary Lyon's biography.[74] Missionaries gave speeches about Lyon's school, while *Jogaku zasshi* published her biography.[75] Caroline Telford, who became a teacher of English at San'yō eiwa jogakkō in Okayama in 1892, wrote that Yegashira Hideko ("my own dear child! the nearest my own that God has ever given me!"), the daughter of the physician to the daimyo of Hizen, had read the biography of Mary Lyon and felt the desire to study in her school and found one like it in Japan.[76] Although one cannot generalize, it is safe to suppose that Mary Lyon's biography presented the hope for higher education and the understanding of how an American woman could establish Mount Holyoke College, while it helps explain why those girls who studied with missionaries wanted to become scholars and found girls' schools.

Here it is also worth considering the "Reasons for the Founding of San'yo eiwa jogakkō," a lengthy document concerning a school that was opened in Okayama in 1886, for it shows what kind of influence missionaries might have over those Japanese interested in female education.[77] The school's educational policy, it stated, was based on Christian morality, and through the teaching of English, classical Japanese, and feminine subjects the school would nurture women's knowledge and virtue and reform "women's society" (*fujin shakai*). The document starts as one would expect, arguing that a nation was formed by individual families and the nature of these families would determine the power or weakness of the nation itself. In order for a nation to prosper, it was necessary for individual families to prosper, and that could be achieved if husband and wife collaborated with each other. Husbands worked outside their homes, and their wives took good care of the household and children. Taking care of children meant being able to teach them, so women had to be educated themselves. The document then somewhat changes tone, stating, "How important is the work done by women for their nation and for society? Nations become strong and peaceful if there are accomplished women. It is women who give birth to a nation's heroes." Cultural development went hand in hand with the spread of female education, so "if men are to learn at universities, then women have to enter universities; if men are to acquire specialized knowledge, then women have to do the same. In Europe and North America

74. Tamura, *Joshi gakuin hachijūnenshi*, 88. Deck's book was translated by someone using the pen name Kōu joshi 香雨女子 and was published in 1882 in Yokohama by Beikoku seisho kaisha 米国聖書会社.

75. Miss Carter, "On Female Education," *Dai nihon fujin kyōikukai zasshi*, no. 4, 20.04.1889, 24; *Jogaku zasshi*, nos. 115, 23.06.1888, 22–23; 116, 30.06.1888, 20–22; 117, 07.07.1888, 213; 118, 14.07.1888, 21–22.

76. LD 7096.6x1890, Telford, letter, April 16, 1904, Archive of Mount Holyoke College and Special Collections, South Hadley, Massachusetts. See also Mochizuki Kōzaburō, ed., *Shiritsu San'yō jogakkō hōkoku 1* (First report on the work of the private San'yō jogakkō) (Okayama: San'yō jogakkō, 1894), 7.

77. *San'yō eiwa jogakkō setsuritsu shushi*. The only copy I have seen is preserved uncataloged in the archive of that school, since renamed San'yo gakuen daigaku.

many men and women study together at universities, and this is the basis of those countries' civilization and power. So, the origin of a country's wealth and power resides firstly in its women's society (*fujin shakai*)." After the Meiji Restoration, Japan had made much progress in a short time, but that progress was not complete. Why was that so? "It is not because there are no valid persons, but because there are no women who can assist them. It is not because there are no children who want to learn, but because there are no mothers who can raise them properly. . . . Newton became Newton because his mother was an accomplished woman, and England and North America are strong and wealthy countries because of their strong women." Were there in Japan, like in Europe and North America, women who were knowledgeable and virtuous, who took care of the home and the children, and supported their husbands? Were there women like Mary Lyon, who, in order to raise women's position in society, had founded a women's university? The problem with Japanese society was that, although "women are loved by God as much as men, and they are to be ranked above all other creatures that populate the world, in reality they are treated like servants or toys for men, and suffer under this despotic behavior." Was there no one who would take pity on "our fellow sisters"? In order to change this situation and help Japanese women become real companions to their husbands, it was necessary to establish girls' schools, and this, among all the urgent tasks Japan had to face, was the most important.

This was certainly an unusual statement compared to the ones issued by Christian girls' schools elsewhere. According to Mochizuki, Onoda Inokichi 小野田伊之吉, a Christian teacher in an elementary school in Okayama, was among the founders of the school. Onoda had compared the regulations of various girls' schools in Tokyo, Osaka, Kobe, and elsewhere and had written a new set of regulations, asking the American missionary Otis Carey, who was then in Okayama, to comment on it. Onoda then contacted Kanemori Kohisa 金森こひさ, who was teaching at Kobe eiwa jogakkō. She eventually quit her job in Kobe and took up a position at the school. Among the supporters were Ōnishi Kinu 大西絹 (1858–1933) and Ishiguro Kan'ichirō 石黒涵一郎 (1854–1917), who organized a meeting with other men and women to discuss the opening of the school.[78] The degree of missionary involvement in the founding of this school is not clear, but many of its Japanese teachers and supporters had been taught by missionaries. It is also worth mentioning that the terminology used and the vehemence of the arguments presented above are very similar to the language used by women who were politically active in Okayama at the time (see chapter 5), and I wonder how

---

78. Kanemori quit her position after a few months and soon thereafter a graduate from Kobe eiwa jogakkō was hired in her stead. Between 1886 and 1893, five North American women were employed as English teachers. Mochizuki, *Shiritsu San'yō jogakkō hōkoku*, 1–2. On Ōnishi, see Okayama joseishi kenkyūkai, ed., *Kindai Okayama no onnatachi* (Women of Okayama during the modern period) (Sanseidō, 1987), 63–76.

much the latter's activities and discourses influenced these founders. Finally, given that the characters for *joshi daigaku* (women's university) used in the document are almost identical to those for *Onna daigaku*, the Edo period book that postulated that women were to acquire an education only insofar as it was of benefit to their families, one wonders what emotions that new term created in the girl students of San'yo eiwa jogakkō, who were used to hearing the latter but not the former.

After Graduation

After graduating, many girls taught at their alma maters or moved within the missionary environment. For example, Mrs. Maria True of the Presbyterian mission was asked to help with the running of Takada jogakkō in Niigata prefecture, which was founded in 1888, and graduates from Joshi gakuin worked there as teachers.[79] Other graduates of missionary schools taught at Maebashi eiwa jogakkō (now Kyōai gakuen 共愛学園), Iai jogakkō 遺愛女学校 in Hakodate, and Bara jogakkō in Shizuoka. Watase Kame 渡瀬香芽, who had attended A-rokuban, opened the Eigo kōshūkai 英語講習会 in Mito.[80] As a final example, Hirata Tsuneko (b. 1865, a graduate of the Tokyo Normal School) worked at Brittain jogakkō and from 1886 to 1890 studied at Western Maryland College in the United States. Back in Japan she was appointed a missionary by the Methodist Board.[81]

We have more detailed information about the girls who studied at Kobe jogakuin (then still called Kobe eiwa jogakkō) and the ways in which they made use of their education. Kobe jogakuin was one of the most famous female missionary schools of the period, with important national and international connections, but it was similar to other well-established missionary schools in Japan and can therefore be considered representative of what girls could achieve through their exposure to the missionary environment.

---

79. Mitani Tamiko henshū iinkai, *Mitani Tamiko*, 26–27.
80. Inoue Yuriko, *Chikara o ataemase: Honda Yōitsu fujin Teiko no shōgai* (Give me strength! The life of Teiko, Honda Yōitsu's wife) (Aoyama gakuin, 2004), 69; Watase, *Watase Torajirōden*, 122; Ōhama, *Joshi gakuin no rekishi*, 147.
81. Hirata arrived in Pittsburgh in September 1886, but I could find no additional information regarding her stay there. Diary of James Thomas Ward, entry for September 16, 1886, Ward/Lewis Collection, Archive of McDaniel College, Maryland. Brittain jogakkō was opened in 1880 by the Methodist Protestant missionary Harriet Brittain and became Yokohama eiwa jogakkō in 1886. It offered primary education and some additional courses, all the subjects being taught in English with English textbooks. Brittain also established a kindergarten, probably the first missionary one in Japan, run by a certain Harada Ryōko, a graduate and teacher from Ferris and the recipient of a three-year training course at the government normal school. In 1882 there were sixty-four students. Brittain seems to have moved to Meiji jogakkō in 1885. John Krummel, "The Methodist Protestant Church in Japan: The Early Years in Yokohama, 1880–1887," *Ronshū*, no. 14 (Aoyama gakuin daigaku, 1973), 1–17; "Missionaries of the Methodist Protestant Church in Japan," *Ronshū*, no. 12 (Aoyama gakuin daigaku, 1971), 114.

Between 1882 and 1889, six classes totaling forty girls graduated from Kobe jogakuin. Thirty-one of the girls married, most to men who either worked as teachers or preachers in the missionary environment or had been students at missionary schools, thus fulfilling the missionaries' hopes for the formation of "Christian homes." Three became involved in the work of the Fujin kyōfūkai, while in their later years others became members and trustees of the board of their alma mater, forming an older generation of Japanese women who could be role models for the students. Thirty became teachers, either for a number of years or as a lifelong occupation, at various schools, mostly missionary, further demonstrating that by the late 1880s, even amid rising nationalistic feelings, women missionaries had established contacts with other missionary and private schools throughout Japan and were using these to find employment for "their" students.[82]

Among the forty-seven girls were the following individuals. Kanemori Kohisa (class of 1882) married a student of Dōshisha and taught at San'yō eiwa jogakkō in Okayama and Kobe eiwa jogakkō and Joshi kōtō shihan gakkō in Tokyo.[83] Hirata Toshiko 平田敏子 (class of 1882) became a teacher at her alma mater and Ferris, and was a student at Mount Holyoke College from 1890 to 1893. She kept in contact with her American classmates and wrote that she was teaching English to her students at Kobe jogakuin but that the girls did not appreciate Shakespeare as much as they should have, the problem being that they thought he spoke too much of love! She also longed to hear once again one of her American female teachers talk "so learnedly" about Hegel, and she tried to "keep up with the times" by reading newspapers and magazines for four or five hours each week.[84] Kōga Fuji (class of 1882) was the first girl to be baptized in the Kobe church. She went to North America to continue her studies to become a kindergarten teacher and worked in a school in Hiroshima.[85] Ōshima Hanako (class of 1889), from a samurai family, was a student of mathematics and science at Mount Holyoke College (class of 1895) and a teacher at various girls' schools in Tokyo. She wrote about the way in which she managed to enroll at Mount Holyoke.

> Dr. Mariana Holbrook visited Tottori once before she came to live there.
> I felt as if she was an angel who brought an answer from Heaven to me.
> After she went back to Okayama, Miss McLennan asked me if I wanted

---

82. Kobe jogakuin, ed., *Kobe jogakuin hyakunenshi: Kakuron* (One hundred years of Kobe jogakuin: A detailed discussion) (Kobe: Kobe jogakuin, 1981), 205–13.

83. Kobe jogakuin, *Kobe jogakuin*, 205. See also Mochizuki, *Shiritsu San'yō jogakkō hōkoku*; and Okayama joseishi kenkyūkai, *Kindai Okayama*, 67.

84. Greet the Unseen with a Cheer, December 1893, letter. Hirata was a Chinese girl adopted by Mr. and Mrs. Orramel Gulick, missionaries in China, who named her Martha. After returning from America she was adopted by a certain Mr. Miyagawa. She married a Japanese pastor of the Yokohama Congregational Church in 1899. Alumnae biographical files (LD 7096.6), class of 1893, Archive of Mount Holyoke College and Special Collections, South Hadley, Massachusetts.

85. Kobe jogakuin, *Kobe jogakuin*, 206.

to come to America. "Yes, I do," I said promptly. "Have you some plan for me?" She told me that Dr. Holbrook had said that she would be very glad to help me to go there if I wanted to. I cannot tell how glad I was to hear it. I spent one summer vacation with Miss C.A. Stone on Hyezan, where I studied a little with her for the entrance examinations at Mt. Holyoke. After she and Dr. Holbrook came to Tottori, they helped me in many ways; Dr. Holbrook as a mother, Miss Stone as my older sister, and a little later Miss Carrie Telford added her interest to theirs, and provided me for vacations in America.[86]

Mori Shizu 森しず (b. 1873, class of 1889) became a student at the Northwestern University Preparatory School and attended Northwestern University from 1892 to 1893, moving to Radcliffe College in 1893 where she studied until 1894.[87] Finally, Tsukamoto Fujiko (class of 1886) was a student at the Doremus School in 1887 and went to Wilson College in Pennsylvania from 1890 to 1894, becoming its first international graduate. She then studied at the University of Pennsylvania, and once back home she taught at her alma mater.[88] Some of her diary entries allow us a glimpse of her encounter with North America. In 1893 she spent the Christmas holidays at the home of a schoolmate, and she recorded that "Several papers noticed my arrival, as if I had been a visitor of distinction. One named me, Losoji Yarkskoo and another, Yusi Teaukeaw Meantean. Probably they were deeply disappointed not to find the long ears or some peculiar appendage that might be expected in a human being born in a semi-civilized land!"[89]

86. Personal memoirs preserved in the Archive of Mount Holyoke College and Special Collections, South Hadley, Massachusetts (original in English). Dr. Mariana Holbrook, a missionary doctor who had worked in China, arrived in Japan in 1889. Her plan was to establish a Japanese version of Mount Holyoke College, where she had studied from 1876 to 1878, with Caroline Telford, Cora Stone, and another young woman. The American Board for Foreign Missions turned down their request, and they worked at Kobe jogakuin instead, where Holbrook established a science department. Johanna M. Selles, "The Role of Women in the Formation of the World Student Christian Federation," *International Bulletin of Missionary Research* 30.4 (2006): 189–94. Telford taught in Tottori in 1890 and became an English teacher at San'yō eiwa jogakkō in Okayama in 1892, probably taking the place of Ida Augusta McLennan (1857–1951), who had studied at Oberlin College and taught there from 1890 to 1892. She left Japan in 1895. Mochizuki, *Shiritsu San'yō jogakkō hōkoku*, 5–7; letter from Caroline Telford to Miss Edwards, undated, Archive of Mount Holyoke College. See also Ishii Noriko, "America josei iryō senkyōshi no chugoku to nihon dendō: Meary Ana Horuburukku no baai (1881–1907)" (American women missionary doctors in China and Japan: The case of Mary A. Holbrook [1881–1907]), *Nihon kenkyū* 30 (2005): 167–91.
87. Alumni Biographical Files, Archive of Northwestern University, Evanston; Archive of Radcliffe College, Schlesinger Library, Harvard University, Subject Files 1894–2006, Japanese students n.d. RG XXIV, series 5.
88. *The Wilson Alumnae Quarterly*, 3–3, May 1927, 4–8: Archive of Wilson College, Chambersburg, Pennsylvania.
89. *Pharetra* (the Wilson students' literary publication), January 1893 (original in English). Other entries show how much she enjoyed life in North America. Archive of Wilson College, Chambersburg, Pennsylvania.

These girls, blessed with the right opportunities, did not repudiate marriage but were careful to retain their jobs, were active in voluntary work, and kept in contact with their former schools and classmates. Once they were given the chance to go abroad to continue their education they seized it and saw with their own eyes what being a woman and student in North America meant. In most cases, they even managed to attend universities, something they would not have been able to do had they remained in Japan. Through chance encounters, the girls' own intelligence, and women missionaries' hard work to help those girls succeed for themselves, and therefore for Christianity and their country, Japanese girls were able to experience different social and educational worlds.

The First Japanese Nurses

Teaching was not the only occupation through which missionaries helped Japanese women to expand their employment opportunities and public position. Meiji women were not the first to nurse or treat ill people, but during the early Meiji years nursing became a recognized profession for women, who found employment in those hospitals willing to hire them.

During the 1870s the Japanese government had started to implement German medical techniques and knowledge by sending Japanese students abroad, translating medical books, and establishing medical examinations, which differed completely from the procedures for entry into the profession that were usual in the Edo period. If it was not difficult for most people to accept the role of nurses trained according to Western medical knowledge, this did not mean that the idea of *female* nurses working in hospitals was widely accepted.[90] Nurses needed to be educated, so at least at the beginning they could only be women from families that had the financial means to pay for such an education. Hirano Tō 平野鐙 (1869–1969), from Aichi prefecture, who graduated from Tokyo jikei iin 東京慈恵医院 in 1891 and went on to write a book containing general knowledge on nursing for women, recalled how nurses in that period were mostly the educated daughters of samurai families.[91] However, how could women of the upper middle classes take care of male patients not related to them in any way? Moreover, it was not easy to reconcile

90. *Jogaku zasshi* tried to support girls who wanted to become nurses by publishing Florence Nightingale's biography in no. 31, 05.08.1886, 12; no. 32, 15.08.1886, 31–33; and no. 37, 05.10.1886, 133–34. It also publicized schools for nurses in Japan and their students. *Jogaku zasshi*, no. 26, 15.06.1886, 227–29; no. 27, 25.06.1886, 247. Nightingale's story fascinated more than one generation of Japanese people, for we find it again in the supplement to *Kokumin shinbun*, no. 62, 03.04.1890, 2.

91. *Kanbyō no kokoroe* (Introduction to nursing), 1896, cited in Tsuboi Yoshiko, ed., *Kindai nihon kango meicho shūsei: Kaisetsuhen* (Famous works on nursing during the modern period: Explanatory volume) (Ōzorasha, 1989), 38–39; Doyōkai rekishi bukai, ed., *Nihon kindai kango no yoake* (The dawn of Japanese modern nursing) (Igaku shoin, 1973), 11–18.

their careers with having a family and children, for nurses were supposed to work in hospitals, could be made to move to war zones, and could become ill through contact with patients. This new occupation increased women's medical knowledge and the boundaries of women's participation in public work, showed that educated women could work with male doctors, offered a good source of income, and was an alternative for those who could not become doctors.

The presence of female nurses in Western hospitals was recorded by Japanese male students and intellectuals who traveled abroad during the early Meiji period, and as early as 1868 a few Japanese hospitals employed a limited number of female nurses.[92] In 1873 Satō Takanaka 佐藤尚中 (1827–82), the founder of the hospital Juntendō iin 順天堂医院, employed Sugimoto Kaneko 杉本兼子 (1838–1915), a widow with two children, and she eventually became the head nurse there.[93] In 1877, the association Hakuaisha 博愛者 was founded by Sano Tsunetami 佐野常民 (1822–1902), who had previously seen the workings of the Red Cross in Europe and thought that a similar organization should be formed in Japan. Kameyama argues that, although documents related to the Hakuaisha state that nurses would be employed, it is not clear whether *women* were employed from the start.[94] In 1883 the Hakuaisha started receiving three hundred yen a year from the empress, who also lent her support to the opening of its hospital in 1886. In 1887, when the Hakuaisha became the Japanese Red Cross, her donation rose to five thousand yen a year, giving it the imperial seal of approval, as in the case of the Tokyo Women's Normal School.[95]

Another important figure in the development of the nursing profession was Takagi Kanehiro 高木兼寛 (1849–1920), who, after studying at the Saint Thomas Hospital Medical School in England, opened the hospital Yūshi kyōritsu Tokyo byōin 有志共立東京病院 in 1882 with Matsuyama Tōan 松山棟庵, a student of J. C. Hepburn and later the director of the medical department at Keiō gijuku, especially for those who could not afford medical care. In 1885, he added to it the Kangofu kyōikusho 看護婦教育所, a training school for nurses. It had proven difficult to raise funds to open it, so upper-class women helped by collecting money at a fund-raising event organized at the Rokumeikan by their group, the Fujin jizenkai 婦人慈善会 (Women's charity association).[96] In 1887, the hospital, which had to

92. See Niiro Kyōko, Yamaguchi Hanae, and Yukinaga Masae, *Kangoshi nenpyō* (Timeline of the history of nursing) (Igaku shoin, 1991), 46.

93. Kameyama Michiko, *Onnatachi no yakusoku: M. T. Tsuru to nihon saisho no kangofu gakkō* (A promise made among women: M. T. True and the first school for female nurses in Japan) (Kyoto: Jinbun shoin, 1990), 86–87.

94. Kameyama Michiko, *Nihon sekijūjisha to kangofu* (The Japanese Red Cross and female nurses) (Domesu, 1983), 12.

95. Kameyama, *Nihon sekijūjisha*, 15–17. The history of the Hakuaisha is outlined in Olive Checkland, *Humanitarianism and the Emperor's Japan, 1877–1977* (Basingstoke: Macmillan, 1994).

96. Among them were Itō Umeko 伊藤梅子, Inoue Takeko 井上武子, Kawamura Haruko 川村春子, Yamakawa Sutematsu, Sasaki Teiko 佐々木貞子 and Matsukata Masako 松方満佐子. Kameyama

be enlarged, changed its name to Tokyo jikei iin, and Yamakawa Sutematsu and her group worked to obtain a donation from the empress.[97] Although the hospital, the school, and the authorization to educate nurses would not have been achieved without the involvement of well-known and respected men, this is one of the very few instances I encountered in which women of the noble class became heavily involved in the building and running of these enterprises and were thus able to change the lives of other women.

Missionaries helped in the development of the nursing profession in order to expand their work in Japan. This new profession also promoted their ideal of women active in society, making use of inherent qualities that enabled them to take better care of the sick.

In Kyoto, the Kyoto kanbyōfu gakkō 京都看病婦学校 (Kyoto Training School for Nurses) was founded in 1886 by Niijima Jō, John Berry (1847–1936), a missionary doctor who had previously been living in Okayama, and other supporters, and was attached to Dōshisha. Much of the money used to erect the buildings and pay the teachers was donated by the American Mission Board.[98] Thus, in this case missionary involvement was a compromise between the missionaries' goal of teaching the Bible in a city where missionary work was difficult to establish because of its strong Buddhist influence and the Japanese need for trained nurses. Linda Richards (1841–1930), who had been working as the head nurse in a hospital in Boston, arrived in Japan in 1886 to join the school. The course lasted two years, and among the first class of five students "two had had all the advantages of a graduate course in the best of the mission schools." One of them was Itō Tetsu 伊藤哲, who had a good command of the English language and helped Richards as a translator. Richards recalled that Itō

> was my assistant as well as pupil during her two years in training, and
> she has continued to be my best loved friend among all the Japanese

Michiko, *Kangofu to ishi* (Female nurses and doctors) (Domesu, 1985), 104–12. The fund-raising event became the subject of a print. Konishi Shirō, *Nishikie Bakumatsu Meiji no rekishi* (*Nishikie:* A history of the Bakumatsu and Meiji periods) (Kōdansha, 1977), vol. 9, 94–95. See also Tsuda Umeko's letter to Adeline Lanman, in Barbara Rose, *Tsuda Umeko and Women's Education in Japan* (New Haven: Yale University Press, 1992), 64–65. The Presbyterian missionary nurse Mary Reade was asked to start work at the Kangofu kyōikusho; the course of study lasted two years, and beginning in 1893 students had to be between twenty and thirty-five years old, but it is possible that the same rule applied in earlier periods. The first class consisted of five students, who graduated in 1888 with the empress herself attending the graduation ceremony. Hirao Machiko, *Shiryō ni miru nihon kango kyōikushi* (What the documents tell us of the history of Japanese nursing education) (Kango no kagakusha, 1999), 15. See also the Web site of the Jikei University School of Medicine, http://www.jikei.ac.jp/eng/our.html, accessed July 25, 2009.

97. *Jogaku zasshi*, no. 64, 14.05.1887, 77–78.
98. Ueno Naozō, ed., *Dōshisha hyakunenshi: Tsūshihen* (One hundred years of Dōshisha: The narrative volume) (Kyoto: Dōshisha, 1979), 288–313.

women I have known. Her story was interesting. Two years before I went to Japan her husband had sent her away because she had become a Christian. . . . She came to live with me, and soon became not only dear to me, but very necessary, as she showed amazing cleverness in assisting me through the many difficulties of daily life and work in this foreign land.[99]

Four girls from the first class graduated in 1888. Two remained to work at the school, and two "were soon happily married." The second class graduated in 1889 with seven students. Of these, four went to work in hospitals around the country, two remained in Kyoto and worked as nurses while also doing some missionary work, and one married a Japanese priest.[100]

In 1886 a school for nurses was opened in Tokyo at Sakurai jogakkō. The wife of the American missionary John Ballagh had been hospitalized, and seeing that there were no female nurses in the hospital, she decided to start raising money to help in the training. The money was handed over to Maria True, who thought that for a country to be strong and wealthy the people had to be strong and nurses could help in this process.[101] Thus, nursing was not only a matter of caring for the sick; it also had profound social and nationalist implications, and women were at the center of its development. There, too, a student (Mineo Eiko 峰尾栄子) helped translate the first English textbook, but the task was difficult, for the book described objects nurses were supposed to use that she had never seen![102]

What did these women want to achieve? Only a small number of women became nurses during these years and even fewer wrote about their experiences and aspirations, but we have some information. One of the girls who graduated with the first class at Sakurai, Sakuragawa Rii 桜川里以 (1866–1938), recalled that it was frowned on for a woman of the upper class to work, but, "as a Christian and as a woman," she had taken the decision to become a good nurse and enrolled in the course.[103] Ōzeki Chikako 大関和子 (of Sakurai school for nurses) was working at the hospital attached to Tokyo Imperial University, and when the wife of an impor-

99. Linda Richards, *Reminiscences of Linda Richards, America's First Trained Nurse* (Boston: Whitcomb and Barrows, 1911), 73, 88; Ueno, *Dōshisha hyakunenshi*, 303. Students gained practical experience in the "wards and among the private patients of the [Kyoto] hospital, where there was a great variety of medical and surgical work, eye diseases being especially prevalent; in the large outpatient department, which we considered most valuable training; in nursing patients in their homes." Nurses were allowed to keep the money earned while conducting private rounds. By 1906, 131 students had graduated from the school. Richards, *Reminiscences*, 71, 81; Ueno, *Dōshisha hyakunenshi*, 307.

100. Richards, *Reminiscences*, 88; Ueno, *Dōshisha hyakunenshi*, 306–7.

101. Cited in Kameyama Michiko, *Shūkyō to kango* (Religion and nursing) (Domesu, 1985), 40.

102. The course lasted two years, including one of practice in a hospital, and Yajima Kajiko taught Bible lessons. Kameyama, *Shūkyō to kango*, 41; Kameyama, *Onnatachi no yakusoku*.

103. Cited in Kameyama, *Shūkyō to kango*, 42.

tant person was hospitalized there around 1888 she was chosen to be her nurse. She spent her days with the patient, feeling particularly conscious of the importance of the task she had been given, and went to church to pray that she would be able to fulfill her mission. Since she had to walk through Tokyo early in the morning when it was still dark, something she did not like to do, sometimes Hirose (Sano) Umeko accompanied her.[104] These girls helped each other and were visible in public spaces at hours hitherto unthinkable for respectable upper-middle-class women.

A striking example of how women used their education and employment opportunities to build more public lives for themselves is that of Suzuki Masako 鈴木雅子 (1857–1940), the daughter of a *shizoku* family from Shizuoka prefecture who studied at Ferris jogakkō, married a military officer, had two children, and became a widow in 1883. She enrolled in Sakurai's school for nurses and was especially welcome because of her fluency in English. She was then employed at the hospital annexed to Tokyo Imperial University, helping Agnes Vetch (1842–1942), the British nurse working there, as a translator. She became a founding member of the Dai nihon fujin eiseikai 大日本婦人衛生会 (Great Japan Women's Hygiene Association) in 1887 with Ogino Ginko, a society that had the goal of increasing women's knowledge of hygiene, and from 1888 on they published the magazine *Fujin eiseikai zasshi*.[105]

Japanese nurses, as well as women teachers, embraced Christianity and sought to use their feminine qualities for the benefit of their society, and by doing so they expanded women's sphere of action. It would be easy to dismiss these few young women who entered a new profession as a small group that had not much influence over society at large, but I argue that they are interesting precisely because they were but a few. By the late Meiji period women as nurses were no longer a rarity and were thoroughly incorporated in the nationalist ideology espoused by the government and supported by society. During this period, instead, they considered themselves pioneers with a sense of a mission who appropriated for themselves spaces that had been hitherto improper for respectable women. It was the missionaries' support that enabled them to achieve their goals, but it was their education that enabled them to translate Western books about medical instruments and practices that Japanese girls had never seen. These girls went one step further and specialized in a new field by banking on the elite education they had already managed to obtain. It is also

104. Tamura and Asada, *Joshi gakuin gojūnenshi*, 4–5. Ōzeki was active in the Fujin kyōfūkai and later became the head of the Kangofukai (Nurses' Association) in Kanda. *Fujo shinbun*, no. 89, 20.1.1902, 2. See also Kameyama Michiko, *Taifū no yōni ikite. Nihon saisho no kangofu Ōzeki Chika monogatari* (Live like a strong wind: The story of the first female Japanese nurse Ōzeki Chika) (Domesu, 1992).

105. Takahashi Masako, *Shashin de miru nihon kindai kango no rekishi: Senkusha o tazunete* (A visual history of the Japanese nursing profession during the modern period: Meeting the pioneers) (Igaku shoin, 1984), 32–35.

important to remember that some of these nurses met the first Japanese woman doctor, established connections with male doctors, founded groups to listen to lectures, and published a magazine to help nurses and women doctors, but also women in general, learn about hygiene and the ways in which they could improve their lives. Maria True had stated that the nursing profession had profound social implications; these girls did learn that lesson and tried to spread their knowledge to the general public.

Girls' Associations and Their Publications

Missionary girls' schools, a new religion, and the jobs missionaries offered allowed girls to widen their horizons. Missionary schools were not disconnected from society, and women's groups, as we will see in the next chapter, established links with girls' schools while girl students formed connections with women's magazines such as *Jogaku zasshi*.

In 1889 and 1890, two new magazines were launched for girl students, demonstrating that they had become a group that could be influenced by competing theories over women's education and position in society. The first was *Kuni no motoi*, inaugurated in May 1889 by a group of professors at Tokyo kōtō jogakkō with the support of Katō Hiroyuki. It published news, articles, and Japanese and foreign literary works, and it carried the article that probably started the discussion about girl students' alleged scandals mentioned in chapter 2. The purpose of the magazine, as stated in the editorial in the first issue, was to provide a forum in which people with similar ideas about girls' education could discuss how to develop a better school system and to teach girls how to become good wives and wise mothers. In contrast, *Jogakusei* 女学生, the brainchild of Iwamoto Yoshiharu and the writer and literary critic Hoshino Tenchi 星野天知 (1862–1950), was launched in May 1890 by *Jogaku zasshisha*. It carried the writings of students belonging to literary societies in various (mostly missionary) schools and commented on them. Members of Atomi, Shinsakae, Kaigan, Meiji, Ferris, Kyōritsu, Rikkyō, Tōyō eiwa, Joshi dokuritsu, Seiritsu gakusha, and other schools contributed to the magazine. An article in the first issue held that these societies had been formed so that girls could express their opinions and extend their circle of acquaintants and to present to the general public girls' achievements and the world of girl students.[106] Thus, whereas the aim of *Kuni no motoi* was to disseminate the theories of a group of scholars on the education of Japanese girls, *Jogakusei* was published to establish links among (missionary) schools, to give girls a space for discussion and making themselves known to the public, and to counter accusations of girl students' improper behavior by presenting a different image of them. Given that Iwamoto was

---

106. *Jogakusei*, no. 1, 21.05.1890, inside front cover. Almost no material related to these societies has survived in the schools' archives.

already busy with *Jogaku zasshi*, to which girl students were contributing in large numbers, it is clear that by this time new venues were considered necessary, and lucrative, for this particular group.

In 1886, *Jogaku zasshi* publicized one such literary society opened at Ferris, the Jishūkai 時習会, and in November 1888 Wakamatsu Shizuko, a Christian and a student at Ferris, wrote a statement in English for the group's anniversary that was published in 1890 in *Jogaku zasshi*. She explained that the society wanted to review and put into practice "in a quiet and unassuming way" the knowledge acquired at school and added:

> We are not far removed from the time when needle and distaff were the insignia of womanly occupation. Indeed the idea is so deep-rooted among us that the most enlightened seem loathe to part with the old idea that womanly virtue requires her to do her "own work" . . . the woman who is capable of sustaining herself by editorial work, for example, should give her washing to her laundress and her sewing to her dressmaker who have no other honest means of livelihood. . . . The intelligent part of the world is haranguing us on our capabilities, and we must neither live beneath our privileges nor withhold our best for the cause of the general good.[107]

And she was not the only young woman holding such opinions. When Mitani Tamiko wrote, "In clearing the table and washing dishes, she [Miss Milliken] was always up and doing and next moment in the recitation hall, she was explaining verses from [Lord Alfred] Tennyson and [Robert] Browning," she clearly agreed with Wakamatsu and believed that, although the burden was heavier, it was still possible to take care of the family *and* have a satisfying life outside it.[108] Wakamatsu Shizuko did not think it improper to express her opinions in public, nor to present a model of womanhood that differed from the one proposed by Mori Arinori and other intellectuals. She put the stress on literary achievements and the "unassuming way" in which girls and women had to live, but she also argued that women who could do better than washing dishes should do so. Like Mitani, she believed that this should not be considered shameful but only the way in which capable persons expressed themselves. Women's writings, the literary societies, and *Jogakusei* show how more and more girls, in both private and missionary schools, were opposed to the idea that they were being educated only to become mothers

---

107. *Jogaku zasshi*, no. 13, 25.01.1886, 30–32, and supplement no. 242, 6.12.1890, 11–12 (original in English). The statement was signed K. S. (Kashi Shimada, i.e., Wakamatsu Shizuko). Wakamatsu also wrote that the name of the association was derived from the teachings of Confucius, who used the word *jishū* to define the "pleasure of acquiring knowledge, and then reviewing or dwelling upon it from time to time."

108. Tamura and Asada, *Joshi gakuin gojūnenshi*, 49.

and companions for their husbands and were as a group publicly expressing their objections. The end of the statement reported above epitomizes this point.

> We are here as a flock of birds all trying our wings. Perhaps some of our sistermembers, like eagles in a flock of geese, may in the future, soar far above us in literary attainment. But for the present, we are all possible eagles, we may all try our wings.

Conclusions

Strong and ambitious female students had existed during the Edo period as well, but it was during the early Meiji years that they began to find different spaces in which to express themselves. During these years, education and its purposes were not only based on the ideas of women such as Atomi Kakei or the school teachers who fulfilled their duties, but were also influenced by foreign (single) women teachers who did not seem to be exceptions in their home countries. Despite the class barriers that limited women's sphere of action, and although in some cases women missionaries considered themselves to be superior to Japanese women, some young Japanese women regarded them as role models.

Many of the girls mentioned in these pages reported that the "love" God felt for human beings had struck them. That love was directed toward both men and women and was presenting girls with the right to be educated and to assume their place in Christian society, a place that was different from, but complementary to, that of men. The fact that women's work complemented men's was nothing new in Japanese society, but in this case missionaries were not referring to women's *labor*. Because of their "natural" feminine qualities, women missionaries argued, Japanese women could teach their children to be good Japanese and Christians, could be companions to their husbands, and could work for the betterment of their society. They proposed a female sphere in which educated women were an irreplaceable part of family and social life. Some students did indeed believe that their education and position in society could be changed, and that such change would benefit Japanese society as a whole, and tried to live Christian lives as teachers, nurses, and wives. Some went to North America to further their studies thanks to the connections they established with women missionaries, who helped them organize their trips. What the missionary environment did, then, was to give them confidence in the value of their education and opinions and a circle of friends that would listen to and support their hopes.

The history of the Meiji period is often told as the history of Japanese missions abroad and Japanese interactions with Westerners at home, but that is too often a male story. Here, instead, we see that international bonds were formed by and for women. Furthermore, although I did not find many articles in the contemporary print media describing these girls' experiences abroad, this does not mean that they were not presented as examples to younger Japanese girls. It is most probable, in fact, that missionaries used these girls' stories as "success stories" in their schools, while the fact that many taught in or were members of their alma maters meant that younger generations of girl students could approach them and ask about their experiences abroad. Finally, and I deal with this point in the conclusion to this work, given the information above, I argue that it is necessary to look carefully at these young women, their experiences abroad, and their work once back in Japan if we really want to understand women's society, and the examples of womanhood circulating in it, during the following decades.

Missionary discourses on women's position and work were not contained within their school walls. Missionaries participated in public activities, and the education they provided to Japanese boys and girls was criticized or praised in public spaces as much as, if not more than, that provided by the government. Girls, too, entered the debate and wrote about their experiences in the print media. If in many cases, irrespective of their social class, girls married after graduation and disappeared from public life, there are also many other cases in which female students and teachers continued their public activities after graduating from missionary schools or while teaching there, and committed themselves to reforming women's position by bringing forth their gendered criticism of society. Women missionaries and their education stimulated debates such as that on the concept of family, and women involved in the missionary effort, such as Yajima Kajiko, brought these teachings to public halls and the pages of magazines, as we will see in the next chapter.

Christianity was surely not intended to produce a generation of feminists, but women missionaries showed that women's place was not only at home. They told Japanese girls that they had the right and power to reform Japanese customs, presenting some of them with reasons that gave them the strength to go public and ask for a different position for women in Japanese society.

4

Women's Groups and Their Activities

Ellen Richards (1842–1911), the first woman to do graduate work in chemistry at the Massachusetts Institute of Technology, wrote:

> I hope in a quiet way, I am winning a way which others will keep open. Perhaps the fact that I am not a Radical or a believer in the all powerful ballot for women to right her wrongs and that I do not scorn womanly duties, but claim it as a privilege to clean up and sort of supervise the room and sew things, etc., is winning me stronger allies than anything else.

Rather than denying the domesticity assigned to women, Blair has argued that Richards "employed it to make her presence tolerable in a field heretofore hostile to women. Her self-conscious use of ladylike qualities is an early example of domestic feminism—women winning a place outside the home using domestic credentials."[1]

What Blair calls domestic feminism can be distinguished among early Meiji women as well. With the development of public spaces, such as schools and magazines, that favored the appearance in public of various models for women, some found employment by opening or teaching in girls' schools, whereas others, who sought change, could access more venues in which to voice their concerns than were available in previous decades. Those women who wanted to become public figures, to work for what they considered to be the public good, and to obtain self-realization and expression also started forming or joining *fujinkai* (women's

---

1. Caroline L. Hunt, *The Life of Ellen H. Richards* (Boston: Whitcomb and Barrows, 1912), 90–91, quoted in Karen Blair, *The Clubwoman as Feminist: True Womanhood Redefined, 1868–1914* (New York: Holmes and Meier, 1980), 10.

groups).[2] The fact that the majority of the young women described in the previous two chapters were members of one or more women's groups shows how associations in which to discuss and confront ideas, and from which to enter public life and discourses, were as important for Meiji women as they were for men.

Male intellectuals had repeatedly stated that women should be "nationalistic" and contribute to society by managing their households and dedicating themselves to their families; the members of some of the groups presented in this chapter wanted to achieve precisely that. Others expanded this basic definition of "nationalistic women" and sought to improve their education, to enhance their social roles as mothers and wives, and to obtain a space outside their homes in which to discuss issues that concerned women and therefore, they argued, Japanese society. They justified their actions with their self-attributed inherent moral qualities, and through their activities in public spaces, carried out under the banner of "good wives, wise mothers" working for the betterment of their country, they influenced social and political discourses by making society and the government discuss their demands.

Women's groups were a new feature of the Meiji period as much as male groups were, and they were linked to girls' schools and women's magazines.[3] By analyzing women's activities and objectives, and the reasons why they felt it necessary to organize themselves, it will become clear how *fujinkai* developed, how they became tools for the expansion of women's activities, how they influenced and shaped public opinion, and what practical skills women obtained by participating in them. By looking in detail at these points, it will also be clear that women's groups were not a subcategory of male groups but were created in their own right and with their own goals.

Women's Groups and Their Aims

 Many *fujinkai* were founded during the second half of the 1880s, and one of their foremost goals was that of educating their members on the new theories on women's education and roles. They provided an additional space and source of information for young women and also one where older women could approach subjects that their daughters were learning at school.[4] Girls who managed to graduate from

2. As I specified in the introduction, *fujinkai* defined the modern way of socializing for upper-middle-class women and men, and they not only included married women but also girl students, divorced women, and men. In this chapter, I use the term *fujinkai* to indicate "women's groups" even though it was not a word used in each and every group's name.

3. On the formation of early Meiji male groups, see Kenneth B. Pyle, *The New Generation in Meiji Japan* (Stanford: Stanford University Press, 1969); and William Braisted, trans., *Meiroku Zasshi: Journal of the Japanese Enlightenment* (Cambridge, Mass.: Harvard University Press, 1976).

4. For example, Harada Yoshiko 原田良子 (perhaps she was the Harada Ryōko mentioned in chapter 3, n. 81) formed the Shukujo ibunkai 淑女以文会 in Kanda with eleven people to learn about Japanese, Chinese, and Western culture and to listen to concerts and speeches. About one hundred women participated in the first meeting. *Iratsume*, no. 5, 12.11.1887, 49–50.

schools formed groups in order to continue learning and to meet with their friends. Some groups were founded in their hometowns by female graduates of the major girls' schools, so they were comparable to today's alumni groups.[5] It could be argued that there was almost no difference between some of these groups and two or three friends getting together to discuss the books they were reading or talk about the latest hairstyle in vogue in the capital. Some of these groups were indeed small, but the fact that they were publicized in newspapers and magazines that did not criticize their existence shows that they were in line with the "enlightened and progressive" policy supported by Meiji society, that they were formed by educated girls who thought that their groups deserved a name, and that they could become examples for other girls to follow.

A crucial reason for the existence of such spaces was that of women learning *together*. The forty members of the Fukuoka fujin kyōkai 福岡婦人協会 (Fukuoka Women's Association), for example, met once a month and argued that society was changing, female education was spreading, and they could learn from Western women's examples. Their goals were to improve their position, teach their children, work with their husbands, and use their energy for the good of their nation. By meeting periodically, by listening to public speeches on subjects that directly concerned women, such as education, hygiene, and household economy, and by discussing these subjects together, they would be able to pursue the *onna no michi*, the "woman's way."[6] It is therefore not surprising to find members of one group participating in the activities of another. The Fujin kōdankai 婦人講談会 (Women's Lecture Group), whose members met in an elementary school in Kōjimachi, Tokyo, was founded by women and men who sought to improve female education. At its first meeting, which was attended by one hundred women, one of the speakers was Kimura Sadako 木村貞子 (1856–1926), who belonged to the Tokyo fujin kyōiku danwakai 東京婦人教育談話会 (Tokyo Women's Educational Conversation Society) and was a teacher at Kazoku jogakkō.[7] The latter group, one of the largest of the period, had the goal of improving women's education. It was set up in 1887 by, among others, Tanahashi Ayako, Kimura herself, and Ishii Fudeko, also a teacher

---

5. The Ōkikai 鴨沂会 was formed by girls who had graduated from Kyoto jogakkō and wanted to remain in contact, organize debates and speeches, and publish a journal. *Iratsume*, no. 2, 13.08.1887, 10. The Echigo Nagaoka joshi shinbokukai 越後長岡女子親睦会 (Echigo Nagaoka Women's Friendship Association) was founded by Makino Kiyoko 牧野きよ子, a graduate of Tokyo joshi shihan gakkō, and three female friends. Thirty-seven women who had already obtained an elementary education participated in the first meeting. *Jogaku zasshi*, no. 32, 15.08.1886, 39.

6. *Jiji shinpō*, no. 1223, 15.03.1886, 3. A similar group was the Joshi kōsaikai 女子交際会 (Women's Meeting Group). Its members stated that women did not know what having social relations meant and did not have enough chances to enlarge their knowledge. This group, which was organized by men in a girls' school, was to become a space where women could meet periodically to exchange information, and there was also a plan to publish a monthly journal. *Chōya shinbun*, no. 3748, 27.04.1886, 4.

7. *Iratsume*, no. 2, 13.08.1887, 10; no. 3, 10.09.1887, 6–7.

at Kazoku jogakkō. In December of the same year it was renamed Dai nihon fujin kyōikukai (Great Japan Women's Education Society), and soon thereafter it started publishing a magazine under the same name. Women founded this group because "the world's knowledge expands daily and men are allowed to pursue their studies and progress together with it" whereas women "have been kept ignorant." In order to change this situation, "women should meet and discuss what they know best, thus furthering their education. By doing so, women's opinions will acquire validity and their social value will rise. This development will benefit first their homes and then also their nation."[8] These women were asking for more education and the possibility of becoming active participants in the development of their society even from within more conservative spaces, such as Kazoku jogakkō (where some of the organizers taught) and Tokyo Imperial University (the exclusive, high-profile university where at least one of their meetings was held).

Finally, *fujinkai* allowed women to realize that working and campaigning together would enhance their chances of spreading their message and attaining their goals. A statement attributed to Sasaki Toyoju, one of the founders of Tokyo fujin kyōfūkai (Tokyo Women's Group for the Reform of Morals), claimed that women had to "reform the customs and laws based on *danson johi* [revere men and despise women], support the formation of monogamous families, abolish prostitution, reform the family system and social relations, and oppose the consumption of alcohol and tobacco, and dissipation and indolence." However, these were difficult and far-reaching goals, so it was necessary to spread awareness by talking or writing about them.[9]

Women of all ages started shaping visible physical and social spaces for themselves as an alternative to those already existing, spaces that supported the development of a different understanding of women's worth within and outside their homes. On the one hand, they learned about female chores and responsibilities, including how to raise children, how to cook new dishes, or the latest rules of hygiene, enlarging their sphere of knowledge and competence. On the other hand, women's groups started to be acknowledged by that part of society that edited, published, and read

8. *Dai nihon fujin kyōikukai zasshi*, no. 1, 21.12.1888, 3, 39–40. See *Dai nihon fujin kyōikukai zasshi*, supplement to no. 22, 13.12.1890, for a list of its members. Three hundred women participated in the first meeting, held in January 1888 at Imperial University. Kimura Sadako welcomed the audience, Ishii Fudeko spoke about women's duty to educate the next generation, Morooka Nobuko 師岡信子 discussed the way to enlarge the woman's sphere, and Mizuno Mineko 水野峰子, a teacher at Tōyō eiwa jogakkō, lamented women's ignorance and stressed the need for women's education. Katō Hiroyuki also considered the changes in the roles of women and men. *Iratsume*, no. 8, 11.02.1888, 65–66.

9. *Jogaku zasshi*, no. 65, 21.05.1887, 27, reprinted in Nihon kirisutokyō fujin kyōfūkai, ed., *Nihon kirisutokyō fujin kyōfūkai hyakunenshi* (One hundred years of the Nihon kirisutokyō fujin kyōfūkai) (Domesu shuppan, 1986), 50–54. Sasaki was born in Sendai and later went to Tokyo, becoming a student of Nakamura Masanao, probably at Dōjinsha, and at Ferris jogakkō. Abe Reiko, "Sasaki Tojoyu oboegaki" (Notes on Sasaki Toyoju), *Nihonshi kenkyū* 171 (1976): 52–65.

the magazines in which their activities were recorded, by the schools in which they met, by the areas in which they operated, and by the people who attended their numerous public meetings. By taking part in these activities, women were finding reasons to leave their homes and meet with other women, creating new possibilities for themselves and others.

Distribution, Membership, and Male Participation

It is impossible to determine how many *fujinkai* were opened during the 1880s, how many women and men took part in their activities, how many joined more than one, how they operated, or how long they existed. The following, however, is clear: *fujinkai* flourished all over Japan and are of fundamental importance for our understanding of the development of Meiji civil society.

In 1887 *Jogaku zasshi* published a list of some eighty *fujinkai* active in places that included Osaka, Nagoya, Shizuoka, Kochi, Sendai, and Kumamoto. Names such as Osaka fujin gakushūkai 大阪婦人学習会 (Osaka Women's Learning Society) and Dai nihon fujin bunshō kairyōkai 大日本婦人文章改良会 (Great Japan Women's Association for the Reform of Writing) give us an indication of the scope of some of them, but the fact that many contain in their names words such as *cooperation, discussion, learning,* and *interaction* confirms that women's aggregation and education were the main reasons for their existence.[10] *7* lim.

[Given that members had to pay a monthly fee, and usually there was no mention of free or reduced membership for those who could not pay, most of these groups consisted of women who had money and free time at their disposal.]Women of the upper classes and nobility were also unlikely to have joined groups whose purpose was to teach women how to manage their households or groups that met in schools or religious places given that they were more limited in their movements and did not need such information as they relied on servants and maids. The founders and targets of such groups tended to be upper-middle-class women.

Men were not excluded and were often invited to become "honorary" members.[11] Male presence in women's groups was not always welcomed; in 1889 a woman from Tosa wrote an article in *Shinonome shinbun* in which she argued, "Women organize themselves in *fujinkai* or *kyōfūkai* [reform societies] in order to free themselves from male oppression and expand women's rights," but "when one asks about the founding and development of such groups, many are based on men's advice, are formed because they are a fashionable undertaking, or their regulations

10. *Jogaku zasshi*, no. 90, 24.12.1887, 194–95.
11. Chino has made a comprehensive study of *fujinkai* founded by men for their wives or in which men participated by giving lectures or helping write the groups' constitutions. Chino Yōichi, *Kindai Nihon fujin kyōiku shi* (A history of Japanese women's education during the modern period) (Domesu shuppan, 1979).

are written by men." Women should not rely on men, this writer stated, and should instead fight to gain their freedom and liberty by cooperating with each other.[12] During the Meiji period, however, only male and female groups that were able to blend nationalistic goals with their own aspirations could flourish, and the presence of respected men in women's groups publicly legitimated their existence and positive contribution to women's and social "advancement." For example, the Tokyo fujin kyōfūkai, the group I concentrate on below, and the connections it created with respected men, initiated a process by which women's activities and speeches were not heavily suppressed by the authorities, as happened with female political speakers such as Kishida Toshiko and Fukuda Hideko, and therefore could be organized more often and attended by more people. Without supporters such as Iwamoto Yoshiharu, women would have encountered more difficulties in forming groups, reaching to a wide audience, and having their demands taken seriously. Thus, when *fujinkai* were set up in order to change women's lot, a male presence, women's willingness to learn in their free time, and the use of a mild rather than fiercely feminist language in the groups' names and statements ensured their survival and expansion.

The Tokyo fujin kyōfūkai

In 1884 Mary Leavitt, a member of the American Woman's Christian Temperance Union (WCTU), assumed the tasks of persuading the world of the need for national governments and local authorities to close down places where alcohol was served and campaigning against the use of tobacco and other drugs.[13] She arrived in Tokyo in June 1886 with a slogan calling for universal sisterhood and asked the Presbyterian missionaries residing in Japan for help. Soon afterward, Leavitt made a speech entitled "Duty of Women in Relation to Intemperance and Other Cognate Vices" at the Jogaku enzetsukai (Public Speech Meeting on Women's Education), promoted by Jogaku zasshisha (the company that published *Jogaku zasshi*), in Tokyo, and Yajima Kajiko (1833–1925), the future president of the Tokyo fujin kyōfūkai (hereafter Kyōfūkai), was among the audience.[14]

---

12. Yamazaki Take (chapter 5) responded in the next issue of the newspaper, arguing that if men were willing to help women reform society there was no reason to refuse their help. These articles are reprinted in Sotozaki Mitsuhiro, *Ueki Emori to onnatachi* (Ueki Emori and women) (Domesu, 1976), 203–14.

13. Rumi Yasutake, "Men, Women, and Temperance in Meiji Japan: Engendering WCTU Activism from a Transnational Perspective," *Japanese Journal of American Studies* 17 (2006): 98.

14. Yajima was born in Kumamoto prefecture. One of her sisters, Yokoi Tsuseko 横井つせ子, was the wife of Yokoi Shōnan and the mother of Ebina Miya. Another sister, Tokutomi Hisako 德富久子 (1829–1919), was the mother of the intellectual and journalist Tokutomi Sohō 德富蘇峰 (1863–1957), and another, Takezaki Junko 竹崎順子 (1825–1905), became the headmistress of Kumamoto jogakkō in 1897. In 1858 Yajima married a man who is said to have abused her. She

Although plenty of *fujinkai* were formed all over Japan during the 1880s, it is crucial to analyze the activities and membership of the Kyōfūkai in particular, for this is one of the groups that proposed the kind of domestic feminism discussed above and for which we have abundant material. The activities of the Kyōfūkai during the Meiji period are well known today because of its local groups all over Japan (it became a national organization in 1893), because it published a magazine, and because it was founded in connection with the arrival of Western women, who became notorious partly due to their role as experts on Western culture. The members of the Kyōfūkai thought that women's inherent nature would allow them to identify and address the "evils" of Japanese society. They combined work in their homes with the spread of their ideas on morality to the general public, and in this new space they created they learned the art of making speeches, writing petitions, establishing relationships with Western women, organizing large meetings, and coordinating activities throughout Japan.[15]

Finally, although the magazine they founded in April 1888, the *Tokyo fujin kyōfū zasshi*, was edited by Iwamoto Yoshiharu, Asai Saku and Sasaki Toyoju were on its editorial board. As the magazine's editorial office was based at first at Sasaki's home and then at Asai's, it is clear that their involvement went beyond that acknowledged on its back cover.[16] In November 1893, the magazine changed its name to *Fujin kyōfū zasshi*. There were no more male names on its editorial board, which instead included, among others, Wakamatsu Shizuko, Asai Saku, Nagamine (Honda) Teiko, and Sasaki Toyoju. The editor was Takekoshi Takeyo (chapter 6)

---

divorced him in 1868 and went to Tokyo around 1872, leaving her three children behind. She obtained a diploma to become elementary teacher and met the Presbyterian missionaries, who offered her a position at Shinsakae jogakkō. When Sakurai and Shinsakae merged to become Joshi gakuin, Yajima was appointed its director. Kubushiro Ochimi, ed., *Yajima Kajiko den* (Yajima Kajiko's biography) (Ōzorasha, [1935] 1988). Tanigawa Kensuke, *Kindai Kumamoto joseishi nenpyō: Meiji gan'nen—Showa nijūnen* (Timeline of Kumamoto women's modern history: From 1868 to 1945) (Kumamoto: Kumamoto shuppan bunka kaikan, 1999), 27.

15. Yajima Kajiko held that in less than a year 180 persons had joined the group. *Jogaku zasshi*, no. 70, 06.08.1887, 190. By the end of 1888 there were 546 members. *Tokyo fujin kyōfū zasshi*, no. 11, 19.02.1889, 20.

16. Katano Masako, "Asai Saku oboegaki" (Notes on Asai Saku), in *Kindai Nihon no kirisutokyō to joseitachi* (Christianity and women in Japan during the modern period), edited by Tomisaka Kirisutokyō Center, 12–50 (Shinkyō shuppansha, 1995), 49. The magazine was publicized in venues that were not Christian. In *Tokyo keizai zasshi* (Tokyo Magazine on Economic Matters), no. 439, it was stated that various magazines for women were being published, and that was something over which to rejoice for the development of women's society (*fujin shakai*), but only the Kyōfūkai's was written by women. Reported in *Tokyo fujin kyōfū zasshi*, no. 7, 20.10.1888, 154. In *Nihon no jogaku* (Japanese Women's Education), no. 16, the magazine was praised because of the space it gave to all sorts of discussions, literary works, and news. The author of the piece lamented the magazine's Christian connection but wrote that the association would not necessarily deter readers from purchasing copies. Reported in *Tokyo fujin kyōfū zasshi*, no. 10, 19.01.1889, 13.

while Yajima was the publisher.[17] For those innumerable women who wanted to have a public voice, this was no small achievement.

Female Speech Making

The art of speaking in public, developed in Japan in the 1870s, was not mastered only by male scholars, politicians, and students in order to shape and put forward their arguments. The members of most women's groups tried to spread their message by organizing and participating in public speech meetings. Thus, women speaking in public also became a common feature of the early Meiji period. The earliest public speech given by a woman that I could find was the one delivered in 1878 at Tōkyō Women's Normal School discussed in chapter 2, but it was with the formation and development of women's groups that this art spread among women, while making public speeches and talking to each other was perceived, as we have seen in the case of the Fukuoka fujin kyōkai, as a way to pursue the *onna no michi*, "the woman's way."[18]

Female public speech meetings were a curiosity because of the peculiarity of hearing *women* speak in front of an audience. The historian Taguchi Ukichi 田口卯吉 (1855–1905), for example, gave a speech in 1886 that opened with the words "I have made many public speeches but this is the first time I speak in front of a female audience," so a woman speaker was even more of a novelty and a surprise.[19] When Leavitt made the speech entitled "Duty of Women in Relation to In-

---

17. There were two pieces of legislation regarding the publication of newspapers and magazines, the Shinbunshi jōrei and the Shuppan jōrei, which were often revised during the Meiji period. The first dealt with newspapers and magazines that were published from time to time and the second with magazines on the sciences (*gakujutsu*) and arts (*gigei*). According to article 7 of the Newspaper Regulation (Shinbunshi jōrei), revised in April 1883, only Japanese men over twenty could become owners, directors, editors, or printers of newspapers. The legislation is reprinted in Matsumoto Sannosuke and Yamamuro Shinichi, *Genron to media* (Debate and the media), vol. 11 of *Nihon kindai shisō taikei* (Collection on modern Japanese thought) (Iwanami shoten, 1990), 416–21. In English, see Jay Rubin, *Injurious to Public Morals: Writers and the Meiji State* (Seattle: University of Washington Press, 1984); and James Huffman, *Creating a Public: People and Press in Meiji Japan* (Honolulu: University of Hawai'i Press, 1997). Apparently, in 1893 the magazine of the Kyōfūkai was included in the *gakujutsu* category of the Shuppan jōrei (in which no mention was made of women). I have not been able to determine why that was so and why it happened in 1893. Kindai josei bunkashi kenkyūkai, ed., *Fujin zasshi no yoake* (The dawn of women's magazines) (Ōzorasha, 1989), 14–15, 31. The Shuppan jōrei is reprinted in Matsumoto and Yamamuro, *Genron to media*, 425–37. The magazine changed its name again in February 1895 and became *Fujin shinpō*. The publisher was Yajima Kajiko, and the editors were Takekoshi Takeyo and then Yamaji Taneko 山路タ子. For a brief history of the magazine, see *Fujin shinpō*, no. 36, 25.04.1900, 1; and no. 370, 01.1929, 27–29. See also Nihon kirisutokyō fujin kyōfūkai, *Nihon kirisutokyō*, 120–28.

18. *Jiji shinpō*, no. 1223, 15.03.1886, 3.

19. *Jogaku zasshi*, no. 24, 25.05.1886, 1.

temperance and Other Cognate Vices" at the Jogaku enzetsukai, women went there out of curiosity because they were attracted by the topic of the speech, because they accompanied acquaintances, but also because it was given by a woman and a North American. Only women could attend this meeting, and, although the organizers had not expected a large audience, it seems to have attracted six hundred women and to have lasted more than four hours.[20] Why could only women participate? And why did six hundred women do so?

Jogaku zasshi continued publicizing such meetings, and we know that the second Jogaku enzetsukai, held in the same venue soon after, attracted more than one thousand women. There were four speakers that we know of: Adaline Kelsey, a doctor who had studied at Mount Holyoke and done missionary work in China and whose speech was interpreted by Suzuki Mitsu 鈴木みつ, a graduate of Kyōritsu jogakkō; Maria True with Mineo Eiko (both teachers of Sakurai jogakkō) as interpreter; Ebina Miya; and Sasaki Toyoju. As with the first meeting, only women were admitted because according to the New Testament it was not considered proper for women to make speeches in public, and even in the West women did not like to speak in front of a mixed audience. In this case, the Western understanding of feminine propriety coincided with the Japanese one, as traditionally Japanese women could not lecture from a podium in front of men.[21] Thus, a first "agreement" was reached according to which women could speak about womanly affairs in front of women only so as not to find themselves in inappropriate situations.

In order to stress this point further, the second Jogaku enzetsukai seems to have been the occasion for the publication of a book titled *Fujin genron no jiyū* 婦人言論の自由 (Women's Freedom of Speech), which was a translation of a book published by the American WCTU. Of three prefaces, the first was written by Tokutomi Sohō, who argued that men had to face the external world while mothers, wives, and sisters should support their male relatives. The translation of the book, he continued, was made by Sasaki Toyoju, the secretary of the Kyōfūkai, and he encouraged women to read it. He approved of the fact that books were being translated by Japanese women but he was also hoping that works by talented women who, like George Sand and George Eliot, loved truth and humanity, would appear in Japan. In the second preface, Iwamoto Yoshiharu wrote that Jogaku zasshisha

---

20. *Jogaku zasshi*, no. 30, 25.07.1886, 305.
21. *Jogaku zasshi*, no. 62, 30.04.1887, 38; no. 63, 07.05.1887, 41–43; no. 64, 14.05.1887, 63–65; no. 65, 21.05.1887, 83–86. Kelsey gave suggestions on food and hygiene and held that women's physical problems were created by the habit of using corsets or binding their feet. The news, content, and names of the speakers were reported in *Mainichi shinbun*, no. 4920, 03.05.1887, 3. Women reading or teaching in front of small groups of women can be found in various periods of Japanese history, but the modern understanding of the value of public speech meetings, coupled with the number of people in the audience, was different from what women had been doing before the Meiji period.

had held a public meeting in which Sasaki and other women had made speeches in front of an entirely female audience. Because of this, people were suspicious, and the book had been translated to prove that there was no reason to oppose women's speeches. The last preface was by Sasaki herself, who stated that in North America and Europe the mistrust of women speaking in front of a male public was based on the New Testament, but as women's knowledge was improving and they were becoming more active they now had the opportunity to reform society's bad habits. Moreover, in the New Testament nothing prevented women from joining in philanthropic activities and obtaining an education since they were working under the benevolence of Christ.[22]

The book explained that women were good teachers, speakers, and thinkers but also good organizers since the WCTU had been born and developed entirely as a result of their work. One of the misunderstood phrases in the New Testament was in the First Letter to the Corinthians, which stated, "As in all the churches of the Saints, the women should keep silence in the churches. For they are not permitted to speak, but should be subordinate, as even the law says. If there is anything they desire to know, let them ask their husbands at home. For it is shameful for a woman to speak in church." The book explained that it was wrong to read everything written in the Bible literally, and people should understand and interpret its teachings, for these were based on the habits and requirements of past ages and therefore were no longer suitable. Women played important roles in the Bible and were active in society and necessary to the Church; as men and women were all children of Christ, they should all be treated with respect.

The book was published in response to criticism of public meetings organized for women in which women were the speakers. Such criticism was based on the notion that, even though they were doing so in order to become better mothers and create better families, women participating in this and other groups were becoming agents of social change by bringing forth private issues in public places, and these concerns were all the more serious because of the sheer number of women attending such meetings.

Why did so many women participate? For most women these meetings were likely to have been one of the few occasions in which they could listen to women's speeches on topics that were geared toward influencing their society and sometimes even government decisions. Women could read about the contents of some public speeches in *Jogaku zasshi* and the newspapers publicizing them, but not everyone had access to such articles, nor was it the same as being present at a speech and then having the chance to talk with like-minded men and women. It is precisely in this way that the Kyōfūkai was formed; the article reporting Leavitt's speech mentioned

22. Sasaki Toyoju, ed. and trans., *Fujin genron no jiyū* (Women's freedom of speech) (Sasaki Toyoju, 1888).

that after the meeting thirty women stayed on and talked about forming a new association to promote temperance.[23]

According to the articles published in various newspapers soon after its formation, the Kyōfūkai was in favor of monogamous families and the extension of women's rights (*joken*). The group was also against prostitution, the custom of despising women and revering men, and alcohol and tobacco. Given that within a year of its founding plenty of local branches were formed, it is clear that there were women and men who had been waiting for this chance and supported the group's aims.[24]

Wang has argued that by embracing nationalism and feminism some Chinese women discovered empowering new discourses. In her opinion, the construction of a new understanding of women's worth is a process that involves the circulation of a new discourse and a group of women unhappy with the status quo since "without an audience made receptive by their own personal experience, even a circulating discourse cannot create new subject positions."[25] Women unhappy with their status had existed during the previous centuries as well, but during the early Meiji period the construction of a new subjectivity could become thinkable because of the possibility of circulating a new discourse throughout Japan. The *enzetsu* was the starting point, but groups could be formed, and women decided to join them, because the media, leaflets, women's groups, churches, and girls' schools publicized such activities widely. Iwamoto Yoshiharu and the other organizers of Leavitt's speeches were not sure about the overall outcome of the first *enzetsukai* she took part in, but if six hundred women really participated, and if the second Jogaku enzetsukai attracted even more women, the publicity they had given these events had clearly been effective and the topics discussed had attracted many listeners. Such publicity

23. *Jogaku zasshi*, no. 32, 15.08.1886, 2. The founding of the Kyōfūkai was delayed until November 1886 because Kimura Tōko (1848–86), who with her husband Kumaji had opened Meiji jogakkō in 1885, had died of cholera while they were organizing the group. *Jogaku zasshi*, no. 37, 05.10.1886, 142. See also Aoyama Nao, *Meiji jogakkō no kenkyū* (A study of Meiji jogakkō) (Keiō tsūshin, 1970). When Leavitt delivered a similar speech in Kobe and left for Osaka, women in Kobe organized to found another temperance group. Kawamoto Sō 川本操 (b. 1841) was the president, Watanabe Tsuneko was the secretary, and there were sixty members. *Jogaku zasshi*, no. 37, 05.10.1886, 142.

24. *Asahi shinbun*, 12.12.1886, reprinted in Suzuki Yūko, ed., *Nihon josei undō shiryō shūsei* (Sources on the Japanese women's movement), vol. 1, *Shisō seiji* (Political thought) (Fuji shuppan, 1996), 85; *Chōya shinbun*, no. 3945, 12.12.1886, 4; *Kyōiku jiron*, no. 91, 25.10.1887, 29. Branches were opened in Sendai and Kumamoto. *Jogaku zasshi*, no. 70, 06.08.1887, 201; no. 89, 17.12.1887, 181. A branch was opened in Hokkaido soon after the founding of the Kyōfūkai because some female graduates from Tokyo who had met Yajima Kajiko were teachers in a school in Hakodate and kept in contact with Tokyo, showing that the bonds formed at school often lasted after the girls' graduation. Inoue Yuriko, *Chikara o ataemase: Honda Yōitsu fujin Teiko no shōgai* (Give me strength! The life of Teiko, Honda Yōitsu's wife) (Aoyama gakuin, 2004), 75.

25. Zheng Wang, *Women in the Chinese Enlightenment: Oral and Textual Histories* (Berkeley: University of California Press, 1999), 279.

ensured that Leavitt's presence in Japan and her speeches did not pass unnoticed and helped spread information about the lives of women in other countries. Without these possibilities, even "empowering new discourses" would not have found such an eager and numerous audience.

Thus, the first *enzetsukai* Leavitt took part in as a speaker should be considered an important moment in Japanese women's history because it was if not the first then one of the very first occasions in which women were present as speakers, as translators, and among the audience and their activities and speeches were recorded in magazines. Furthermore, the fact that the papers reported about women's public speech meetings throughout the Meiji period means that even if a certain part of society considered such activities lightly, or regarded women on a podium as an abhorrence, women making speeches were recognized as an integral part of modern Japan.

Women as Interpreters of Women's Speeches and Translators of Different Cultures

The employment of young women translators or interpreters who acted as speakers by delivering in Japanese the message voiced by a Western woman was also a new feature of the early Meiji period. Graduating from a girls' school was already an achievement for these girls, but standing in front of an audience and rendering into Japanese concepts that were familiar to Japanese women, such as alcoholism and prostitution, while using the English language that they had so painstakingly learned at school was a comparably important experience. Leavitt's first speech, for example, was interpreted by Wakamatsu Shizuko of Ferris jogakkō and Watase Kame 渡瀬香芽, a graduate of Shinsakae jogakkō.[26] When Leavitt arrived in Kobe, she was helped by Watanabe Tsuneko (1864–1946), who also acted as her interpreter.[27] Both Watase and Watanabe went on to hold prominent positions in Japanese women's history, the former lobbying the participants at the 1930 London Naval Conference to reduce the arms race, the latter teaching at Kobe jogakuin and becoming the head of the Kobe branch of the Kyōfūkai after studying with private funds as the first non-Western student at Carleton College in Minnesota from 1889 to 1891.[28] Finally, when in Osaka, Leavitt was helped by Sakurai Chika, Ukita Fuku 浮田ふく, and Etō Hide 江頭ひで. I could not find information on Ukita, but Etō was sixteen years old at the time, and after graduating from Baika jogakkō she

---

26. *Jogaku zasshi*, no. 29, 15.07.1886, 278; no. 30, 25.07.1886, 305. See also Watase Masakatsu, ed., *Watase Torajirōden* (The biography of Watase Torajirō) (Watase Dōzoku, 1934), 120.

27. *Kobe yūshin nippō*, 03.12.1886, 6.

28. See http://acad.carleton.edu/campus/archives/history/chrono/chrono1866–1891.html, accessed February 27, 2010. On Watase and the London Naval Conference, see Manako Ogawa, "The 'White Ribbon League of Nations' Meets Japan: The Trans-Pacific Activism of the Woman's Christian Temperance Union, 1906–1930," *Diplomatic History* 31.1 (2007): 21–50. On Watanabe,

studied in North America and taught at her alma mater, so it is probable that Ukita was also a student of some missionary school in the area.[29]

Among the members of the Kyōfūkai up to July 1887 there were some familiar names, including Asai Saku, whose articles were published in the magazine *Haishō* 廃娼 (Abolishing Prostitution); Ogino Ginko; and Tokutomi Hisako, Yajima's sister. There were also many young women studying, for example, at Sakurai, Meiji, Ferris, Kaigan, and Kirisuto jogakkō.[30] It is thus probable that other students were asked to translate for the Western women and women missionaries participating in the activities of the Kyōfukai, also because of the involvement of their teachers. For example, given that Sakurai Chika, who at the time was teaching at Osaka jogakuin, was Leavitt's interpreter when Leavitt was in Osaka, it is probable that her students helped as well. By 1886 Japanese and Western women had strengthened their connections and had links all over Japan, links that could be used to organize events such as those mentioned above, while the girls studying with missionaries were also asked to help.

The Kyōfūkai was not the only *fujinkai* employing female interpreters, thus showing that women had begun specializing in this new skill even though it was probably not a lucrative one. At a meeting of the Dai nihon fujin kyōikukai, the speech on women's education given by a certain Miss Carter, who had done missionary work in India, was interpreted by Ishii Fudeko. Miss Carter concluded her speech by stating that she had come to Japan and seen what education meant to Japanese women and it was now their turn to go to North America, learn about the life of female students there, and talk to them about the education of Japanese women in Japan.[31] This was not an impossible dream, for we have seen that numerous girls had crossed the ocean and studied in North America. Carter's exhortation was also taken up by Ishii Fudeko, who left Japan a year later and accomplished exactly that.

Speech Making and the Print Market

The fact that a sizable number of women had begun to appear as speakers, listeners, and interpreters also had an impact on the print market, for publishing companies were quick to reach out to this new female readership.

see Haga Noboru, Ichibangase Yasuko, Nakajima Kuni, and Soda Kōichi, eds., *Nihon josei jinmei jiten* (Biographical dictionary of Japanese women) (Nihon tosho Center, 1993); and *Jogaku zasshi*, no. 285, 03.10.1891, 25.

29. *Jogaku zasshi*, no. 37, 05.10.1886, 142; Tamura Naoomi and Asada Mikako, eds., *Joshi gakuin gojūnenshi* (Fifty years of Joshi gakuin) (Joshi gakuin dōsōkai, 1928), 83.

30. Their names and addresses were published in *Jogaku zasshi*, no. 71, 13.08.1887, 22; and no. 78, 01.10.1887, 163. They are reprinted in Nihon kirisutokyō fujin kyōfūkai, *Nihon kirisutokyō*, 43–49. On Asai, see Katano Masako, "Asai Saku oboegaki."

31. *Dai nihon fujin kyōikukai zasshi*, no. 4, 20.04.1889, 21–33; no. 5, 18.05.1889, 23–30.

Jogaku enzetsushū 女学演説集 (Collection of Public Speeches on Women's Education) was a collection of speeches already published in *Jogaku zasshi* and reprinted in book format in 1888. In the same year Nakai Tatsu 中井タツ edited a small volume, *(Tottori fujinkai) enzetsu hikki* 鳥取婦人会演説筆記 (Transcription of the Public Speeches of the Tottori Women's Group), containing three *enzetsu* made by men at the meetings of the Tottori fujinkai.[32]

Joshi dokuritsu enzetsu hikki 女子独立演説筆記 (Transcription of the Public Speech on Women's Independence, 1888), on the other hand, was a transcription of a speech by Fukuoka Teruko. Fukuoka opened her speech by stating that although she wanted to discuss Western women's lifestyles this was not because she had the "American fever" (*America netsu*) or because she had been overcome by an "uncontrollable desire to go abroad" (*yōkōbyō*), as some critics might argue, but because talking about the lifestyles of Western women would highlight something important about her country and be of help to her sisters. "The bad customs that have made us women suffer in the past centuries are being swept away," she said, "and theories on the reformation of women's status and education have gained credit. At the same time, the use of Western clothes and hairstyles has increased." This progress for women was something to rejoice in, for, Fukuoka made clear, women's progress was always linked to social advancement (*wareware fujin ippan no tame, mata shakai no tame*), so much so that she believed "the main starting point for social reforms are women." It was so because women's duties were to marry, take care of the household, help their husbands, entertain relations, and, when mothers, teach their children. Yet motherhood was not a good reason to keep women at home, as had happened in the past. People were surprised when Millicent Fawcett and other Western women surpassed some male colleagues in their fields. These women had managed to do so because of their husbands' support, and "it is thanks to this kind of husband that such women arise, while it is these circumstances [intelligent women and supportive husbands] that make parity of rights a reality." So, Fukuoka implied, Japanese husbands' perceptions of their wives' worth had to change if women were to find suitable occupations. Would this development simply favor women? England (where Fawcett was born) was "a wealthy

32. Ōmizo Kichizō, *Jogaku enzetsushū* (Collection of public speeches on women's education) (Isogai shobō, 1888); Nakai Tatsu, ed., *(Tottori fujinkai) enzetsu hikki* (Transcription of the public speeches of the Tottori Women's Group) (Tottori: Nakai Tatsu, 1888). In Nakai's volume two speeches dealt with child rearing and education, and one discussed the custom of despising women and revering men. The names of the 117 members of the group were listed at the end of the volume. I could not find information about Nakai, but another member of the group was Ozawa Saki 小沢咲 (1863–1948), a graduate of Tottori Women's Normal School. In 1887 the Christian Tottori eiwa jogakkō was founded (it closed in 1902), and a year later this group started raising funds to open Tottori jogakkō, where Ozawa worked as a teacher. Kaneda Susumu, ed., *Tottori-ken hyakketsuden: Kindai hyakunen* (One hundred eminent lives in Tottori prefecture: One hundred years of the modern period) (Tottori: San'in hyōronsha, 1970), 211–17.

country with a strong army who has no enemy in the world." There were various reasons for England's success, Fukuoka argued, but the determination, nobility, and education of its women were some of the most important.[33] Thus, "if we want our country to become the England or North America of the East, we have to find a way to reform motherhood, for mothers are the ones that teach the customs of our people. To do so, we cannot halt women's education at a basic level but have to allow women to obtain a higher or university education," a possibility available in other countries. Thus, Fukuoka's domestic feminism consisted of maintaining women's roles within the home while enhancing women's public positions for the good of the nation. If Japan wanted to become an enlightened country, she argued, women had to be educated, obtain more social rights, and therefore gain a public position. Fukuoka was lending her voice to the discourse on women's education we have seen in the previous two chapters, but she was also helping to enlarge the limits of such discourse, for in her opinion obtaining a higher or even university education also meant being able to aspire to different, more prestigious kinds of employment. For example, she mentioned that in Europe and North America there were female doctors, students of science and law, women elected to local assemblies, and women who were employed as clerks in law courts. The fact that a Frenchwoman had even been employed by the French Ministry of Education was, Fukuoka argued, "a steppingstone in the history of the advancement of women's rights."[34]

Finally, given the growing number of women making speeches, it is only logical that a book such as *Fujin enzetsu shinan* 婦人演説指南 (Instructions for Women Making Public Speeches, 1887) should have appeared. It contained advice for women speakers and stressed the necessity of presenting oneself as a modest person and choosing the order of the various points in one's presentation and the right register to use. The language used in a public speech, the author pointed out, was important because through its proper use the speaker could make the audience experience different emotions. Speakers should read newspapers in order to have material for their *enzetsu*, remember what parts of a speech the public appreciated and use them again, and be prepared to answer direct criticism at *enzetsukai.*[35]

33. Fukuzawa Yukichi made a similar comment in "On Japanese women," serialized in his newspaper, *Jiji shinpō*, in 1885. He stated, "Because it will be impossible to expect women today to bring forth a posterity of better physique, our first necessity is to make our women more active mentally and physically. To make them more active, they must be given more responsibilities and more enjoyments." Kiyooka Eiichi, ed. and trans., *Fukuzawa Yukichi on Japanese Women: Selected Works* (Tokyo: University of Tokyo Press, 1988), 36.
34. Fukuoka Teruko, *Joshi dokuritsu enzetsu hikki* (Transcription of the public speech on women's independence) (Nisshindō, 1888). The book was publicized in *Jogaku zasshi*, no. 108, 05.05.1888, 24.
35. Kagawa Rinzō. *Fujin enzetsu shinan* (Instructions for women making public speeches) (Osaka: Shinshindō, 1887).

During the early Meiji period the print market expanded to include not only numerous books for women written by men and novels written by women but also new "genres" in which women were active as writers and speakers. Although some contemporary critics and intellectuals did not like the idea of women becoming public figures, especially when speaking in public, there was a growing interest in women making speeches; they were acknowledged in the print media, represented in novels written by men (chapter 5), and supported by a publishing industry providing for a female readership.

Women's Discourses

What were the discourses women initiated and participated in when attending the meetings of these groups? Here I deal mostly with those that relate to the shaping of a (domestic) feminist discourse and focus specifically on the Kyōfūkai because of the abundance of material on this group. These discourses were not in contraposition, but rather complementary, to those I introduced in the chapters that focus on female education and political rights.

Temperance

In the first speech she made after arriving in Japan, Mary Leavitt argued that people who drank alcohol would die early because of the various physical problems it caused. This was a social problem that afflicted rich as well as poor classes, and it was shocking to see that Japan had even started importing foreign liquors. As women raised children they could influence the opinions of the next generation, and that was why women should take an active part in the fight, talking about this matter with everybody. Tobacco, too, was a social problem that affected men as well as women, and, whereas in North America few women smoked, in Japan many had acquired this bad habit.[36] Although alcohol and tobacco were not considered by Japanese women to be the most important "evils" to fight in Japanese society, Leavitt's was, nevertheless, a topical speech. Here was a woman who had come to tell Japanese women that they should start speaking up in public, without worrying about the audience's social class, since the feminine qualities they possessed were those that could reform Japanese society. This corroborated the Protestant message many had already received in schools and churches, namely, that women were more pious and pure than men.[37] Japanese women's opinions on the position of Western

---

36. *Jogaku zasshi*, no. 31, 05.08.1886, 1–3; no. 32, 15.08.1886, 21–22.
37. On the ideological influence of Protestantism on the American WCTU, see Rumi Yasutake, "Transnational Women's Activism: The Woman's Christian Temperance Union in Japan and the United States," in *Women and Twentieth-Century Protestantism*, edited by Margaret Lamberts Bendroth and Virginia Lieson Brereton, 93–112 (Champaign: University of Illinois Press, 2002).

women in their countries shifted from idealization (they are equal to their husbands, they talk about politics with them, they are well educated, they participate in public society) to the recognition that Western and Japanese women led lives that were not so dissimilar. Although for some who went to listen to what Leavitt had to say Western women's realities had nothing in common with theirs, and they therefore remained "foreigners," for others Leavitt was speaking of familiar problems. Alcoholism had wrecked more than a few Japanese women's lives, not least that of Yajima Kajiko, the head of the Kyōfūkai, and they could identify common ground in Leavitt's speech, as well as common future goals.

The Meiji Empress

Fujitani has written that during the late Meiji period the women of the imperial family emerged as public figures, supporting their husbands.[38] This process had already started in the early Meiji period. Clara Whitney, for example, wrote in 1878 that the empress "is exceedingly intelligent and is so anxious to cultivate virtue and good deeds that she has collected all the notices of good deeds and qualities among her subjects—especially women—and has published them in three volumes as an incentive to great exertions."[39]

The figure of the empress seems to have been a powerful one for Japanese women to use. A text outlining the aims of the Kyōfūkai signed by Yajima Kajiko stated that the Meiji emperor had bestowed freedom and the possibility of enjoying equal rights to the people, which had never been granted by the emperors of the past. However, "[F]rom ancient times, because of the practice of respecting men and despising women, women have been used by men in various ways." A new period had begun in which women were valued, the text continued, and this was thanks to the benevolence of the emperor and empress. There were plenty of evil practices and habits that afflicted women in the private and public ways of socializing and in relation to hygiene, education, and employment. With the benevolence of the emperor and empress, their duty was to quickly eradicate them.[40] By marking

---

38. One reason for the empress's "appearance" in public life was the emulation of European monarchies, where monarchs and their consorts were often seen together in public. Fujitani Takashi, *Splendid Monarchy: Power and Pageantry in Modern Japan* (Berkeley: University of California Press, 1996), 183.

39. M. William Steele and Tamiko Ichimata, eds., *Clara's Diary: An American Girl in Meiji Japan* (Kodansha International, 1979), 201. The volume Clara mentioned was probably *Meiji kōsetsuroku* 明治孝節録 (An account of filial piety and integrity during the Meiji period), a collection of biographies of virtuous men and women compiled in 1877 and consisting of four volumes. Midori Wakakuwa, "The Gender System of the Imperial State," *U.S.-Japan Women's Journal* 20–21 (2001): 27–30.

40. *Jogaku zasshi*, no. 70, 06.08.1887, 190–92. The statement was also published in *Chōya shinbun*, no. 4148, 06.08.1887, 3.

a distinction between the past and the present, Yajima was arguing that women should become active and change the society in which they lived also because of the unchallengeable support the emperor and empress had demonstrated in favor of women's involvement.

Wakamatsu Shizuko, who played an important part in the life of Ferris jogakuin and participated in students' literary societies, writing about them in *Jogaku zasshi*, was also involved at some level in the Kyōfūkai. In 1895 she wrote an essay entitled "Our Beloved Empress," which described the differences between past and present emperors as follows. "It is with feelings of deep joy that we realize in this gradual change the fact that our Sovereign and his worthy Consort live very much nearer to the hearts of the people than did any of their illustrious ancestors." While this was a general statement about the relationship between the emperor and the people, in 1868, Wakamatsu continued, people believed that the emperor had chosen the future empress as his consort because of "her high character and unusual attainments, rather than her personal beauty." Theirs was a happy union, and the empress had been "invited to go up the stairs of the Shishinden, the august Audience Hall, where the Mikado of old used to administer public affairs, and where no female had yet set foot." However, she was also a good wife, anticipating "every wish of her sovereign lord," and did not want any of the maids of the household "to do him the slightest service" when she herself was there. And she was always interested in social matters, from questions related to rice crops to diplomatic issues.[41] This was the portrait of a person who, in her private as well as her public role, was seen to embody all the good qualities a woman should have. Like Miss Milliken at Joshi gakuin, who washed dishes between lectures on Tennyson, or Wakamatsu's model woman, who would give her domestic work to someone else if she had literary abilities that were worth cultivating, the empress was not defined by her personal appearance, and her proper place was not only within "the home" as a mother and wife. Her official role as *the* model of educated womanhood working for her society, for example, rolling bandages for the Red Cross during the Sino-Japanese War or supporting women's education, was as important as her private one.[42] In her case, "going public" was not a reprehensible action; on the contrary, she was perceived to be working for her nation while bringing forth a different model of woman and wife.

Wakamatsu's only regrets about the imperial family were that it was not "blessed with any issue, and that according to the custom of the country his Impe-

---

41. Iwamoto Yoshiharu, ed., *In Memory of Mrs. Kashi Iwamoto with a Collection of Her English Writings* (Jogaku Zasshisha, 1896), 11–18 (in English).
42. Ibid., 22. A woodblock triptych of Empress Haruko and her ladies-in-waiting rolling Red Cross bandages during the Sino-Japanese War is reproduced in Dorothy Robins-Mowry, *The Hidden Sun: Women of Modern Japan* (Boulder: Westview Press, 1983), 32–33.

rial Majesty is unable to give undivided attention to his noble consort." Concubines were a necessary presence only when the continuation of the family line was at risk, which in the case of the imperial family was considered a question of supreme importance. By describing the behavior of the emperor in this way, Wakamatsu seems to imply that there was no reason for common Japanese people to have concubines. She also said, "Religion, we mean *the* Religion, will have a hard fight against the national usage handed down from centuries, before this source of grief shall disappear."[43]

Marriage and the Home

Fujitani has also argued that the publicity around the celebrations of the imperial marriage was a way for the government to emphasize the value of marriage as a sacred institution since during the early Meiji period, when legal and moral restrictions on divorce were slim, the divorce rate was quite high.[44] "Marriage" and "family composition" were important topics for missionaries, who taught their students that the family was based on Christian love, and the Christian home was the place where husband and wife worked together to make that union fruitful, following God's teachings and transmitting them to their children. By stating this, they were always, even if not openly, marking their opposition to all the "evil customs," as they termed them, that were so widespread in Japanese society such as concubinage and arranged marriages that were done for the sake of the family's fortunes. These topics were also taken up by the men and women who wanted to reevaluate their position within Japanese society, many of whom were members of the Kyōfukai.

For example, in the text outlining the aims of the Kyōfukai signed by Yajima Kajiko, women were urged "to assist their husbands in the home and to help men in the world," for it was their responsibility to "work in public and private life (*naigai kōshi*)" and create good relationships between husbands and wives since many evils were born within the family. Some bad customs had been caused by women's behavior, but women also had to accept them because they were traditionally rooted

43. Iwamoto, *In Memory*, 15. The Imperial House Law, drafted in 1886 by Itō Hirobumi, had the intent of protecting the emperor system "from political change and to ensure the permanency of the imperial family." It made it legal for the emperor to have more than one wife. Wakakuwa, "The Gender System," 17–18. Sakatani Shiroshi, a member of Meirokusha, argued that there were men who cited the emperor's example as support for keeping concubines. He condemned them for trying to disguise their misconduct while not understanding the difference between theirs and the emperor's position. "On Concubines," *Meiroku zasshi*, issue 32, March 1875, translated in Braisted, *Meiroku Zasshi*, 398.
44. Fujitani, *Splendid Monarchy*, 187–88. Fuess contests those numbers during the 1880s and 1890s. Harald Fuess, *Divorce in Japan: Family, Gender, and the State, 1600–2000* (Stanford: Stanford University Press), 2004, 120–3.

in Japanese society. Women had to fight prostitution, alcohol, and tobacco, which were destroying their families and weakening the country.[45]

Intellectuals were stating that women needed to become educated in order to help in the development of their nation, but Yajima was arguing that corruption, the use of alcohol, and the restrictions placed on women were hindering progress in achieving this goal. If women remained ignorant, or if their homes were awash with "evils," or again if they were not allowed to make full use of their abilities, how could they be expected to educate the next generation, be virtuous, and work for their nation? It was not possible for women to become household managers only in relation to their children and helpers; women had to be able to criticize their husbands' behavior and request change. By incorporating government ideologies in their discourses, but also by arguing that certain practices were not only detrimental to women but also to their nation's interests, they were articulating a nationalistic feminist ideology.

Rev. Tamura Naoomi, a Christian who had studied in North America and the husband of Mineo Eiko, a graduate of Sakurai and a student at Elmira College in New York, wrote two books, in 1889 and 1893, about the different ways the family was considered in North America and Japan.[46] He argued that in America marriages were based on love, whereas in Japan people married only to have children and thus continue the family name. The Japanese father was considered the highest authority, and women did not have to learn about relations with the male sex before marriage. Mothers taught girls that they were inferior to boys, that they should not be talkative, and that they had to obey their parents-in-law. Girls were separated from boys from childhood, had little chance to interact with them, and had no reason to be educated in politics, literature, or other subjects since they were not supposed to discuss such things. Tamura considered these practices to be deleterious to Japanese society and supported the American and Christian way of viewing male-female relations in which women were highly educated and were supposed to contribute to the formation of a happy family.

A similar opinion was held by Wakamatsu Shizuko, who wrote that "The English word 'home' is suggestive of all that makes sacred the name of motherhood and of the many and varied relations associated with the same." In Japan instead,

---

45. *Jogaku zasshi*, no. 70, 06.08.1887, 192, also published in *Chōya shinbun*, no. 4148, 06.08.1887, 3.

46. See Fujisawa Matoshi and Umemoto Junkō, eds., *Tamura Naoomi: Nihon no hanayome, Beikoku no fujin, shiryōshū* (Tamura Naoomi's *The Japanese Bride, American Women* and other related materials) (Ōzorasha, 2003); and Emily Anderson, "Tamura Naoomi's *The Japanese Bride*: Christianity, Nationalism, and Family in Meiji Japan," *Japanese Journal of Religious Studies* 34.1 (2007): 203–28. Mineo Eiko left for North America in 1887 with Sakurai Mineko, a student of Kyōritsu jogakkō, who was going to study at Syracuse University in New York. No information could be found in the archives of Syracuse University, but it is possible that Sakurai audited courses alongside regularly enrolled full-time students. Mineo's trip to North America was reported in *Jogaku zasshi*, no. 67, 16.07.1887, 144.

when a couple married they were united under one family name and became "joint guardians of that ancestral name and family prestige, their individual interests being of secondary importance." Thus, the wife was to become "common property of the house" rather than "the sole helpmate of her husband."[47]

For the members of the Kyōfukai, one of the major problems regarding family life was the existence of concubines, a presence that was possible not only because of old-fashioned customs but also because of the law. The *Shinritsu kōryō* 新律綱領 (Summary of New Stipulations), promulgated in 1870, had legally defined "the degree of relationship of certain categories of kin to a householder." It stated that the wife and concubines of the head of the household "were both placed in the second degree of kinship" vis-à-vis the male head of the household, giving them equal status under the law.[48] Even after the word *mekake* (concubines, mistresses) was erased in the revised Civil Code of 1882, and *mekake*'s legal recognition removed, that does not mean they ceased to exist.[49]

The most startling example of concerted action I have found regarding the issue of concubinage was a petition signed by eight hundred people and sent in 1889 to the Genrōin 元老院 (a national assembly that reviewed proposed legislation) to plead for the reform of "the family." Signatures came from all over Japan, and among those who signed it were Ueki Emori, Tsuda Sen, Ozaki Kōyō, Shimada Saburō 島田三郎, Tamura Naoomi, Shimizu Toyoko 清水豊子 (aka Shikin 紫琴, 1868–1933), and Ogino Ginko.[50] It is not clear who drafted this petition, and the petition itself seems to have been lost; what I found was an article written in *Jogaku zasshi* by Yuasa Hatsuko, Yajima's niece, which is probably if not the petition itself then something that comes very close to its main points. Having more than one "wife," it stated, was against nature because the number of women was less than that of men. Since the institution of marriage was there for men and women to love one another, if men had more than one wife the relationship between husband and wife would be destroyed; even the Mormons, who originally followed this practice, were now strictly forbidden from doing so. The relationship between husband and wife in upper-middle-class families where concubines were present was ruined because of the sexual needs of the husband and because the concubines wanted to

---

47. The same was true for men who married into their wives' families. Iwamoto, *In Memory*, 34–43.
48. Wakakuwa, "The Gender System," 20; Mary Louise Nagata, "Mistress or Wife? Fukui Sakuzaemon vs. Iwa, 1819–1833," *Continuity and Change* 18.2 (2003): 288–9.
49. Nagata states that there was no linguistic distinction between concubines and mistresses, and both were termed *mekake*, the difference being whether they lived with the man and his wife or not. Nagata, "Mistress or Wife?" 291.
50. *Jogaku zasshi*, no. 168, 29.06.1889, 300; no. 171, 20.07.1889, 384. Four women promoted it in Sapporo, and one of them was at Sumisu jogakkō. Their names and addresses were also reported to enable readers to contact them. *Hokkaido mainichi shinbun*, no. 577, 18.06.1889, 2. For other articles discussing the petition, see *Hokkaido mainichi shinbun*, no. 580, 21.06.1889, 3, and no. 586, 28.06.1889, 2; and *Jogaku zasshi*, no. 170, 13.07.1889, 28.

become rich and make their own children the heirs of the families.[51] Seeing this, the legitimate children could not grow up with sound moral examples and would bring this evil into the next generation. As the family was the basis of the country, if the family was not harmonious then Japan would regret the consequences. How could this situation be changed? It was necessary to legislate that illegitimate children could not become legitimate heirs. Unlike Buddhism and Confucianism, Christianity was a powerful tool in the formation of monogamous families. A second step was to legislate against adulterous relationships. The women and men who signed this petition wanted article 252 of the Penal Code, which stated that a wife committing adultery and her partner could be punished by up to two years of imprisonment and hard labor, to be changed. They wanted it to stipulate that if a husband or wife committed adultery each would be subject to the same punishment. Moreover, they wanted the government to define an "adulterous relationship" as a wife or husband having an extramarital relationship, a woman or man having a relationship with a married man or woman, and a husband having a concubine or entertaining himself with geishas or maidservants. Once a husband or a wife was found guilty of adultery, the couple should go to court and the guilty party should pay the other party a sum of money that should be no more than half of his or her property as compensation. Moreover, adultery would be considered sufficient grounds for divorce.[52]

Similar thoughts were probably entertained by previous generations of women as well, while some of this discussion echoed the debates on wives and concubines started by the male members of Meirokusha and published in *Meiroku zasshi* and *Jiji shinpō* in the 1870s and 1880s.[53] The difference between the Edo and Meiji periods was that Edo women were not empowered to make their thoughts public

51. Children of the wife were in the first degree of kinship to their father, whereas children of the *mekake* were in the third degree. Unless the wife could not give birth to a male son, the lawful heir of the family, the first male child of the wife, was the one who inherited the family fortune. Nagata, "Mistress or Wife?" 289. See also Katō Mihoko, "Shoshi seido kara mita Meiji zenki no hōsei saku" (The legislative policies of the early Meiji period as seen from the perspective of the system of illegitimate children), in *Kindai nihon no kazoku. Seisaku to hō* (The modern Japanese family: Policies and the law), edited by Fukushima Masao, 43–88, vol. 6 of *Kazoku. Seisaku to hō* (The family: Policies and the law) (Tokyo daigaku shuppankai, 1984), for a detailed study of these laws.

52. "Rinri no motoi no yōshi" 倫理の基の要旨 (Key points on "The Root of Moral Behavior"), *Jogaku zasshi*, no. 161, 11.05.1889, 30, reprinted in Nihon kirisutokyō fujin kyōfūkai, *Nihon kirisutokyō*, 62–65. Yuasa was also the editor of a book or pamphlet entitled "The Root of Moral Behavior," which was publicized in *Jogaku zasshi*, no. 161, 11.05.1889, 10. It dealt with issues related to the abolition of prostitution and male and female relations and was probably an expanded version of the article in *Jogaku zasshi*, but I could not find it. On Yuasa, see Kubushiro Ochimi, *Yuasa Hatsuko* (Ōzorasha, [1937] 1995).

53. Mori Arinori lamented the way husbands treated their wives as slaves. It was so barbaric, he stated, that children of concubines could be adopted as legal heirs if the wife failed to give birth to a male child. Mori Arinori, "On Wives and Concubines," *Meiroku zasshi*, issues 8 (May 1874, 104–5), 11 (June 1874, 143–5), 15 (August 1874, 189–191), and 20 (November 1874, 252–3), translated in William Braisted, *Meiroku Zasshi*. He also proposed a marriage contract in which if a spouse

or start a movement for the reformation of society while by the 1880s women were able to participate in male discussions about women's issues and shape the ways in which such issues were debated. The eight hundred signatories of the petition spelled out publicly that if women's roles were to change then so, too, must those of their husbands and the other women of the family. They wanted husbands to be prohibited from having sexual relationships outside the family unit, but they also claimed the right to be freed from marriage and allowed compensation in cases of adultery. The fact that Mary Crawford Fraser, the wife of Hugh Fraser, who headed the British legation in Tokyo, wrote about this petition in her letters shows how powerful this demand was and how successful the publicity devoted to the petition by the Japanese newspapers had been.[54]

Women did not obtain what they were hoping for. The Meiji Civil Code of 1898 recognized the needs and rights of the male head of household over and above every other member of his family. Specifically, it decreed that a marriage was legally recognized from the moment in which it was recorded in the family register. As for divorce, an adulterous wife could be prosecuted by her husband, but an adulterous husband could only be prosecuted by the husband of the adulterous woman. If he was sentenced for illicit sexual intercourse, then his wife could sue for and obtain a divorce. Divorce could also be initiated if the spouse had committed bigamy (articles 775 and 813). Furthermore, as Mackie states, there was no provision for alimony for the woman in case of divorce, and the father usually retained custody of his offspring.[55] Women remained unprotected under the Civil Code in other ways. Although the figure of the female head of household was recognized, especially when there was no alternative, it was also implied that such a woman would at some point marry. Her husband would become head of the household (article 736) and have the right to manage his wife's property (article 801). Women

---

had intimate relations with a third person or made the other spouse "suffer unbearably immoral treatment" the latter could sue and receive a monetary settlement together with a divorce. Ibid., issue 27, February 1875, 332. In "Nippon fujin ron" (On Japanese Women) which was serialized in *Jiji shinpō* in 1885, Fukuzawa Yukichi wrote, "In many Western countries, the divorce law is very strict. . . . It does not tolerate a husband divorcing his wife without proper reason. . . . When the husband is dissolute and has relations with another woman and brings her into the house where his legal family lives or keeps her secretly elsewhere, or if he is unkind and gives his wife no attention even though he lives with her—in such cases, the wife has the right to openly demand legal divorce in the court." Translated in Kiyooka, *Fukuzawa Yukichi*, 31.

54. The Society for the Correction of Morals was "preparing to petition the Government for a change of the laws relating to marriage, asking that unfaithfulness in a husband shall be punished as severely as the same crime in a wife, for which the penalties here are very heavy." Mary C. Fraser, *A Diplomat's Wife in Japan: Sketches at the Turn of the Century* (New York: Weatherhill, 1982), 38. News of the petition was reported in *Fukuoka nichinichi shinbun*, no. 3614, 22.12.1889, 1; and no. 3615, 24.12.1889, 1. *Shinonome shinbun*, 04.06.1889, published a similar version of the text presented. It is reprinted in Suzuki Yūko, *Nihon josei undō shiryō*, 87.

55. Vera Mackie, *Feminism in Modern Japan: Citizenship, Embodiment, and Sexuality* (Cambridge: Cambridge University Press, 2003), 24.

could not buy or sell property without the husband's consent (article 14), and if the husband died all of "his" property was to go to the male heir. As Mackie argues, under a system in which suffrage was dependent on the ownership of land, not having property rights and not being able to buy property meant that it was impossible for women to obtain political rights.[56]

These women failed to change the law, but, as Nagy reminds us, in 1919 some members of the commission established by Prime Minister Hara Kei 原敬 (1856–1921) to consider revision of the Civil Code supported measures that would have given women more rights within the family. They proposed requiring women's legal permission for the entry of illegitimate children into the household, making infidelity by the husband a cause for legal divorce and restricting the parental consent for marriage.[57] Early Meiji women's demands were based on sound arguments but were ahead of their time; some three decades later male scholars and politicians would discuss the proposals that had already been voiced by them.

The "prostitution discourse," however, needs to be considered from another angle as well. Prostitution, concubinage, and the way in which Japanese society should eradicate them were topics discussed in print by male intellectuals from the very beginning of the Meiji period because of their impact on hygiene, social morals, law, and international relations, while the petition discussed above shows that women addressed this issue in public and at length from 1888–89 onward.[58] Why were women's groups not involved in the issue of prostitution before 1889? To be sure, as Yuval-Davis and Anthias have put it, in every country "Women actively participate in the process of reproducing and modifying their roles as well as being actively involved in controlling other women," and this was no less true in Japan, since the petition and this chapter in general show that early Meiji women despised concubines and were in effect creating a discourse that addressed the concerns of their own class.[59] Yet, when in November 1890 Iwamoto Yoshiharu added a new column to *Jogaku zasshi* in order to discuss news related to the movement to abolish

56. Ibid., 23. Part of the Civil Code is reprinted in Yuzawa Yasuhiko, ed., *Nihon fujin mondai shiryō shūsei* (Sources on the "woman's problem" in Japan), vol. 5, *Kazoku Seido* (The family system) (Domesu shuppan, 1976), 239–276.

57. Margit Maria Nagy, "'How Shall We Live?': Social Change, the Family Institution, and Feminism in Prewar Japan," PhD diss., University of Washington, 1981, 198–218.

58. To give but a couple of examples, Tsuda Mamichi criticized the "bad custom" (*akufū*) of prostitution in 1869. The Maria Luz incident of 1872 led to a great deal of discussion about the difference between slavery and prostitution and to an ordinance liberating prostitutes in 1872 that freed all indentured prostitutes and prohibited the buying and selling of people. See Sotozaki Mitsuhiro, *Meiji zenki fujin kaihō ronshi* (Theories on the movement for women's liberation during the early Meiji period) (Kochi: Kochi shiritsu shimin toshokan, 1963), 169–226; Sheldon Garon, *Molding Japanese Minds: The State in Everyday Life* (Princeton: Princeton University Press, 1997), 91.

59. Nira Yuval-Davis and Flora Anthias, "Introduction," in *Woman-Nation-State*, edited by Nira Yuval-Davis and Flora Anthias, 1–15 (New York: Macmillan, 1989), 11.

prostitution and other venues were opened for this purpose, women indeed became an important group in the movement. The reason why women did not participate in the "prostitution debate" before 1889 is that during the 1870s and 1880s prostitution was a "sensitive issue" for upper-middle-class women that could not be discussed in public. This seems to have been Ushioda Chiseko's 潮田千勢子 (1845–1903) implied reasoning.[60] In an interview published in *Fujo shinbun* in 1901, she stated, "The reform of social customs has to be done by women. Given that the basic element forming a society is the family, if we want to reform society it is necessary to start from the family. Women are the ones who have the power of influencing the family, so they are extremely important in inspiring social change." She then described the birth and work of the Kyōfūkai, and stated that, as a result of the efforts of its members, in 1900 the government had made it legal for prostitutes to freely leave their trade. That was something to rejoice about "for women and for our society."[61] She recalled that during the mid-1880s arguments against prostitution had been put forward and public speech meetings were organized on the subject. However, her feeling was that during the 1880s the time was not ripe for the movement to abolish prostitution. For example, Ushioda remembered, when an *enzetsu* was organized on the topic and Shimada Saburō and Ueki Emori gave interesting speeches, the audience was not inspired. Yet, when Shimada gave a speech based on the same notes some fifteen years later, the audience was moved. He noted that the same speech had elicited two completely different responses from the audience and stated that the reason for such different reactions was "timing" (*jiun*). The audience was more receptive to his arguments the second time, Shimada continued, because of the work carried out by the Kyōfūkai.[62]

60. Ushioda was the daughter of a physician from Ida domain. She was baptized in 1882, lost her husband in 1883, and moved to the capital with her five children soon after, where she enrolled in Sakurai jogakkō. She was a founding member of the Kyōfūkai, and in June 1889, with Sasaki Toyoju, she founded a group to discuss legal and government matters. *Fujin shinpō*, no. 35, 25.03.1900, 18–20; no. 75, 25.07.1903, 1–3, 7–9.

61. In 1872 the selling of women into prostitution was made illegal, but if one "wanted" to be a prostitute that "possibility" was legally recognized. Prostitution was legal only when carried out in licensed quarters such as the Yoshiwara in Tokyo. "Illegal" prostitutes did exist but, if found, could be arrested. Women were often sold to brothel owners by their families or guarantors who received a sum of money in exchange. That was considered an advance payment, and the woman was supposed to pay it back, together with any other expenses incurred on her behalf, by "working" in the brothel. Licensed prostitutes were to live and work inside brothels within the licensed quarters and were bound by their contracts to work until they had repaid the money. In 1900, the Rules Regulating Licensed Prostitutes (Naimushō rei, article 44, Shōgi torishimari kisoku 娼妓取締規則) and the Supreme Court recognized the right of prostitutes to freely cease working and invalidated the provisions of contracts that bound prostitutes to continue their trade. As Garon states, however, it remained difficult for them to leave the trade at will because of their debts, which in any case had to be repaid. Garon, *Molding Japanese Minds*, 712–13. See also Fujime Yuki, *Sei no rekishigaku* (A history of sexuality) (Fuji Shuppan, 1997).

62. Supplement to *Fujo shinbun*, no. 49, 08.04.1901, 1.

As Wakamatsu Shizuko pointed out, women were often made to share not only their husbands but also their homes with other women, and consenting to a concubine could have been a compromise whereby a woman would not be sent away for failing to give birth to an heir. Wakamatsu also wrote that "some barren women have even gone so far as to choose a mistress for their husbands."[63] Women were in large measure powerless against social customs and patriarchal dominance within their homes, and it is not difficult to understand why they would consider prostitutes and concubines responsible for their situation rather than attributing the cause of such "evil," as they termed prostitutes and prostitution, to patriarchal society. After all, the understanding that prostitutes are not enemies of upper-middle-class women but often the victims of patriarchy is a feminist concept women arrived at only a few decades ago. Only by 1890, and especially with the work of the Kyōfūkai, did upper-middle-class women, helped by women missionaries, start to address the problem from a different point of view. For example, during the early 1890s they opened a house in Tokyo, the Jiaikan 慈愛館 (Home of Mercy and Love), where former prostitutes could try to change their lives by learning a trade; the newly formed Zenkoku haishō dōmeikai 全国廃娼同盟会, a coalition of associations that promoted the abolition of prostitution, started organizing *enzetsukai* in Tokyo to promote its work; the magazine *Haishō* (Abolishing Prostitution), where women such as Asai Saku voiced their opinions, was published; and the Kyōfūkai published an article in the magazine of the association stating that poverty was also a reason why women ended up as prostitutes. By helping women to obtain proper work rather than pontificating against their moral behavior, the members of the Kyōfūkai could try to help them.[64]

Finally, the increase in the number of activities related to the abolition movement during the 1890s might also have been a way to overcome newly implemented legislation that prohibited women from participating in political meetings and political discourses while taking an active stance in discussions about topics that were at the core of government legislation concerning the value and rights of women.

---

63. Iwamoto, *In Memory*, 37. Enchi Fumiko 円地文子 (1905–86) presented this very situation at the beginning of her novel *Onnazaka* 女坂 (translated in English as *Waiting*), which is set in the Meiji period.

64. On the Jiaikan, see Manako Ogawa, "Rescue Work for Japanese Women: The Birth and Development of the Jiaikan Rescue Home and the Missionaries of the Woman's Christian Temperance Union, Japan, 1886–1921," *U.S.-Japan Women's Journal* 26 (2004): 98–133; and *Fujin kyōfū zasshi*, no. 8, 02.06.1894, 1–2. Ushioda stated that when *enzetsu* were held on the topic of the abolition of prostitution in 1886 she thought that such way of spreading ideas was praiseworthy but that it was also necessary to open a home to help women who had slipped into prostitution to get back on the right path. Supplement to *Fujo shinbun*, no. 49, 08.04.1901, 1. On the individual groups that composed the Zenkoku haishō dōmeikai, see Sotozaki, *Meiji zenki*, 212.

Employment

The new understanding of women's position in society and of the relationship between husband and wife was closely linked to the issues of women's employment and property rights, as is clear from the speech entitled "Fujin bunmei no hataraki" (Women's Enlightened Occupations) 婦人文明の働 given by Sasaki Toyoju at the second Jogaku enzetsukai. Women might have been working hard, Sasaki argued, but their jobs could not be called "enlightened occupations." They were managing households and raising children, but *bunmei no hataraki* were occupations in which women could make use of their intellect. The female doctor Kelsey who made a speech at the same *enzetsukai*, Sasaki continued, came from a country in which women worked as teachers, journalists, and telegraph operators, and many were members of Christian temperance groups. In Japan there were various schools for girls, but it was still not enough. She did not believe that Japan was an enlightened country, for Japanese people were simply following Western patterns and customs without understanding the deeper meaning of those customs. Another problem was that of prostitution. The area closest to Tokyo Imperial University was a red-light district. Could that be called an example of civilization? It was necessary to change this situation and fight the evil of prostitution.[65]

Sasaki criticized various practices that she did not consider *bunmei* and accused Japanese men and women of merely following the customs of the age in the hope that by doing so they would achieve something for themselves and for Japan. For some, *bunmei* were the activities held at the Rokumeikan or learning English, what Ebina Miya called *haikara* (high collar, fashionable), namely, everything that was styled after the West, and there were plenty of women supporting that way of life.[66] In Sasaki's view, this was deleterious not only to Japanese society in general but also to those girls and women who considered themselves part of an enlightened and progressive social group just because they were going to balls and meetings. By the mid-1880s Christian education and "westernization" were being criticized by

65. *Jogaku zasshi*, no. 63, 07.05.1887, 56; no. 65, 21.05.1887, 86–88. The political thinker Baba Tatsui recalled how male students of Keiō gijuku (those who were supposed to become the new generation of Meiji Japan) were spending their money and time with prostitutes and becoming ill. Murakami Nobuhiko, *Meiji joseishi* (History of Meiji women), vol. 2 (Rironsha, 1970), 63–64. Articles published in *Tokyo fujin kyōfū zasshi* were informing readers about new occupations and training courses available to foreign women. For example, one told of a new school opened in North America where girls were being trained as journalists. *Tokyo fujin kyōfū zasshi*, no. 7, 20.10.1888, 163.

66. See Ebina's interview in Nakajima Masukichi, ed., *Meien no gakusei jidai* (Famous ladies' school days) (Yomiuri shinbunsha, 1907), 73–79. Itō Umeko, the wife of Itō Hirobumi, was known for ordering dresses from Europe, learning English, and participating in the charity bazaars and costume balls of the Rokumeikan. Sharon Sievers, *Flowers in Salt: The Beginnings of Feminist Consciousness in Modern Japan* (Stanford: Stanford University Press, 1983), 93.

some Japanese intellectuals, and the government responded to such criticism also by changing the curricula of girls' schools. However, Sasaki was not condemning Christianity or westernization in general but the way in which these were being adopted without serious consideration, including by the government and its officials.

Moreover, by arguing that the low-paid jobs women typically held offered additional money to their families but could not solve women's problems, she was agreeing with those intellectuals who held that women should obtain an education as well as better employment because only then could they use their intellect, acquire public recognition, and earn good salaries. However, according to the members of the Kyōfukai, educated women's lives would not improve if their money was not protected by the law by making it the possession of the women who earned it and not of the men they married.

This was the topic of an article published in *Tokyo fujin kyōfū zasshi* in 1889. It argued that the main reason why women held little power in Japanese society was because they lacked property rights. That was caused by the law in general and by the unfairness of the inheritance law in particular, and it was necessary to redress this situation by allowing the legal practice of granting property to women that would remain theirs even after marriage.[67] In a public speech meeting two years before, Tamura Naoomi had strongly criticized those parents who wanted their daughters to be married as soon as possible and who did not value their education. Japanese intellectuals were always talking about *bunmei kaika* (civilization and enlightenment), but where was the enlightenment? There were men who thought, "That is a good woman, I want to marry her," and they would do so only to send her back to her family after a while, even without good grounds for divorce. Others would marry educated girls who had rich parents and after a couple of years divorce them and keep their money. It was necessary to give women property rights so that in case of divorce husband and wife would keep what was originally theirs.[68]

The home was the foundation of society, but how could women work for society when living in such homes? And if daughters were supposed to become the future mothers of Japan, how could they fulfill their roles when parents were not interested in their education but only in marrying them off as soon as possible?

67. *Tokyo fujin kyōfū zasshi*, no. 13, 20.04.1889, 12.
68. *Jogaku zasshi*, no. 61, 23.04.1887, 4–5; no. 62, 30.04.1887, 25–27. Fukuzawa Yukichi made a similar comment in "Nippon fujin ron" (On Japanese women) serialized in *Jiji shinpō* in 1885. He argued, "Even for a daughter of a good family, when she marries into another family and that family's fortune declines, there is no guarantee that she would not lose her own clothing and jewelry. In an extreme case, the husband may be a dissolute and vicious playboy, and he might empty his wife's closet and trunks, and in the end, contrive to divorce her. . . . As long as there is no law against it and the way is open for men, even if cruelty is not actually perpetrated, for women there is no true security and their safety will be a matter of accidental good fortune." Translated in Kiyooka, *Fukuzawa Yukichi*, 10–11. He also stated, "Among government officials, too, if there are to be new revisions in the Civil Law, give consideration to the problem of property ownership between a husband and a wife, or new regulations for marriage and divorce." Ibid., 31.

Tamura considered girls to be the "victims" of their families, which were practicing a socially accepted behavior that was harmful to the girls, and of men, who chose their wives frivolously or because of the wealth of their families. This state of affairs was possible because the law permitted it, so the solution was not only to change people's behavior but also to give women a legal status that would put an end to this situation. Some women during the early Meiji period tried to change existing legislation in order to obtain property rights so as to protect themselves, but Tamura's speech pointed to different reasons why women needed property rights. He argued that if women had rights this would curb the practices described above and Japanese society would become more civilized as a whole. People like Tamura were not only putting forward their requests with sound arguments but were also attacking those men who opposed women's rights because it was convenient for them.

The members of the Kyōfūkai were aspiring to the creation of a class of educated, intelligent women who would have a position in public society not only through philanthropic work but also through well-paid and valued jobs. These women had to be protected from unprincipled men, and even from their husbands, through legislation that would grant them female property rights and the right to divorce. These were the central tenets of the Kyōfūkai during the first years of its existence, but here the limitations of the group also become clear since at that point only upper-middle-class women could hope to obtain an education, earn more money, fight for property rights, and through all this try to reform society.

Conclusions

While most articles on public speeches published in early Meiji newspapers centered on male activities, a considerable number were about female public speeches. By the late 1880s, public speech making was no longer an overwhelmingly male activity but had been appropriated by women as well. In the same way, while male groups such as the Meirokusha tried to shape new institutions and practices to form a modern Japan, women also contributed to this process from within their *fujinkai*, which had been founded all over the country, by taking an interest in public questions and by allowing for a sociability between men and women that had not previously existed.

Similar to what Eger has argued in the case of English women, early Meiji women were not merely "icons of national pride." They were involved in the "process of definition taking place in new cultural institutions" while access to public spaces made women's activities also occasions for identity formation.[69] Women

---

69. Elizabeth Eger, "Representing Culture: *The Nine Living Muses of Great Britain* (1779)," in *Women, Writing, and the Public Sphere, 1700–1830*, edited by Elizabeth Eger, Charlotte Grant, Cliona O Gallchoir, and Penny Warburton, 104–32 (Cambridge: Cambridge University Press, 2006), 118.

7

participating in *fujinkai* started to take control of their own agendas and funds, to build their own networks, and to vote during the elections of committee members in their groups. These were activities that a small number of men could carry out from within their political associations and parties that excluded women, but regardless of whether women considered this a sufficient substitute, through their participation in *fujinkai* women were learning to be active citizens. These women initiated a process that blurred the distinctions between political institutions and spaces and the home.

That they were able to make demands and influence male behavior under the banner of "good wives, wise mothers," all the while avoiding openly violating the canons of upper-middle-class domesticity, is clear if we look at the following petition. In 1890 the first elections were held for the Diet, the popular assembly established for the first time under the Imperial Constitution of 1889. Women were left out, however, since the Law on Assembly and Political Associations (1890) restricted people's freedom of speech in general but also stipulated that women were barred from promoting (article 3) or, together with other social categories such as military men, policemen, teachers and students, participating in political meetings (article 4) and joining political associations (article 25).[70] Women were thus prohibited from attending the meetings of the newly opened Diet as auditors.

Reacting against this legislation, a group of twenty-one women, among whom Yajima Kajiko, Tokutomi Hisako, Sasaki Toyoju, Ogino Ginko, Yokoi Tamako, Takekoshi Takeyo, and Ushioda Chiseko, petitioned the Jiyūtō 自由党, a constitutionalist party opposed to absolutist government, to abolish the restriction.[71] The following is their petition.

> Having read that article 165 of the regulations of the Lower House stipulates that women are not allowed to attend sessions as auditors, we are feeling downcast. What can be the reason for such a decision? We have asked learned people how this regulation could have been passed, but we have not heard any reasonable explanation, and, feeling more distressed than ever, we hope that our grave misgivings will be allayed by asking you [the members of the Jiyūtō] for your valuable opinion.

70. The law (Shūkai oyobi seisha hō 集会及政社法) was a revised version of the Shūkai jōrei, promulgated in April 1880, which I discuss in chapter 5. It is reprinted in Matsumoto and Yamamuro, *Genron to media*, 447–50.
71. The petition was published in *Tokyo nichinichi shinbun*, 24.10.1890 (reprinted in Suzuki, *Nihon josei undō shiryō shūsei*, 129–30) and publicized in *Dai nihon fujin kyōikukai zasshi*, no. 21, 8.11.1890, 36. The latter is reprinted in Nihon joishi hensan iinkai, ed., *Nihon joishi* (History of Japanese women doctors) (Nihon joikai, 1991), 96–97. Shimizu Toyoko, reading an article in which it was suggested that women would be a distraction to the lawmakers, could not refrain from laughing. See "Naite aisuru shimai ni tsugu" 泣いて愛する姉妹に告ぐ (To my beloved sisters in tears), supplement to *Jogaku zasshi*, no. 234, 11.10.1890, 2, reported in Sievers, *Flowers in Salt*, 101.

The emperor, listening to the opinion of the people and submitting the affairs of the state to public debate, has devolved a considerable part of his authority. His wish to convene the Diet, which in our country is being attempted for the first time, is an act of extraordinary benevolence, and all the people are grateful for the emperor's divine virtue. The members of the Diet are chosen in accordance with the desire of the people, and it is extraordinary that those members work day and night to give substance to the emperor's desires and exert their strength to lead the people in accordance with the emperor's wishes. Although this is work undertaken out of your loyalty to His Majesty, what our 40,000,000 compatriots have been given is immense, and we have no words to convey our gratitude. We, as women, cannot do anything but cultivate ourselves skillfully, take care of the household economy, work for the well-being of our country, and comfort our brothers in their grief. We do all this because we are aware of our lot ordained by heaven, and, encouraging each other, we never stop learning. Although for some time we have been looking forward to this day so that we might, even if from the shadows, hear wise men talking and get a deeper sense of our duty, lately this horrible new rule has been promulgated stipulating that women, just because they are women, are prohibited from the glory of being admitted to the Diet as listeners. We weep tears at something deeply regrettable for our whole lives and we do not know what to do. . . . With the exception of people carrying weapons and drunkards, all are allowed to attend the Lower House sessions, including not only teachers and students but even stable boys, old men selling candy, and farmers. But we think it quite extraordinary that women, just because they are women, are excluded from taking part in its sessions, and our misgivings will not be assuaged. There surely is some reason for this decision, and we wish to hear your opinion so that we can dispel our gloom, reconcile ourselves to unchangeable circumstances, and at last console ourselves.

This was by no means the only reaction to such legislation. In *Jogaku zasshi* we find an editorial in which the writer (possibly Iwamoto Yoshiharu) argued that, although it was understandable that military men and teachers were excluded from participating in political activities, and although it was also possible to understand why women "were not supposed to enter the political world," this did not mean that women should not become educated in politics. After all, how were women supposed to support and help their husbands if they only knew things pertaining to household matters?[72] In another article published in *Jogaku zasshi* entitled "Naniyue ni joshi wa seidan shūkai ni sanchō suru to o yurusarezaruka" 何故に

---

72. *Jogaku zasshi*, no. 225, 09.08.1890, 1–2.

女子は、政談集会に参聴するとを許されざる乎 (Why Is It That Women Are Not Allowed to Participate in Political Meetings as Listeners?) Shimizu Toyoko decided to present the problem from a different perspective. She argued that "by adding the two characters for *women* to articles 4 and 24 of the Law on Assembly and Political Associations, we, twenty million women [living in Japan], have become crippled." Was that really necessary? Because of this decision, "[A]lthough we women live in this world, are human beings, and have spirits (*reikon*) and senses (*kan'no*), we have nevertheless all been put under the one category of *women* and because of this are deprived, even more than men, irrespective of social class, of the freedom to use our spirits and senses. What are the reasons for this decision?" While the government had to protect its people and preserve social order, it was the duty of male and female subjects to participate in discussions related to their country. "But if women are prohibited by law from attending political meetings that are important for the people, is this really the way for the government to achieve the goal of protecting people's rights and developing their knowledge?" Some people thought that if women busied themselves with political matters they would neglect their duties of child rearing and housework; that, Sasaki stated, was absurd.[73]

To be sure, these were all expressions of dissatisfaction with the newly issued legislation, but the petition translated above is significant for several other reasons. Although it is not clear who wrote it, it was obviously a concerted action; those women sat down, probably with male sympathizers, and decided to oppose a piece of government legislation through the only means they had at their disposal, their voices. The phrase "women, just because they are women, are prohibited" shows that this was a reasoned reaction to discriminatory legislation and a feminist protest. Furthermore, Zaeske has cited women's signatures as an example of women attempting to influence national policy as a group. The twenty-one women who signed the petition, together with the eight hundred men and women who signed the earlier petition for the reformation of the concept of family, came from all over Japan, and their signatures were a visible sign that they considered themselves rightful citizens rather than just subjects accepting what was imposed on them. As Zaeske has argued, when married women signed petitions they defied not only the general assumption that women did not need to express their political opinions but also that there was no need for women to speak independent of their husbands.[74] Theirs was a public act geared toward changing a political decision, and their ability to respond immediately as a group to what they considered unjust was proven.

True, the Civil Code of 1898 did not give women legal authority in marriage, nor were they granted property rights, but what early Meiji women did achieve

73. *Jogaku zasshi*, no. 228, 30.08.1890, 5–8.
74. Susan Zaeske, *Signatures of Citizenship: Petitioning, Antislavery, and Women's Political Identity* (Chapel Hill: University of North Carolina Press, 2003), 12, 108.

and pass on to the next generation were the ability to organize themselves around issues of common concern and the possibility of establishing a dialogue with intellectuals and institutions, even if not on equal terms. Petitions had been used during the Edo period to protest against what were perceived to be unjust decisions, but, as Roberts has written, during the Meiji period petitioners "gave a new and a truly modern meaning to this old form of political activity by publishing their petitions, ostensibly addressed to the emperor or the government, but really as a vehicle for forming public opinion."[75] In this case, they won on both counts; not only did they manage to influence public opinion, but they were also soon allowed to attend the meetings of the Diet.

75. Luke Roberts, "The Petition Box in Eighteenth-Century Tosa," *Journal of Japanese Studies* 20.2 (1994): 456.

5

Women's Political Participation

What would happen if women [in Japan] joined political associations or engaged in political discussions? Family education would be hindered terribly. . . . If they are allowed to join political associations, they will neglect their duties as women (*joshi no honbun*). Such a situation would greatly disturb household management, as well as harm family education.

—Kiyoura Keigo 清浦奎吾,
*chief of the Home Ministry's Police Bureau
and later prime minister, 1890[1]*

Analyzing early Meiji women's political activities and opinions means highlighting the opportunities women had to make political statements, to work politically at the local level, and to politicize their existences in the public sphere. "Women's involvement in political activities" did not mean that there was a *national* women's movement fighting for political rights or political participation in the same way that there was no national male movement. As Japan was still characterized by great regional diversity, which also manifested itself in the political arena, it makes sense to examine, as far as the sources allow, the activities of groups of women working in different geographic areas, which were often strongly influenced by the male-centered Jiyū minken undō (Movement for Freedom and Popular Rights), rather than trying to form a national picture of women's political activities, which did not exist.

---

1. First Diet, Lower House, 01.03.1890, in Dai nihon teikoku gikaishi kankōkai, ed., *Dai nihon teikoku gikaishi* (Records of the Imperial Diet of Greater Japan), vol. 1 (Dai nihon teikoku gikaishi kankōkai, 1926), 1049, 1058, translated in Sheldon Garon, *Molding Japanese Minds: The State in Everyday Life* (Princeton: Princeton University Press, 1997), 119.

Women's involvement in politics during the early Meiji period came about in different ways. Some met famous female or male political activists, others were part of women's groups whose activities grew out of their husbands' participation in the Movement for Freedom and Popular Rights, while others regarded political rights as part of their quest for women's advancement.

What did "involvement in politics" mean for the early Meiji women presented here? For some, the goal was the right to vote. For the majority, it meant the possibility of becoming members of political associations, of participating in political discussions, of collecting funds for male political activities, of supporting local reading rooms opened by the Movement for Freedom and Popular Rights, of publishing small-scale journals featuring their opinions on political matters, and of discussing female political rights abroad.

There are two main reasons why I did not include political activities among the "topics" discussed by early Meiji women presented in chapter 4, writing instead a separate chapter. First of all, with the notable exception of the Kyōfūkai, whose petitions provide us with some of the most striking examples of Meiji period women's ability to influence political decisions through public actions, I have not found among the *fujinkai* covered in chapter 4 groups clearly stating that they were interested in "political education" or "political participation." Second, the terms used by the women presented here in their groups' statements and their speeches often differed from those used by the women discussed earlier; these women used the same gendered words, but in addition we also find in these groups' statements phrases such as "equal rights between men and women," *danjo dōken* 男女同権, or "women's rights," *joken* 女権. Only a few women explained what they meant when they used such expressions, so I decided to take them to also mean *"political* rights for women" only when their speeches or writings allowed for it. For example, when Kishida Toshiko wrote, "In the West, in order to win political rights women are actively engaged in various movements such as submitting petitions to their parliament. Undoubtedly they will soon win the right to participate in politics and make equal rights between men and women a reality," it is clear that for her equal rights included political rights as well.[2] In most cases, however, women used such terms in a wider context. Given that words such as "parity" or "equality" of rights were often used in tandem with requests for more education, employment opportunities, and free spaces in which to confront and debate ideas with other women and men, I assumed these terms to mean precisely that, the acknowledgment of women's legal disabilities in various fields and their active participation in redressing their situation. Even so, given that most of the women presented below used such terms while

2. Kishida Toshiko, "To My Fellow Sisters," (*Dōhō shimai ni tsugu*) published in installments in *Jiyū no tomoshibi* in 1884, translated in Mikiso Hane, *Reflections on the Way to the Gallows: Rebel Women in Prewar Japan* (Berkeley: University of California Press, 1988), 17. This article is discussed in more detail below.

participating in political activities, it is important to recognize the political nuances attached to them. Sekiguchi provides us with proof of this. She argues that during the Edo period the term *joken* was used to define the (political) power of court ladies. By 1873 the English word *gynecocracy* was translated as *onna seiji* (women's government) and *joken* (power of women). The elimination of this power, Sekiguchi continues, was considered necessary by Meiji oligarchs, who did not want to replicate the errors of their political predecessors. Although by 1877, when Ozaki Yukio 尾崎行雄 translated Herbert Spencer's *Social Statics* (1851) under the title *Kenri teikō* 権理提綱 (Outline of Civil Rights), *joken* was used to render the English expression "the rights of women," the word itself never lost its political power.[3]

What distinguishes most of these women from those presented in the previous chapters is the fact that they reelaborated the "domestic feminism" ideology discussed in chapter 4. Women had to become good companions for their husbands and good teachers for their sons and work for the betterment of their country in public society, but the knowledge they had to acquire in order to succeed in this task also included knowledge about political developments, and this knowledge could be acquired only through participation in political activities.

Before proceeding, two additional caveats are necessary. First, given that the political activities and opinions of Kishida Toshiko (1861–1901) and Kageyama Hideko (aka Fukuda Hideko, 1865–1927) have been extensively discussed elsewhere, I introduce them here only when they are relevant to a discussion of other women's activities and opinions.[4] Second, although women participated in political *agitation* before and after the Meiji Restoration, I consider here only those women who were driven by the gendered dimension of their activities in the political sphere and tried to change the patriarchal society in which they lived. I do not, therefore, look at female involvement in peasant and other uprisings, for which, so far as I could ascertain, this was not the case.

The Creation of New Political Spaces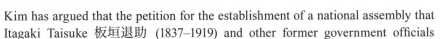

Kim has argued that the petition for the establishment of a national assembly that Itagaki Taisuke 板垣退助 (1837–1919) and other former government officials

---

3. Sumiko Sekiguchi, "Gender in the Meiji Renovation: Confucian 'Lessons for Women' and the Making of Modern Japan," *Social Science Japan Journal* 11.2 (2008): 201–21.
4. Most recently on Kishida, see Noriko Sugano, "Kishida Toshiko and the Career of a Public-Speaking Woman in Meiji Japan," in *The Female as Subject: Reading and Writing in Early Modern Japan*, edited by P. F. Kornicki, Mara Patessio, and G. G. Rowley, Michigan Monograph Series in Japanese Studies, no. 70 (Ann Arbor: Center for Japanese Studies, University of Michigan, 2010), 171–89. Hane has translated part of Fukuda Hideko's autobiography in *Reflections*, 34–50. See also Sharon Sievers, *Flowers in Salt: The Beginnings of Feminist Consciousness in Modern Japan* (Stanford: Stanford University Press, 1983), chap. 3. Vera Mackie, *Feminism in Modern Japan: Citizenship, Embodiment, and Sexuality* (Cambridge: Cambridge University Press, 2003), ch. 2.

presented to the government in 1874 was the first attempt to mobilize public opinion in order to challenge the legitimacy of the Meiji state. To be sure, a great deal of political discussion on this topic was carried out in the press and among the members of male groups.[5]

From as early as 1871 the authorities tried to control public opinion with the various Newspaper Regulations that censored the discussion of political topics in print and inflicted penalties on those who did not comply. Furthermore, during these years only the opinions of intellectuals and members of the wealthier classes survived in print because they had the means of creating and participating in new public spaces in which to debate what was best for Japan. They were also the only individuals with the prospect of political participation, for even those who were in favor of a popularly elected assembly did not intend to give *all* male citizens political rights. As Soejima Taneomi 副島種臣 (1828–1905), Gotō Shōjirō 後藤象二郎 (1838–1897), and Itagaki Taisuke put it in 1874, "[W]e do not propose that the franchise should at once be made universal. We would only give it in the first instance to samurai and the richer farmers and merchants, for it is they who produced the leaders of the revolution of 1868."[6] For these reasons, at this early stage women's chances of gaining political rights were negligible, but their exclusion from political discussion was not total, as the following examples show.

In 1874 Itagaki Taisuke and others founded the political groups Risshisha 立志社 (Self-Help Society) and Risshi gakusha 立志学舎 (Self-Help School) in Kochi, where students read original texts written by John Stuart Mill, Jeremy Bentham, and Bertrand Russell.[7] In 1876 the Risshisha started organizing public speech meetings in Kochi, and soon it was reported that at these meetings the number of seats allocated to women was insufficient. The members of the group wondered whether to increase it.[8]

A woman who attended some of those speeches was Kusunose Kita, who by 1878 was the legal head of her family. Laws regulated that men who were heads of families could vote in ward assemblies, but this did not apply to women. Probably also because of the speeches she heard there, Kusunose decided to write to the prefectural office in Kochi and to the Ministry of Home Affairs asking why, if a

5. For an analysis of the petition and the discussions that followed, see Kyu Hyun Kim, *The Age of Visions and Arguments: Parliamentarianism and the National Public Sphere in Early Meiji Japan* (Cambridge, Mass.: Harvard University Press, 2007), 134; see also chapter 3. The petition and other documents related to the establishment of a national assembly are translated in David J. Lu, *Japan: A Documentary History—the Late Tokugawa Period to the Present* (London: M. E. Sharpe, 1997), 326–7.

6. Translated in Walter W. McLaren, ed., *Japanese Government Documents*, vol. 42, part 1, of *Transactions of the Asiatic Society of Japan* (London: Kegan Paul, 1914), 445.

7. Mita Munesuke, ed. *Jiyū to minken* (Freedom and popular rights), vol. 5 of *Meiji no gunzo* (The Meiji group) (San'ichi shobō, 1968), 195–99.

8. Miyagi no joseishi kenkyūkai, ed., *Miyagi no joseishi* (Miyagi women's history) (Sendai: Kahoku shinpōsha, 1999), 381.

woman who was head of her family was supposed to pay taxes, she was not allowed to vote.[9] As an additional example, the socialist Kinoshita Naoe 木下尚江 (1869–1937) recalled in his autobiography the time in his childhood when he attended public lectures at a local temple. He stated, "At that time the laws concerning public assembly were not in effect, and women and children could freely attend these lecture meetings. My grandmother used to say, 'These lectures are so energetic, they are much more fun than the priest's boring sermons.' So she took me almost every time there was a meeting."[10]

The number of women who attended political meetings rose with the introduction of prefectural assemblies, and their presence was recorded in the newspapers.[11] The government chose to give the right to vote or be elected in local elections to a small percentage of men while starting to educate the populace about how to be active participants in national politics. Newspaper articles on women's presence at political meetings prove that women, too, were getting an education in local politics. Furthermore, scholars have uncovered examples of female heads of households who were given the right to vote and be elected in local assemblies during the same years, explaining that this was mainly due to the fact that among the members of those assemblies there were men linked to the Movement for Freedom and Popular Rights who had taken a confrontational stand against the government.[12] Such rights were soon withdrawn when the central government decided that only men who paid a certain amount of taxes could vote in local elections.

If a handful of women were allowed to vote, and if some could listen to male debates in prefectural assemblies, others also started to take an active political stance. In 1880 the *Tokyo Yokohama mainichi shinbun* reported that, like the Frenchwomen who had helped men during the French Revolution, women in Tsuwano, Shimane prefecture, were raising money to meet the expenses men would incur when the Diet opened. It also added that in February, when the Jinsetsusha 尽節社, a society formed by people who were supporting the opening of the Diet, was founded in

9. *Tokyo nichinichi shinbun*, 31.01.1879, reprinted in Suzuki Yūko, ed., *Nihon josei undō shiryō shūsei* (Sources on the Japanese women's movement), vol. 1, *Shisō seiji* (Political thought) (Fuji shuppan, 1996), 55; *Osaka Nippō*, no. 883, 26.01.1879, 2–3. Most of her letter is translated in Hiroko Tomida, *Hiratsuka Raichō and Early Japanese Feminism* (Leiden: Brill, 2004), 63–65.

10. Kinoshita Naoe, *Zange* (Confessions) (1906), translated in Kim, *The Age of Visions*, 225.

11. Women could attend the prefectural assembly in Aichi (*Yokohama mainichi shinbun*, 05.06.1879, reprinted in Suzuki, *Nihon josei undō shiryō shūsei*, 52) and the ward assembly in Kanda (*Chōya shinbun*, 10.09.1880, reprinted in Suzuki, *Nihon josei undō shiryō shūsei*, 53), and thirty-two women had recently participated for the first time in the prefectural assembly in Fukuoka (*Fukuoka nichinichi shinbun*, no. 1370, 17.04.1884, 2).

12. See Ōki Motoko, *Jiyu minken undō to josei* (The Movement for Freedom and Popular Rights and women) (Domesu shuppan, 2003), 87; Satō Ken'ichi, "Joshi sanseiken o meiki shita Meiji jūsannen no 'Nagamachi mura sonkai kisoku'" (The 1880 village regulation of Nagamachi mura that specified women's voting rights), *Shishi sendai* 1 (1992): 47; and Ichihara Masae, *Shizuoka onna hyakunen* (One hundred years of Shizuoka women's history) (Domesu, 1982), vol. 1, 8.

Gunma prefecture, one Matsushima Jū 松島ぢう, who was nineteen, had donated five yen to help meet the expenses of the association.[13] During the years 1882 and 1883 newspapers also reported instances in areas such as Gunma and Chiba prefectures in which women either wanted to become or were accepted as members of the Jiyutō.[14]

I could not find anything more about these women, nor where the money they donated came from, but even these short mentions present examples of women who were visible in public spaces in which men discussed politics and participated in activities that were not prohibited to them. What they lacked during the early 1870s was a wider discourse that could accommodate the demands made by women such as Kususe while offering others the possibility of doing something more than listening to men or raising funds to support their activities.

Theories on Women's Rights

Perhaps partly because of the news of women's presence in political spaces, a discourse on women's political inclusion started to be developed by men who had also been influenced by Western translations.

In 1876, Doi Kōka 土居光華, a supporter of the Movement for Freedom and Popular Rights, published *Bunmeiron onna daigaku* 文明論女大学 (Enlightened Theory on the *Greater Learning for Women*). In its preface he argued that, according to the English scholar John Stuart Mill, freedom was a right of mankind, and that was valid for women as well. Criticizing the *Onna daigaku* for its bigoted teachings, he based his new work on women's learning in Western civilizations and argued in favor of women's education, property and marriage rights, and the encouragement of harmonious relations between husbands and wives.[15]

In 1877, Ozaki Yukio's abridged translation of Herbert Spencer's *Social Statics* (1851) was published with the title of *Kenri teikō* (Outline of Civil Rights). Spencer stated that people had the right to resist unlawful authority and that equal freedom included free speech, sexual equality, and equal educational rights. In his opinion, human happiness was a divine right and this was valid for men as well as women since there was no difference between the sexes and both had to work for the well-

13. *Tokyo Yokohama mainichi shinbun*, 06.04.1880, reprinted in Suzuki, *Nihon josei undō shiryō shūsei*, 52.
14. Ōki, *Jiyu minken undō to josei*, 12.
15. Doi Kōka, *Bunmeiron onna daigaku* (Enlightened theory on the *Greater Learning for Women*) (1876), in *Onna daigaku shū* (Collection of works related to the *Greater Learning for Women*), edited by Ishikawa Matsutarō, 119–50 (Heibonsha, 1977). Doi moved to Shizuoka in 1881 and founded a group that promoted the movement for popular rights. The speeches he organized were attended by large crowds, so it is possible that there were women among them. Ichihara, *Shizuoka onna hyakunen*, vol. 1, 10–11; Kaneko Sachiko, *Kindai nihon joseiron no keifu* (A genealogy of theories on Japanese women during the modern period) (Fuji shuppan, 1999), 51.

being of their country. The only major difference he could name, in fact, was that women had not been allowed the same education as men, and therefore it was normal for their intellectual development to be crippled.[16]

A year later, in 1878, Suzuki Yoshimune 鈴木義宗 published *Fujo hōritsuron* 婦女法律論 (Legal Theories on Women), a translation of the English jurist Sheldon Amos's *Difference of Sex as a Topic of Jurisprudence and Legislation* (1870). Amos, who supported women's participation in public and political life as a way to teach them how to be responsible citizens, argued that women should be granted property rights and more education so that they could obtain better jobs. In his preface, Suzuki wrote that, although numerous legal theories had been introduced, few people were concerned with laws affecting women. Considering this regrettable, he had undertaken the task of translating the book.[17]

In 1878 the Kakumeisha 鶴鳴社 (Society of the Crying Crane), one of the constituent groups of the Movement for Freedom and Popular Rights, was founded in Sendai by Fukamauchi Motoi 深間内基 (b. 1846), a student and teacher at Keiō gijuku and Risshi gakusha. In the same year he translated and published part of Mill's *The Subjection of Women* (1869) under the title *Danjo dōkenron* 男女同権論 (Parity of Rights between the Sexes), which was also the topic of a speech he gave in 1879 at one of the Kakumeisha's public speech meetings that was open to both men and women.[18] In *The Subjection of Women* Mill had written that human development was crucial to achieving a better society, for only in their most developed state could people enjoy the highest forms of happiness. Women were slaves in their homes, and they had to tolerate the situation, Mill argued, because they had no alternative means, such as jobs with which to earn a living or property and voting rights.[19]

Another collection translated into Japanese was Theodore Stanton's *The Woman Question in Europe*, published in 1884. This was comprised of essays written by famous Danish, Spanish, British, Italian, Greek, Austrian, and French feminists who were involved in female education, suffrage, medicine, philanthropy, and

---

16. In 1881, Inoue Tsutomu 井上勤 translated part of Spencer's *Social Statics* with the title *Joken shinron* 女権真論 (True theory on women's rights), and in the same year Matsushima Kō 松島剛 translated it in its entirety as *Shakai heikenron* 社会平権論 (On the social equality of rights). See Sotozaki Mitsuhiro, *Meiji zenki fujin kaihō ronshi* (Theories on the movement for women's liberation during the early Meiji period) (Kochi: Kochi shiritsu shimin toshokan, 1963), 18; Kaneko, *Kindai nihon joseiron*, 54; and Roger Bowen, *Rebellion and Democracy in Meiji Japan: A Study of Commoners in the Popular Rights Movement* (Berkeley: University of California Press, 1980), 203.

17. Suzuki Yoshimune, trans., *Fujo hōritsuron* (On legislation concerning women) (Suzuki Yoshimune, 1878); Sheldon Amos, *Difference of Sex as a Topic of Jurisprudence and Legislation* (London: Longmans, Green, 1870), esp. 26, 32, 40.

18. Miyagi no joseishi kenkyūkai, *Miyagi no joseishi*, 382.

19. John Stuart Mill, *The Subjection of Women*, edited by Susan Moller Okin (Indianapolis: Hackett, 1988), iv–xiii.

journalism such as Millicent Garrett Fawcett, Frances Power Cobbe, Aurelia Cimino Folliero De Luna, and Princess Helene Kaltzoff-Massalsky. The collection was translated by Sumida Yorinosuke 住田頼之助 and published in 1887 as *Saigoku fujin risshi hen* 西国婦人立志編 (Collection of Biographies of Successful Western Women). I have not found essays or books written by those Western women that were translated into Japanese with the exception of the works of Millicent Garrett Fawcett (1847–1929), the British activist who devoted her life to the cause of women's advancement and suffrage. Millicent Fawcett was married to a man who supported her ideas and activities—Henry Fawcett, a Radical member of Parliament for Brighton—and was the sister of Elizabeth Garrett Anderson, who opened the medical profession for women in England. She was also part of the movement for higher education for women in Cambridge, and we have seen how Cambridge and women's university education were topics dear to many Japanese women. Fawcett wrote a series of books during her lifetime.[20] In particular, in *Essays and Lectures on Social and Political Subjects* (translated as *Seijidan* 政治談 [Tales of Political Affairs]), published with her husband in 1872, she included an essay titled "The Electoral Disabilities of Women," arguing for the need for female political rights and refuting point by point the criticisms levied against it.[21]

Fawcett's theories on women's position in society were well known to Japanese female political activists, but she was not the only foreign woman active in

20. See, for example, *Political Economy for Beginners* (1870), translated in an abridged version as *Keizaigaku kaitei* 経済学階梯 (Primer in political economy) in 1877 by Tazawa Shizutarō 田沢鎮太郎; and *Tales in Political Economy* (1874), translated by Kanezaki Shigeki 兼崎茂樹 and published in 1885 with the title *Keizairon mondai shū* 経済論問題集 (Collection of theories on political economy). Information regarding these Japanese translations is collated in Sekiguchi Sumiko, "Enzetsu suru onna tachi" (Women who make public speeches), *Mirai* 399 (1999): 36–39. Fawcett's name appears also as the author of *Keizaigaku* 経済学 (Political economy), translated by Nagata Kensuke 永田健助 in 1887, which was reprinted in its third edition in 1888. They are both available online at the Japanese National Diet Library's Kindai digital library (http://kindai.ndl.go.jp/), but the quality of the reproduction is poor, and I have not been able to view these volumes elsewhere.

21. She pointed out that those who were against political rights for women argued that women were sufficiently represented by their husbands, that they were intellectually and physically inferior to men, that a woman's proper sphere was the family, that women's moral superiority would be destroyed by contamination in the public sphere, that they did not want the franchise, that they could not be soldiers, that there was nothing in the Bible supporting such a demand, that it would be like giving two votes to a woman's nearest male relative, and that there was only one head in the family—the man—so family life would be destroyed if women were given voting rights. Millicent Garrett Fawcett, "The Electoral Disabilities of Women," in *Essays and Lectures on Social and Political Subjects*, by Henry Fawcett and Millicent Garrett Fawcett, 230–61 (London: Macmillan, 1872), 230–32. The Japanese translation was published in 1883; chapters 8 and 9 discuss women's education, whereas chapters 10 and 11 of the second volume are dedicated to women's political rights. Shibuya Zōji, trans., *Seijidan* (Tales of political affairs), 2 vols. (Jiyū shuppan, 1883). Fawcett's activities in England were reported in *Tōkyō fujin kyōfū zasshi*, no. 11, 16.02.1889, 12–13. Her biography was published in *Fujo zasshi*, no. 17, 10.10.1891, 14–15.

the political sphere discussed in the Japanese papers. For example, readers of *Doyō shinbun* knew that British women such as Alice Westlake, a member of the Central Committee of the National Society for Women's Suffrage, were petitioning members of Parliament in order to obtain more political rights and were organizing public speeches on the topic. Westlake, it was reported, argued that it was irrational to include women in the category of people not allowed to vote as it was otherwise composed of criminals, children, and the disabled.[22]

Whether or not women read these works, and if they did what they thought of the theories presented in them, which were at variance with many practices regulating the lives of Japanese women, is unclear. These works nevertheless show that it was becoming conceivable for male intellectuals to challenge the existing patriarchal order by translating and explaining such theories in public meetings and print. Thus, the importance of women's participation in men's public speeches at this early stage, and of those first women's groups that were organized mainly with the aim of supporting male activities, lies also in the fact that it is probably there that they heard lectures on Mill or Fawcett for the first time.

Moreover, many of the articles describing female participation in political activities were published in newspapers that openly supported the Movement for Freedom and Popular Rights, and it appears that such women were not considered to be engaging in activities outside their proper sphere. For example, the En'yō fujo jiyūtō 遠陽婦女自由党 (En'yō Women's Liberal Party) was founded in 1883 in Hamamatsu by the wives of members of the En'yō Liberal Party; it had the aim of collecting money each month that would be saved until 1890, when it would be used to fund the activities of the party.[23] *Chōya shinbun* also reported that when men linked to the Movement for Freedom and Popular Rights held a public meeting delivering speeches in Kashiwazaki, among those who took the podium there was a girl of sixteen who argued for the parity of rights between men and women. The girl, the reporter wrote, was beautiful but also eloquent, and at the end of her speech many people approached her to learn who she was.[24]

This girl was probably Nishimaki Sakuya 西巻開耶 (1866–1908), a primary school teacher from Kashiwazaki who also participated in a public speech meeting organized at the Saifuku temple in Kashiwazaki in 1883 in which she read out a congratulatory address and was arrested by the authorities. I have not been able to access the contents of her speech, but the papers reported that, although she was a teacher who was involved in "political" activities, article 85 of the Criminal law

---

22. British women, it was also reported, could obtain higher education at Oxford. *Doyō shinbun*, no. 563, 17.07.1884, 1.

23. *Chōya shinbun*, 01.04.1883, reprinted in Suzuki, *Nihon josei undō shiryō shūsei*, 72; *Doyō shinbun*, no. 191, 10.04.1883, 1.

24. *Chōya shinbun*, 28.09.1881, reprinted in Suzuki, *Nihon josei undō shiryō shūsei*, 53; *Niigata shinbun*, no. 1335, 25.09.1881, 2.

ruled that for women between sixteen and twenty years of age the penalty was reduced by one degree, and so the fine of one yen and fifty sen was to be waived.[25] Nishimaki was arrested because of the Shūkai jōrei 集会条例 (Ordinance on Public Assembly), which was promulgated in April 1880 to limit the activities of the Movement for Freedom and Popular Rights in particular but the spread of "dangerous ideas" in general. It stipulated that students, teachers, policemen, and military men were not allowed to participate in political meetings or join political associations (art. 7) while organizers of political meetings had to obtain prior approval from the police by providing the authorities with the contents of their speeches, the speakers' names and domiciles, and the locations and times when the speeches would be made (art. 1). No specific mention was made of women. The law was revised in 1882, the year before Nishimaki made her speech, and again in 1890, when it became the Law on Assembly and Political Associations, discussed in chapter 4, against parts of which the members of the Kyōfūkai rallied.

Women's Work for Women's Rights

In 1882 newspapers started to publish a large number of articles describing women's political activities. Whether the large number of articles was directly responsible for the increase in women's involvement in politics or vice versa is unclear; however, it is in this period that women's political activities started to spread and women began a dialogue with other women on political matters.

In 1882 and 1883 Kishida Toshiko toured Japan to deliver a series of public speeches. Her movements were reported in the papers, and women read about her.[26] Yoshioka Yayoi was one of Kishida's admirers. She enjoyed reading the newspapers her father bought when she was living in a small town in Shizuoka prefecture,

---

25. *Eiri chōya shinbun*, no. 1, 22.01.1883, 3. Nishimaki went to Tokyo and was involved in a number of *fujinkai*. In 1888 she founded with her husband a school in Fukushima prefecture where girls were taught subjects designed to help them become financially independent. Tanaka Kazunori, "Josei minkenka Nishimaki Sakuya no shōgai" (The life of the popular rights female activist Nishimaki Sakuya), *Niigata kenritsu rekishi hakubutsukan kenkyū kiyo* 4 (2003): 25–48. See also by the same author, "Josei kaihō ni tsukushita Nishimaki Sakuya no ashidori" (The path of Nishimaki Sakuya, who exerted herself for the liberation of women), *Kashiwazaki kariha* 26 (1999): 32–57.

26. Kishida went to Tokushima (*Chōya shinbun*, 26.07.1882, reprinted in Suzuki, *Nihon josei undō shiryō shūsei*, 60) and Kumamoto prefecture (*Kumamoto shinbun*, 31.10 and 01, 02, 03, 08.11.1882, reprinted in Suzuki, *Nihon josei undō shiryō shūsei*, 60), attracting large crowds. In Kyoto she participated in a public speech meeting where even an eight-year-old girl was among the speakers, and since such meetings were rare attendance was large. *Chōya shinbun*, no. 2994, 09.10.1883, 2; *Kyōto eiri shinbun*, 04.10.1883, reprinted in Suzuki, *Nihon josei undō shiryō shūsei*, 67. In Ōtsu she made the famous speech entitled "Daughters in Boxes" (Hakoiri musume) in which she criticized parents who denied their daughters the possibility of experiencing intellectual development and which was understood to constitute a metaphorical criticism of government

but she was particularly interested in the reports on political speech meetings, feeling inspired by Kishida Toshiko and Fukuda Hideko and discussing the news with her female friends.[27]

During the same period, an office of the Liberal Party was opened in Okayama, and Takeuchi Hisako 竹内寿子, fifty-three years old, and Tsuge Kumeko 津下久米子, forty-eight years old, respectively the mother and wife of two members of the movement, visited Itagaki Taisuke in Osaka where they met Kishida.[28] This meeting led to the founding of the Okayama joshi konshinkai 岡山女子懇親会 (Okayama Women's Friendship Society, sometimes referred to as Okayama joshi shinbokukai 岡山女子親睦会) in 1882. The thirty initial members included Uemori Misao 上森操 (1858–1942), the daughter of a Chinese studies scholar and later the founder of a private school for girls; Yamamoto Uji 山本宇志, who had married Yamamoto Ken, a member of the Liberal Party, and was involved in the Jōkō gakusha, discussed below; Fukuda Hideko, then seventeen, and her mother; Ishiguro Obi 石黒織尾, an eighteen-year-old Christian and later a founding member of the Okayama fujin kyōfūkai; and Okada Yaeko 岡田八重子, the sister of Okada Masamichi, a journalist for the *Okayama mainichi shinbun*.[29] As early as 1882, women of different ages and religious beliefs were traveling to meet influential men and opening spaces from which to launch their activities.

What was the scope of the Konshinkai? During the second meeting of the group, it was reported in the papers, Tsuge Kumeko stated that although men were working for their country there was no reason for women to be excluded. They met "to protect women's honor (*sessō*), to reform bad customs, and to find a proper way of educating children"; they wanted to give women a space in which to talk and

---

practices toward the people of Japan. For that speech she was arrested, jailed, and fined. *Jiyū shinbun*, 19.10.1883, and *Nihon rikken seitō shinbun*, 15.11.1883, both reprinted in Suzuki, *Nihon josei undō shiryō shūsei*, 68–69. Sugano, *Kishida Toshiko*, includes a detailed study of these speeches. Rebecca Copeland and Aiko Okamoto MacPhail translate "Daughters in Boxes" in *The Modern Murasaki: Writing by Women of Meiji Japan*, edited by Rebecca Copeland and Melek Ortabasi, 62–71 (New York: Columbia University Press, 2006).

27. Yoshioka Yayoi, *Yoshioka Yayoi den* (Yoshioka Yayoi's biography) (Nihon tosho Center, [1967] 1998), 70.

28. *Nihon rikken seitō shinbun*, 06.05.1882 and 09.05.1882, reprinted in Aoki Mitsuko and Mitsuda Kyōko, eds., *Minkenki Okayama joseishi kankei shiryō* (Historical records related to the history of women in Okayama during the Minken period), vol. 4 of *Okayama minken undōshi kankei shiryōshū* (Collection of historical records related to the history of the Okayama Minken movement) (Okayama: Okayama minken undō hyakunen kinen gyōji jikkō iinkai, 1982), 30.

29. Okayama joseishi kenkyūkai, ed., *Kindai Okayama no onnatachi* (Women of Okayama during the modern period) (Sanseidō, 1987), 26–28. The complete list of members can be found in *Nihon rikken seitō shinbun*, 16.05.1882, reprinted in Suzuki, *Nihon josei undō shiryō shūsei*, 58. News of the group was also reported in *Doyō shinbun*, no. 44, 18.05.1882, 3; and *San'yō shinpō*, 13.05.1882, reprinted in Suzuki, *Nihon josei undō shiryō shūsei*, 57. The articles on the Okayama joshi konshinkai are reprinted in Aoki and Mitsuda, *Minkenki Okayama*, 25–33.

exchange opinions and information and in that way to become more knowledgeable about social issues.[30]

In order to achieve these goals, the group used all the means available; they met twice a month, made public speeches, and opened a school, the Jōkō gakusha 蒸紅学舎, where women of every age, many of them poor, and also some boys, were taught subjects useful for finding a job for six sen a month, a low fee compared to that charged by other schools. The school had boarding facilities and provided evening courses for those who were busy during the day, and on Saturdays meetings were held to discuss women's position in society.[31]

Little information has survived on the public speech meetings these women held, but we know that they participated in a two-day political meeting organized in Okayama in 1882. Here Kishida Toshiko gave a speech entitled "To the Women of Okayama," arguing in favor of a society built by men and women together, since in her opinion for the common good and progress it was necessary to achieve equal rights between the sexes (danjo dōken), and emphasizing that even in the West movements had risen to this end. The audience was very large, and on the first day Kishida also gave a speech entitled "The Government Rules over the People and Men over Women," which was followed by speeches by members of the Liberal Party. One was Kobayashi Kusuo 小林樟雄, the brother of Kobayashi Tei 小林貞 (another member of the group, then twenty-one years old), who was also the translator of a biography of Joan of Arc that Fukuda Hideko had read and enjoyed.[32] The group held public speech meetings in September 1882 in which only women were allowed (about fifty were present), and in November, when Fukuda Hideko was among the speakers.[33]

The lives of two women who participated in the Konshinkai show how women from considerably different backgrounds were entertaining the same hopes and could find common ground in which to develop their ideas concerning the position of women in Japanese society. One was Sumiya Koume 炭谷小梅 (1850–1920), who was born in Okayama to a family of low-ranking samurai and lost her par-

---

30. *Asahi shinbun*, no. 981, 31.05.1882, 2; *Nihon rikken seitō shinbun*, 01.08.1882, reprinted in Suzuki, *Nihon josei undō shiryō shūsei*, 71.

31. Okayama joseishi kenkyūkai, *Kindai Okayama no onnatachi*, 30. The school closed in September 1884, apparently because the government deemed the students' involvement in the activities organized by the Movement for Freedom and Popular Rights contrary to public peace, and no more news on the group was reported in the papers. *Jiyū shinbun*, no. 629, 13.08.1884, 2. See also Fukuda's description of these events in her autobiography, reprinted in Murata Shizuko and Ōki Motoko, eds., *Fukuda Hideko shū* (Collection of documents by and about Fukuda Hideko) (Fuji shuppan, 1998), 17.

32. *San'yō shinpō*, 9, 11, 13, 16.05.1882, reprinted in Aoki and Mitsuda, *Minkenki Okayama*, 25–26; Hane, *Reflections*, 30.

33. *Nihon rikken seitō shinbun*, no. 116, 01.08.1882, 3; *San'yō shinpō*, 23.09.1882, and 18.11.1882, both reprinted in Aoki and Mitsuda, *Minkenki Okayama*, 27.

ents at an early age. She became the concubine of Nakagawa Yokotarō 中川横太郎 (1836–1903), who in 1875 had helped some Western missionaries settle in Okayama and often asked her to read to him books such as Fukuzawa Yukichi's *Gakumon no susume*. Sumiya went to Kobe girls' school in 1878 but was called back by Nakagawa, who wanted her in Okayama. She went back, but then left him, was baptized, and found a job as a Japanese-language teacher for a woman missionary. She joined the Konshinkai and made speeches with Kishida, and in 1886 she opened a school, the Fujin eigakusha 婦人英学舎 (English School for Women), which taught older and poor women Christianity, English, and arts useful for finding employment such as Western dressmaking and knitting.[34] From 1887 on, Sumiya helped Ishii Jūji, who had just opened the Okayama orphanage, and this collaboration was to be a long-lasting one, for in 1901, when a public speech meeting was convened in Tokyo in support of his work, she participated as well.[35]

Another woman active in the Konshinkai was Kageyama Umeko, the mother of Fukuda Hideko. Umeko was born in 1826, and after attending her father's private school she married Hideko's father, who had also opened a private school, where she worked. Umeko worked hard inside and outside her home because of her family's precarious financial condition, but she also paid close attention to her daughter's education. Hideko, probably because of her mother's example, had learned that a woman could have an education, a job, and a family to take care of, but also personal beliefs that should be pursued. According to Hideko, Umeko opened a school, probably the Jōkō gakusha, where she taught prostitutes, and around 1882 she also read Fukuzawa Yukichi's *Gakumon no susume* and *Seiyō jijō* (Conditions in the West).[36]

In *Seiyō jijō*, Fukuzawa argued that Western governments promoted liberty, religious tolerance, trade, arts, the development of human talent, peace, security, and benevolent institutions for the poor. He wrote that "literacy, reasoned discussion, and ambitious effort" were the characteristics that made for a superior man and that "The great fundamental of human interaction is that free and independent people assemble, employing strength and laboring minds, attaining goals and achieving

34. *Jogaku zasshi* (no. 113, 09.06.1888, 24) reported that about forty students attended the school and that among the teachers there was a woman missionary and graduate of Kobe jogakkō, Oshioi Kyōko 鹽井京子. In 1891 there were forty students. *Jogaku zasshi*, no. 249, 24.01.1891, 28.

35. Okayama joseishi kenkyūkai, *Kindai Okayama*, 105–17; *Fujo shinbun*, no. 52, 06.05.1901, 2. Details about Sumiya's collaboration with Ishii were reported in *Jogaku zasshi*, no. 380, 19.05.1894, 10. Both Sumiya and Ishii supported the founding of San'yō eiwa jogakkō, the school opened in Okayama in 1886 discussed in chapter 3. Mochizuki Kōzaburō, ed., *Shiritsu San'yō jogakkō hōkoku 1* (First report on the work of the private San'yō jogakkō) (Okayama: San'yō jogakkō, 1894), 11, 14.

36. Fukuda Hideko, "Kageyama Umeko no omoide" (Remembering Kageyama Umeko), *Sekai fujin*, no. 34, 05.03.1909, reprinted in Aoki and Mitsuda, *Minkenki Okayama* 43–45. See also Hane, *Reflections*, 34–36; and Okayama joseishi kenkyūkai, *Kindai Okayama*, 36–50.

rewards, in an effort to preserve an order and to plan for the general benefit of all."[37] Could it be that Kageyama Umeko considered these points also applicable to women? Fukuzawa's works were advocating social changes that could appeal to women with an education and the strength of their convictions, and Kageyama clearly was the female counterpart of Fukuzawa's "superior man." Moreover, if Kageyama and Sumiya could read *Gakumon no susume* and *Seiyō jijō*, they may also have been reading similar books, and, since the women helping at the school were also members of the Konshinkai, they may well have discussed together the books they read. Thus, even at schools in which girls learned vocational subjects, such as those opened by Kageyama and Sumiya, the possibility of accessing various theories on women's position in society was not so remote.

These women were part of a growing public that was being educated in political matters, but there are others that merit attention because they wanted to publish their own journals and in so doing were seeking to reach a broader audience. For example, forty-six-year-old Narita Ume 成田梅 (b. 1838) from Miyagi prefecture, a widow and teacher of *kiyomoto* ballads whose son was a member of the Liberal Party, helped form the Sendai joshi jiyūtō 仙台女子自由党 (Sendai Women's Liberal Party) in 1883, held public speech meetings, and aspired to publish a magazine.[38] In the same year, some women living in Shibata, Miyagi prefecture, who were ardent supporters of the Movement for Freedom and Popular Rights, opened the Joshi jiyūkan 女子自由館 (Hall of Freedom for Women) where they made speeches, discussed contemporary matters, and considered publishing a journal.[39] When a reading room opened in Shibata by supporters of the Movement for Freedom and Popular Rights, in which there were newspapers from various provinces, was closed, two *shōgi* (prostitutes) started raising money to have it reopened; it is possible that women of the Joshi jiyūkan, living nearby, also helped.[40]

Access to newspapers and public libraries helps to explain how women came to know about political theories and activities elsewhere, while the fact that they wanted to publish their own journals (which, if they ever existed, were probably similar to newsletters) shows that they were aware of the importance of publiciz-

37. Fukuzawa Yukichi, *Seiyō jijō* (Conditions in the West), in *Fukuzawa Yukichi zenshū* (Collected works of Fukuzawa Yukichi), edited by Keiō gijuku, vol. 1, 275–608 (Iwanami shoten, 1958), 290–91, 393, translated in Douglas Howland, *Translating the West: Language and Political Reason in Nineteenth-Century Japan* (Honolulu: University of Hawai'i Press, 2002), 34, 102, 106.
38. *Chōya shinbun*, 14.03.1883, reprinted in Suzuki, *Nihon josei undō shiryō shūsei*, 72; *Yūbin hōchi shinbun*, no. 3004, 15.03.1883, 5. Given that the Kakumeisha's public speech meetings, where Fukamauchi Motoi gave the speech entitled "Parity of Rights between the Sexes" in 1879, took place near Narita's home, it is possible that she attended them. Miyagi no joseishi kenkyūkai, *Miyagi no joseishi*, 382.
39. *Doyō shinbun*, 10.08.1883, in Miyagi no joseishi kenkyūkai, *Miyagi no joseishi*, 380; *Chōya shinbun*, 04.08.1883, reprinted in Suzuki, *Nihon josei undō shiryō shūsei*, 72.
40. *Ōu hibi shinbun* 19.02.1883, in Miyagi no joseishi kenkyūkai, *Miyagi no joseishi*, 381.

ing their existence and political opinions. If they were becoming known because newspapers published a few lines on their activities, an ambitious few were seeking to create additional publicity and gain followers. These journals can also be considered the precursors of the well-known magazines that appeared some years later, targeting a female audience, and help to explain the promulgation of laws that prohibited women from becoming publishers of print media, for it was clear that many wanted to do just that.

Fujo Kyōkai and Fujin Tokugikai: Looking beyond Groups' Names

The groups described above were established during the years leading up to 1883, when the Movement for Freedom and Popular Rights was at its peak. In 1884, when the Liberal Party dissolved, the government started to directly oppose the activities of the people involved in the movement and to fine or jail those who voiced demands in opposition to the government line. As a consequence, after 1884 women lost part of the main source of support for their activities, but they were not silenced. On the contrary, the following pages show that it was precisely in the mid-1880s that women started to refine their arguments and voice even stronger criticism of their political exclusion.

Perhaps also to deflect government criticism, some women justified their activities by arguing that they would help women become good mothers and wives, while more power and rights outside the home meant that they could better support their nation. Interesting are, for example, the Aikō fujo kyōkai (Aikō Women's Association) 愛甲婦女協会, founded in Ogino, Kanagawa prefecture, probably in 1884, most certainly by the wives and daughters of members of the Movement for Freedom and Popular Rights, and the Toyohashi fujo kyōkai 豊橋婦女協会 (Toyohashi Women's Association), launched in 1883 in Aichi prefecture by Murasame Nobu 村雨のぶ (1856–1939), Nishikawa Sato 西川さと, Kaneko Tō 金子とう, and others. Given the similarities between these two groups' names and statements, it seems likely that there were connections between them.

The women of the former group argued that Western women "collaborate with men for the well-being of the people and the progress of their nation. . . . Instead, in our country if we look at women's position, they are men's playthings and slaves." They wanted to change the way in which relationships between husbands and wives were structured, as well as to take care of the home, keep themselves informed, and raise their children, all "for the sake of women's happiness and the progress of our country," but in order to do so they needed knowledge, which could be obtained by attending male public speeches and meetings. The latter group had very similar goals. It was founded in order to bring together those women who wanted to support and work "for their country and for their family" by helping their husbands and raising their children, who would then become the pillars on which Japan would rest.[41]

Both groups placed emphasis on women's duties inside the home, and by carefully emphasizing their roles as mothers and wives they sought to be accepted by society. However, they also made a comparison with Western women and stated that Japanese women were treated like playthings by men. My research indicates that this phrasing was used when women wanted to radically transform their condition. Furthermore, in October 1884 Murasame cooperated with her husband, a member of the Jiyutō, in the Chichibu incident (and we find her name again at the end of this chapter linked to that of Ueki Emori and Sasaki Toyoju), while in the spring of 1885 Fukuda Hideko went with Tomii Tora to Ogino to raise funds among the supporters of the Movement for Freedom and Popular Rights, probably meeting the women of the Aikō fujo kyōkai.[42] At first glance, and especially because of their names, these two groups do not seem to have challenged women's status, but in reality some of their members were interested in political matters and involved in political unrest.

The Fujin tokugikai 婦人徳義会 (Association for [the Protection of] Women's Morality) is another good example. The rules of the association united the need for the development of women's rights and the elimination of social customs that despised women with the need to reinforce and promote morality and women's true nature. This association published the magazine *Joken* 女権 (Women's Rights) in September 1891, *after* women were banned from participating in public political meetings and joining political associations.[43] The female contributors to the first issue (among them Fukuda Hideko) published articles in defense of women's political

41. See Suzuki, *Nihon josei undō shiryō shūsei*, 72–73, for the former founding statement. For the latter, see *Doyō shinbun*, 3.11.1883, reprinted in Suzuki, *Nihon josei undō shiryō shūsei*, 73–74; and *Nihon rikken seitō shinbun*, 30.10.1882, reprinted in Ōhata Tetsu, "Meiji joseishi ni kansuru futatsu no shinshiryō" (Two new documents on the history of Meiji women), *Kanagawa kenshi kenkyū* 28 (1975): 62. See also Kanagawa-ken, ed., *Kanagawa kenshi* (History of Kanagawa prefecture), vol. 13 (Yokohama: Kanagawa-ken, 1977), 87–88.

42. The Chichibu incident occurred in 1884 when peasants, artisans, and members of the Movement for Freedom and Popular Rights rebelled against newly introduced taxes. On the significance of this and other peasant rebellions during the modern period, see Stephen Vlastos, "Opposition Movements in Early Meiji, 1868–1885," in *The Cambridge History of Japan*, edited by Marius B. Jansen, vol. 5, *The Nineteenth Century*, 367–431 (Cambridge: Cambridge University Press, 1989), 421–5. On Fukuda and Tomii's trip, see the brief description Fukuda includes in her autobiography, reprinted in Murata and Ōki, *Fukuda Hideko shū*, 26; and Ōhata, *Meiji joseishi ni kansuru*.

43. The magazine was publicized in *Jogaku zasshi*, no. 286, 10.10.1891, 20. The publisher and editor was Fujii Tsunenosuke 藤井常之助, and the signed contributions to the first issue were mainly from women. Kindai josei bunkashi kenkyūkai states that in reality the editor of the magazine was Fujii Yoshiko 藤井美子. Kindai josei bunkashi kenkyūkai, ed., *Fujin zasshi no yoake* (The dawn of women's magazines) (Ōzorasha, 1989), 38. I have not been able to find information

and social participation and asked readers to send in material related to women's activities in schools, associations, and workplaces in order to create a new space in which women could form a community.[44] Unfortunately, I have been unable to locate other issues of the magazine, so it is possible that, even though these women had specifically chosen to name their group Fujin tokugikai in an attempt to avoid government action, its publication was blocked by the authorities.[45]

There was a plethora of groups with similar names during the Meiji period, some of which were cited in chapter 4. Although their names are all that remain, and so it is tempting to assume that they engaged in activities deemed proper for Meiji women, the evidence suggests that women could have been challenging the official ideology of womanhood in much greater numbers than would appear a priori.

Ueki Emori's *Danshi Shakai* (Male Society) and Kishida Toshiko's *Fujin Shakai* (Female Society)

Even after the dissolution of the Liberal Party in 1884, one of the major figures who discussed the expansion of women's rights was Ueki Emori, a renowned member of the Movement for Freedom and Popular Rights. Ueki had read Mill, Spencer, Jean-Jacques Rousseau, and Fawcett, and in 1879 he had written *Minken jiyūron* 民権自由論 (On Freedom and People's Rights), in which he had argued that "in the past, people have been in poor spirits, have been concentrating merely on one's own business and family, and have not taken an interest in their world and country, knowing very little of all public matters." It was time for a change, though, "for we have to concern ourselves with our world and society, expand people's rights and freedom, spread that wisdom, and help the development of our world."[46]

---

regarding these two individuals, but given that they have the same surname it is possible that Yoshiko was related to Tsunenosuke and that he was used by the group as a figurehead.

44. Ōki writes that Fukuda's article, entitled "Joshi no honbun" (Women's duties), was originally published in *Rikken jiyū shinbun*, so it is possible that her participation was minimal. Murata and Ōki, *Fukuda Hideko shū*, 646. She seems, however, to have been interested in actively participating in the publication of magazines for women years before *Sekai fujin*, which I discuss in chapter 6. *Yūbin hōchi shinbun* (14.10.1891, reprinted in Suzuki, *Nihon josei undō shiryō shūsei*, 97–98) reported that Fukuda had the plan of publishing a magazine for women and the employees and journalists would all be female; the magazine would support parity of rights between men and women.

45. In 1893 *Yomiuri shinbun* published a short article on Fujii Yoshiko, who was referred to as "the editor in chief of *Joken*," so it is possible that the magazine had a longer life but that its issues have been lost. *Yomiuri shinbun*, no. 5662, 21.04.1893, 2.

46. Ueki Emori, *Minken jiyūron* (On freedom and people's rights) (Fukuoka: Shūbundō, 1879), 3, 8, 9.

To be sure, some women who sought the help of male intellectuals associated with the Movement for Freedom and Popular Rights were dissatisfied with their behavior. Fukuda Hideko, for one, wrote that her male partners in the movement thought nothing of spending money to buy drinks and the services of geishas. Shimizu Shikin wrote a similar criticism in 1890 in an article entitled "To My Beloved Sisters in Tears," stating that many men involved in the movement "are pseudo-scholars who know full well that only the principle of equal rights between the sexes accords with the truth, and yet for their own convenience they hold to the old practice of treating women as inferior to men."[47] Ueki's support was nevertheless important for women because, unlike those intellectuals who discussed women with other men, he talked to them as well as about them. Furthermore, although some women who knew Ueki were appalled by the discrepancy between his theoretical views and his behavior toward women, this does not mean that his theories were not well received by those women who had access to his writings.

In a series of articles published in *Doyō shinbun* beginning in 1886, Ueki argued that women with an education could obtain better jobs, as had happened in North America. They could enlarge their circle of acquaintances, open schools, make public speeches, be employed in newspapers and magazines or publish their own, and obtain greater political rights.[48] Japan had to revise its laws concerning the rights of inheritance, property rights, and the rights of husbands and wives since marriage should be a bond between two equal people.[49] Men and women could not attain happiness without rights, and, although there were physical differences between them and some also argued that male and female mental abilities were different, rights were not based on mental or physical strength. He pointed out that in *Social Statics* Spencer had shown that there were women who had greater intellectual abilities than common men, and therefore the only obstacle to women's participation in public society was that they did not have the same opportunities.[50] Ueki also wrote about *danshi shakai* (male society), stating that even after the establishment of the Diet the franchise would be given only to "male society" and

47. For Fukuda's criticism, see Hane, *Reflections*, 37. Shimizu's article is reprinted in Aoki and Mitsuda, *Minkenki Okayama*, 47–49, and translated in Yukiko Tanaka, *Women Writers of Meiji and Taishō Japan* (Jefferson: McFarland, 2000), 49.
48. Ueki Emori, "Fujin joshi shōrai no tenchi" (The future position of women), reprinted in Sotozaki Mitsuhiro, *Ueki Emori kazoku seidō ronshū* (Collection of Ueki Emori's theories on the family system) (Kochi: Kochi shiritsu shimin toshokan, 1957), 105–11.
49. See "Minpōjō ni tsuki fufu no fudōken o ronsu" (On the disparity of rights between husbands and wives from the perspective of the Civil Law), "Keihōjō ni tsuki fufu no fudōken o ronsu" (On the disparity of rights between husbands and wives from the perspective of the Criminal Law), and "Sōzokuhō ni tsuki fufu no fudōken o ronsu" (On the disparity of rights between husbands and wives from the perspective of the Inheritance Law), all reprinted in Sotozaki, *Ueki Emori kazoku seidō ronshū*, 117–23, 124–27, 128–33.
50. Ueki Emori, "Danjo no dōken" (Male and female parity of rights), reprinted in Sotozaki, *Ueki Emori kazoku seidō ronshū*, 315–52.

women would be left out.[51] He was acknowledging the existence of a reality that protected male privileges and therefore could not be called a society proper.

The idea of a male society is particularly interesting when analyzed in tandem with Kishida Toshiko's "woman's society." In an article entitled, "To My Fellow Sisters," Kishida argued that she wanted to talk to her fellow sisters because of her devotion to her country and her hope for "the expansion of my sisters' happiness and freedom." "Humankind is created by men and women together" so "our society should not be shaped only by men. . . . But given that people think that men are strong and women are weak, equality between the sexes, they say, is not achievable." Kishida argued that one could not differentiate between men and women purely on the basis of physical strength as among men there were both strong and weak individuals. Similarly, it was not possible to distinguish them on the basis of mental ability as was evident from the fact that many famous and intelligent women had existed in the past, including Murasaki Shikibu, Sei Shōnagon, Izumi Shikibu, Elizabeth Browning, Catherine the Great, Madame Roland, Mary Somerville, Madame de Staël, and others. (With the exception of the Japanese names, these women were those Spencer had named in *Social Statics*.)[52] Furthermore, men, too, possessed different intellectual abilities while certain women were more intelligent than men, a point made by both Spencer and Millicent Fawcett.[53] "The mental powers of men and women are different" Kishida continued, "and men have always excelled [in various fields] more than women," but that was due to the fact that men "could obtain an education, whereas women could not, and because they could associate in public, whereas women could not." This had naturally led to differences in the intellectual development of men and women. Furthermore, education was not always a good thing. "In our country, the way in which women have been educated has been in most cases deleterious" and this had "prevented the development of our women's society." It was necessary for "her sisters" to obtain parity of rights and property rights, and it was foolish to think that if women obtained the same rights men had (*danjo dōken*) family happiness would be ruined since conflicts between husbands and wives were not always the wife's fault. She wrote that parity of rights did not exist even in the "enlightened West," since men could take part in the government of their country and divorce their wives if they committed adultery, whereas women could not, but she also named Millicent Fawcett and praised her work toward redressing legislation that disadvantaged women.[54]

---

51. Ueki, "Fujin joshi shōrai no tenchi," 109–10.
52. Herbert Spencer, *Social Statics* (London: Routledge and Thoemmes Press, [1851] 1996), 157.
53. Ibid., 158; Fawcett, "The Electoral Disabilities of Women," 243.
54. Kishida, "To my fellow sisters", published in installments in *Jiyū no tomoshibi*, 18, 21, and 27.05.1884; 04, 06, 12, 17, 18, 21, and 22.06.1884, reprinted in Suzuki, *Nihon josei undō shiryō shūsei*, 74–85.

As in the case of Japanese male intellectuals, some Japanese women looked to the West as a source of learning when discussing prostitution, higher education, and women's right to vote.[55] For male intellectuals, this was perceived as the way to consider and select the "best" form of government, technology, or school system, but for Japanese women the argument that their participation in politics was possible, and that even if their demands were not met women still had to bring them forward, drew force from the demonstrable fact that they were not the only ones doing so, thus forming an ideological bond between Western and Japanese women and showing that Japan's comparability with other nations did not concern only *male* economic and political matters. "The West" could thus be used as a comparative tool in debating what kind of relationship between the sexes should be advocated in Japan.

Moreover, while male intellectuals were trying to build a nation based on institutions and ideologies that were described as "enlightened," Japanese female political activists were producing examples such as that of the Heian period female writer Murasaki Shikibu to prove that educated and intelligent women had existed in the past, to create a tradition of active women in spheres other than the private, and to justify their nationalistic and political activities.

Finally, it is in the mid-1880s, by which time women had studied in girls' schools, had participated in women's activities, and had read about female activities in women's magazines, that they started addressing each other as *shimai* (sisters) living in a *fujin shakai* (woman's world), acknowledging the existence of separate spheres of female and male culture that had always been there. Now, for the first time, they could discuss those separate spheres in public spaces and extend the discussion to women in various geographic areas. *Fujin shakai* was an ideological space, in contraposition to Ueki Emori's *danshi shakai*, showing how male and female exchange of opinions on women's political rights was a fertile ground from which to develop new ideas and terminology. It was the creation of this separate culture, together with the formation of separate public spaces from which women discussed and voiced their ideals and demands, that allowed women of later generations to forcefully impose their presence in public society.

Fictional Women? Female Characters in Political Novels

The new phenomenon of female participation in political life was recognized by the authors of *seiji shōsetsu* (political novels). Some scholars have argued that female

---

55. An article in *Doyō shinbun* explained that three French "women politicians" (*onna seijika*) had submitted their candidature for the general election of members to the National Assembly. They were young and good looking and were seeking office to represent women who shared their ideas, but they were not the first ones since in 1885 six women had tried as well. *Doyō shinbun*, no. 2100,

characters in Meiji political novels allegorically represented the nation as a whole; women are understood to have appeared in them as metaphors for the choices confronting the nation, and this understanding is certainly justified by some of the fictional female characters' names (e.g., Otami, which means "the people").[56] There are indeed Meiji political novels that play on the relationship between men and women in order to represent people's political struggles against the government.[57] However, that is not the only reading one can extract from such novels, and below I give a gendered interpretation of some Meiji novels. My aim is not to criticize literary studies on 1880s political novels but to add to our understanding of why these novels were written and how they could have been read.

In 1887 Uchimura Gijo 内村義城 wrote an unfinished work entitled *Nijūsan-nen mugen no kane* 二十三年夢幻之鐘 (Year 23: The Dream Bell). After the opening of the Diet in 1890, Otami ("the people"), a young woman of twenty-three who supported the Liberal Party, wanted nevertheless to establish a women's party, which, in her opinion, would better voice women's demands. It was crucial, she argued, to "divorce oneself from one's own interests for the public good," and men and women should work together toward this goal. She believed that people should act to change their circumstances instead of merely "waiting" for something to be done by others, and she knew that women and the nonruling class had to protect their rights and interests themselves.[58]

Sumiko Sekiguchi has analyzed *Bunmei no hana: Joken bidan* 文明之花.女権美談 (The Flower of Civilization: A Praiseworthy Story of Women's Rights), written in 1887 by Sugiyama Tōjirō 杉山藤次郎, a member of the Kaishintō political party. The heroine of the novel, Sakuragi Hanako 桜木花子, another good-looking and intelligent young woman, wanted to organize a public exhibition where women could present their work given that one she had visited in Ueno included only men's artifacts. She wrote to newspapers to express her opinions on the topics debated at public speech meetings and rephrased theories of Western scholars such as Mill and Fawcett, stating that the way in which women were

---

12.11.1889, 1. Articles on women's political activities in Europe and North America were also reported in *Tokyo fujin kyōfu zasshi*. See, for example, no. 7, 20.10.1888, 163.

56. Iwamoto Yoshio, "Suehiro Tetchō: A Meiji Political Novelist," in *Japan's Modern Century*, edited by Edmund Skrzypczak, 83–114 (Sophia University and Charles E. Tuttle, 1968), 102. John Pierre Mertz, *Novel Japan: Spaces of Nationhood in Early Meiji Narrative, 1870–1888*, Michigan Monograph Series in Japanese Studies, no. 48 (Ann Arbor: Center for Japanese Studies, University of Michigan, 2003).

57. See, for example, the description of Toda Kindō's *Jōkai haran* in Christopher Hill, "How to Write a Second Restoration: The Political Novel and Meiji Historiography," *Journal of Japanese Studies* 33.2 (2007): 342.

58. "Women as the Nation's Conscience: A Study of Feminism in Shūfū Dōjin's 秋風道人 (Uchimura Gijo's) *Nijūsan-nen mugen no kane*," unpublished paper by Kyoko Kurita. I would like to thank Professor Kurita for providing me with a copy.

treated by their nation was an accurate indication of that nation's level of civilization. So, she continued, for Japan to accept female political rights would not only be a sign of civilization but also a way of showing the country's enlightened path to the rest of the world. Sakuragi also decided to publish a magazine, *Joken kakuchō zasshi* 女権拡張雑誌 (Magazine for the Expansion of Women's Rights), to promote her ideas.[59]

Similar novels were written by the better-known Suehiro Tetchō 末広鉄腸, a journalist working for *Chōya shinbun* and a member of the Liberal Party. In 1886 he published *Setchūbai* 雪中梅 (Plum Blossoms in the Snow) in which Tominaga Haru 富永春 (Spring of Eternal Wealth), the heroine of the novel, was portrayed as an educated girl who went to political meetings, believed that "in today's world women too need to know a little about politics in order to help men stand abreast with the countries of Europe and America," and decided to marry the man she loved, Kunino Motoi 国野基 (Foundation of the Nation), a young and handsome man who spoke at political meetings.[60]

In 1887 Hirotsu Ryūrō 廣津柳浪 (1861–1928) published *Joshi sansei shinchūrō* 女子参政蜃中樓 (On Women's Suffrage) in *Tokyo eiri shinbun*. The novel was set in the period following the promulgation of the Constitution, and Yamamura Satoko 山村敏子, the nineteen-year-old daughter of Count Yamamura Takakiyo 山村高潔, was depicted as a young, good-looking university graduate who was a supporter of women's political rights and an active public speaker. Yamamura went to Osaka as a representative of the Joshi sanseitō 女子参政党 (Party for Female Political Participation) and made a public speech in support of women's political rights, arguing that human beings had the right to use the "senses" (*kannō* 官能) bestowed on them by heaven and that this was true for women as well as men.[61]

The term *kannō* was also used in *Sen'enjō* 嬋艶嬢 (The Story of Miss Senko and Miss Enko), written by a certain Mr. Kosaka 小坂 and serialized in *Doyō shinbun* beginning in May 1890.[62] I could only find the first ten installments of this novel, but his opinions on women's issues are nevertheless clear. The first installment introduced two young women graduates of a girls' school in Osaka, Sawai Enko 澤井艶子 and Hanayama Senko 花山嬋子, who were talking about the expansion of women's rights. One argued that they were unattainable at that particular historical moment but that society could be changed, and women's rights enlarged, by educating girls who would then become teachers, since male students, seeing women in their formal and public role, would begin to respect them and,

59. Sekiguchi, "Enzetsu suru onna tachi," *Mirai* 401 (2000): 16–17. See also Sekiguchi Sumiko, *Go-isshin to jendaa* (Gender and the Meiji Restoration) (Tokyo Daigaku Shuppankai, 2005), 304–9.

60. Hill, "How to Write a Second Restoration," 350.

61. See Sekiguchi, "Enzetsu suru onna tachi," *Mirai* 401 (2000): 14–16.

62. *Doyō shinbun* from n. 2239 (02.05.1890, 3) to n. 2255 (21.05.1890, 3).

as a consequence, women in general. The theory of *jiyū kekkon* 自由結婚 (free marriage) was also presented, and it was argued that girls should be allowed to choose their husbands. Sawai and Hanayama formed a group to expand women's rights and talked about temperance movements and the abolition of prostitution. The novel mentioned the debate about people's rights and declared that those rights were predicated on the possibility of expressing one's needs (*kannō*), the first prerequisite for obtaining happiness, thus rephrasing Spencer's theory, expressed in *Social Statics*, that people should be free to satisfy their mental and physical needs. *Kannō* meant that a person was free to look, listen, talk, think, and move. However, since women had fewer rights than men, they were limited in their freedom to use *kannō*, and this meant that half of the population was excluded from the "benefits of heaven." Some argued that women had fewer rights because they had weaker minds, but this theory was mistaken, as was clear from the fact that there had been cases of women in the past who were involved in government and literary pursuits.

As I stated at the beginning of this section, some scholars have argued that the use of female characters in political novels was a way to allegorically represent the nation as a whole. When Otami in *Year 23: The Dream Bell* spoke about the well-being of the people and the meetings of the Diet as something in which she was interested, they argue, she was representing the opinion of "the people" rather than that of "Japanese women," and a similar analysis can be considered valid for *Setchūbai* as well. Women did read these novels; Sōma Kokkō, for one, wrote that her brother had urged her to become like Fukuda Hideko and given her a copy of *Setchūbai* and she was particularly impressed by it.[63] Although it is unclear whether Sōma appreciated the allegories more than the actual female characters, it is not possible to understand such characters only in allegorical terms. For example, Satoko is depicted in *Joshi sansei shinchūrō* as a young woman who has graduated from a university, and we know that Japanese girl students were asking for more educational rights. When in *Sen'enjō* the two girls argue that male students, seeing educated women teachers, will start respecting women in general, they were but presenting the opinions of Meiji educators. Finally, it is not at all surprising that Otami in *Year 23: The Dream Bell* wants to establish a women's party, for we have seen similar examples in this chapter. Male novelists were influenced by social change when writing their works, and material for their political novels could be found in Japanese society. It was easier, when depicting "the people" versus "the institutions," to take *real life* examples of women struggling for more political participation.

---

63. Sōma Kokkō, *Hirosegawa no hotori* (The banks of the Hirose river) (Josei jidaisha, 1939), 111–12, reprinted in Karasawa Tomitarō, *Gakusei no rekishi* (A history of students) (Sōbunsha, [1955] 1980), 35.

The Late 1880s [[

Despite the legislation barring women from participating in political meetings or giving political speeches, during the late 1880s women seem to have been very active in political spaces. A cursory look at Meiji newspapers provides quite a few examples, although they do not present us with the details. In 1889 Fukuda Hideko helped launch the Fujin daikonshinkai 婦人大懇親会 (Women's General Meeting Society) in Osaka and then went to Kyoto to help women organize there.[64] Although it is not clear what this group wanted to achieve, it is safe to assume that if Fukuda was involved some degree of political interest was present. In the same year, admittance to a political meeting convened in Tokyo by Ōi Kentarō, Ueki Emori, and others was free of charge for women.[65] In Kumamoto prefecture, again in 1889, the Fujin shinbokukai 婦人親睦会 (Women's Friendship Association) was formed at the home of Watanabe Junki 渡邊順喜 for women interested in learning about politics, while in Hakodate some women were organizing to found a political party and in Yokohama women were delivering political speeches with the help of men.[66] An advertisement to recruit five female speakers also appeared in the papers. Speeches, the reporter wrote, were considered by many as a way to change society and contribute to the progress of the nation, and women speakers would attract a good number of listeners since they were still an unusual presence at public speech meetings. The advertisers were looking for young women between fifteen and thirty years old who were supporters of the theories of the Liberal Party, reliable and respectable, had a good basic education, and were able to make speeches.[67] Women were pushing for more political participation, and some men who understood this point were willing to acknowledge women's political needs if only for personal or political gain.

To be sure, some of the articles published during this period, like the ones mentioned above, may have been entirely or partially fabricated, and until more details regarding those women's activities come to light it will not be possible to argue one way or the other, but there are other activities that can be more easily traced, as the following example shows.

One of the most interesting cases of how the line between real and fictional women was blurred is the Kochi fujinkai. In March 1887 the Fujin kōsaikai 婦人交際会 (Group for Women's Association) was opened in Kochi at the home of Sakamoto Naohiro 坂本直寛 by the wives of liberal activists, and Ueki Emori was

---

64. *Yomiuri shinbun*, no. 4329, 11.06.1889, 1.
65. *Yomiuri shinbun*, no. 4382, 11.08.1889, 2.
66. *Yomiuri shinbun*, no. 4407, 10.09.1889, 1; *Shinonome shinbun*, 25.07.1889, reprinted in Suzuki, *Nihon josei undō shiryō shūsei*, 116; *Yomiuri shinbun*, no. 4547, 16.02.1890, 3.
67. *Shinonome shinbun*, 14.06.1889, reprinted in Suzuki, *Nihon josei undō shiryō shūsei*, 114. The same article appeared in *Hokkaido mainichi shinbun*, no. 582, 23.06.1889, 3.

among the supporters. This group then changed its name to Joshi (sometimes Fujin) kyōfūkai 女子興風会 and in 1889 merged with the Fujin shōfūkai 婦人尚風会 and the Nagaoka fujin kairyōkai 長岡婦人改良会 (Nagaoka Women's Group for Reform) to become the Kochi fujinkai 高知婦人会.[68]

In 1889 *Doyō shinbun* published an article detailing the reasons for the founding of this group. It was argued that women's responsibilities were heavier compared to earlier periods. As daughters they had to learn and be virtuous, as wives they had to help their husbands and new families, and as mothers they had to raise and teach their children. However, women were often treated like slaves, were not allowed to educate themselves, could not help their husbands or teach their children, and knew little about the world. The members of this group thought that this state of affairs should be changed; they met once a month in order to learn together, "reform women's society," and advance the progress of their country.[69]

One of the founders of the Joshi kyōfūkai was Tominaga Raku 富永楽 (1866–1938), who was born in present-day Kochi and in 1886 opened a midwifery there.[70] Soon afterward she met Ueki Emori and Kishida Toshiko. She became the head of another group, the Tamamo joshi konshinkai 玉藻女子懇親会, founded in Takamatsu, Kagawa prefecture, in December 1887, and together with her mother and sisters she became a member of the Kochi fujinkai.[71] With Shimizu Shikin and Fukuda Hideko, she planned to publish a magazine, *Joken no sakigake* 女権の魁 (Pioneers of Women's Rights), but I was unable to locate it.[72] She married a doctor from Mori village in 1889 and became a teacher at the local girls' school, but when her husband died in 1892 she moved to Tokyo where she worked as a midwife and wrote articles for *Hōchi shinbun*.[73]

Another member was Yamazaki Take 山崎竹 (1866–1908) from Sagawa in Kochi prefecture. Yamazaki graduated from Kochi Women's Normal School in

---

68. *Doyō shinbun*, no. 1922, 14.04.1889, 2; no. 1940, 05.05.1889, 3. The public speeches of the Joshi kyōfūkai 女子興風会 were publicized in *Doyō shinbun*, no. 1508, 27.11.1887, 2; and no. 1509, 29.11.1887, 2. The Fujin shōfūkai was formed by thirty-two students and teachers of the female section of the Kochi Normal School. Mita, *Jiyū to minken*, 210. Possibly as a way to stop younger women from joining the already vibrant women's movement in the area, students of the female department of Kochi jinjō chūgakkō were prohibited from participating in the meetings and public speeches of the Joshi kyōfūkai 女子興風会, Fujin kyōfūkai 婦人矯風会, and Jofū kairyōkai 女風改良会 (Group for the Reform of Women's Customs). *Doyō shinbun*, no. 1544, 11.01.1888, 3; *Kijo no tomo*, no. 12, 25.01.1888, 1–2. The Jofū kairyōkai's public speeches were publicized in *Doyō shinbun*, no. 1516, 07.12.1887, 3, and no. 1520, 11.12.1887, 3; and *Kōchi nippō*, no. 1425, 11.12.1887, 3, and no. 1426, 13.12.1887, 3.
69. *Doyō shinbun*, no. 1940, 05.05.1889, 3–4.
70. *Doyō shinbun*, no. 1077, 13.05.1886, 4; no. 1664, 03.06.1888, 2.
71. Sotozaki Mitsuhiro, *Ueki Emori to onnatachi* (Ueki Emori and women) (Domesu, 1976), 100–102.
72. *Doyō shinbun*, no. 1919, 11.04.1889, 2.
73. See Sotozaki, *Ueki Emori to onnatachi*, 102.

1882, married a dentist the same year, and worked as a teacher in local elementary schools.[74]

Before the launch of the Kochi fujinkai, a woman from Tosa wrote the article I mentioned in chapter 4 in which she argued that women founded associations and met every month to free themselves from male oppression and to obtain more rights but many such associations were formed with the help of men or men were writing the groups' rules. In her opinion, women had to found groups in cooperation with each other and using only their own strength while fighting men who imposed their ideas on them. Yamazaki responded in the next issue, apparently because she considered the accusations to be directed at the group of which she was a member, arguing that if men were willing to help women reform society there was no reason to refuse their help; on the contrary, men and women should work together to reform the status of women.[75] In an article entitled "Genkon fujo no kyūmu" 現今婦女の急務 (Urgent Work for Today's Women), she explained this concept further. She addressed her "fellow sisters" and lamented that women did not know anything about the state of their nation even though they were "persons born in the same world and possessing the same brains" as men. If women "show a little interest in participating in public service (*shakai no kōmu*) or argue about national welfare" they are called *namaiki* (impertinent). "Society is the society of the people, and the nation is the nation of the people. What would our society and our country be like if those who argue about these matters included women as well as men?" How could women participate in the development of their country? They had to "reform the bad customs of old, develop our knowledge, find employment that will grant us independence, and help capable men."[76]

Yamazaki probably wrote this article after discussing her opinions with other members of her group, and the influence of the Movement for Freedom and Popular Rights is visible in the concepts she proposed. Yamazaki, like Otami in *Year 23: The Dream Bell*, argued that instead of relying upon their husbands women themselves had to fight for the same share of responsibilities and rights; they should be instructed in political matters and be good teachers not merely for their sons but also for themselves. Although men's help was important, the ultimate goal was to become independent. Finally, by asking what kind of society would develop from the complete inclusion of women, she went beyond her contemporaries' demands and hopes and envisioned a reality that feminists are still debating nowadays.

In an article published in *Doyō shinbun* in 1889, Yamazaki also criticized the regulations for the elections in cities, towns, and villages. Addressing "her sisters"

74. Mita, *Jiyū to minken*, 195–214.
75. *Shinonome shinbun*, no. 349, 15.03.1889, 3. Yamazaki's reply was published in no. 391, 05.05.1889, 2; and no. 392, 07.05.1889, 3. The articles are reprinted in Sotozaki, *Ueki Emori to onnatachi*, 203–7 (see also 103–5); and Suzuki, *Nihon josei undō shiryō shūsei*, 104–110.
76. *Doyō shinbun*, no. 1578, 22.02.1888, 3–4.

directly and throughout, Yamazaki wrote that half the population had been denied citizenship and "was considered as persons without any rights whatsoever." This was because the law regulated that only male "imperial subjects" (*teikoku shinmin*) who had citizenship (*kōken*) and fulfilled other requirements were eligible to vote and be elected. Non-Japanese residents and women were not considered citizens (*kōmin*). Given this situation, "How can women develop their understanding of governmental issues? How can they promote love for their country?" According to Japanese legislation, Yamazaki continued, women could not be considered citizens, could not participate in government, could not enter universities, and could not become editors or publishers of magazines and newspapers. Women were encouraged to obtain an education but were then forced to repress their feelings and interrupt their intellectual development.[77]

Soon after writing this article, Yamazaki and the other members of the Kochi fujinkai accepted an offer from Sasaki Toyoju, one of the founders of the Kyōfūkai and the publisher of Ueki Emori's *Tōyō no fujo* 東洋の婦女 (Women of the East), who invited them to write some prefaces for Ueki's book.[78] The book itself did not break new ground, for it rehearsed arguments Ueki had already made in other venues, but the seventeen prefaces are interesting. They were signed by women from Tokyo, Kochi prefecture, Higo Takaoka, Aichi prefecture, and Niigata, and, although I could not find information about many of the contributors, their writings reinforce the assumption that the politically active women presented here are merely examples of the many more we know little about and that, although legislation was being implemented against women's public and political participation, there were women who resisted it.[79]

One of these writers was nineteen-year-old Yoshimatsu Masuko 吉松ます子 (b. 1870), from Kami-gun in Kochi prefecture, who had lost both her parents at an early age and had been involved, at least as a listener, in the political discussions carried out in her area. I have found an article she wrote in *Doyō shinbun* in 1887 entitled "Urgent Work for Women" in which she also addressed her "fellow sisters." Although the world of science and culture was evolving and progressing all over Japan, she complained, it could not be said that women had advanced with the rest of the world. This was in part due to the fact that women were treated like "property" and "playthings" by men, but it was also women's fault, for women submitted to such treatment and oppression. Even "when individual women come forward with the desire to participate even only a little in public matters (*shakai no kōji*), to discuss contemporary topics, or to debate political matters (*ikkoku no*

---

77. *Doyō shinbun*, 31.05.1889; 01.06.1889, reprinted in Sukuzi, *Nihon josei undō shiryō shūsei*, 121–22.

78. *Doyō shinbun*, no. 2100, 12.11.1889, 2; Sotozaki, *Meiji zenki*, 259.

79. The prefaces are reprinted in Sotozaki, *Ueki Emori to onnatachi*, 181–202. See also Sotozaki, *Ueki Emori kazoku seidō ronshū*, 462–66.

seiji)," they were called impertinent. "The most urgent work for our women today" she concluded, is "to join forces with other like-minded women and change the old customs of women's society (*fujin shakai*)."[80] It is difficult to read this text without hearing echoes of the words of Yamazaki and the Kyōfukai, a point that suggests that the same discourses were taken up by women in different parts of the country and were influencing people's way of looking at contemporary society. Not only that, but Yoshimatsu had also learned the lesson taught by early Meiji women that if women wanted to change society they had to work together.

One of the prefaces in *Tōyō no fujo* was written by Sasaki Toyoju herself, who argued that in Japan only men could acquire rights, freedom, happiness, and knowledge. "If Japan wants to become an enlightened country," she wrote, "when men are respected then women have to be respected too. When men are educated, then women have to obtain an education as well." Ueki was one of the few men working for women's society, Sasaki wrote, and she hoped that his book would become "a light that shines upon women's society and that our women will embrace its aims and quickly start on the path of reforming [our society]."[81]

Shimizu Shikin wrote, "The problems of nineteenth-century society are the problems of women, the history of civilization [*bunmei*] in the nineteenth century is the history of the advancement of women's rights, and the nineteenth century is the century in which women's society is changing in Europe and North America." The publication of the book, then, "is not something to rejoice over only for East Asian women, but for East Asian civilization in general." The book, Ueki Emori, and the women who participated in its publication knew that "without reforming the old custom [of *danson johi*] speedily and thoroughly it will not be possible to continue on the path of East Asian civilization." There were two reasons why Ueki Emori was publishing the book: "because of his sincere desire to thoroughly expand women's rights [*joken*] and allow women to attain happiness, and because of his patriotism [*aikokushin*]," for he knew that the improvement of women's condition meant the progress of East Asian civilization.[82]

---

80. *Doyō shinbun*, no. 1268, 11.01.1887, 3. Little is known about her activities afterward. She enrolled in Kochi eiwa jogakkō in 1888 but did not graduate. She went to Tokyo instead, where she was photographed with Shimizu Shikin in 1890 and in 1895 married an activist in the Movement for Freedom and Popular Rights. Kumon Gō, "Tosa no josei minkenka Yoshimatsu Masu" (Yoshimatsu Masu, a female activist in the Movement for Freedom and Popular Rights of Tosa), *Tosa shidan* 161 (1983): 115–20.

81. Reprinted in Sotozaki, *Ueki Emori to onnatachi*, 183–4.

82. Ibid., 184–7. Shimizu was not the only one to argue that the nineteenth century was the century of women. An article written in English in *Kuni no motoi* entitled "Woman's Opportunity" made the same point, stating, "It arises from looking at women as wives and mothers only, taking it for granted that all their interests and emotions, all their hopes, fears, aspirations, ambitions, struggles, triumphs, and defeats, are connected with men, as their wives or mothers. This is looking at them on only one side of their existence, and leaving the other side quite undevel-

Finally, to mention one more preface, Murasame Nobu argued that, although there obviously were differences between men and women, both were human beings and it was necessary to reform bad customs and form a new society in which men and women would be considered equals. That work was to be carried out by them all.

Conclusions

As mentioned in the introduction to this work, Walthall has examined the lives of Edo women who challenged conventional restrictions about what they were allowed to know about politics; by bringing their demands to the authorities, they managed to invade public spaces. However, the worlds in which they moved were almost entirely male, and their activities were not critical of patriarchal institutions and customs. As in the case of Edo women, the cases presented here reveal women reflecting on political issues of which they considered themselves a part, but, in contrast to Edo women, these women made public their struggles against a society in which they were not allowed to participate because they were women and tried to attract an audience. Early Meiji women were also able to form networks with like-minded women and therefore form the basis for a woman's movement. Early Meiji women raised gendered political issues in their groups and the print media while considering themselves to be acting as patriotic citizens working for the development of their country's political institutions. They did not see political rights and education as hindrances to Japan's development; on the contrary, they were a necessary step toward that development.

Few of these women attained national prominence; they were able to craft local spaces for themselves from which to make statements on political issues, but it is clear that national political participation was beyond their reach. The groups presented here were limited in their scope, and the public they reached was also limited because their activities were organized locally and many of their articles were published in regional newspapers that were unlikely to have reached a national audience. Nevertheless, the activities and opinions presented show many common strands that suggest a certain degree of interaction between the groups mentioned

---

oped. Granting that this assumption was correct for the earlier periods of civilization, will it stand the test of the present phase in this 'Woman's Century,' as the nineteenth has been so happily called. The opportunity of women, has just come to the surface, the gates are wide open, and any work of which any individual woman thinks herself capable, and for which she has received a proper education, she is at liberty to try, and thus prove herself a success or a failure." *Kuni no motoi*, no. 1, 01.04.1889, 20–21. I have been unable to identify the author of this piece, but given that it was published in English, was signed with the initials I. G. P., and did not mention *Japanese* women, it is possible that it was first published abroad or was part of a speech given by a foreigner in Japan.

in this chapter and those presented in chapter 4. It is also important to note that, if women's "social groups" developed particularly from 1885 onward, their "political groups" were founded in the early 1880s. It is therefore possible that the women who participated in the Kyōfūkai, for example, knew about these women's political activities but were consciously trying to find less confrontational spaces from which to present their opinions. *All* of these groups, however, helped women to develop their own ideas about feminism and nationalism and were training grounds for women who wanted to obtain a public position—paving the way for a *national* women's movement.

A further characteristic all these groups had in common is that some of their members were involved in the work of Western missionaries either as students or as teachers in missionary schools. This adds another dimension to the work of women missionaries in Japan. I could not discover whether women missionaries openly spoke to Japanese women about female political activities in their countries, but at the very least such missionary environments do not seem to have opposed the idea of female political activities, and provided a fertile backdrop for their development, while "political women's" involvement in missionary schools or groups shows how early Meiji women were able to move from one ideological space to the other and benefit from each.

Early Meiji women were able to create and spread a *discourse* that resisted opposition to female participation in public and political life and education. The Japanese government wanted to educate *subjects* and gave citizenship to a very limited number of men, but in this chapter, too, early Meiji women have demonstrated that they considered themselves to be Japanese *citizens.* They did not have political rights, but they argued that political education for women would support the development of their country. The language women used in the writings we have seen in the last few pages shows that they felt optimistic and confident in their abilities, so much so that in the process they developed the concept of *fujin shakai*. They started to create a different vision, one in which women were active in public society, asking for more rights while working within the home to educate the new generation.

All these activities were not considered mutually exclusive and were perceived as fundamental to *bunmei, fujin shakai*, and *aikokushin* (love for one's country). For them—and this is where their feminist nationalism and the difference between their own and government ideas of nationalism become clear—*aikokushin* developed when women were allowed to demonstrate their abilities and put them to good use, but they could work for their country only if they possessed the rights, happiness, and freedom that men enjoyed. They had come to believe that the nineteenth century was the century of women's advancement and that those intellectuals who thought they could build a strong Japan without the help of women did not understand the meaning of *bunmei*.

Finally, despite all the restrictions placed on them, this chapter shows that the extent of women's involvement in politics was impressive, and this from the very beginning of the Meiji period. Supported and encouraged by some male groups, politicians, and intellectuals, women were able to extend their activities and establish groups in their towns and cities in which they could discuss gendered issues and voice a gendered critique of society.

In light of these points, and even allowing for a decrease in the number of women and women's groups discussing politics and participating in political meetings, is it really believable that, come 1890 and because of the legislation banning women from political participation, women were silenced and lost all the channels they had opened?

6
Conclusions and a Step Forward

During the early Meiji period, the first steps toward the formation of a civil society were taken, more democratic forms of government were discussed, new public spaces were developed in which people could debate all sorts of issues, a full-fledged print industry was formed, and a dialogue with foreign institutions and individuals was initiated. The activities of girl students described in chapters 2 and 3, the founding and spread of women's groups and women's public speeches seen in chapters 4 and 5, as well as the discussion of women's publications and agency across boundaries and across regions, demonstrate that female activities were not simply corollary to, or a result of, male activities. Early Meiji women were fully involved in debating social and cultural issues and creating a new Japan. Furthermore, these activities were not carried out only by few women, but by a relatively large number of young and adult women.

The women introduced in this book became involved in current debates, opened new avenues for women, and made it into print either because of chance encounters or because they belonged to groups that supported their activities. They were but a minority compared to the larger number of women who participated in public life and the print media without challenging male authority, and their number was minuscule compared to the overall number of women living in Japan at the time. Moreover, they often did not manage to achieve the goals they had set for themselves. However, this was also the case for the men who participated in Meiji public society, who formed political groups and made public speeches. Thus, rather than regarding these women as a social minority and powerless group or focusing on what they did not attempt or achieve it is more fruitful for our understanding of the development of Meiji society to focus on what they did achieve. It was the right to express opinions in public settings, to be listened to, and to start a dialogue with others and the government that was important for them, and this, it is now clear, they did obtain. By becoming participants in the Meiji public sphere, they managed to promote their ideas and reach out to a large audience and readership while at the same time establishing a dialogue with the authorities.

These women found in the new notion of womanhood and motherhood a basis for a new affirmation of women's potential power within the home but also a new confidence outside it. This initially happened in a practical way because going to school meant that girls could extend their circle of acquaintances, and learn about the associations organized by women that were meeting at schools and about women's presumed position in society. It happened also because if, according to government authorities and male intellectuals, women's position was to be reformed, by the mid-1880s women started to voice what *they* wanted to change. They organized themselves in groups, publicized their activities in the print media, and recruited new members. Although during the 1870s and early 1880s the spaces they formed were separate, by the late 1880s, and because of the publicity they received, many of these groups and individual women had formed links with each other. These links, in turn, promoted a growing number of venues where women could gather to discuss issues and demand rights in ways that would not have been possible for individuals. In so doing, they publicly started to question the assumptions they were supposed to accept, and the place society had hitherto given them, some by fighting them and living their lives in ways that openly rejected the conventions of their time. By the late 1880s these women had forcefully entered the public sphere, making it also their own, and had started arguing for a "women's way," or *onna no michi*, addressing a public called "sisters," thus showing how conscious of their position they had become. Finally, throughout this book I have mentioned the names of women of whom little or nothing is known because they appeared in relation to interesting groups, activities, or geographic areas. Although we lack information about them and their connections, it is still important to record their names as they serve as evidence of early Meiji women's involvement with one another and with Meiji society.

Early Meiji women were also quick to establish real and ideological links with Western and missionary women. If at first girls in missionary schools considered Western women as alien, soon "international bonds of womanhood" were created that helped many Japanese women progress in their careers and lives. In a few cases, they even became translators and interpreters for the Western women who had taken the bold step of going to Japan to spread their message. Through the publicity their presence, ideas, and activities generated in the Japanese press, Western women became examples to follow or ideological supporters of the causes Japanese women had embraced.

The women discussed here were conscious of the gendered dimensions of their lives. In the political sphere, they were seen as curiosities when standing on a podium and were excluded from the right to participate in political discussions. In the social sphere, they were considered the mothers of the new generation and the only ones who could teach their children sound moral values, in that way saving Japanese society from indecent and immoral behavior. In the economic sphere, this awareness rested on the fact that they were not allowed to dispose of their property as they thought fit and were excluded from a variety of rewarding jobs. In the educational sphere, as a result of the progress they achieved in schools founded by the government, of their setbacks when asking for more educational opportunities, and of their encounters with North American female university students.

This consciousness, together with the publicity created by their activities, produced three important results that I have discussed throughout this book. First, it helped Japanese women establish social networks of women who did not necessarily know one another but shared similar ideas and hopes for the development of women's society, empowering them to become a vocal presence in Japanese society. Second, it helped them define their own vision of the Japanese imagined community and their own idea of nationalistic Japanese women. Early Meiji women were not legally entitled to political or social rights, but they nevertheless expressed their opinions on political and social issues affecting Japanese women. They concerned themselves with the discourses on how Japan could become a modern, enlightened, and powerful country initiated by the Meiji government and male intellectuals and embraced those goals. They believed and publicly argued, however, that without women's full and free participation in the formation of a new Japan such goals would be unattainable. Third, it helped them bring to the fore topics, such as concubinage and family composition, that they felt needed to be addressed but male society wanted to keep private. Early Meiji women, I have shown, endowed the next generation of feminists with two decades of gendered social and political experience and consciousness.

This is what happened during the early Meiji period, but my research becomes much more interesting when linked to the following periods of Japanese history. I devote the rest of this final chapter to bringing my arguments forward and proposing new lines of inquiry and research.

Meiji Women and Japanese Women's History

The heuristic value of the concept of the "public sphere" that has informed the arguments of this book is important if we want to link early Meiji women to women of the following decades. During the Taishō period (1912–26), groups of women such as the Seitōsha gained much public recognition, but how indebted were they to the groups that, before them, had voiced feminist demands in public spaces? Could Taishō women have published magazines if the women who came before them had not written articles critiquing social, political, and economic issues in the print media and if they had not already tried to publish their own magazines? Could Taishō women have found men who supported their different understanding of women's position in society if these same men had not already become acquainted with a culture of women's social and political unrest? And how are we to explain the "Seitō phenomenon" if *Jogaku zasshi* had only a small female readership, *Tokyo fujin kyōfu zasshi* was read only by Christian followers, and the other women's magazines published during the early Meiji period were produced solely for good wives and wise mothers?[1]

Late Meiji Women

These questions raise other questions that are yet to be answered satisfactorily. First of all, if early Meiji women formed the first feminist movement active in public spaces, *who belonged to the next generation*, for between early Meiji women and the Seitō group there spans twenty years that have yet to be fully explored.

Mackie and Sievers, among others, have done important work to help us answer this question. They have shown how Fukuda Hideko moved from participating in the jiyū minken undō to actively working in the socialist movement. She joined the Heiminsha 平民社 (Commoners' Society, founded in 1903) and edited a magazine, *Sekai fujin* 世界婦人 (Women of the World, 1907–9) in which women's issues were discussed from a socialist perspective.[2] She was not the only one, for various women gathered around Fukuda and the socialist group, and their history is important not only within the history of Japanese women but also for our understanding of the socialist movement as a whole.[3] *Sekai fujin* was not the first socialist women's journal either, *Nijūseki no fujin* 二十世紀の婦人 (Twentieth Century Woman, 1904) and *Suiito homu* (Sweet Home, 1904) having been published previously.[4] Between 1904 and 1909 these women petitioned for the revision of article 5 of the Public Peace Police Law (Chian keisatsu hō 治安警察法, 1900), which prohibited women from joining political associations or attending political meetings, proving that efforts to stop women from concerning themselves with political matters were opposed by many.[5]

---

1. On the Seitō group, see Sharon Sievers, *Flowers in Salt: The Beginnings of Feminist Consciousness in Modern Japan* (Stanford: Stanford University Press, 1983), 163-88; Vera Mackie, *Feminism in Modern Japan: Citizenship, Embodiment, and Sexuality* (Cambridge: Cambridge University Press, 2003), 45-58; and Jan Bardsley, *The Bluestockings of Japan: New Woman Essays and Fiction from Seito, 1911–1916,* Michigan Monograph Series in Japanese Studies, no. 60 (Ann Arbor: Center for Japanese Studies, University of Michigan, 2007).

2. Sievers, *Flowers in Salt,* chap. 6; Vera Mackie, *Creating Socialist Women in Japan: Gender, Labour, and Activism, 1900–1937* (Cambridge: Cambridge University Press, 1997), chap. 3.

3. Mackie, *Creating Socialist Women,* chap. 3; Nishikawa Fumiko, *Heiminsha no onna: Nishikawa Fumiko jiden* (A woman of the *Heiminsha*: The autobiography of Nishikawa Fumiko), edited by Amano Shigeru (Aoyamakan, 1984).

4. Mackie, *Creating Socialist Women,* 15.

5. Mackie, *Feminism in Modern Japan,* 32–33.

Even so, if come the late 1880s women were silenced by the government in many ways, how did they manage to reappear so forcefully in the 1900s? Were the women of the Heiminsha a social and political "anomaly" compared to the rest of the female population? Given that early Meiji individual female activists were but part of a larger network of women and women's groups, it seems likely that the women active in the Heiminsha and their petitions were similarly supported by a network of politically informed women, a network that waits to be thoroughly uncovered.

Perhaps the most famous female group founded during the late Meiji period and before women joined the Heiminsha was the Aikoku fujinkai 愛国婦人会 (Patriotic Women's Association). This group, which was founded in 1901 by Okumura Ioko 奥村五百子, the daughter of a chief Buddhist priest, with the assistance of the Home Ministry and Army Ministry, had the aim of comforting wounded soldiers and the families of those who fell in battle but also of educating women and collaborating with the state.[6] To be sure, the rise of nationalist and militarist discourses, which became much stronger during the 1890s, worked directly against the diversity of public spaces and the topics discussed in them, while those women who embraced their country's war efforts were left with much less space from which to define women's needs independent of their country's needs. Even considering that some (a substantial percentage?) of the women presented in this work turned toward the Aikoku fujinkai and other conservative female associations, what does this tell us about women's need to associate, feel part of a civil society, and, at least in some cases, to defend from within nationalist associations the freedom of action and speech they had gained? Supporting the war was a way to behave as dutiful subjects but also of reclaiming for themselves a certain degree of citizenship. More work needs to be done on the Aikoku fujinkai in order to link it to other women's organizations of the time, but even if, for argument's sake, we consider the Aikoku fujinkai merely as a conservative organization that did not support women's society, or even hindered its development, what are we left with? Did feminist action shift elsewhere or did it (partly) disappear?

Hastings writes that Hatoyama Haruko's first involvement in political campaigning came shortly after the 1890 election, when her husband agreed to run for the office of Diet representative from the Kita Toyoshima district in Tokyo. She went from house to house campaigning for her husband and, according to Hastings, this was not the only time she did so.[7] Was she the only one? Was she, a woman, taken seriously by the members of the households she visited? Did she talk mostly

---

6. There were 464,000 members in 1905 and 807,000 in 1911. Sheldon Garon, *Molding Japanese Minds: The State in Everyday Life* (Princeton: Princeton University Press, 1997), 122.
7. Sally A. Hastings, "Hatoyama Haruko: Ambitious Woman," in *The Human Tradition in Modern Japan*, edited by Anne Walthall, 81–98 (Wilmington: Scholarly Resources, 2002), 89.

to women? And if so, why were these women politically educated or interested in politics? If they were not, how did they feel about a woman who was? What issues did she address? Women seem to have continued to obtain a political education and discuss political matters within their homes. In a period of repressive government gendered policies, rather than large gatherings and meetings they were more likely to have attended smaller ones. Furthermore, given that it was through women's active involvement in early Meiji society that a feminist consciousness was born, and Hatoyama's work shows that such involvement was still possible for some to a certain degree during the 1890s, it becomes easier to understand why women's activism resurfaced during the 1900s, when the time was ripe.

Similarly, what about all those girls who wanted to pursue higher education during the 1880s and those who left Japan to study in North America? Though small in number, given that they were part of a constant flow, that they were provided with more and better organized facilities in which to study, and that a female student culture had already formed around them, it is inconceivable that they did not have an impact on their educational institutions. They were, most probably, the teachers of those twelve thousand students in the fifty-two high schools for girls that Furuki reports existed in 1900.[8] In 1900 Yoshioka Yayoi founded the first school for young women who wanted to become doctors, Tokyo joi gakkō 東京女医学校 (Tokyo Women's Medical School), and Tsuda Umeko opened Joshi eigaku juku 女子英学塾, which offered girls a higher qualification with which to find employment. What background did these young women have? What were they thinking, and how did they regard themselves in relation to society at large?

Finally, Chatterjee has argued that in India the battle for the new ideal of womanhood in the era of nationalism was waged in the home, and this suggests further lines of inquiry. What do the private writings of the young women who studied abroad and in Japan, and of late Meiji women in general, tell us about the battles they fought and the ways in which they lived?[9] One example of a woman who voiced her opinion about the way relationships between the sexes were structured was Shimizu Shikin's female character in *Koware yubiwa* こわれ指輪 (The Broken Ring, 1891), in which a strong critique of contemporary marriage and society was presented. There were many other female novelists during the 1890s and 1900s; the literary value of their works might not have been as high as those of famous women writers, and for this reason they have not stood the test of time, but in them we might find important information concerning their aspirations and dreams.[10]

---

8. Yoshiko Furuki, *The White Plum: A Biography of Ume Tsuda, Pioneer in the Higher Education of Japanese Women* (New York: Weatherhill, 1991), 102–3.
9. Partha Chatterjee, *The Nation and Its Fragments: Colonial and Postcolonial Histories* (Princeton: Princeton University Press, 1993), 133.
10. Rebecca Jennison, trans., "The Broken Ring," in *The Modern Murasaki: Writing by Women of Meiji Japan*, edited by Rebecca Copeland and Melek Ortabasi, 232–39 (New York: Columbia

If we want to find out what women who wanted to change Japanese society did when they "retreated to their homes" once public life was not easily accessible to them anymore, the debate over the issue of prostitution is another good place in which to look. Shimada Saburō argued at the beginning of the 1900s that the work carried out by the Kyōfūkai on the abolition of prostitution had raised public awareness on the topic.[11] Mihalopoulos writes that every year from 1890 to 1927 the Kyōfūkai petitioned the Japanese government to stop the flow of *karayuki-san*, Japanese women going abroad to work as prostitutes.[12] Ogawa, on the other hand, has analyzed the work undertaken at the Jiaikan (Home of Mercy and Love), a "rescue home" for prostitutes opened in 1894 by the Kyōfūkai.[13] Although scholars have done important work on the issue of prostitution during the late Meiji period, this topic has not been sufficiently analyzed. For example, we still do not know enough about the debates on prostitution that took place in the female periodical press during the 1890s and 1900s and how women participated in them.

I started my research in order to find out whether, during the early Meiji period, famous individual Japanese feminists such as Kishida Toshiko or Fukuda Hideko were representatives of a larger women's movement. The answer to this question has proven to be affirmative. My research, however, raises even more questions that remain to be answered. In order to start addressing those questions, I discuss below the activities of four women who lived and worked during the period analyzed in this book but who showed a feminist awareness and initiative even after the government issued laws that hampered women's participation in society. These women are extremely powerful examples of a feminist current that awaits discovery.

Women Journalists

In chapter 4 we saw how Sasaki Toyoju argued that women should obtain positions that could be defined as "enlightened jobs," and she was probably pleased when she heard that Meiji women were beginning to be employed as journalists, for it

University Press, 2006); and, in Japanese, Yamaguchi Reiko, *Naite aisuru shimai ni tsugu: Kozai Shikin no shōgai* (To my beloved sisters in tears: The life of Kozai Shikin) (Sōdo bunka, 1977). On Meiji women writers, see Rebecca Copeland and Melek Ortabasi, eds., *The Modern Murasaki: Writing by Women of Meiji Japan* (New York: Columbia University Press, 2006).

11. Interview with Ushioda Chiseko, supplement to *Fujo shinbun*, no. 49, 08.04.1901, 1, discussed in chapter 4.

12. Bill Mihalopoulos, "Mediating the Good Life: Prostitution and the Japanese Woman's Christian Temperance Union, 1880s–1920s," *Gender and History* 21.1 (2009): 8; "Modernization as Creative Problem Making: Political Action, Personal Conduct, and Japanese Overseas Prostitutes," *Economy and Society* 27.1 (1998): 50–73.

13. Manako Ogawa, "Rescue Work for Japanese Women: The Birth and Development of the Jiaikan Rescue Home and the Missionaries of the Woman's Christian Temperance Union, Japan, 1886–1921," *U.S.-Japan Women's Journal* 26 (2004): 98–133.

was precisely during the 1890s and 1900s that such an opportunity arose. In 1890, *Jogaku zasshi* announced, "The editing of the paper will be under the general superintendence and responsibility of Miss T. [Toyoko, aka Shikin] Shimizu."[14] We know of Shimizu's activism, and Iwamoto's support for women's employment, but what about the other women who were employed by newspapers? Were they simply doing a man's job in a male environment or were they bringing something different to the journalistic profession? What background did they have?

Take, for example, the cases of Takekoshi Takeyo 竹越竹代 (1870–1944) and Ōzawa Toyoko 大沢豊子 (1873–1937). I came across Takekoshi's name for the first time in the petition signed by twenty-one women demanding the right to attend meetings of the Diet discussed in chapter 4. Takekoshi Takeyo was born in Okayama in 1870, and around 1877 she entered a local elementary school. Her father died, and her mother, Nakamura Shizuko 中村静子 (1850–1909), who later became a Christian and the head of the Okayama branch of the Kyōfūkai (founded in 1889), started teaching female chores to children at home and Japanese to some missionaries in the area.[15] Nakamura was a close acquaintance of Sumiya Koume and Ōnishi Kinu 大西絹, Nakagawa Yokotarō's sister-in-law and one of the founders of San'yō eiwa jogakkō, where Nakamura taught needlework and Takekoshi studied.[16] Takekoshi was baptized in Okayama but then moved to Baika jogakkō in Osaka, graduating in 1887. She must have been a very good student, for one of her schoolmates remembered that when Takekoshi's friend Kajiro Yoshi 上代淑 (1871–1976) was accepted at Mount Holyoke College in 1893 everyone thought that she would be the next one to study in North America.[17]

In 1889 Takekoshi married Takekoshi Yosaburō 竹越与三郎, who was working for *Kokumin shinbun* 国民新聞, and in 1890 she started working for the paper as well. Although male journalists continued to write about women in their articles, by the early 1890s newspapers were willing to employ educated women (who could be paid less) to write about women's matters. Under the pen name Takemura 竹村,

---

14. *Jogaku zasshi*, no. 244, 20.12.1890, inside front cover. See also Mara Patessio, "Readers and Writers: Women and Magazines in the Late Nineteenth Century," in *The Female as Subject: Reading and Writing in Early Modern Japan*, edited by P. F. Kornicki, Mara Patessio, and G. G. Rowley, Michigan Monograph Series in Japanese Studies, no. 70 (Ann Arbor: Center for Japanese Studies, University of Michigan, 2010), 191–213.

15. Takekoshi Kumasaburō, *Takekoshi Takeyo no shōgai* (The life of Takekoshi Takeyo) (Takekoshi Tatsugorō, 1965), 1–2. A brief account of Nakamura's travels while head of the Okayama fujin kyōfūkai was published in *Jogaku Zasshi*, no. 253, 21.02.1891, 27.

16. On Ōnishi, see Okayama joseishi kenkyūkai, ed., *Kindai Okayama no onnatachi* (Women of Okayama during the modern period) (Sanseidō, 1987), 63-76.

17. Takekoshi, *Takekoshi Takeyo*, 12. Kajiro studied at Baika jogakkō in Osaka, and from 1889 she taught English at San'yō eiwa jogakkō. She studied at Mount Holyoke College until 1897, obtaining a bachelor of science degree. She went back to teaching in Okayama after returning from North America. Kajiro Yoshi kenkyūkai, *Kajiro Yoshi kenkyū* (A study of Kajiro Yoshi), vol. 1 (Okayama: San'yō gakuen daigaku, 1996), 49.

Takekoshi conducted a series of interviews with famous women, including the educator Shimoda Utako,[18] the nurses Suzuki Masako 鈴木雅子 and Ōzeki Chikako,[19] Kishida Toshiko,[20] and Toyoda Fuyuko, who had just returned from Italy.[21]

One interesting article probably written by Takekoshi was a report on a day spent at Meiji jogakkō, where she attended lectures and interviewed Iwamoto Yoshiharu, who told her that the aim of the school was to nurture "women educators" (*fujin no kyōikuka*). Educated women would be able to find suitable jobs while their employment was closely related to the expansion of women's rights. Iwamoto explained that women were oppressed by men because of a habit born in the past, and to break this tradition it was necessary to provide women with a different kind of education. In order to really promote women's advancement, Iwamoto continued, people should be taught to respect women, and that could be done by raising the new generation, a task that women teachers could begin to fulfill at the elementary level. Not only that, it had been proved that in elementary schools women were much more effective than men in keeping children quiet.[22] During the Meiji period, elementary schools were established all over Japan in order to educate the next generation of Japanese *subjects*, and teaching became the first occupation available to educated women. Teachers were supposed to embrace the government ideology and transmit it to their students, but here Iwamoto was proposing different reasons for becoming elementary teachers; it is likely that his opinion was shared by women who were either already employed in elementary schools or wanted to be.

In 1892, Takekoshi published *Fujin risshi hen* 婦人立志篇 (Subtitled, Self-Help for Women), a collection of biographies of famous Western women, including Florence Nightingale, the writers Harriet Beecher Stowe and Lucy Hutchinson, the scientist Mary Somerville, the traveler Ida Pfeiffer, and the poet, educator, and writer Hannah More. In 1871, Nakamura Masanao had published *Saigoku risshi hen* 西国立志編 (Tales of Successful Men in Western Countries), a translation of Samuel Smiles's *Self Help*, and it is hard not to link Takekoshi's collection to those of Smiles and Nakamura. Nakamura was a supporter of women's education

---

18. Supplement to *Kokumin shinbun*, no. 30, 02.03.1890, 2.
19. Supplement to *Kokumin shinbun*, no. 26, 26.02.1890, 1–2.
20. Supplement to *Kokumin shinbun*, no. 49, 21.03.1890, 1.
21. *Kokumin shinbun*, no. 169, 19.07.1890, 2; no. 170, 20.07.1890, 1. *Kokumin shinbun* (no. 199, 18.08.1890, 2) published an unsigned article, probably written by Takekoshi, reporting on a public speech meeting sponsored by the Joshi danwakai 女子談話会 (Women's Conversation Society) in Ueno. There were about two hundred listeners, mostly girl students but also older women, and the first two speeches were given by two young women. The third was delivered by a certain Kawaguchi Kumoi 河口雲井, who delivered a fierce speech critical of Fukuda Hideko, arguing that she was a slave of the Jiyūtō who wanted to put Kawaguchi's group at its service. I could not find any more information about Kawaguchi.
22. *Kokumin shinbun*, supplement to no. 37, 09.03.1890, 1.

and improvement, and Takekoshi's choice of title seems to have been an answer to his call. Biographies of women were published during the Edo and Meiji periods, but they presented and supported feminine virtues and described as models of womanhood mothers who raised their children, wives who supported their husbands, and daughters who were faithful to their parents' desires. By 1892, the time had come for women to read books centered on female, rather than only male, past and future achievements.[23]

This was not the only time that Takekoshi's name appeared in a book. In 1893, after Mary Allen West, a member of the directorate of the WCTU, died as she was engaged in a series of public speeches in Japan, Takekoshi edited a book entitled *The late Mrs. West's teachings*, a collection of essays on her activities and opinions. Beginning in November 1893, we also find Takekoshi's name listed as the editor of *Fujin kyōfu zasshi*.[24]

Takekoshi was a prolific writer, translator, and activist who found employment in a newspaper company and defined herself as the first Japanese woman journalist. She visited and interviewed many people and recalled that they would give her tips when the interviews were over. Given that she was one of the few women working as journalist, she continued, everyone was nice to her, for example, lending her an umbrella if it rained.[25]

Ōzawa Toyoko, on the other hand, wrote about the difficulty of feeling comfortable in a newspaper company, a wholly male environment. Born in Gunma prefecture, in 1888 she enrolled in the Sokkihō joshi kenkyūkai 速記法女子研究会, a private school that taught shorthand opened in the same year in Tokyo by Tsukuda Yojirō 佃興次郎. Tsukuda was also employed at Meiji jogakkō in 1890 to teach shorthand courses.[26]

---

23. The volume was publicized in *Jogaku zasshi*, no. 365, 03.02.1894, 27, and no. 370, 10.03.1894, 27; and *Fujin kyōfu zasshi*, no. 1, 20.11.1893, 55. Another woman, Sakurai Fukiko 桜井ふき子, edited *Fujin risshi den* 婦人立志伝 (Biographies of successful women) (Hifumi-kan, 1893), which included biographies of Japanese as well as Western women. Female "success stories" were becoming a genre that was finding a market in Meiji Japan.

24. Takekoshi Takeyo. ed. *Westo joshi ikun* (The late Mrs. West's teachings) (Tokyo fujin kyōfūkai, 1893). Interviews with West conducted by Takekoshi were published in *Kokumin shinbun*, no. 823, 21.09.1892, 3; and no. 824, 22.09.1892, 3. Her death was reported in *Kokumin shinbun*, no. 884, 06.12.1892, 1.

25. "Taku o kakonde" 卓をかこんで (Around the table), in *Fujin shinpō*, no. 370, 01.1929, 31.

26. Esashi Akiko, *Onna no kuse ni: Kusawake no josei shinbun kisha tachi* (Only a woman: Pioneer women newspaper journalists) (Impacto, 1997), 88. *Jogaku zasshi* (no. 198, 01.02.1890, inside front cover, in English) reported, "We have hinted again and again on the advisability of training girls, in short-hand writing. Since the beginning of this term, short-hand is taught by Mr. Tsukuda in the Meiji Jo-Gakko to a class of some thirty girls who specially wish to be instructed in the same." Of the nine students who took courses in shorthand and graduated from Meiji jogakkō after March 1891 (the exact date is not clear), one was hired by *Jogaku zasshisha* and

Kokumin shinbun published an article in 1890 outlining the reasons why note taking was a suitable job for women. It stated that in a country with a constitutional government, speeches and discussions were the tools for the creation of new laws. It followed that note taking was a crucial service and that note takers' value would rise sharply.[27] This was probably another job that Sasaki Toyoju considered "enlightened," as it enabled women to listen to speeches on all sorts of topics while earning a living.

Ōzawa became the note taker for *Fujin eisei zasshi*, the journal of the Dai nihon fujin eisei kai (Great Japan Women's Hygiene Association), edited by Iwamoto Yoshiharu (the editorial board included the nurse Suzuki Masako and the doctor Ogino Ginko), in September 1889, and in 1899 she began work for *Jiji shinpō* in the same capacity, where she remained for the next twenty-five years.[28] Ōzawa was not sure whether to accept the job at *Jiji shinpō*, so she visited the famous educator Shimoda Utako, whom she already knew. Shimoda told her to give it a try and always remember that even if she could not achieve equality with male journalists, as a woman she nevertheless had distinctive qualities useful for her job. Although in the case of other newspapers the situation might be different, Shimoda continued, *Jiji shinpō*, which had been founded by Fukuzawa Yukichi, was a respectable venue, and Ōzawa should do her best. While working for *Jiji shinpō*, Ōzawa eventually interviewed women such as Shimoda Utako herself, Ushioda Chiseko, and Miwada Masako.

Given the length of her employment in the media industry, it is clear that Ōzawa enjoyed her job (or at least was determined to succeed in it), and her recollections offer us a glimpse into the life of a woman working in a thoroughly male environment, an experience that was partly shared by Takekoshi Takeyo as well. Ōzawa could not move freely in the office because there were always hundreds of eyes looking at her. She had to refrain from drinking water during office hours for fear of having to go to the toilet and from eating until very late at night when there was extra work to do, and, of course, she could not socialize with colleagues outside the office for fear of attracting criticism and gossip. This last self-imposed rule, Ōzawa remembered, was relaxed only at the end of her employment there, when another woman joined the company and times had changed. Then she felt it necessary to set an example for the other woman and participated in the various

---

another remained at the school as a teacher. *Fujin kyōkai zasshi*, no. 39, 03.04.1891, 24; *Yomiuri shinbun*, no. 4920, 24.2.1891, 3. The course lasted three months, and some of its first students found employment either in the school or at magazines. *Jogaku zasshi*, no. 295, 12.12.1891, 21.

27. *Kokumin shinbun*, no. 38, 10.02.1890, 1.

28. See *Fujin eiseikai zasshi*, no. 1, 02.02.1888, for its editorial board; and *Fujin eiseikai zasshi*, no. 8, 17.09.1889, for Ōzawa. Before Ōzawa, Tsukuda was the note taker. See also Esashi, *Onna no kuse ni*, 88-108.

parties organized by the company. However strict her behavior was during her years of work, Ōzawa concluded, that did not preclude her from becoming a *otenba* (tomboy) in her old age![29]

Meiji women's freedom was restricted in all sorts of ways, but Takekoshi and Ōzawa were neither daughters kept in boxes nor women who lived exclusively for their households. Ōzawa, and probably Takekoshi as well, put up with these conditions because they wanted to succeed in their occupations, and their tenacity and hard work are one of the reasons why women were able to become full-fledged journalists during the Meiji period.

The Ashio Copper Mine and Female Activism

A third woman who merits attention is Matsumoto Eiko 松本英子 (1866–1928), for her life story demonstrates that women besides those involved in the socialist Heiminsha were interested in political action during the early 1900s. Matsumoto was born in Chiba prefecture and studied at her father's private school before enrolling in Kaigan jogakkō and Joshi kōtō shihan gakkō in Tokyo. She was baptized and went on to translate essays and speeches for women missionaries, as well as literature, publishing, among other things, a translation of Henry Wadsworth Longfellow's writings in *Yomiuri shinbun* and a free translation of the Edo period novel *Murasaki no hitomoto* 紫の一本 (A Spring of Purple) by Toda Mosui 戸田茂睡. She married Ienaga Toyokichi 家永豊吉, who was employed by the Ministry of Foreign Affairs, but their marriage did not last, and in 1898 she became a teacher at Kazoku jogakkō.[30] Matsumoto was the third woman, together with Tsuda Umeko and Ishii Fudeko (discussed below) to teach at this elite government school for the daughters of the nobility. Clearly, even spaces that were not feminist at all allowed women to articulate opinions that differed from the official ideology on Japanese womanhood, while women could choose, or move within, different ideological spaces while at the same time maintaining their ideological integrity.

Matsumoto left Kazoku jogakkō in 1900, and the next year she was hired by *Mainichi shinbun*, a progressive newspaper in which Shimada Saburō, a member of the Constitutional Progressive Party, and the socialist Kinoshita Naoe worked. Under the pen name Midoriko みどり子, Matsumoto recorded the activities of women who criticized the lack of government support for those whose lives had been destroyed by the pollution caused by the Ashio copper mine in Tochigi prefecture.

---

29. Ōzawa's memoir, "Hisareta onna no kokoro" 秘された女の心 (The secret heart of a woman) was published in *Fujin kōron*, no. 125, 01.01.1940, 130–40. Esashi, in *Onna no kuse ni*, 93, mentions this article, but her bibliographical reference is mistaken. This is the correct one.
30. See Fuma Kiyoshi, *Matsumoto Eiko no shōgai* (The life of Matsumoto Eiko) (Shōwa tosho shuppan, 1981).

The mine had existed since the Edo period, but during the Meiji period it started dumping toxic materials into a nearby river, which flooded periodically, sending polluted water into cultivated fields. The fields became sterile, with disastrous consequences for the local population, and, although petitions were addressed to the local and central governments, no solution was found.[31] In 1900, individuals such as Tanaka Shōzō 田中正造, a member of the Lower House, Shimada Saburō, Kinoshita Naoe, Abe Isoo, and Iwamoto Yoshiharu, established the Kōdoku chōsa yūshikai 鉱毒調査有志会 (Volunteer Society to Investigate Mine Pollution), and in 1901 they were joined by the women of the Kyōfūkai who, after visiting the areas affected and witnessing the level of distress of those living there, established the Kōdokuchi kyūsai fujinkai 鉱毒地救済婦人会 (Women's Association for the Relief of Mine-Polluted Areas). Rather than an alternative to the Kōdoku chōsa yūshikai, this was a sister group, for the members of the two organizations worked closely together, and similar local women's groups were also established in order to raise funds.[32]

Among the women who participated in activities of this group were Ushioda Chiseko, Shimada Nobuko 島田信子, Mitani Tamiko, Yamawaki Fusako, Kinoshita Misaoko, Uemura Kikuko, Miwada Masako, and Yajima Kajiko.[33] These women went to the areas affected by the mine, taking food and clothing. They also publicized the problem through public speech meetings, collected donations, and organized visits to the area.[34] Some of them went on a public speech tour and could count on the local branches of the Kyōfūkai and missionary schools for support. They visited schools in the affected areas and reported that in one town with three hundred school-age children only eighty were attending school and were being taught by just one teacher; of these eighty, only three were girls.[35] The Kōdokuchi kyūsai fujinkai brought some girls between the ages of nine and fourteen to Tokyo to study, but this undertaking was not entirely successful, for several were homesick and left quite soon.[36] In 1903, Ushioda established a successful vocational

31. See Elizabeth Dorn Lublin, "Pollution Relief and the Japan Woman's Christian Temperance Union," *Asian Cultural Studies: International Christian University* 27 (2001): 49–58; and Fred George Notehelfer, "Japan's First Pollution Incident," *Journal of Japanese Studies* 1.2 (1975): 351–83.
32. The Chiba fujin kōdokuchi kyūsai was formed in 1902. *Fujo shinbun*, no. 93, 17.02.1902, 2.
33. *Fujo shinbun*, no. 83, 09.12.1901, 2; no. 89, 20.01.1902, 2.
34. See, for example, the amounts donated and the names of the donors in *Mainichi shinbun*, no. 9497, 25.12.1901, 3; and no. 9509, 06.01.1902, 3. See also *Fujo shinbun*, no. 81, 25.11.1901, 4; and no. 87, 06.01.1902, 4. Their public speeches were publicized in *Fujo shinbun*, no. 93, 17.02.1902, 2.
35. *Fujo shinbun*, no. 82, 02.12.1901, 4. The article was written by Ushioda. Ushioda also published articles describing the situation to which many families were reduced in *Fujo shinbun*, no. 81, 25.11.1901, 4; and no. 82, 02.12.1901, 4.
36. *Mainichi shinbun*, no. 9497, 25.12.1901, 3; no. 9513, 10.01.1902, 3.

school in one area of the polluted region, where women learned to weave material used in the manufacture of Western hats.[37]

Students were also involved and organized public speech meetings.[38] When the students of Tottori eiwa jogakkō read a statement issued by the Kōdokuchi kyūsai fujinkai explaining the situation, they raised twenty yen for the group.[39] Another supporter was Nishikawa Fumiko 西川文子 (later a member of the Heiminsha), a student of Kyoto-fu jogakkō. She went to a fund-raising event where Kinoshita Naoe, Tamura Naoomi, and Ushioda Chiseko gave speeches and was so deeply moved that she managed to persuade the headmaster to invite Ushioda to give a public speech for the students of her own school.[40]

In the meantime, Matsumoto was reporting everything in *Mainichi shinbun*. She portrayed the level of disease, decay, dirt, and death; she pushed "her sisters" to help and encouraged them to go and see for themselves what was happening; she described the lack of schooling for children and the problems that were affecting women's lives; and she introduced individuals and families, detailing their miserable lifestyles and the problems they had to face daily.[41]

As I have argued in this book, "political activity" did not necessarily coincide with the suffrage movement. It could often be found at the local level and in groups of people who were trying to influence public matters or oppose government activities, concentrating on what women could do. The women of the Kōdokuchi kyūsai fujinkai did just that. Their collective participation reinforced their convictions and spurred them to accuse Japanese society of wrongdoings, even though issuing such public statements was by then against the law. Matsumoto and Ushioda were summoned by the police after they issued a particularly critical statement, which confirms that the government was aware of the power of women's voices and considered their writings and actions to be detrimental to public "peace."[42] Let us look at this statement, which was published by the Kōdokuchi kyūsai fujinkai as a plea for help.

> The voice of the Ashio mine pollution disaster is shaking the world. . . .
> For the past twenty years our society has been committing a heinous crime by ignoring the grieving of those 300,000 citizens living in the

37. Dorn, "Pollution Relief," 56.
38. *Mainichi shinbun*, no. 9509, 06.01.1902, 2.
39. *Fujo shinbun*, no. 94, 24.02.1902, 2.
40. Nishikawa, *Heiminsha no onna*, 26.
41. See, for example, *Mainichi shinbun*, no. 9467, 25.11.1901, 3; no. 9470, 28.11.1901, 3; no. 9507, 04.01.1902, 1; no. 9508, 05.01.1902, 3; no. 9526, 23.01.1902, 3; and no. 9530, 27.01.1902, 3. These articles were often accompanied by drawings portraying those people, their homes, and their broken objects of daily use. Descriptions of individuals or families continued to be published until February 1902 for a total of fifty-nine articles. Esashi, *Onna no kuse ni*, 115.
42. *Fujo shinbun*, no. 92, 10.02.1902, 2.

areas affected by this problem. This heinous crime has not been committed by only one individual person or one government, but by the whole of society.

They concluded by stating that if there was anyone who still did not know how bad the situation was, that person should take a day off and go and see it with his or her own eyes.[43]

These women petitioned the authorities, organized and were asked to speak at meetings in order to raise awareness of the situation, published articles in magazines and newspapers, and collected donations. They even published a volume on their movement.[44] They were not afraid of stepping up and publicly accusing society as a whole, as well as the government, of wrongdoings. These were the same women who had been educated or were active during the 1880s; they knew how to organize themselves when they found out about the pollution problem, how to make speeches, how to collect money, how to write for the print media, and how to pull the strings of a network of male and female acquaintances.

Ishii Fudeko

The women involved in the Kōdokuchi kyūsai fujinkai decided to speak in favor of those who had been abandoned by the Japanese government, but in the same period there was one more woman who devoted her life to safeguarding the well-being of another group of neglected people, and it is with her story that I conclude my work.

I first came to know about Ishii Fudeko 石井筆子 (1861–1944) in the summer of 2006 when I visited Takinogawa gakuen 滝乃川学園, the school for disabled children where she worked with her husband. While there, I met Ms. Miyazaki Nobue 宮崎信恵, who had just finished making the movie *Mumyō no hito, Ishii Fudeko no shōgai* 無名のひと—石井筆子の生涯 (An Unknown Person, Ishii Fudeko's Life). Since then, another movie on Ishii Fudeko has been completed by the director Yamada Hisako 山田火砂子 entitled *Fudeko, sono ai, tenshi no piano* 筆子・その愛—天使のピアノ (Fudeko, Her Love, the Pianoforte of an Angel).

In 1898 Ishii Fudeko (wherever possible, I will refer to her simply as Fudeko because her surname changed more than once) wrote an article on Florence

---

43. The Kōdokuchi kyūsai fujinkai signed the statement asking that money be sent to the Mainichi company and items for the people affected to the general headquarters of the group. *Mainichi shinbun*, 17.01.1902, in Tanaka Shōzō, *Kōdoku jiken* (The mine pollution incident), in *Gijin zenshū* (The complete works of a righteous man), edited by Kurihara Hikosaburō, vols. 3–4 (Chūgai shinronsha, 1925–27), vol. 4, 772–74. It was also published in *Fujo shinbun*, no. 89, 20.01.1902, 6.
44. Matsumoto Eiko, ed., *Kōdokuchi no sanjō* (The pitiful situation of the land polluted by the mine), vol. 1 (Kyōbunkan, 1902).

Nightingale, yet another model of womanhood for Japanese women, stating that Nightingale was a gentle, sincere, and refined person born to a well-to-do family. She obtained a very good education, but she used it to help others by becoming a nurse. Not only that, she also established the first educational institution for nurses. She believed that "Irrespective of differences in gender or wealth, people have their own missions to accomplish in life," and she pursued what she thought was her mission: working as a nurse and helping to develop the nursing profession.[45]

Florence Nightingale was an example for Japanese women not only because she was a pioneer in the nursing profession but also because of how she came to follow this path. Like Fudeko, Nightingale was born to a rich family and was not satisfied with the usual philanthropic and charity work undertaken by affluent women. Fudeko paraphrased Nightingale's life to present her own opinion of women's position in Japanese society; like Wakamatsu Shizuko, she believed that women had missions to follow and that such missions were more important than clothing or appearance. Whether Fudeko considered herself, in a way, the Japanese "version" of Florence Nightingale is unclear, but her perception of Nightingale's life and aims and her own activities form a striking parallel.

Fudeko was born in Ōmura, in present-day Nagasaki prefecture, to a family of upper-class samurai. After the Meiji Restoration, her father, Watanabe Kiyoshi 渡邊清, served in various posts in the newly formed government, but Fudeko was left in Ōmura with the rest of her family. She eventually arrived in Tokyo in 1872 and enrolled in Tokyo jogakkō a year later. Fudeko's upbringing was meant to make her a good upper-class wife and mother, and her education during her teens was geared toward that goal. In 1877, before being called to Fukuoka by her father, who by that time was the provincial governor there, she briefly studied English and the Bible with Clara Whitney. As Clara mentioned in her diary, Fudeko had been promised in marriage to an official of her domain, Ogashima Hatasu 小鹿島果. This was an arranged marriage in which Fudeko had no say, and because of it, Clara recalled, Fudeko was unhappy.[46]

When former American president Ulysses S. Grant arrived in Nagasaki on a world tour in 1879, Fudeko was presented to him at a formal event; she wrote that Grant was impressed with her ability to speak English and gave her a signed pho-

45. Ishii Fudeko, "Furorensu Naichingeru jō to sekijūjisha jigyō" (Florence Nightingale and the work of the Red Cross) *Dai nihon fujin kyōiku kai zasshi*, no. 102, 13.03.1898, reprinted in Ichibangase Yasuko, Tsumagari Yūji, and Kawao Toyoshi, eds., *Mumyō no hito: Ishii Fudeko* (An unknown person: Ishii Fudeko) (Domesu, 2004), 135.

46. At that time Ogashima was still a student, but he would be employed by the Engineering Ministry in Tokyo. Clara also wrote that parents who gave away their children to strangers in that way were committing despicable acts. Clara Whitney, *Clara no Meiji nikki* (Clara's Meiji diary) (Kodansha, 1976), vol. 2, entry for 21.09.1878, 25. The English version does not contain this section. William M. Steele and Tamiko Ichimata, eds., *Clara's Diary: An American Girl in Meiji Japan* (Kodansha International, 1979).

tograph, which is now preserved with her other belongings at Takinogawa gakuen, as a memento.[47] English was not the only language in which she was proficient. She was well versed in French and Dutch, too, making her the only polyglot woman of the Meiji period I have encountered.[48]

Fudeko married Ogashima in February 1880 and in July left Japan on a two-year trip to Holland and France with Nagaoka Moriyoshi 長岡護美 (1842–1906), the son of the former lord of Kumamoto domain, who had married Chikuko, the daughter of the lord of Ōmura domain, and at that time was Japanese envoy extraordinary to Holland. Apparently, it was the empress herself who had expressed her wish for Fudeko to go to France; while there she fulfilled the role of lady-in-waiting to Chikuko.[49]

Once back home, Fudeko enjoyed the evenings and parties organized in the capital for the upper classes and became a teacher of French at Kazoku jogakkō.[50] In 1886 Fudeko and her daughter Sachiko were baptized, and Sachiko's godmother was Tsuda Umeko. Tsuda and Fudeko must have been confidantes as they both came from privileged backgrounds, had lived abroad, and were working at the same school. One of the interests common to both Fudeko and Tsuda was the education of women. In 1892, while working at Kazoku jogakkō, Fudeko also helped found and run Jokō gakko 女紅学校, a vocational school opened by the Dai nihon fujin kyōikukai for poor girls, whereas in 1900 Tsuda became the founder and headmistress of Joshi eigaku juku, a school that was highly regarded by her contemporaries.[51] Whereas Tsuda focused on female education throughout her life, Fudeko shifted her energies (though not her interest) from female education to disabled people's well-being in a society in which little was done for them and among whom many were female. Yet, before being able to focus on her life's mission, Fudeko had

---

47. Ishii Fudeko, *Suginishi hi no ryokō nikki* (A diary of travels past) (Sawada Hironori, 1932), 35. Gustave Boissonade, who arrived in Japan in 1873 to work as a legal adviser to the government, and his daughter Louise presented her with similar carte de visite, which are also preserved at Takinogawa gakuen.

48. Erwin Baelz commented, "Yesterday evening Aoki, the assistant minister for foreign affairs, gave a ball. . . . I was fascinated by the appearance of Madame Ogashima, one of the most charming women I have ever met. She speaks English, French, and Dutch fluently, and had had the courage to adapt Japanese hakama as part of a European dress!" Erwin Baelz, *Awakening Japan: The Diary of a German Doctor, Erwin Baelz*, edited by Toku Baelz (Bloomington: Indiana University Press, 1974), 84, entry for March 2, 1889.

49. She seems to have arrived at the Hague on August 25, 1880, and returned to Yokohama on May 23, 1882. Tsumagari Yūji, *Ishii Fudeko* (Ōzorasha, 2006), 55–60. Unfortunately, no relevant material has yet been found on her trip to Europe.

50. Tsuda Umeko, who in 1885 was teaching English there, was earning an annual salary of 420 yen; it is possible that Fudeko's salary was similar. Barbara Rose, *Tsuda Umeko and Women's Education in Japan* (New Haven: Yale University Press, 1992), 70.

51. Since Jokō gakkō did not charge fees, it is possible that Fudeko (and Tsuda?) spent some of the money she was earning at Kazoku jogakkō to help keep it running. *Tokyo asahi shinbun*, no. 2685, 03.11.1893, 1. See also Tsumagari, *Ishii Fudeko*, 107–9.

to endure much pain and suffering. Her husband died in 1892, leaving her with two children with disabilities to bring up alone (a third one had died in 1890, and the youngest of the surviving two would die in 1898).

Her links to Kazoku jogakkō help explain why in June 1898, a few months after one of her children died, we find Fudeko going to North America with Tsuda Umeko to attend as Japanese delegates the International Convention of the General Federation of Women's Clubs. The formal request for representatives had arrived from the head of the federation addressed to the Japanese Ministry of Education. Given that both women resigned from their positions as teachers of Kazoku jogakkō soon after returning to Japan from this trip, it is worth exploring what they did in the United States.

The conference was only part of a much longer trip, for Fudeko and Tsuda visited all sorts of places in Boston, Denver, Chicago, Philadelphia, and elsewhere. Fudeko was told to make a point of meeting Jane Addams, a graduate of Rockford Female Seminary who had been doing charitable and educational work, including the founding of Hull House in Chicago. While there, Tsuda and Fudeko heard women graduates speak on art history, visited homes for abandoned children, crèches for children whose parents had to work, schools for disabled children, bathhouses where poor workers could bathe for little money, libraries for children, and, finally, the University of Chicago, where girls and boys were studying the same subjects and attending the same courses in the same lecture rooms! An invitation to participate in a similar "educational tour" was sent from England, but only Tsuda went, visiting women's colleges in London, Cambridge, and Oxford and having extensive discussions with women educators there, whereas Fudeko continued her trip around North America. Once back home, she made a presentation based on her trip at a meeting of the Dai nihon fujin kyōikukai in May 1899.[52]

Fudeko married Ishii Ryōichi 石井亮一 (1864–1937) in 1903. She was forty-two, he was in his thirties, and theirs would become a lifelong partnership. Ishii had studied at Rikkyō daigakkō from 1883, was baptized there, and was a teacher at Rikkyō jogakkō. When the Nobi earthquake shook the area around Gifu and Nagoya in October 1891, *Jogaku zasshi* and the Kyōfūkai, fearing that girls who had lost their parents because of the earthquake could be sold into prostitution, published a call for help. Ishii answered it, gathering some twenty girls and giving them a place to stay and be educated; Kojo gakuin 孤女学院 was founded for those orphan girls, some of whom were disabled.[53] The school was renamed Takinogawa gakuen in 1897, the year in which Fudeko enrolled Sachiko in it, and it still cares for people with disabilities today. Fudeko would become an indispensable part of

---

52. Ishii, *Suginishi*. A transcript of her presentation is reprinted in the same volume (77–88).
53. See *Jogaku zasshi*, no. 294, 05.12.1891, 1–4. All sorts of charitable activities to help those hit by the earthquake were organized all over Japan by private people and groups and were publicized

that institution, taking up its directorship when Ishii died, but right from the start she helped by organizing and participating in fund-raising events for this and other institutions such as the Okayama orphanage and Tokyo jikei iin.[54]

Here we have a woman who had obtained a superb education, had interacted with some of the most educated people in Japan, had married the man her parents chose for her, had given birth to children with disabilities, and had lost her husband. She had managed to support herself and her children with her work and had met a man who thought she deserved the right to a life lived fulfilling her mission. Fudeko visited other countries and met foreign women, exchanged opinions on all sorts of topics, enriched her life, developed her intellectual abilities, and found inspiration for her plans. By dedicating herself to a cause, by obtaining (international) support, and by having print outlets for her ideas, she was able to live her life to the full.

We can hear Fudeko "speak" through a lengthy article she published in *Dai nihon fujin kyōikukai zasshi*. At first glance, the magazine does not seem to have been particularly innovative or feminist, but the piece she wrote for it suggests that Fudeko was willing to talk about delicate topics with women of the upper classes and to enter into a conversation over the meaning of "proper womanhood."[55] It is worth citing it at length.

> Our country's women are praised for their gentle and docile character, their loyalty and filial piety, and their support of public morality. Filial piety is the basis of human conduct; people should be filial toward their parents, loyal to their sovereign, and sincere toward other people. It is indeed true that filial piety is the source of all virtues. Parents should not take advantage of their children's filial piety, forget the importance of their responsibility as guardians, and indulge in self-interest using their infinite authority. The children, too, if they are not admonished when necessary, and are granted their every wish, fall into immoral conduct, and this cannot be called dutiful behavior. The virtues of gentility and docility are beautiful and good, but because the women of our country are gentle and obedient, the men, using that as a lever, are prone to wrongdoing. . . . Women cannot stand vis-à-vis men for knowledge and experience, and only in exceptional cases can they manage to break free and remonstrate against their parents and husbands; otherwise they

in *Jogaku zasshi* during the same period. See, for example, *Jogaku zasshi*, no. 293, 28.11.1891, 24–25; and no. 294, 05.12.1891, 24–25. By 1901 there were about fifty girls at the school. *Fujo shinbun*, no. 52, 06.05.1901, 2. Wakamatsu Shizuko described the orphanage two years after its founding. Iwamoto Yoshiharu, ed., *In Memory of Mrs. Kashi Iwamoto with a Collection of Her English Writings* (Jogaku Zasshisha, 1896), 44-60. Sometimes the school was referred to by the name Kojoin or Kojo gakuen.

54. Tsumagari, *Ishii Fudeko*, 143–47.
55. Ishii Fudeko, "Omohi izuru mama" (My thoughts), *Dai nihon fujin kyōikukai zasshi*, nos. 97–100, 10.1897–01.1898, reprinted in Ichibangase, Tsumagari, and Kawao, *Mumyō no hito*, 104–32.

have no courage, no spirit, they choke in tears of regret for their lives and are reduced to distress.

Whether Fudeko is here drawing from her personal experience is unclear, but her criticism of parents and husbands who mistreated the women in their families because those women were virtuous but powerless is evident.

> One day, an American [missionary?] came to visit and said that one of her girls had died prematurely. She was thinking of organizing a memorial and argued that it was necessary to rescue those young women who found themselves in sad circumstances. In order to inquire about the circumstances [of her death], she had gone to the Tokyo police, where she was told that her parents or her guardian had exchanged her for money and she was seeing many men every day. . . . That American, seeing my anguish, told me not to grieve over this episode, for the same was happening in China and India. Those words, spoken to console me, had the opposite effect and were like a dagger in my breast. Ah, our country, which is praised as the enlightened country of the East and yet in regard to this matter is placed on the same level of India and China. . . . The girl who has to sell her body for her parents, who should instead love and cherish her, will one day arrive to confide in her teacher and come to think that she wants to study to become like her teacher or a nurse and work for other people.

Here Fudeko inverts the usual argument about filial daughters and states that "women's education" was also a way to redress parents' wrongdoings. Some daughters had to undertake unspeakable acts because of their parents, who should have been their guardians, but could then find their own way in life with the support of other women and by exploring the jobs available to women. Female education and employment, then, were means through which women could escape, or avoid, what their families (and Japanese society) were making them do. Furthermore, Japan might have won a war against China, but when it came to women's position it was no more "civilized" than China.

> But men and women have equal rights; women are not made for men, and men are not made for women. If women were really made to be men's possessions, then men would be made to be women's. It has been argued that if women obtain higher education they will detest marriage. In reality, that is just a male prejudice. . . . In North America there are plenty of adult women who lead independent lives. . . . The unmarried women of our country, instead, are derided because they are considered to be men's belongings, and therefore those who are unmarried are looked down on as persons unworthy of men's selection. . . . Further-

more, parents think that when their daughters have reached the age of fifteen or sixteen it is time to marry them off, and they end up treating them as if they were goods; this is appalling. . . . Among our fellow sisters there are many who are right now living such lives. . . . If even one of today's women can sacrifice herself for the expansion of the rights of future women, then our country will indeed achieve happiness.

The debate over the proper composition of the family in Japan begun during the mid-1870s was still being addressed during the late 1890s. Fudeko argued that parents were treating their girls as perishable goods that had to be sold quickly. Women were educated to become part of other families rather than for education's sake, while marriage was sought because of the need to continue one's family line rather than for other, more important reasons that should bind two human beings together. Fudeko stated that women were not men's belongings, men and women had equal value, and it was only by forming a family based on love and respect that women and men could work together for a better society.

The debates that early Meiji women started and participated in were still seen as important for Japanese society and were continued in public spaces by late Meiji women. Early Meiji women (and a few men) had used the dichotomy and gendered division of society into men and women, male and female spaces, rights, and employment to bring forth their feminist demands, and we have seen in the conclusion to chapter 5 that by 1889 the women who wrote prefaces for Ueki Emori's *Tōyō no fujo* (Women of the East) thought that *aikokushin*, "love of one's country," meant for men and women to use their qualities together, without difference. Fudeko made the same points in her article in a more forceful way, arguing that men and women were *persons* whose abilities and missions should complement each other. This concept was based on a vision of the future; during Fudeko's time it was still necessary for women to sacrifice their lives in order to create a fairer world for their daughters and granddaughters. The words used to express these ideas, however, were taken from the past; we have seen how Kishida Toshiko and other women used the term *shimai*, "sisters," to address their readers, and Fudeko was doing the same.

Fudeko's vision proves that the late 1890s were not years of repression for all Japanese women. On the contrary, they were years in which men, the issue of prostitution, social wrongs, women's missions, and women's futures could be discussed and influenced by women. The call Fudeko made was also a call to herself, for soon after publishing this article she would leave for North America.

Bibliography

Unless otherwise stated, the Japanese books listed below were published in Tokyo. Articles in Meiji period newspapers and magazines cited in the footnotes are not included here.

Archives Consulted

Archive of Aoyama gakuin, Tokyo.
Archive of the Church Mission Society (CMS) Special Collections Department, University of Birmingham, Birmingham.
Archive of Dōshisha joshi daigaku, Kyoto.
Archive of Ferris jogakuin, Yokohama.
Archive of Joshi gakuin, Tokyo.
Archive of Kobe jogakuin daigaku, Kobe.
Archive of the Ladies' Association for the Promotion of Female Education in India and other Heathen Countries (LAPFE), Rhodes House Library, Oxford.
Archive of McDaniel College, Westminster, Maryland.
Archive of Mount Holyoke College and Special Collections, South Hadley, Massachusetts.
Archive of Northwestern University, Evanston, Illinois.
Archive of Radcliffe College, Schlesinger Library, Harvard University, Cambridge, Massachusetts.
Archive of San'yō gakuen daigaku, Okayama.
Archive of the Society for Promoting Female Education in China, India and the East (FES), Special Collections Department, University of Birmingham, Birmingham.
Archive of Takinogawa gakuen, Tokyo.
Archive of the U.S. Presbyterian Missions, Records of U.S. Presbyterian Missions, Yokohama Kaikō Shiryōkan, Yokohama.
Archive of Wilson College, Chambersburg, Pennsylvania.
Archive of Yokohama kyōritsu gakuen, Records of the Woman's Union Missionary Society of America for Heathen Lands (WUMS), Yokohama.
Ibaragi kenritsu rekishikan, Mito.
Meiji shinbun zasshi bunko, University of Tokyo.
Yokohama kaikō shiryōkan, Yokohama.

Online Archival Material

Japanese National Diet Library, Kindai Digital Library, http://kindai.ndl.go.jp.

Other Sources

Abe Reiko 阿部玲子. "Ashio kōdoku mondai to Ushioda Chiseko" 足尾鉱毒問題と潮田千勢子 (The problem of the Ashio mine pollution and Ushioda Chiseko). *Rekishi hyōron* 歴史評論 347 (1979): 98–117.

―――. "Sasaki Tojoyu oboegaki" 佐々城豊寿覚え書 (Notes on Sasaki Toyoju). *Nihonshi kenkyū* 日本史研究 171 (1976): 52–65.

Akie Shōko 秋枝蕭子. "'Rokumeikan jidai' no josei kyōiku ni tsuite" 鹿鳴館時代の女性教育について (On female education during the Rokumeikan period). *Bungei to shisō* 文芸と思想 29 (1966): 37–54.

Amos, Sheldon. *Difference of Sex as a Topic of Jurisprudence and Legislation.* London: Longmans, Green, 1870.

Anagol, Padma. "Indian Christian Women and Indigenous Feminism, c.1850–c.1920." In *Gender and Imperialism*, edited by Clare Midgley, 79–103. Manchester: Manchester University Press, 1998.

Anderson, Benedict. *Imagined Communities: Reflections on the Origins and Spread of Nationalism.* London: Verso, 1991.

Anderson, Emily. "Tamura Naoomi's *The Japanese Bride*: Christianity, Nationalism, and Family in Meiji Japan." *Japanese Journal of Religious Studies* 34.1 (2007): 203–28.

Anderson, Marnie. "A Woman's Place: Gender, Politics, and the State in Meiji Japan." PhD. diss., Ann Arbor, University of Michigan, 2005.

Aoki Mitsuko 青木充子 and Mitsuda Kyōko 光田京子, eds. *Minkenki Okayama joseishi kankei shiryō* 民権期岡山女性史関係史料 (Historical records related to the history of women in Okayama during the Minken period), vol. 4. of *Okayama minken undōshi kankei shiryōshū* 岡山民権運動史関係史料集 (Collection of historical records related to the history of the Okayama Minken movement), Okayama: Okayama minken undō hyakunen kinen gyōji jikkō iinkai, 1982.

Aoyama gakuin 青山学院, ed. *Aoyama gakuin kyūjūnenshi* 青山学院九十年史 (Ninety years of Aoyama gakuin). Aoyama gakuin, 1965.

Aoyama Nao 青山なを. *Yasui Tetsu to Tokyo joshi daigaku* 安井てつと東京女子大学 (Yasui Tetsu and Tokyo Women's University). Keiō tsūshin, 1982.

―――. *Meiji jogakkō no kenkyū* 明治女学校の研究 (A study of Meiji jogakkō). Keiō tsūshin, 1970.

Aoyama sayurikai 青山さゆり会, ed. *Aoyama jogakuin shi* 青山女学院史 (History of Aoyama jogakuin). Aoyama sayurikai, 1973.

Arinori, Mori, ed. *Education in Japan: A Series of Letters Addressed by Prominent Americans to Arinori Mori.* New York: D. Appleton Century, 1873.

Ashikari, Mikiko. "The Memory of the Women's White Faces: Japaneseness and the Ideal Image of Women." *Japan Forum* 15.1 (2003): 55–79.

Bacon, Alice Mabel. *Japanese Girls and Women*. Rev. and enlarged ed. London: Houghton–Mifflin, 1902.

———. *A Japanese Interior*. London: Gay and Bird, 1893.

Badran, Margot. *Feminists, Islam, and Nation: Gender and the Making of Modern Egypt*. Princeton: Princeton University Press, 1995.

Baelz, Erwin. *Awakening Japan: The Diary of a German Doctor, Erwin Baelz*. Edited by Toku Baelz. Bloomington: Indiana University Press, 1974.

Baker, Frances J. *The Story of the Woman's Foreign Missionary Society of the Methodist Episcopal Church, 1869–1895*. Cincinnati: Cranston and Curts, 1896.

Baker, Paula. "The Domestication of Politics: Women and American Political Society, 1780–1920." *The American Historical Review* 89.3 (1984): 620–47.

Ballhatchet, Helen. "Christianity and Gender Relationships in Japan: Case Studies of Marriage and Divorce in Early Meiji Protestant Circles." *Japanese Journal of Religious Studies* 34.1 (2007): 177–201.

Ban Naonosuke 伴直之助. *Nihon fujo no chii* 日本婦女之地位 (Japanese women's position). Kobayashi Shinbei, 1888.

Bardsley, Jan. *The Bluestockings of Japan: New Woman Essays and Fiction from Seito, 1911–1916*. Michigan Monograph Series in Japanese Studies, no. 60. Ann Arbor: Center for Japanese Studies, University of Michigan, 2007.

Beaver, Robert Pierce. *American Protestant Women in World Mission: History of the First Feminist Movement in North America*. Grand Rapids, Mich.: William B. Eerdmans, 1980.

Beckmann, George. *The Making of the Meiji Constitution: The Oligarchs and the Constitutional Development of Japan, 1868–1891*. Lawrence: University Press of Kansas, 1957.

Beichman, Janine. *Embracing the Firebird: Yosano Akiko and the Birth of the Female Voice in Modern Japanese Poetry*. Honolulu: University of Hawai'i Press, 2002.

Bernstein, Gail Lee, ed. *Recreating Japanese Women, 1600–1945*. Berkeley: University of California Press, 1991.

Berry, Mary Elizabeth. *Japan in Print. Information and Nation in the Early Modern Period*. Berkeley: University of California Press, 2006.

———. "Public Life in Authoritarian Japan." *Daedalus* 127.3 (1998): 133–65.

Bitō, Masahide. "Thought and Religion, 1550–1700." In *The Cambridge History of Japan*, edited by John Whitney Hall, vol. 4, 373–424. Cambridge: Cambridge University Press, 1991.

Blair, Karen. *The Clubwoman as Feminist: True Womanhood Redefined, 1868–1914*. New York: Holmes and Meier, 1980.

Bowen, Roger. *Rebellion and Democracy in Meiji Japan: A Study of Commoners in the Popular Rights Movement*. Berkeley: University of California Press, 1980.

Boyd, Julia. *Hannah Riddell: An Englishwoman in Japan*. Rutland, Vt.: Charles E. Tuttle, 1996.

Braisted, William, trans. *Meiroku Zasshi: Journal of the Japanese Enlightenment*. Cambridge, Mass.: Harvard University Press, 1976.

Calhoun, Craig, ed. *Habermas and the Public Sphere*. Cambridge, Mass.: MIT Press, 1999.

――――. *Critical Social Theory: Culture, History, and the Challenge of Difference*. Oxford: Blackwell, 1995.

Carrothers, Julia. *The Sunrise Kingdom; or, Life and Scenes in Japan, and Woman's Work for Woman There*. Philadelphia: Presbyterian Board of Publication, 1879.

Chalmers, Rhoderick. "'We Nepalis': Language, Literature, and the Formation of a Nepali Public Sphere in India, 1914–1940." PhD diss., School of Oriental and African Studies, 2003.

Chambers, Simone. "Discourse and Democratic Practices." In *The Cambridge Companion to Habermas*, edited by Stephen K. White, 233–59. Cambridge: Cambridge University Press, 1995.

Chatterjee, Partha. *The Nation and Its Fragments: Colonial and Postcolonial Histories*. Princeton: Princeton University Press, 1993.

Checkland, Olive. *Humanitarianism and the Emperor's Japan, 1877–1977*. Basingstoke: Macmillan, 1994.

Chino Yōichi 千野陽一. *Kindai nihon fujin kyōiku shi* 近代日本婦人教育史 (A history of Japanese women's education during the modern period). Domesu shuppan, 1979.

Clapp, Frances Benton. *Mary Florence Denton and the Doshisha*. Kyoto: Dōshisha University Press, 1955.

Cohen, Philip N. "Nationalism and Suffrage: Gender Struggle in Nation–Building America." *Signs: Journal of Women in Culture and Society* 21.3 (1996): 707–27.

Colley, Linda. *Britons: Forging the Nation, 1707–1837*. London: Vintage, 1996.

Copeland, Rebecca, trans. "Warbler in the Grove." In *The Modern Murasaki: Writing by Women of Meiji Japan*, edited by Rebecca Copeland and Melek Ortabasi, 80–125. New York: Columbia University Press, 2006.

――――. *Lost Leaves: Women Writers of Meiji Japan*. Honolulu: University of Hawai'i Press, 2000.

Copeland, Rebecca, and Aiko Okamoto MacPhail, trans. "Daughters in Boxes." In *The Modern Murasaki: Writing by Women of Meiji Japan*, edited by Rebecca Copeland and Melek Ortabasi, 62–71. New York: Columbia University Press, 2006.

Copeland, Rebecca, and Melek Ortabasi, eds. *The Modern Murasaki: Writing by Women of Meiji Japan*. New York: Columbia University Press, 2006.

Cortazzi, Hugh, ed. *Britain and Japan: Biographical Portraits*. Vol. 6. Folkestone: Global Oriental, 2007.

Cott, Nancy. *The Bonds of Womanhood: "Woman's Sphere" in New England, 1780–1835*. New Haven: Yale University Press, 1977.

Czarnecki, Melanie. "Bad Girls from Good Families: The Degenerate Meiji Schoolgirl." In *Bad Girls of Japan*, edited by Laura Miller and Jan Bardsley, 49–64. New York: Palgrave Macmillan, 2005.

Dai nihon teikoku gikaishi kankōkai 大日本帝国議会誌刊行会, ed. *Dai nihon teikoku gikaishi* 大日本帝国議会誌 (Records of the Imperial Diet of Greater Japan). Vol. 1. Dai nihon teikoku gikaishi kankōkai, 1926.

Davidoff, Leonore. "Gender and the 'Great Divide': Public and Private in British Gender History." *Journal of Women's History* 15.1 (2003): 11–27.

————. *Worlds Between: Historical Perspectives on Gender and Class.* Cambridge: Polity Press, 1995.

Davies, Kate. "A Moral Purchase: Femininity, Commerce, and Abolition, 1788–1792." In *Women, Writing, and the Public Sphere, 1700–1830*, edited by Elizabeth Eger, Charlotte Grant, Cliona O Gallchoir, and Penny Warburton, 133–159. Cambridge: Cambridge University Press, 2006.

DeForest, Charlotte B. *History of Kobe College, 1875–1950.* Chicago: Kobe College Corporation, 1950.

Doi Kōka 土居光華. *Bunmeiron onna daigaku* 文明論女大学 (Enlightened theory on the Greater Learning for Women) 1876. In *Onna daigaku shū* 女大学集 (Collection of works related to the *Greater Learning for Women*), edited by Ishikawa Matsutarō 石川松太郎, 119–50. Heibonsha, 1977.

Donaldson, Margaret. "'The Cultivation of the Heart and the Moulding of the Will . . .': The Missionary Contribution of the Society for Promoting Female Education in China, India, and the East." In *Women in the Church*, edited by W. J. Shiels and Diana Wood, 429–42. Oxford: Basil Blackwell, 1990.

Dorn Lublin, Elizabeth. "Crusading against Prostitution: The Woman's Christian Temperance Union in Meiji Japan." *Japanese Religions* 29.1/2 (2004): 29–43.

————. "Pollution Relief and the Japan Woman's Christian Temperance Union." *Asian Cultural Studies: International Christian University* 27 (2001): 49–58.

Doyōkai rekishi bukai 土曜会歴史部会, ed. *Nihon kindai kango no yoake* 日本近代看護の夜明け (The dawn of Japanese modern nursing). Igaku shoin, 1973.

Eder, Elizabeth. *Constructing Opportunity: American Women Educators in Early Meiji Japan.* Lanham, Md.: Lexington Books, 2003.

Eger, Elizabeth. "Representing Culture: *The Nine Living Muses of Great Britain* (1779)." In *Women, Writing, and the Public Sphere, 1700–1830*, edited by Elizabeth Eger, Charlotte Grant, Cliona O Gallchoir, and Penny Warburton, 104–32. Cambridge: Cambridge University Press, 2006.

Eger, Elizabeth, Charlotte Grant, Cliona O Gallchoir, and Penny Warburton. "Introduction: Women, Writing and Representation." In *Women, Writing, and the Public Sphere, 1700–1830*, edited by Elizabeth Eger, Charlotte Grant, Cliona O Gallchoir, and Penny Warburton, 1–23. Cambridge: Cambridge University Press, 2006.

Eger, Elizabeth, Charlotte Grant, Cliona O Gallchoir, and Penny Warburton, eds. *Women, Writing, and the Public Sphere, 1700–1830.* Cambridge: Cambridge University Press, 2006.

Egusa Mitsuko 江種満子. "Shimizu Toyoko/Shikin (1), 'joken' no jidai" 清水豊子/紫琴(一)「女権」の時代 (Shimizu Toyoko/Shikin (part 1), the era of women's rights). *Bungakubu kiyō* 文学部紀要. Bunkyō daigaku bungakubu 17.1 (2003): 1–21.

Eley, Geoff. "Nations, Publics, and Political Cultures: Placing Habermas in the Nineteenth Century." In *Habermas and the Public Sphere*, edited by Craig Calhoun, 289–339. Cambridge, Mass.: MIT Press, 1999.

Ellis, Markman. "Coffee–women, the *Spectator,* and the Public Sphere in the Early Eighteenth Century." In *Women, Writing, and the Public Sphere, 1700–1830,* edited by Elizabeth Eger, Charlotte Grant, Cliona O Gallchoir, and Penny Warburton, 27–52. Cambridge: Cambridge University Press, 2006.

Esashi Akiko 江刺昭子. *Onna no kuse ni: Kusawake no josei shinbun kisha tachi* 女のくせに. 草分の女性新聞記者たち (Only a woman: Pioneer women newspaper journalists). Impacto, 1997.

Fawcett, Millicent Garrett. "The Electoral Disabilities of Women." In *Essays and Lectures on Social and Political Subjects,* by Henry Fawcett and Millicent Garrett Fawcett, 230–61. London: Macmillan, 1872.

Ferris Jogakuin フェリス女学院, ed. *Kidaa shokanshū* キダー書簡集 (Collection of Kidder's letters). Kyōbunkan, 1975.

Ferris Jogakuin hyakunenshi henshū iinkai フェリス女学院百年史編集委員会, ed. *Ferris jogakuin hyakunenshi* フェリス女学院100年史 (One hundred years of Ferris jogakuin). Yokohama: Ferris jogakuin, 1970.

Flint, Kate. *The Woman Reader, 1837–1914.* Oxford: Clarendon Press, 1993.

Foucault, Michel. *The Archaeology of Knowledge.* London: Routledge, 2003.

Fraser, Mary C. *A Diplomat's Wife in Japan: Sketches at the Turn of the Century.* New York: Weatherhill, 1982.

Fraser, Nancy. "Rethinking the Public Sphere: A Contribution to the Critique of Actually Existing Democracy." In *Habermas and the Public Sphere,* edited by Craig Calhoun, 109–42. Cambridge, Mass.: MIT Press, 1999.

———. "Politics, Culture, and the Public Sphere: Toward a Postmodern Conception." In *Social Postmodernism: Beyond Identity Politics,* edited by Linda Nicholson and Steven Seidman, 287–314. Cambridge: Cambridge University Press, 1995.

———. *Unruly Practices: Power, Discourse, and Gender in Contemporary Social Theory.* Minneapolis: University of Minnesota Press, 1989.

Freedman, Estelle. "Separatism as Strategy: Female Institution Building and American Feminism, 1870–1930." *Feminist Studies* 5.3 (1979): 512–29.

Fuess, Harald. *Divorce in Japan: Family, Gender, and the State, 1600–2000.* Stanford: Stanford University Press, 2004.

Fujime Yuki 藤目ゆき. *Sei no rekishigaku* 性の歴史学 (A history of sexuality). Fuji Shuppan, 1997.

Fujimura–Fanselow, Kumiko, and Atsuko Kameda, eds. *Japanese Women: New Feminist Perspectives on the Past, Present, and Future.* New York: Feminist Press, 1994.

Fujisawa Matoshi 藤澤全 and Umemoto Junkō 梅本順子, eds. *Tamura Naoomi: Nihon no hanayome, Beikoku no fujin, shiryōshū* 田村直臣日本の花嫁米国の婦人資料集 (Tamura Naoomi's *The Japanese Bride, American Women,* and other related materials). Ōzorasha, 2003.

Fujita Yoshimi 藤田美実. *Meiji jogakkō no sekai* 明治女学校の世界 (The world of Meiji jogakkō). Seieisha, 1984.

———. "'Meiji jogakkō' ni kansuru oboegaki: Meiji ki roman shūgi to kirisutokyō" 『明治女学校』に関する覚え書—明治期ロマン主義とキリスト教 (Notes on Meiji jogakkō:

Romanticism and Christianity during the Meiji period). *Rissho daigaku bungakubu ronsō* 立正大学文学部論叢 71 (1981): 27–51.

Fujitani Takashi. *Splendid Monarchy: Power and Pageantry in Modern Japan.* Berkeley: University of California Press, 1996.

"Fujo Shinbun" o yomu kai 『婦女新聞』を読む会, ed. *"Fujo shinbun" to josei no kindai* 『婦女新聞』と女性の近代 (*Fujo shinbun* and women in the modern period). Fuji shuppan, 1997.

Fukaya Masashi 深谷昌志 and Fukaya Kazuko 深谷和子. *Jokyōshi mondai no kenkyū: Shokugyō shikō to katei shikō* 女教師問題の研究: 職業志向と家庭志向 (A study of women teachers: The conflict between employment and family). Nagoya: Reimei shobō, 1971.

Fukuda Hideko 福田英子. "Kageyama Umeko no omoide" 景山楳子の思い出 (Remembering Kageyama Umeko). *Sekai fujin* 世界婦人, no. 34, 05.03.1909. In *Minkenki Okayama joseishi kankei shiryō* 民権期岡山女性史関係史料 (Historical records related to the history of women in Okayama during the Minken period), edited by Aoki Mitsuko 青木充子 and Mitsuda Kyōko 光田京子, vol. 4 of *Okayama minken undōshi kankei shiryōshū* 岡山民権運動史関係史料集 (Collection of historical records related to the history of the Okayama Minken movement), 43–45. Okayama: Okayama minken undō hyakunen kinen gyōji jikkō iinkai, 1982.

_____. *Warawa no hanseigai* 妾の半生涯 (My life so far). Iwanami Shoten, [1904] 1958.

Fukuoka Teruko 福岡照子. *Joshi dokuritsu enzetsu hikki* 女子独立演説筆記 (Transcription of the public speech on women's independence). Nisshindō, 1888.

Fukuzawa Yukichi 福沢諭吉. *Seiyō jijō* 西洋事情 (Conditions in the West). In *Fukuzawa Yukichi zenshū* 福沢諭吉全集 (Collected works of Fukuzawa Yukichi), edited by Keiō gijuku 慶応義塾, vol. 1, 275–608. Iwanami shoten, 1958.

Fuma Kiyoshi 府馬清. *Matsumoto Eiko no shōgai* 松本英子の生涯 (The life of Matsumoto Eiko). Shōwa tosho shuppan, 1981.

Furuki, Yoshiko. *The White Plum: A Biography of Ume Tsuda, Pioneer in the Higher Education of Japanese Women.* New York: Weatherhill, 1991.

Furuya, Tsunatake. "Meiji Women: Landmarks They Have Left." *Japan Quarterly* 14 (1967): 318–25.

Gagan, Rosemary. *A Sensitive Independence: Canadian Methodist Women Missionaries in Canada and the Orient, 1881–1925.* Montreal: McGill–Queen's University Press, 1992.

Garon, Sheldon. *Molding Japanese Minds: The State in Everyday Life.* Princeton: Princeton University Press, 1997.

_____. "The World's Oldest Debate? Prostitution and the State in Imperial Japan, 1900–1945." *The American Historical Review* 98.3 (1993): 710–32.

Gauntlett, Saiko. "Edward Gauntlett (1868–1956), English Teacher, Explorer and Missionary." In *Britain and Japan: Biographical Portraits*, edited by Hugh Cortazzi, vol. 6, 299–306. Folkestone: Global Oriental, 2007.

Gauntlett, Tsune ガントレット恒. *Shichijūshichinen no omohide* 七十七年の想ひ出 (Memories of my seventy–seven years). Ōzorasha, [1949] 1989.

Gellner, Ernest. *Nations and Nationalism*. Oxford: Basil Blackwell, 1983.

Gendaigo de yomu Niijima Jō henshū iinkai 現代語で読む新島襄編集委員会, ed. *Gendaigo de yomu Niijima Jō* 現代語で読む新島襄 (Reading the writings of Niijima Jō in contemporary Japanese). Maruzen, 2000.

Gluck, Carol. *Japan's Modern Myths: Ideology in the Late Meiji Period*. Princeton: Princeton University Press, 1985.

Gonda, Caroline. "Misses, Murderesses, and Magdalens: Women in the Public Eye." In *Women, Writing, and the Public Sphere, 1700–1830*, edited by Elizabeth Eger, Charlotte Grant, Cliona O Gallchoir, and Penny Warburton, 53–71. Cambridge: Cambridge University Press, 2006.

Goodwin, Janet R., Bettina Gramlich–Oka, Elizabeth A. Leicester, Yuki Terazawa, and Anne Walthall. "Solitary Thoughts: A Translation of Tadano Makuzu's *Hitori Kangae*." *Monumenta Nipponica* 56.1–2 (2001): 21–38, 173–95.

Gramlich–Oka, Bettina. "Tadano Makuzu and Her *Hitori Kangae*." *Monumenta Nipponica* 56.1 (2001): 1–20.

Habermas, Jürgen. *Between Facts and Norms: Contributions to a Discourse Theory of Law and Democracy*. Oxford: Polity Press, 1996.

––––––. *The Structural Transformation of the Public Sphere: An Inquiry into a Category of Bourgeois Society*. Cambridge, Mass.: MIT Press, 1991.

Haga Noboru 芳賀登, Ichibangase Yasuko 一番ケ瀬康子, Nakajima Kuni 中嶌邦, and Soda Kōichi 祖田浩一, eds. *Nihon josei jinmei jiten* 日本女性人名辞典 (Biographical dictionary of Japanese women). Nihon tosho Center, 1993.

Haggis, Jane. "'A Heart That Has Felt the Love of God and Longs for Others to Know It': Conventions of Gender, Tensions of Self, and Constructions of Difference in Offering to Be a Lady Missionary." *Women's History Review* 7.2 (1998): 171–93.

––––––. "'Good Wives and Mothers' or 'Dedicated Workers'? Contradictions of Domesticity in the 'Mission of Sisterhood', Travancore, South India." In *Maternities and Modernities: Colonial and Postcolonial Experiences in Asia and the Pacific*, edited by Kalpana Ram and Margaret Jolly, 81–113. Cambridge: Cambridge University Press, 1998.

Hakuhō gakuen hoiku Center 白峰学園保育センター, ed. *Hoiku no shakaishi: Kanagawa kindai no kiroku* 保育の社会史: 神奈川近代の記録 (A social history of child care: The records of Kanagawa in the modern period). Chikuma shobō, 1987.

Hane, Mikiso. *Peasants, Rebels, Women, and Outcastes: The Underside of Modern Japan*. Lanham, Md.: Rowman and Littlefield, 2003.

––––––. "Fukuzawa Yukichi and Women's Rights." In *Meiji Japan: Political, Economic, and Social History, 1868–1912*, edited by Peter Kornicki, vol. 2, 200–16. London: Routledge, 1998.

––––––. *Reflections on the Way to the Gallows: Rebel Women in Prewar Japan*. Berkeley: University of California Press, 1988.

Hani Motoko 羽仁もとこ. *Hansei o kataru* 半生を語る (Telling my life so far). Fujin no tomosha, 1928.

Hara, Kimi "Challenges to Education for Girls and Women in Modern Japan: Past and Present." In *Japanese Women: New Feminist Perspectives on the Past, Present, and Fu-*

ture, edited by Fujimura–Fanselow Kumiko and Kameda Atsuko, 93–106. New York: Feminist Press, 1995.

Harada Tomohiko 原田伴彦, ed. *Meiji no josei* 明治の女性 (Meiji women). Vol. 10 of *Gendai nihon kiroku zenshū* 現代日本記録全集 (Collection of records on contemporary Japan). Chikuma shobō, 1968.

Harrington, Ann. "The First Women Religious in Japan: Mother Saint Mathilde Raclot and the French Connection." *The Catholic Historical Review* 87.4 (2001): 603–23.

———. "Women and Higher Education in the Japanese Empire." *Journal of Asian History* 21.2 (1987): 169–86.

Hastings, Sally A. "Hatoyama Haruko: Ambitious Woman." In *The Human Tradition in Modern Japan*, edited by Anne Walthall, 81–98. Wilmington: Scholarly Resources, 2002.

———. "The Empress' New Clothes and Japanese Women, 1868–1912." *The Historian* 55.4 (1993): 677–92.

Hatoyama Haruko 鳩山春子. *Waga jijoden* 我が自叙伝 (Telling my life). Nihon tosho Center, [1929] 1997.

Hill, Christopher. "How to Write a Second Restoration: The Political Novel and Meiji Historiography." *Journal of Japanese Studies* 33.2 (2007): 337–56.

Hirai, Atsuko. "The State and Ideology in Meiji Japan. A Review Article." Review of Carol Gluck, *Japan's Modern Myths: Ideology in the Late Meiji Period. Journal of Asian Studies* 46.1 (1987): 89–103.

Hirao Machiko 平尾真智子. *Shiryō ni miru nihon kango kyōikushi* 資料にみる日本看護教育史 (What the documents tell us of the history of Japanese nursing education). Kango no kagakusha, 1999.

Hirata Yumi 平田由美. *Josei hyōgen no Meiji shi – Higuchi Ichiyō izen* 女性表現の明治史–樋口一葉以前 (A history of women's expressions in the Meiji period: Before Higuchi Ichiyō). Iwanami shoten, 1999.

Hiratsuka Masunori 平塚益徳, ed. *Jinbutsu o chūshin to shita joshi kyōikushi* 人物を中心とした女子教育史 (Case studies in the history of women's education). Teikoku chihō gyōsei gakkai, 1965.

Hirota, Masaki. "Notes on the 'Process of Creating Women' in the Meiji Period." In *Gender and Japanese History*, edited by Wakita Haruko, Anne Bouchy, and Ueno Chizuko, vol. 2, 197–219. Osaka: Osaka University Press, 1999.

Honda Masuko 本田和子. *Jogakusei no keifu: Saishiki sareru Meiji* 女学生の系譜: 彩色される明治 (A genealogy of girl students: A vivid representation of the Meiji period). Seidosha, 1990.

Hoston, Germaine A. "Civil Society and the Public Sphere in the Construction of Modernity in Japanese Political Thought." Paper presented at the annual meeting of the American Political Science Association, Washington, D.C., 2005, http://www.allacademic.com//meta/p_mla_apa_research_citation/0/4/2/6/8/pages42684/p42684-1.php, accessed January 17, 2010.

Howarth, David R. *Discourse*. Buckingham: Open University Press, 2000.

Howland, Douglas. *Translating the West: Language and Political Reason in Nineteenth–Century Japan*. Honolulu: University of Hawai'i Press, 2002.

Huffman, James. *Creating a Public: People and Press in Meiji Japan*. Honolulu: University of Hawai'i Press, 1997.

Hunt, Caroline L. *The Life of Ellen H. Richards*. Boston: Whitcomb and Barrows, 1912.

Ichibangase Yasuko 一番ケ瀬康子, Tsumagari Yūji 妻曲裕次, and Kawao Toyoshi 河尾豊司, eds. *Mumyō no hito: Ishii Fudeko* 無名の人. 石井筆子 (An unknown person: Ishii Fudeko). Domesu, 2004.

Ichihara Masae 市原正恵. *Shizuoka onna hyakunen* 静岡おんな百年 (One hundred years of Shizuoka women's history). 2 vols. Domesu, 1982.

Ignatieff, Michael. *Blood and Belonging: Journeys into the New Nationalism*. London: Vintage, 1994.

Inoue Hisao. "A Historical Sketch of the Development of the Modern Educational System for Women in Japan." *Education in Japan: Journal for Overseas* 6 (1971): 15–35.

Inoue Kennosuke 井上健之助. *Tōyō eiwa jogakuin shichijūnenshi* 東洋英和女学院七十年誌 (Records of Tōyō eiwa jogakuin during the past seventy years). Tōyō eiwa jogakuin, 1954.

Inoue Nao 井上直, ed. *Nihon fujin sanron* 日本婦人纂論 (Collection of theories on Japanese women). Privately published, 1886.

Inoue Yuriko 井上ゆり子. *Chikara o ataemase: Honda Yōitsu fujin Teiko no shōgai* 力を与えませ：本多庸一夫人貞子の生涯 (Give me strength! The life of Teiko, Honda Yōitsu's wife). Aoyama gakuin, 2004.

Ion, A. Hamish. *The Cross and the Rising Sun: The Canadian Protestant Missionary Movement in the Japanese Empire, 1872–1931*. Waterloo, Ont.: Wilfrid Laurier University Press, 1990.

Ishii Fudeko 石井筆子. *Suginishi hi no ryokō nikki* 過にし日の旅行日記 (A diary of travels past). Sawada Hironori, 1932.

Ishii, Kazumi, and Nerida Jarkey. "The Housewife Is Born: The Establishment of the Notion and Identity of the *Shufu* in Modern Japan." *Japanese Studies* 22.1 (2002): 35–47.

Ishii Noriko 石井紀子. "America josei iryō senkyōshi no chugoku to nihon dendō: Meary Ana Horuburukku no baai (1881–1907)" アメリカ女性医療宣教師の中国と日本伝道 – メアリ・アナ・ホルブルックの場合 (1881–1907) (American women missionary doctors in China and Japan: The case of Mary A. Holbrook [1881–1907]). *Nihon kenkyū* 日本研究 30 (2005): 167–91.

Itoya Toshio 絲屋寿雄. *Meiji ishin to josei no yoake* 明治維新と女性の夜明け (The Meiji Restoration and women's awakening). Chōbunsha, 1976.

Iwamoto Yoshiharu 巌本善治, ed. *In Memory of Mrs. Kashi Iwamoto with a Collection of Her English Writings*. Jogaku zasshisha, 1896.

Iwamoto Yoshio. "Suehiro Tetchō: A Meiji Political Novelist." In *Japan's Modern Century*, edited by Edmund Skrzypczak, 83–114. Sophia University and Charles E. Tuttle, 1968.

Izuyama Atsuko 伊豆山敦子. "Takeda (Katō) Kin: Meiji ki no kokusai kōryu to joshi kyōiku" 武田(加藤)錦—明治期の国際交流と女子教育 (Takeda [Katō] Kin: International relations and women's education during the Meiji period). *Dokkyō daigaku kyōyō shogaku kenkyū* 独協大学教養諸学研究 23 (1988): 18–37.

Jacob, Margaret. "The Mental Landscape of the Public Sphere: A European Perspective." *Eighteenth–Century Studies* 28.1 (1994): 95–113.

Jennison, Rebecca, trans. "The Broken Ring." In *The Modern Murasaki: Writing by Women of Meiji Japan*, edited by Rebecca Copeland and Melek Ortabasi, 232–39. New York: Columbia University Press, 2006.

Jiyū minken hyakunen zenkoku shūkai jikkō iinkai 自由民権百年全国集会実行委員会, ed. *Jiyū minken undō to gendai* 自由民権運動と現代 (The Movement for Freedom and Popular Rights and the present time). Sanseidō, 1985.

Joshi bijutsu daigaku 女子美術大学, ed. *Joshi bijutsu daigaku hachijūnenshi* 女子美術大学八十年史 (Eighty years of Joshi bijutsu daigaku). Joshi bijutsu daigaku, 1980.

Joshi gakuin shiryōshitsu iinkai 女子学院資料室委員会, ed. *Me de miru Joshi gakuin no rekishi* 目で見る女子学院の歴史 (Graphic history of Joshi gakuin). Joshi gakuin, 2000.

Kagawa Rinzō 香川倫三. *Fujin enzetsu shinan* 婦人演説指南 (Instructions for women making public speeches). Osaka: Shinshindō, 1887.

Kajiro Yoshi kenkyūkai 上代淑研究会. *Kajiro Yoshi kenkyū* 上代淑研究 (A study of Kajiro Yoshi). Vol. 1. Okayama: San'yō gakuen daigaku, 1996.

Kakita Junrō 垣田純朗, ed. *Fujin oyobi kasei* 婦人及家政 (Women and household management). Min'yūsha, 1888.

Kameyama Michiko 亀山美知子. *Taifū no yōni ikite. Nihon saisho no kangofu Ōzeki Chika monogatari* 大風のように生きて.日本最初の看護婦大関和物語 (Live like a strong wind: The story of the first female Japanese nurse Ōzeki Chika). Domesu, 1992.

———. *Onnatachi no yakusoku: M. T. Tsuru to nihon saisho no kangofu gakkō* 女たちの約束: M. T.ツルーと日本最初の看護婦学校 (A promise made among women: M. T. True and the first school for female nurses in Japan). Kyoto: Jinbun shoin, 1990.

———. *Kangofu to ishi* 看護婦と医師 (Female nurses and doctors). Domesu, 1985.

———. *Shūkyō to kango* 宗教と看護 (Religion and nursing). Domesu, 1985.

———. *Nihon sekijūjisha to kangofu* 日本赤十字社と看護婦 (The Japanese Red Cross and female nurses). Domesu, 1983.

Kanagawa–ken, ed. *Kanagawa kenshi* 神奈川県史 (History of Kanagawa prefecture). Vol. 13. Yokohama: Kanagawa–ken, 1977.

Kanbe Yasumitsu 神辺靖光. *Meiji shoki Tokyo no jogakkō* 明治初期東京の女学校 (Girls' schools in Tokyo during the early Meiji period). Unknown publisher, 1964.

———. "Meiji shoki Tokyo ni okeru shiritsu gakkō no keiei" 明治初期東京における私立学校の経営 (The development of private schools in Tokyo during the early Meiji period). *Shigaku kenshū* 私学研修 13 (1961): 128–37.

———. *Meiji zenki Tokyo no shijuku* 明治前期東京の私塾 (Private schools in Tokyo during the early Meiji period). Jōō kōtō gakkō, 1960.

Kaneda Susumu 金田進, ed. *Tottori–ken hyakketsuden: Kindai hyakunen* 鳥取県百傑伝: 近代百年 (One hundred eminent lives in Tottori prefecture: One hundred years of the modern period). Tottori: San'in hyōronsha, 1970.

Kaneko Sachiko 金子幸子. *Kindai nihon joseiron no keifu* 近代日本女性論の系譜 (A genealogy of theories on Japanese women during the modern period). Fuji shuppan, 1999.

Kanzaki Kiyoshi 神崎清. *Yoshioka Yayoi den* 吉岡弥生伝 (Yoshioka Yayoi's biography). Ōzorasha, [1941] 1989.

———. *Gendai fujin den* 現代婦人傳 (Biographies of contemporary women). Chūō kōronsha, 1940.

Karasawa Tomitarō 唐澤富太郎. *Gakusei no rekishi* 学生の歴史 (A history of students). Sōbunsha, [1955] 1980.

———. *Joshi gakusei no rekishi* 女子学生の歴史 (A history of female students). Mokujisha, 1979.

———. *Kyōshi no rekishi: Kyōshi no seikatsu to rinri* 教師の歴史：教師の生活と倫理 (A history of teachers: Their lifestyle and ethics). Sōbunsha, 1955.

Katano Masako 片野真佐子. "Asai Saku oboegaki" 浅井柞覚書 (Notes on Asai Saku). In *Kindai nihon no kirisutokyō to joseitachi* 近代日本のキリスト教と女性たち (Christianity and women in Japan during the modern period), edited by Tomisaka kirisutokyō Center 富坂キリスト教センター, 12–50. Shinkyō shuppansha, 1995.

———. "Ryōsai kenbo shugi no genryū" 良妻賢母主義の源流 (The origins of the *ryōsai kenbo* policy). In *Onnatachi no kindai* 女たちの近代 (The modern period for women), edited by Kindai joseishi kenkyūkai 近代女性史研究会, 32–57. Kashiwa shobō, 1978.

Katayama Seiichi 片山清一. *Kindai nihon no joshi kyōiku* 近代日本の女子教育 (Female education in Japan during the modern period). Kenpakusha, 1984.

Katō Mihoko 加藤美穂子. "Shoshi seido kara mita Meiji zenki no hōsei saku" 庶子制度からみた明治前期の法政策 (The legislative policies of the early Meiji period as seen from the perspective of the system of illegitimate children). In *Kindai nihon no kazoku. Seisaku to hō* 近代日本の家族.政策と法 (The modern Japanese family: Policies and the law), edited by Fukushima Masao 福島正夫, 43–88, vol. 6 of *Kazoku: Seisaku to hō* 家族.政策と法 (The family: Policies and the law). Tokyo daigaku shuppankai, 1984.

Kazokushi kenkyūkai 家族史研究会, ed. *Kindai Kumamoto no onnatachi* 近代熊本の女たち (Women in Kumamoto during the modern period). 2 vols. Kumamoto: Kumamoto nichinichi shinbunsha, 1981.

Kelly, Gary. "Bluestocking Feminism." In *Women, Writing, and the Public Sphere, 1700–1830*, edited by Elizabeth Eger, Charlotte Grant, Cliona O Gallchoir, and Penny Warburton, 163–80. Cambridge: Cambridge University Press, 2006.

Kelsky, Karen. *Women on the Verge: Japanese Women, Western Dreams.* Durham: Duke University Press, 2001.

Kerber, Linda. "Separate Spheres, Female Worlds, Woman's Place: The Rhetoric of Women's History." *The Journal of American History* 75.1 (1988): 9–39.

"Kidaa joshi dendō kyoku ate kōshiki shokan" キダー女史伝道局宛公式書簡 (The official correspondence of the missionary Ms. Kidder). Unpublished material. Ferris jogakuin daigaku.

Kido Wakao 木戸若雄. *Fujin kyōshi no hyakunen* 婦人教師の百年 (One hundred years of women teachers). Meiji tosho shuppan, 1968.

Kim, Kyu Hyun. *The Age of Visions and Arguments: Parliamentarianism and the National Public Sphere in Early Meiji Japan*. Cambridge, Mass.: Harvard University Press, 2007.

Kimura Hideko 木村秀子. *Kōsairon* 交際論 (On interpersonal relations). Seibundō, 1888.

Kindai josei bunkashi kenkyūkai 近代女性文化史研究会, ed. *Fujin zasshi no yoake* 婦人雑誌の夜明け (The dawn of women's magazines). Ōzorasha, 1989.

Kinmonth, Earl. "Nakamura Keiu and Samuel Smiles: A Victorian Confucian and a Confucian Victorian." In *Meiji Japan: Political, Economic, and Social History, 1868–1912*, edited by Peter Kornicki, vol. 2, 280–302. London: Routledge, 1998.

Kiyooka Eiichi, ed. and trans. *Fukuzawa Yukichi on Japanese Women: Selected Works*. Tokyo: University of Tokyo Press, 1988.

Kobe jogakuin 神戸女学院, ed. *Kobe jogakuin hyakunenshi: Kakuron* 神戸女学院百年史. 各論 (One hundred years of Kobe jogakuin: A detailed discussion). Kobe: Kobe jogakuin, 1981.

Kohiyama Rui 小桧山ルイ. *America fujin senkyōshi* アメリカ婦人宣教師 (American women missionaries). Tokyo daigaku shuppankai, 1992.

Koizumi Takashi 小泉仰. *Nakamura Keiu to kirisutokyō* 中村敬宇とキリスト教 (Nakamura Keiu and Christianity). Hokuju shuppan, 1991.

Kokuritsu Kokkai Toshokan Toshobu 国立国会図書館図書部, ed. *Kokuritsu kokkai toshokan zōsho mokuroku: Meiji–ki* 国立国会図書館蔵書目録明治期 (Catalog of the collection of Meiji period books in the National Diet Library). 8 vols. Kokuritsu kokkai toshokan, 1994–95.

Kokusho sōmokuroku 国書総目録 (Catalog of national books). 9 vols. Iwanami Shoten, 1989–91.

Konishi Shirō 小西四郎. *Nishikie Bakumatsu Meiji no rekishi* 錦絵幕末明治の歴史 (*Nishiki–e:* A history of the Bakumatsu and Meiji periods). 12 vols. Kōdansha, 1977–78.

Kornicki, Peter. "Women, Education, and Literacy." In *The Female as Subject: Reading and Writing in Early Modern Japan*, edited by P. F. Kornicki, Mara Patessio, and G. G. Rowley, Michigan Monograph Series in Japanese Studies, no. 70, 7–37. Ann Arbor: Center for Japanese Studies, University of Michigan, 2010.

――――. "Manuscript, Not Print: Scribal Culture in the Edo Period." *Journal of Japanese Studies* 32.1 (2006): 23–52.

――――. "Unsuitable Books for Women? Genji monogatari and Ise monogatari in Late Seventeenth–Century Japan." *Monumenta Nipponica* 60.2 (2005): 147–93.

――――. *The Book in Japan: A Cultural History from the Beginnings to the Nineteenth Century*. Leiden: Brill, 1998.

――――. "Public Display and Changing Values: Early Meiji Exhibitions and Their Precursors." *Monumenta Nipponica* 49.2 (1994): 167–96.

Kornicki, P. F., Mara Patessio, and G. G. Rowley, eds. *The Female as Subject: Reading and Writing in Early Modern Japan*. Michigan Monograph Series in Japanese Studies, no. 70. Ann Arbor: Center for Japanese Studies, University of Michigan, 2010.

Kosaka, Masaaki, ed. *Japanese Thought in the Meiji Era*. Tokyo: Pan–Pacific Press, 1958.

Koyama Shizuko 小山静子. *Ryōsai kenbo to iu kihan* 良妻賢母という規範 (The "good wife wise mother" standard). Keisō shobō, 1991.

Krummel, John. "The Methodist Protestant Church in Japan: The Early Years in Yokohama, 1880–1887." *Ronshū* 論集, no. 14 (Aoyama gakuin daigaku, 1973): 1–17.

———. "Methodist Protestant Beginnings in Japan. Part 1: The Development of the Methodist Protestant Foreign Missions." *Ronshū* 論集, no. 13 (Aoyama gakuin daigaku, 1972): 1–16.

———. "Missionaries of the Methodist Protestant Church in Japan." *Ronshū* 論集, no. 12 (Aoyama gakuin daigaku, 1971): 105–21.

Kubushiro Ochimi 久布白落実. *Yuasa Hatsuko* 湯浅初子 (Yuasa Hatsuko). Ōzorasha, [1937] 1995.

———, ed. *Yajima Kajiko den* 矢島楫子伝 (Yajima Kajiko's biography). Ōzorasha, [1935] 1988.

Kume Kunitake. *The Iwakura Embassy, 1871–1873: A True Account of the Ambassador Extraordinary and Plenipotentiary's Journey of Observation through the United States of America and Europe.* 5 vols. Princeton: Princeton University Press, 2002.

Kumon Gō 公文豪. "Tosa no josei minkenka Yoshimatsu Masu" 土佐の女性民権家吉松ます (Yoshimatsu Masu, a female activist in the Movement for Freedom and Popular Rights of Tosa). *Tosa shidan* 土佐史談 161 (1983): 115–20.

Kuno Akiko. *Unexpected Destinations: The Poignant Story of Japan's First Vassar Graduate.* Kodansha International, 1993.

Kyōritsu joshi gakuen 共立女子学園, ed. *Kyōritsu joshi gakuen hyakunenshi* 共立女子学園百年史 (One hundred years of Kyōritsu joshi gakuen). Kyōritsu joshi gakuen, 1986.

Laird, M. A. *Missionaries and Education in Bengal, 1793–1837.* Oxford: Clarendon Press, 1972.

Landes, Joan. "Further Thoughts on the Public/Private Distinction." *Journal of Women's History* 15.2 (2003): 28–39.

———. *Women and the Public Sphere in the Age of the French Revolution.* Ithaca: Cornell University Press, 1988.

Lerner, Gerda. "The Lady and the Mill Girl: Changes in the Status of Women in the Age of Jackson." *Midcontinent American Studies Journal* 10.1 (1969): 5–15.

Lu, David J. *Japan: A Documentary History—the Late Tokugawa Period to the Present.* London: M. E. Sharpe, 1997.

Mackie, Vera. *Feminism in Modern Japan: Citizenship, Embodiment, and Sexuality.* Cambridge: Cambridge University Press, 2003.

———. *Creating Socialist Women in Japan: Gender, Labour, and Activism, 1900–1937.* Cambridge: Cambridge University Press, 1997.

Mainichi Communications 毎日コミュニケーションズ and Meiji nyūsu jiten hensan iinkai 明治ニュース事典編纂委員会, ed. *Meiji nyūsu jiten* 明治ニュース事典 (Encyclopedia of Meiji news). 9 Vols. Mainichi Communications, 1983–6.

Marran, Christine L. *Poison Woman: Figuring Female Transgression in Modern Japanese Culture.* Minneapolis: University of Minnesota Press, 2007.

Matsumoto Eiko 松本英子, ed. *Kōdokuchi no sanjō* 鑛毒地の惨状 (The pitiful situation of the land polluted by the mine). Vol. 1. Kyōbunkan, 1902.

Matsumoto Sannosuke 松本三之介, ed. *Yoshida Shōin* 吉田松陰 (Yoshida Shōin). Vol. 31 of *Nihon no meicho* 日本の名著 (Japanese famous authors). Chūō kōronsha, 1973.

Matsumoto Sannosuke and Yamamuro Shinichi 山室信一. *Genron to media* 言論とメディア (Debate and the media). Vol. 11 of *Nihon kindai shisō taikei* 日本近代思想大系 (Collection on modern Japanese thought). Iwanami shoten, 1990.

Matsuura Masayasu 松浦政泰. *Dōshisha romansu* 同志社ローマンス (Dōshisha romance). Keiseisha shoten, 1918.

Maza, Sarah. "Women, the Bourgeoisie, and the Public Sphere: Response to Daniel Gordon and David Bell." *French Historical Studies* 17.4 (1992): 935–50.

McClintock, Anne. "Family Feuds: Gender, Nationalism, and the Family." *Feminist Review* 44 (1993): 61–80.

McClintock, Martha. "Okuhara Seiko (1837–1913): The Life and Arts of a Meiji Period Literati Artist." 3 vols. PhD diss., Ann Arbor, University of Michigan, 1991.

McLaren, Walter W., ed. *Japanese Government Documents*. Vol. 42, part 1, of *Transactions of the Asiatic Society of Japan*. London: Kegan Paul, 1914.

Meehan, Johanna, ed. *Feminists Read Habermas: Gendering the Subject of Discourse*. London: Routledge, 1995.

Mehl, Margaret. *Private Academies of Chinese Learning in Meiji Japan: The Decline and Transformation of Kangaku Juku*. Copenhagen: Nordic Institute of Asian Studies, 2003.

———. "Women Educators and the Confucian Tradition in Meiji Japan (1868–1912): Miwada Masako and Atomi Kakei." *Women's History Review* 10.4 (2001): 579–602.

Melton, James Van Horn. *The Rise of the Public in Enlightenment Europe*. Cambridge: Cambridge University Press, 2001.

Mertz, John Pierre. *Novel Japan: Spaces of Nationhood in Early Meiji Narrative, 1870–1888*. Michigan Monograph Series in Japanese Studies, no. 48. Ann Arbor: Center for Japanese Studies, University of Michigan, 2003.

Mihalopoulos, Bill. "Mediating the Good Life: Prostitution and the Japanese Woman's Christian Temperance Union, 1880s–1920s." *Gender and History* 21.1 (2009): 19–38.

———. "Modernization as Creative Problem Making: Political Action, Personal Conduct, and Japanese Overseas Prostitutes." *Economy and Society* 27.1 (1998): 50–73.

Mill, John Stuart. *The Subjection of Women*. Edited by Susan Moller Okin. Indianapolis: Hackett, [1869] 1988.

Mills, Sara. *Discourse*. London: Routledge, 1997.

Mita Munesuke 見田宗介, ed. *Jiyū to minken* 自由と民権 (Freedom and popular rights). Vol. 5 of *Meiji no gunzo* 明治の群像 (The Meiji group). San'ichi shobō, 1968.

Mitani Tamiko henshū iinkai 三谷民子編集委員会, ed. *Mitani Tamiko: Shōgai, omoide, iboku* 三谷民子:生涯, 思い出, 遺墨 (Mitani Tamiko: Her life, memories, and writings). Jogakuin dōsōkai, 1991.

Mitsui Reiko 三井礼子. *Gendai fujin undōshi nenpyō* 現代婦人運動史年表 (Timeline of the contemporary women's movement). San'ichi shobō, 1963.

Mitsui Tametomo 三井為友, ed. *Nihon fujin mondai shiryō shūsei* 日本婦人問題資料集成 (Collection of documents on the 'woman's problem' in Japan). Vol. 4, *Kyōiku* 教育 (Education). Domesu shuppan. 1977

Miwada Masako 三輪田眞佐子. *Miwada Masako: Oshiegusa/hoka* 三輪田眞佐子 教へ草／他 (Miwada Masako: *Oshiegusa* and other writings). Nihon tosho Center, 2005.

Miyagi no joseishi kenkyūkai みやぎの女性史研究会, ed. *Miyagi no joseishi* みやぎの女性史 (Miyagi women's history). Sendai: Kahoku shinpōsha, 1999.

Miyatake Gaikotsu 宮武外骨. *Meiji enzetsushi* 明治演説史 (A history of speaking in public during the Meiji period). Yūgensha, 1926.

Mochizuki Kōzaburō 望月興三郎, ed. *Shiritsu San'yō jogakkō hōkoku 1* 私立山陽女学校報告. 第 1 (First report on the work of the private San'yō jogakkō). Okayama: San'yō jogakkō, 1894.

Monbushō 文部省, ed. *Gakusei hyakunenshi* 学制百年史 (History of the educational system during the past one hundred years). 2 vols. Gyōsei, 1972.

―――, ed. *Gakusei hachijūnenshi* 学制八十年史 (History of the educational system during the past eighty years). Ōkurashō insatsukyoku, 1954.

Montgomery, Helen Barrett. *Western Women in Eastern Lands*. New York: Macmillan, 1910.

Morita Hideko 森田英子. *Bunkyōku yukari no joseitachi* 文京区ゆかりの女性達 (Women connected to the Bunkyō ward). Morita shigetoshi jimusho, 1986.

Morosawa Yōko もろさわようこ, ed. *Dokyumento onna no hyakunen* ドキュメント女の百年 (One hundred years of documents on women). Vol. 2, *Onna to kyōiku* 女と教育 (Women and education). Heibonsha, 1978.

Morris–Suzuki, Tessa. *Re–inventing Japan: Time, Space, Nation*. London: M. E. Sharpe, 1998.

Moses, Claire Goldberg. *French Feminism in the Nineteenth Century*. Albany: State University of New York Press, 1984.

Motoyama Yukihiko. *Proliferating Talent: Essays on Politics, Thought, and Education in the Meiji Era*. Edited by J. S. A. Elisonas and R. Rubinger. Honolulu: University of Hawai'i Press, 1997.

Mouer, Elizabeth Knipe. "Women in Teaching." In *Women in Changing Japan*, edited by Joyce Lebra, Joy Paulson, and Elizabeth Powers, 157–90. Stanford: Stanford University Press, 1976.

Mulhern, Chieko Irie, ed. *Heroic with Grace: Legendary Women of Japan*. London: M. E. Sharpe, 1991.

Murakami Nobuhiko 村上信彦. *Meiji joseishi* 明治女性史 (History of Meiji women). Vol. 1. Kōdansha, [1969] 1977.

―――. *Meiji joseishi* 明治女性史 (History of Meiji women). Vol. 2. Rironsha, 1970.

Murakami Tadashi 村上直. "Kinsei Zōjōji ryō ni okeru 'Jogakkō hokki no shuisho' ni tsuite" 近世増上寺領における「女学校発起之趣意書」について (On the "Reasons for the establishment of *jogakkō*" in the land belonging to the Zōjōji temple in the early modern period). *Hōsei shigaku* 法政史学 30 (1978): 16–31.

Murakami Toshiaki 村上俊亮 and Sakata Yoshio 坂田吉雄, eds. *Kyōiku, dōtoku hen* 教育, 道徳篇 (On education and morals). Vol. 3 of *Meiji bunka shi* 明治文化史 (A cultural history of the Meiji period), edited by Kaikoku hyakunen kinen bunka jigyōkai 開國百年記念文化事業會. Yōyōsha, 1955.

Murao Akiko 村尾昭子. "Hashutsu kangofu no ayumi" 派出看護婦のあゆみ (The development of visiting nurses). In *Onnatachi no kindai* 女たちの近代 (The modern period for women), edited by Kindai joseishi kenkyūkai 近代女性史研究会, 255–80. Kashiwa shobo, 1978.

Murata Shizuko 村田静子. *Fukuda Hideko: Fujin kaihō undō no senkusha* 福田英子: 婦人解放運動の先駆者 (Fukuda Hideko: Pioneer of the movement for women's liberation). Iwanami shoten, 1959.

Murata Shizuko and Ōki Motoko, eds. *Fukuda Hideko shū* 福田英子集 (Collection of documents by and about Fukuda Hideko). Fuji shuppan, 1998.

Nagata, Mary Louise. "Headship and Succession in Early Modern Kyoto: The Role of Women." *Continuity and Change* 19.1 (2004): 73–104.

———. "Mistress or Wife? Fukui Sakuzaemon vs. Iwa, 1819–1833." *Continuity and Change* 18.2 (2003): 287–309.

Nagatoya, Yoji. "Dr. Keiko Okami: Japan's First Female Medical Student Who Studied Abroad." *Journal of the American Medical Women's Association* 15.12 (1960): 1175–77.

Nagy, Margit Maria. "'How Shall We Live?' Social Change, the Family Institution, and Feminism in Prewar Japan." PhD diss., University of Washington, 1981.

Najita, Tetsuo. *Visions of Virtue in Tokugawa Japan: The Kaitokudō Merchant Academy of Osaka*. Chicago: University of Chicago Press, 1987.

Najmabadi, Afsaneh. "Crafting an Educated Housewife in Iran." In *Remaking Women: Feminism and Modernity in the Middle East*, edited by Lila Abu–Lughod, 91–125. Princeton: Princeton University Press, 1998.

Nakai Tatsu 中井タツ, ed. *(Tottori fujinkai) enzetsu hikki* (鳥取婦人会)演説筆記 (Transcription of the Public Speeches of the Tottori Women's Group). Tottori: Nakai Tatsu, 1888.

Nakajima Masukichi 中鳥益吉, ed. *Meien no gakusei jidai* 名媛の学生時代 (Famous ladies' school days). Yomiuri shinbunsha, 1907.

Nakamura, Momoko. "Discursive Construction of the Ideology of 'Women's Language': 'Schoolgirl Language' in the Meiji Period (1868–1912)." *Shizen Ningen Shakai* 自然人間社会 36 (2004): 43–80.

Natori Takao 名取多嘉雄. "Hishūkyō gakkō ni okeru Kirisutōkyō kyōiku no mondai" 非宗教学校におけるキリスト教教育の問題 (The problem of Christian education in secular schools). *Rikkyō jogakuin tanki daigaku kiyo* 立教女学院短期大学紀要 16 (1984): 1–23.

Nihon joishi hensan iinkai 日本女医史編纂委員会, ed. *Nihon joishi* 日本女医史 (History of Japanese women doctors). Nihon joikai, 1991.

Nihon joshi daigaku joshi kyōiku kenkyūsho 日本女子大学女子教育研究所, ed. *Meiji no joshi kyōiku* 明治の女子教育 (Women's education in the Meiji period). Kokudosha, 1967.

Nihon kirisutokyō fujin kyōfūkai 日本キリスト教婦人矯風会, ed. *Nihon kirisutokyō fujin kyōfūkai hyakunenshi* 日本キリスト教婦人矯風会百年史 (One hundred years of the Nihon kirisutokyō fujin kyōfūkai). Domesu shuppan, 1986.

Niiro Kyōko 新納京子, Yamaguchi Hanae 山口花江, and Yukinaga Masae 雪永政枝. *Kangoshi nenpyō* 看護史年表 (Timeline of the history of nursing). Igaku shoin, 1991.

Nirazuka Ichisaburō 韮塚一三郎. *Saitama no onnatachi: Rekishi no naka no 24 nin* 埼玉の女たち.歴史の中の24人 (Women of Saitama: Twenty–four case studies). Urawa: Sakitama shuppankai, 1979.

Nishikawa Fumiko 西川文子. *Heiminsha no onna: Nishikawa Fumiko jiden* 平民社の女: 西川文子自伝 (A woman of the *Heiminsha*: The autobiography of Nishikawa Fumiko). Edited by Amano Shigeru 天野茂. Aoyamakan, 1984.

Nishimura Ayako 西村絢子, Arai Yoshiko 新井淑子, and Tachi Kaoru 館かおる. "Kōtō jogakkō no kenkyū, setsuritsu katei o chūshin ni" 高等女学校の研究―設立過程を中心に (A study of Kōtō jogakkō with particular reference to the period in which it was founded). *Ochanomizu joshi daigaku josei bunka shiryō kanpō* お茶の水女子大学女性文化資料館報 5 (1984): 91–111.

Nolte, Sharon, and Sally Hastings. "The Meiji State's Policy toward Women, 1890–1910." In *Recreating Japanese Women, 1600–1945*, edited by Gail Lee Bernstein, 151–74. Berkeley: University of California Press, 1991.

Notehelfer, Fred George. *American Samurai: Captain L. L. Janes and Japan*. Princeton: Princeton University Press, 1985.

———. "Japan's First Pollution Incident." *Journal of Japanese Studies* 1.2 (1975): 351–83.

Ochanomizu joshi daigaku hyakunenshi kankō iinkai お茶の水女子大学百年史刊行委員会, ed. *Ochanomizu joshi daigaku hyakunenshi* お茶の水女子大学百年史 (One hundred years of Ochanomizu Women's University). Ochanomizu joshi daigaku, 1984.

Ōe Mitsuru 大江満. *Senkyōshi Uiriamuzu no dendō to shōgai: Bakumatsu Meiji beikoku seikōkai no kiseki* 宣教師ウイリアムズの伝道と生涯―幕末・明治米国聖公会の軌跡 (The life and work of the missionary Williams: The American Episcopal Church during the Bakumatsu and Meiji periods). Tōsui shobō, 2000.

Ogawa, Manako. "The 'White Ribbon League of Nations' Meets Japan: The Trans–Pacific Activism of the Woman's Christian Temperance Union, 1906–1930." *Diplomatic History* 31.1 (2007): 21–50.

———. "Rescue Work for Japanese Women: The Birth and Development of the Jiaikan Rescue Home and the Missionaries of the Woman's Christian Temperance Union, Japan, 1886–1921." *U.S.–Japan Women's Journal* 26 (2004): 98–133.

Ogawa Sumie 小川澄江. *Nakamura Masanao no kyōiku shisō* 中村正直の教育思想 (The educational philosophy of Nakamura Masanao). Tochigi: Ogawa Sumie, 2004.

Ōhama Tetsuya 大濱徹也, ed. *Joshi gakuin no rekishi* 女子学院の歴史 (The history of Joshi gakuin). Joshi gakuin, 1985.

———. *Ōe Sumi sensei* 大江スミ先生 (On the teacher Ōe Sumi). Tokyo kasei gakuin kōenkai, 1978.

Ōhata Tetsu 大畑哲. "Meiji joseishi ni kansuru futatsu no shinshiryō" 明治女性史に関する二つの新資料 (Two new documents on the history of Meiji women). *Kanagawa kenshi kenkyū* 神奈川県史研究 28 (1975): 57–65.

Ohyama, Tsunao. "Sarah C. Smith of Elmira: A Missionary to Japan." *Chemung Historical Journal* 23 (1977): 2741–45.

Okayama joseishi kenkyūkai 岡山女性史研究会, ed. "Okayama joshi konshinkai ni tsuite" 岡山女子懇親会について (On the Okayama joshi konshinkai). In *Josei to undō 女性と運動* (Women's activism). Vol. 10 of *Nihon joseishi ronshū 日本女性史論集* (Collection of essays on Japanese women's history), edited by Sōgō joseishi kenkyūkai 総合女性史研究会, 191–214. Yoshikawa kobunkan, 1998.

———, ed. *Kindai Okayama no onnatachi 近代岡山の女たち* (Women of Okayama during the modern period). Sanseidō, 1987.

Okazaki–Ward, Lola. "Women and Their Education in the Tokugawa Period of Japan." MPhil thesis, University of Sheffield, 1993.

Ōki Motoko 大木基子. *Jiyu minken undō to josei 自由民権運動と女性* (The Movement for Freedom and Popular Rights and women). Domesu shuppan, 2003.

Ōkubo Toshiaki 大久保利謙, ed. *Kindaishi shiryō 近代史史料* (Sources on modern history). Yoshikawa Kōbunkan, 1965.

Okuma, Shigenobu, comp. *Fifty Years of New Japan*. 2 vols. Translated by Marcus B. Huish. London: Smith, Elder, 1909.

Ōmizo Kichizō 大溝吉蔵. *Jogaku enzetsushū 女学演説集* (Collection of public speeches on women's education). Isogai shobō, 1888.

Orsini, Francesca. *The Hindi Public Sphere, 1920–1940: Language and Literature in the Age of Nationalism*. Oxford: Oxford University Press, 2002.

Osaka jogakuinshi kenkyū iinkai 大阪女学院史研究委員会, ed. *Osaka jogakuinshi kenkyū 大阪女学院史研究* (History of Osaka jogakuin). Osaka: Osaka jogakuin, 1984.

Oxford Dictionary of National Biography: From the Earliest Times to the Year 2000. Edited by H. C. G. Matthew and Brian Harrison. Oxford: Oxford University Press, 2004.

Ozkirimli, Umut. *Theories of Nationalism: A Critical Introduction*. New York: St. Martin's Press, 2000.

Passin, Herbert. *Society and Education in Japan*. New York: Columbia University Press, 1982.

Patessio, Mara. "Readers and Writers: Women and Magazines in the Late Nineteenth Century." In *The Female as Subject: Reading and Writing in Early Modern Japan*, edited by P. F. Kornicki, Mara Patessio, and G. G. Rowley, Michigan Monograph Series in Japanese Studies, no. 70, 191–213. Ann Arbor: Center for Japanese Studies, University of Michigan, 2010.

Patessio, Mara, and Mariko Ogawa. "To Become a Woman Doctor in Early Meiji Japan (1868–1890): Women's Struggles and Ambitions." *Historia Scientiarum* 15.2 (2005): 159–76.

Peiss, Kathy. "Going Public: Women in Nineteenth–Century Cultural History." *American Literary History* 3.4 (1991): 817–28.

Platt, H. L. *The Story of the Years: A History of the Woman's Missionary Society of the Methodist Church, Canada, from 1881 to 1906*. 2 vols. Canada: Woman's Missionary Society, 1908–9.

Poate Stebbins, Richard, ed. *The Japan Experience: The Missionary Letters of Belle Marsh Poate and Thomas Pratt Poate, 1876–1892*. New York: Peter Lang, 1992.

Poovey, Mary. *Uneven Developments: The Ideological Work of Gender in Mid–Victorian England*. Chicago: University of Chicago Press, 1988.

Bibliography

Proceedings of the General Conference of the Protestant Missionaries of Japan, Osaka. Vol. 1. Yokohama: R. Meikle John, 1883.

Pyle, Kenneth B. *The New Generation in Meiji Japan.* Stanford: Stanford University Press, 1969.

Rabinovitch, Eyal. "Gender and the Public Sphere: Alternative Forms of Integration in Nineteenth–Century America." *Sociological Theory* 19.3 (2001): 344–70.

Racioppi, Linda, and Katherine O'Sullivan See. "Engendering Nation and National Identity." In *Women, States, and Nationalism: At Home in the Nation?* edited by Sita Ranchod–Nilsson and Mary Ann Tetreault, 18–34. London: Routledge, 2000.

Ranchod–Nilsson, Sita, and Mary Ann Tetreault. *Women, States, and Nationalism: At Home in the Nation?* London: Routledge, 2000.

Rendall, Jane. "Women and the Public Sphere." *Gender and History* 11.3 (1999): 475–88.

———. *The Origins of Modern Feminism: Women in Britain, France, and the United States, 1780–1860.* Chicago: Lyceum Books, 1985.

Richards, Linda. *Reminiscences of Linda Richards, America's First Trained Nurse.* Boston: Whitcomb and Barrows, 1911.

Roberts, Luke. "The Petition Box in Eighteenth–Century Tosa." *Journal of Japanese Studies* 20.2 (1994): 423–58.

Robins–Mowry, Dorothy. "Westernizing Influences in the Early Modernization of Japanese Women's Education." In *Foreign Employees in Nineteenth–Century Japan*, edited by E. R. Beauchamp and A. Eriye, 121–36. Boulder: Westview Press, 1990.

———. *The Hidden Sun: Women of Modern Japan.* Boulder: Westview Press, 1983.

Rose, Barbara. *Tsuda Umeko and Women's Education in Japan.* New Haven: Yale University Press, 1992.

Rowbotham, Judith. "'Soldiers of Christ'? Images of Female Missionaries in Late Nineteenth–Century Britain— Issues of Heroism and Martyrdom." *Gender and History* 12.1 (2000): 82–106.

———. "'Hear an Indian Sister's Plea': Reporting the Work of Nineteenth–Century British Female Missionaries." *Women's Studies International Forum* 21.3 (1998): 247–61.

Rubin, Jay. *Injurious to Public Morals: Writers and the Meiji State.* Seattle: University of Washington Press, 1984.

Ryan, Mary. "The Public and the Private Good: Across the Great Divide in Women's History." *Journal of Women's History* 15.2 (2003): 10–27.

———. "The Power of Women's Networks: A Case Study of Female Moral Reform in Antebellum America." *Feminist Studies* 5.1 (1979): 66–85.

Saitō Junkichi 斎藤醇吉. "Edo jidai no kazoku kyōiku" 江戸時代の家庭教育 (Home education during the Edo period). *Nihon shigaku kyōiku kenkyūsho kiyō* 日本私学教育研究所紀要 21.1, 22.1, 23.1 (1986–88): 349–80, 419–454, 443–475.

Sakamoto Kiyone 坂本清音. "Dōshisha jogakkō shodai fujin senkyōshi A. J. Starkweather no kutō" 同志社女学校初代婦人宣教師A.J.スタークウエザーの苦闘 (The struggle of the woman missionary A. J. Starkweather in the early days of Dōshisha jogakkō). In *Rainichi America senkyōshi: American bo–do– senkyōshi shokan no kenkyū 1869–1890* 来日アメリカ宣教師. アメリカンボード宣教師書簡の研究*1869–1890* (American missionaries in Japan: A study of the correspondence of the American Board,

1869–1890), edited by Dōshisha daigaku jinbun kagaku kenkyūsho 同志社大学人文科学研究所, 303–26. Kyoto: Gendai shiryō shuppan, 1999.

———. "Beikoku dendōkai senkyōshi bunsho: A. J. Starkweather shokan (4)" 米国伝道会宣教師文書 A. J. Starkweather 書簡 (The documents of the missionaries of the American Board of Commissioners for Foreign Missions: The correspondence of A. J. Starkweather, part 4). In *Sōgō bunka kenkyūsho kiyō* 総合文化研究所紀要, vol. 10, 69–96. Kyoto: Dōshisha joshi daigaku, 1993.

Sakuma Shōzan 佐久間象山. *Jokun* 女訓 (Moral text for women). In *Nihon kyōiku bunko* 日本教育文庫 (Collection of books on education in Japan). Vol. 5, *Jokunhen* 女訓篇 (Moral texts for women), edited by Kurokawa Mamichi 黒川眞道, 729–39. Dōbunkan 1910.

Sakurai Fukiko 桜井ふき子, ed. *Fujin risshi den* 婦人立志伝 (Biographies of successful women). Hifumi–kan, 1893.

Sakurai Junji 櫻井淳司, ed. *Sakurai Chika shōden: Sakurai jojuku no rekishi* 櫻井ちか小伝. 櫻井女塾の歴史 (A short biography of Sakurai Chika: History of the Sakurai private school for women). Sagamihara: Sakurai Junji, 1976.

Sarkar, Tanika. *Hindu Wife, Hindu Nation: Community, Religion, and Cultural Nationalism*. New Delhi: Permanent Black, 2001.

Sasaki Toyoju 佐々城豊壽, ed. and trans. *Fujin genron no jiyū* 婦人言論の自由 (Women's freedom of speech). Sasaki Toyoju, 1888.

Satō Ken'ichi 佐藤憲一. "Joshi sanseiken o meiki shita Meiji jūsannen no 'Nagamachi mura sonkai kisoku'" 女子参政権を明記した明治十三年の「長町村々会規則」 (The 1880 village regulation of Nagamachi mura that specified women's voting rights). *Shishi sendai* 市史せんだい 1 (1992): 46–52.

Savage, David W. "Missionaries and the Development of a Colonial Ideology of Female Education in India." *Gender and History* 9.2 (1997): 201–21.

Scalapino, Robert. *Democracy and the Party Movement in Pre–war Japan: The Failure of the First Attempt*. Berkeley: University of California Press, 1967.

Scheiner, Irwin. "Christian Samurai and Samurai Values." In *Modern Japanese Leadership*, edited by B. S. Silberman and H. D. Harootunian, 171–94. Tucson: University of Arizona Press, 1996.

———. *Christian Converts and Social Protest in Meiji Japan*. Berkeley: University of California Press, 1970.

Schwartz, Frank J., and Susan J. Pharr, eds. *The State of Civil Society in Japan*. Cambridge: Cambridge University Press, 2003.

Seki Reiko 関礼子. *Kataru onnatachi no jidai. Ichiyō to meiji josei hyōgen* 語る女たちの時代一葉と明治女性表現 (The time in which women spoke: Ichiyō and the representation of Meiji women). Shinyōsha, 1997.

Seki Tamiko 関民子. *Edo kōki no joseitachi* 江戸後期の女性たち (Women of the late Edo period). Aki shobō, 1980.

Sekiguchi, Sumiko 関口すみ子. "Gender in the Meiji Renovation: Confucian 'Lessons for Women' and the Making of Modern Japan." *Social Science Japan Journal* 11.2 (2008): 201–21.

————. *Go–isshin to jendaa* 後一新とジェンダー (Gender and the Meiji Restoration). Tokyo Daigaku Shuppankai, 2005.

————. "Enzetsu suru onna tachi" 演説する女たち (Women who make public speeches). *Mirai* 未来 396, 399, 401, 403, 406 (1999–2000): 32–38, 36–39, 14–21, 30–37, 20–36.

Selles, Johanna M. "The Role of Women in the Formation of the World Student Christian Federation." *International Bulletin of Missionary Research* 30.4 (2006): 189–94.

Senju Katsumi. "The Development of Female Education in Private Schools." *Education in Japan: Journal for Overseas* 6 (1971): 37–46.

Shakry, Omnia. "Schooled Mothers and Structured Play: Child Rearing in Turn–of–the–Century Egypt." In *Remaking Women: Feminism and Modernity in the Middle East*, edited by Lila Abu–Lughod, 126–70. Princeton: Princeton University Press, 1998.

Shiba Keiko 柴桂子. *Kinsei onna tabi nikki* 近世おんな旅日記 (Early modern women's travel diaries). Yoshikawa kōbunkan, 1997.

Shibukawa, Hisako. "An Education for Making Good Wives and Wise Mothers." *Education in Japan: Journal for Overseas* 6 (1971): 47–57.

Shibuya Zōji 渋谷慥爾, trans. *Seijidan* 政治談 (Tales of political affairs). 2 vols. Jiyū shuppan, 1883.

Shirai Takako 白井尭子. *Fukuzawa Yukichi to senkyōshitachi* 福沢諭吉と宣教師たち (Fukuzawa Yukichi and foreign missionaries). Miraisha, 1999.

Sievers, Sharon. "Feminist Criticism in Japanese Politics in the 1880s: The Experience of Kishida Toshiko." In *Meiji Japan: Political, Economic, and Social History, 1868–1912*, edited by Peter Kornicki, vol. 2, 36–50. London: Routledge, 1998.

————. *Flowers in Salt: The Beginnings of Feminist Consciousness in Modern Japan.* Stanford: Stanford University Press, 1983.

Smith, Anthony. *National Identity.* New York: Penguin, 1991.

Smith, Henry D. "The History of the Book in Edo and Paris." In *Edo and Paris: Urban Life and the State in the Early Modern Era*, edited by James L. McClain, John M. Merriman, and Ugawa Kaoru, 332–52. Ithaca: Cornell University Press, 1994.

Sōma Kokkō 相馬黒光. *Hirosegawa no hotori* 広瀬川の畔 (The banks of the Hirose river). Josei jidaisha, 1939.

————. *Mokui* 黙移 (Silent passing). Josei jidaisha, 1939.

Sotozaki Mitsuhiro 外崎光広. *Ueki Emori to onnatachi* 植木枝盛と女たち (Ueki Emori and women). Domesu, 1976.

————. *Kochi–ken fujin kaihō undōshi* 高知県婦人解放運動史 (History of the movement for women's liberation in Kochi prefecture). Domesu, 1975.

————. *Meiji zenki fujin kaihō ronshi* 明治前期婦人解放論史 (Theories on the movement for women's liberation during the early Meiji period). Kochi: Kochi shiritsu shimin toshokan, 1963.

————. *Ueki Emori fujin kaihō ronshū* 植木枝盛婦人解放論集 (Collection of Ueki Emori's theories on women's liberation). Kochi: Kochi shiritsu shimin toshokan, 1962.

————. *Ueki Emori kazoku seidō ronshū* 植木枝盛家族制度論集 (Collection of Ueki Emori's theories on the family system). Kochi: Kochi shiritsu shimin toshokan, 1957.

Spencer, Herbert. *Social Statics.* London: Routledge and Thoemmes Press, [1851] 1996.

Steele, M. William, and Tamiko Ichimata, eds. *Clara's Diary: An American Girl in Meiji Japan*. Kodansha International, 1979.

Stephen, Lynn. "Gender, Citizenship, and the Politics of Identity." *Latin American Perspectives* 28.6 (2001): 54–69.

Stone, Lawrence. *The Past and the Present*. London: Routledge, 1981.

Sugano, Noriko 菅野則子. "Kishida Toshiko and the Career of a Public-Speaking Woman in Meiji Japan." In *The Female as Subject: Reading and Writing in Early Modern Japan*, edited by P. F. Kornicki, Mara Patessio, and G. G. Rowley. Michigan Monograph Series in Japanese Studies, no. 70, 171–89. Ann Arbor: Center for Japanese Studies, University of Michigan, 2010.

———. "Terakoya to onna shishō" 寺子屋と女師匠 (Terakoya and women teachers). In *Kyōiku to shisō* 教育と思想 (Education and ideology). Vol. 8 of *Nihon joseishi ronshū* 日本女性史論集 (Collection of essays on Japanese women's history), edited by Sōgō joseishi kenkyūkai, 140–58. Yoshikawa kōbunkan, 1998.

Sugimoto, Etsu. *A Daughter of the Samurai*. North Clarendon: Tuttle, 1990.

Sumida Yorinosuke 住田頼之助. *Saigoku fujin risshi–hen* 西国婦人立志編 (Biographies of successful Western women). Kinkōkan, 1887.

Suzuki Mitsujirō 鈴木光次郎, ed. *Meiji keishū bidan* 明治閨秀美譚 (Admirable stories of accomplished Meiji ladies). Tokyodō, 1892.

Suzuki Yoshimune 鈴木義宗, trans. *Fujo hōritsuron* 婦女法律論 (On legislation concerning women). Suzuki Yoshimune, 1878.

Suzuki Yūko 鈴木裕子, ed. *Nihon josei undō shiryō shūsei* 日本女性運動資料集成 (Sources on the Japanese women's movement). Vol. 1, *Shisō seiji* 思想政治 (Political thought). Fuji shuppan, 1996.

Tachi Kaoru 舘かおる. "Ryōsai kenbo" 良妻賢母 (Good wives, wise mothers). In *Kōza joseigaku* 講座女性学 (Lectures on women's studies). Vol. 1, *Onna no imeji* 女のイメージ (Images of women), edited by Joseigaku kenkyūkai 女性学研究会, 184–209. Keisō shobō, 1984.

Takahashi, Aya. *The Development of the Japanese Nursing Profession: Adopting and Adapting Western Influences*. London: Routledge, 2004.

Takahashi Educational Institution Volunteer Centre. *Fukunishi Shigeko and Her Life: Never Ending Challenges and Dedication to Women's Education and Women in Development (WID)—the Junsei Spirit*. Takahashi: Okayama gakuen, 2001.

Takahashi Masako 高橋政子. *Shashin de miru nihon kindai kango no rekishi: Senkusha o tazunete* 写真でみる日本近代看護の歴史：先駆者を訪ねて (A visual history of the Japanese nursing profession during the modern period: Meeting the pioneers). Igaku shoin, 1984.

Takeda Kinko 武田錦子. *Joshi eigo yomihon* 女子英語読本 (English reader for women), 4 vols. Kinkōdō, 1902.

Takekoshi Kumasaburō 竹越熊三郎. *Takekoshi Takeyo no shōgai* 竹越竹代の生涯 (The life of Takekoshi Takeyo). Takekoshi Tatsugorō, 1965.

Takekoshi Takeyo 竹越竹代. ed. *Westo joshi ikun* ウェスト女史遺訓 (The late Mrs. West's teachings). Tokyo fujin kyōfūkai, 1893.

———. *Fujin risshi hen* 婦人立志篇 (Self–help for women). Vol. 1. Keiseisha, 1892.

Tamura Hikari 田村光, ed. *Joshi gakuin hachijūnenshi* 女子学院八十年史 (Eighty years of Joshi gakuin). Joshi gakuin, 1951.

Tamura Naoomi 田村直臣. *Shinkō gojūnenshi* 信仰五十年史 (Fifty years of faith). Keiseisha, 1924.

Tamura Naoomi and Asada Mikako 浅田みか子, eds. *Joshi gakuin gojūnenshi* 女子学院五十年史 (Fifty years of Joshi gakuin). Joshi gakuin dōsōkai, 1928.

Tanaka Kazunori 田中和徳. "Josei minkenka Nishimaki Sakuya no shōgai" 女性民権家西巻開耶の生涯 (The life of the popular rights female activist Nishimaki Sakuya). *Niigata kenritsu rekishi hakubutsukan kenkyū kiyō* 新潟県立歴史博物館研究紀要 4 (2003): 25–48.

———. "Josei kaihō ni tsukushita Nishimaki Sakuya no ashidori" 女性解放に尽くした西巻開耶の足どり (The path of Nishimaki Sakuya, who exerted herself for the liberation of women). *Kashiwazaki kariha* 柏崎刈羽 26 (1999): 32–57.

Tanaka Shōzō 田中正造. *Kōdoku jiken* 鉱毒事件 (The mine pollution incident). In *Gijin zenshū* 義人全集 (The complete works of a righteous man), edited by Kurihara Hikosaburō 栗原彦三郎. Vols. 3–4. Chūgai shinronsha, 1925–27.

Tanaka, Yukiko. *Women Writers of Meiji and Taishō Japan.* Jefferson: McFarland, 2000.

Tanigawa Kensuke 谷川憲介. *Kindai Kumamoto joseishi nenpyō: Meiji gan'nen—Showa nijūnen* 近代熊本女性史年表:明治元年(1868)–昭和20年(1945) (Timeline of Kumamoto women's modern history: From 1868 to 1945). Kumamoto: Kumamoto shuppan bunka kaikan, 1999.

Taylor, Sandra C. "The Sisterhood of Salvation and the Sunrise Kingdom: Congregational Women Missionaries in Meiji Japan." *Pacific Historical Review* 48.1 (1979): 27–45.

Thapar, Suruchi. "Women as Activists, Women as Symbols: A Study of the Indian Nationalist Movement." *Feminist Review* 44 (1993): 81–96.

Tocco, Martha. "Made in Japan: Meiji Women's Education." In *Gendering Modern Japanese History*, edited by Barbara Molony and Kathleen Uno, 39–60. Cambridge, Mass.: Harvard University Press, 2005.

———. "Norms and Texts for Women's Education in Tokugawa Japan." In *Women and Confucian Cultures in Premodern China, Korea, and Japan*, edited by Dorothy Ko, Jahyun Kim Haboush, and Joan Piggott, 193–218. Berkeley: University of California Press, 2003.

———. "School Bound: Women's Higher Education in Nineteenth–Century Japan." PhD diss., Stanford University, 1995.

Tokushima–ken kyōikukai 徳島県教育会, ed. *Tokushima–ken kyōiku enkakushi* 徳島県教育沿革史 (A history of Tokushima prefecture's educational system). Tokushima: Tokushima–ken kyōikukai, 1959.

Tokuza, Akiko. *The Rise of the Feminist Movement in Japan.* Keio University Press, 1999.

Tokyo daigaku igakubu 東京大学医学部. *Kango no ayumi: Meiji, Taishō, Shōwa o tōshite* 看護のあゆみ:明治,大正,昭和を通して (The development of the nursing profession during the Meiji, Taishō, and Shōwa periods). Tokyo daigaku igakubu fuzoku byōin kangobu, 1991.

Tokyo joshi kōtō shihan gakkō 東京女子高等師範学校, ed. *Tokyo joshi kōtō shihan gakkō rokujūnenshi* 東京女子高等師範学校六十年史 (Sixty years of the Tokyo women's higher normal school). Daiichi shobō, 1981.

Tokyo–to. *Tokyo no joshi kyōiku* 東京の女子教育 (Female education in Tokyo). Tokyo–to, 1961.

Tomaselli, Sylvana. "The Most Public Sphere of All: The Family." In *Women, Writing, and the Public Sphere, 1700–1830,* edited by Elizabeth Eger, Charlotte Grant, Cliona O Gallchoir, and Penny Warburton, 239–56. Cambridge: Cambridge University Press, 2006.

Tomasi, Massimiliano. "Oratory in Meiji and Taishō Japan: Public Speaking and the Formation of a New Written Language." *Monumenta Nipponica* 57.1 (2002): 43–71.

Tomida, Hiroko. *Hiratsuka Raichō and Early Japanese Feminism.* Leiden: Brill, 2004.

Tomida, Hiroko and Gordon Daniels. *Japanese Women: Emerging from Subservience, 1868–1945.* Folkestone: Global Oriental, 2005.

Tomisaka kirisutokyō Center 富坂基督教センター, ed. *Kindai nihon no kirisutokyō to joseitachi* 近代日本のキリスト教と女性たち (Christianity and women in Japan during the modern period). Shinkyō shuppansha, 1995.

Tomita Hitoshi 富田仁, ed. *Jiten kindai nihon no senkusha* 事典近代日本の先駆者 (A dictionary of pioneers in modern Japan). Nichigai Associates, 1995.

Tsuboi Yoshiko 坪井良子, ed. *Kindai nihon kango meicho shūsei: Kaisetsuhen* 近代日本看護名著集成.解説編 (Famous works on nursing during the modern period: Explanatory volume). Ōzorasha, 1989.

Tsumagari Yūji 津曲裕次. *Ishii Fudeko* 石井筆子 (Ishii Fudeko). Ōzorasha, 2006.

Tsurumi, Patricia. *Factory Girls: Women in the Thread Mills of Meiji Japan.* Princeton: Princeton University Press, 1990.

Tōyō eiwa jogakuin shiryōshitsu iinkai 東洋英和女学院史料室委員会, ed. *Tōyō eiwa jogakuin shiryōshū* 東洋英和女学院資料集 (Sources on Tōyō eiwa jogakuin). Vols. 1–3. Tōyō eiwa jogakuin shiryōshitsu iinkai, 1984, 1985, 1987.

Ueki Emori 植木枝盛. *Tōyō no fujo* 東洋之婦女 (Women of the East). Sasaki Toyoju, 1889.

———. *Minken jiyūron* 民権自由論 (On freedom and people's rights). Fukuoka: Shūbundō, 1879.

Ueno Naozō 上野直蔵, ed. *Dōshisha hyakunenshi: Tsūshihen* 同志社百年史. 通史編 (One hundred years of Dōshisha: The narrative volume). Kyoto: Dōshisha, 1979.

Umihara Tōru 海原徹. *Kinsei no gakkō to kyōiku* 近世の学校と教育 (Early modern schools and education). Kyoto: Shibunkaku, 1988.

Uno, Kathleen S. "The Death of 'Good Wife, Wise Mother'?" In *Postwar Japan as History*, edited by Andrew Gordon, 293–322. Berkeley: University of California Press, 1993.

Usui Chizuko 碓井知鶴子. "Meiji kaikaki ni okeru Margaret Griffis no yakuwari" 明治開化期におけるマーガレット・グリフィスの役割 (The role of Margaret Griffis during the "civilization and enlightenment" period in the Meiji era). In *Za Yatoi: Oyatoi gaikokujin no sōgōteki kenkyū* ザ・ヤトイお雇い外国人の総合的研究 (The yatoi: A comprehensive study of foreign employees in Japan), edited by Shimada Tadashi 嶋田正, 130–50. Shibunkaku, 1987.

Vlastos, Stephen. "Opposition Movements in Early Meiji, 1868–1885." In *The Cambridge History of Japan*, edited by Marius B. Jansen. Vol. 5, *The Nineteenth Century*, 367–431. Cambridge: Cambridge University Press, 1989.

Wakakuwa, Midori. "The Gender System of the Imperial State." *U.S.–Japan Women's Journal* 20–21 (2001): 17–82.

————. "Three Women Artists of the Meiji period (1868–1912): Reconsidering Their Significance from a Feminist Perspective." In *Japanese Women: New Feminist Perspectives on the Past, Present, and Future*, edited by Kumiko Fujimura–Fanselow and Atsuko Kameda, 61–74. New York: Feminist Press, 1995.

Walthall, Anne. "Women and Literacy from Edo to Meiji." In *The Female as Subject: Reading and Writing in Early Modern Japan*, edited by P. F. Kornicki, Mara Patessio, and G. G. Rowley. Michigan Monograph Series in Japanese Studies, no. 70, 215–35. Ann Arbor: Center for Japanese Studies, University of Michigan, 2010.

————. *The Weak Body of a Useless Woman: Matsuo Taseko and the Meiji Restoration*. Chicago: University of Chicago Press, 1998.

————. "Devoted Wives/Unruly Women: Invisible Presence in the History of Japanese Social Protest." *Signs* 20.1 (1994): 106–36.

————. "Edo Riots." In *Edo and Paris: Urban Life and the State in the Early Modern Era*, edited by James L. McClain, John M. Merriman, and Ugawa Kaoru, 407–28. Ithaca: Cornell University Press, 1994.

Wang, Zheng. *Women in the Chinese Enlightenment: Oral and Textual Histories*. Berkeley: University of California Press, 1999.

Warburton, Penny. "Theorising Public Opinion: Elizabeth Hamilton's Model of Self, Sympathy, and Society." In *Women, Writing, and the Public Sphere, 1700–1830*, edited by Elizabeth Eger, Charlotte Grant, Cliona O Gallchoir, and Penny Warburton, 257–73. Cambridge: Cambridge University Press, 2006.

Watanabe Masao 渡辺正雄 and Enomoto Emiko 榎本恵美子, trans. *Kai to jūjika: Shinkaronja senkyōshi J. T. Gyurikku no shōgai* 貝と十字架—進化論者宣教師J・T・ギュリックの生涯 (The shellfish and the cross: The life of J. T. Gulick, evolutionist and missionary man). Yūshōdō Shuppan, 1988.

Watase Masakatsu 渡瀬昌勝, ed. *Watase Torajirōden* 渡瀬寅次郎傳 (The biography of Watase Torajirō). Watase Dōzoku, 1934.

Whitney, Clara ホイットニー・クララ. *Clara no Meiji nikki* クララの明治日記 (Clara's Meiji diary). 2 vols. Kodansha, 1976.

Yamada Yūsaku 山田有策. *"Iratsume" kaidai, sōmokuji, sakuin* 「以良都女」解題・総目次・索引 (*Iratsume*: Introduction, table of contents, index). Fuji Shuppan, 1983.

Yamaguchi Reiko 山口玲子. *Naite aisuru shimai ni tsugu: Kozai Shikin no shōgai* 泣いて愛する姉妹に告ぐ.古在紫琴の生涯 (To my beloved sisters in tears: The life of Kozai Shikin). Sōdo bunka, 1977.

Yamakawa Kikue 山川菊栄. *Nihon fujin undō shōshi* 日本婦人運動小史 (A short history of the Japanese women's movement). Daiwa shobo, [1979] 1981.

———. *Onna nidai no ki* 女二代の記 (Two generations of women). Heibonsha, [1956] 1972.

Yamamoto Hideteru 山本秀煌, ed. *Ferris waei jogakkō rokujūnenshi* フェリス和英女学校六十年史 (Sixty years of Ferris waei jogakkō). Yokohama: Ferris waei jogakkō dōsōkai, 1931.

Yasutake, Rumi. "Men, Women, and Temperance in Meiji Japan: Engendering WCTU Activism from a Transnational Perspective." *Japanese Journal of American Studies* 17 (2006): 91–111.

———. "Transnational Women's Activism: The Woman's Christian Temperance Union in Japan and the United States." In *Women and Twentieth–Century Protestantism*, edited by Margaret Lamberts Bendroth and Virginia Lieson Brereton, 93–112. Champaign: University of Illinois Press, 2002.

Yokogawa Shūtō 横河秋壽. *Kaika no iriguchi* 開化乃入口 (Passage to enlightenment). Osaka: Matsumura bungaidō, 1874.

Yokohama kyōritsu gakuen 横浜共立学園. *Yokohama kyōritsu gakuen hyakunijūnen no ayumi* 横浜共立学園120年の歩み (One hundred and twenty years of Yokohama kyōritsu gakuen). Yokohama: Yokohama kyōritsu gakuen, 1991.

Yokota Fuyuhiko. "Imagining Working Women in Early Modern Japan." In *Women and Class in Japanese History*, edited by Hitomi Tonomura, Anne Walthall, and Wakita Haruko, 153–66. Michigan Monograph Series in Japanese Studies, no. 25. Ann Arbor: Center for Japanese Studies, University of Michigan, 1999.

Yoshimi Kaneko 吉見周子. *Fujin sansei ken* 婦人参政権 (Women's political rights). Kajima kenkyūjo shuppankai, 1971.

Yoshimura Akira 吉村昭. *Nihon ikaden* 日本医家伝 (Biographies of Japanese doctors). Kōdansha, 1971.

Yoshioka Yayoi 吉岡弥生. *Yoshioka Yayoi den* 吉岡弥生伝 (Yoshioka Yayoi's biography). Nihon tosho Center, [1967] 1998.

Yoshizumi Junzō 善積順蔵, ed. *Onna kyōkun yomeiri dōgu* 女教訓嫁入道具 (A dowry of moral lessons for brides-to-be). Osaka: Satō Shingi, 1880.

Yuasa Kōzō 湯浅興三, ed. *Yuasa Hatsuko* 湯浅初子 (Yuasa Hatsuko). Yuasa Tasuke, 1936.

Yuval–Davis, Nira. *Gender and Nation*. London: Sage Publications, 1997.

Yuval–Davis, Nira, and Flora Anthias. "Introduction." In *Woman–Nation–State*, edited by Nira Yuval–Davis and Flora Anthias, 1–15. New York: Macmillan, 1989.

Yuzawa Yasuhiko 湯沢雍彦, ed. *Nihon fujin mondai shiryō shūsei* 日本婦人問題資料集成 (Sources on the "woman's problem" in Japan). Vol. 5, *Kazoku Seido* 家族制度 (The family system). Domesu shuppan, 1976.

Zaeske, Susan. *Signatures of Citizenship: Petitioning, Antislavery, and Women's Political Identity*. Chapel Hill: University of North Carolina Press, 2003.

Zwicker, Jonathan. *Practices of the Sentimental Imagination: Melodrama, the Novel, and the Social Imaginary in Nineteenth–Century Japan*. Cambridge, Mass.: Harvard University Press, 2006.

Index

Abe Isoo, 61, 185
Addams, Jane, 190
Amos, Sheldon, 147
Anagol, Padma, 77
Anderson, Benedict, 19, 22
Anderson, Elizabeth Garrett, 148
Anthias, Flora, 21, 130
Aoyama gakuin, 53n66, 54
Asada Mikako, 43n31, 89
Asai Saku, 53, 53n66, 113, 119, 132
Ashio copper mine, 184–87
Atomi Kakei, 47, 47n45, 104

Baba Tatsui, 133n65
Bacon, Alice Mabel, 25–26, 66–67
Badran, Margot, 22
Baelz, Erwin, 189n48
Ballagh, John, 100
Beecher Stowe, Harriet, 181
Bentam, Jeremy, 144
Berry, John, 99
Berry, Mary Elizabeth, 17
Bickersteth, Edward, 82
Blair, Karen, 107
Boissonade, Gustave, 189n47
Brittain, Harriet, 94n81
Brown, Emily, 89
Browning, Elizabeth, 159
Browning, Robert, 103
Bunmeiron onna daigaku, 146

Carey, Otis, 93
Carrothers, Julia, 41, 53, 75, 84, 84n45
Cartmell, Martha J., 75
Catherine the Great (Catherine II), 159
Chatterjee, Partha, 178
Chichibu incident, 156, 156n42

Christian missions: American Board of Commissioners for Foreign Missions, 72n3, 76n16; American Methodist Episcopal Mission, 75; American Mission Board, 99; American Reformed Church, 73; Church Mission Society, 72n3, 73, 77; Ladies' Committee of the London Missionary Society, 74; Methodist Episcopal Church, 79n27, 85n48; Methodist Protestant Church, 79n28, 94n81; Paris Foreign Mission Society, 73n6; Presbyterian mission, 53, 73, 79n28, 94, 112, 112n14; Society for Promoting Female Education in China, India, and the East, 73n6, 74; Society for the Propagation of the Gospel, 72n3; Soeurs de l'Enfant-Jesus, 73n6; Woman's Foreign Missionary Society of the Methodist Episcopal Church, 85n50, 87n56; Woman's Missionary Society of the Canadian Methodist Church of Canada, 75, 79; Woman's Union Missionary Society of America for Heathen Lands, 73n6, 79, 80n29; Yokohama Congregational Church, 95n84
Cimino Folliero De Luna, Aurelia, 148
Civil Code, 12, 127, 129–30
Clark, William Smith, 28
Cobbe, Frances Power, 148
Cochran, George, 55
Colley, Linda, 31
concubines (*see also* prostitution), 125–28, 127n49, 128n51, 128n53, 132, 153, 175
Copeland, Rebecca, 2, 23

Cott, Nancy, 29–31, 62
Crosby, Julia, 80

Daigaku nankō, 53n65
Daniels, Gordon, 3
danjo dōken (parity of rights between
    men and women), 47, 120, 142, 152,
    157n44, 158–59
Danjo dōkenron, 147
danshi shakai, 158–60
danson johi, 63, 66, 110, 168
(Madame) De Staël (Anne Louise
    Germaine de Staël-Holstein), 159
Deck, Amy Catherine, 91–92, 92n74
*Difference of Sex as a Topic of
    Jurisprudence and Legislation,*
    147
Doi Kōka, 146, 146n15
Dōjinsha, 27, 59, 110n9
Doremus, Sarah, 80n29
Dōshisha, 54, 95, 99
Dudley, Julia, 76n16, 80n33

Ebina Danjō, 51
Ebina Miyako, 51, 54, 76, 88, 112n14,
    115, 133
Eger, Elizabeth, 135
Eigo kōshūkai, 94
Eliot, George, 115
Enchi Fumiko, 132n63
Enomoto Takeaki, 66
*Essays and Lectures on Social and
    Political Subjects,* 148
Etō Hide, 118

Fawcett, Henry, 148
Fawcett, Millicent Garrett, 120, 148,
    148n20, 157, 159, 161,
feminism, 22–23; domestic feminism,
    107, 113, 121–22, 143
foreign schools: Boston Normal School
    of Gymnastics, 54; Carleton College,
    56, 118; Elmira College, 126; Mount
    Holyoke College, 43n30, 56, 89n65,
    95, 95n84, 96, 96n86, 180, 180n17;
    Newnham College, Cambridge, 52,
    55; Northfield University, 84n45;
    Northwestern University, 96; Oxford

University, 84n45; Radcliffe College,
    96; Saint Thomas Hospital Medical
    School, 98; Salem Normal School, 55;
    Syracuse University, 126n46;
    University of Chicago, 190;
    University of Pennsylvania, 96;
    Wellesley College, 55–56; Western
    Maryland College, 94; Wilson
    College, 56, 96
Foucault, Michel, 16
Fraser, Mary Crawford, 129
Fraser, Nancy, 10
Fuess, Harald, 125n44
Fujii Tsunenosuke, 156n43
Fujii Yoshiko, 156n43, 156n45
Fujin enzetsu shinan, 121
Fujin genron no jiyū, 115
Fujinkai. See women's groups
Fujin risshi den, 182n23
Fujin risshi hen, 181
Fujin shakai, 92–93, 113n16, 159–60, 168,
    170
Fujita Tōko, 56
Fujita Yukiko, 56
Fujitani, Takashi, 18–19, 123, 125
Fujo hōritsuron, 147
Fujo kagami, 52
Fujo no kagami, 52
Fukamauchi Motoi, 147, 154n38
Fukuba Bisei, 50
Fukuda Hideko/Kageyama Hideko, 45n35,
    112, 143, 143n4, 151–52, 152n31, 153,
    156, 157n44, 158, 158n47, 163, 164–
    65, 176, 179, 181n21
Fukuoka Teruko, 56, 120–21
Fukuzawa Yukichi, 15, 15n34, 37n10, 41,
    50, 58n82, 63, 81, 83, 121, 128n53,
    134n68, 153–54, 183
Furuki Yoshiko, 178

Gakumon no susume, 41, 50, 153–54
Gakunōsha nōgakkō, 59
Gakusei, 40–41, 49
Garon, Sheldon, 131n61
Gauntlett, George Edward, 87
Gauntlett (Yamada) Tsuneko, 87, 88n58,
    90
Genrōin, 127

girl students: criticism of, 24–25, 43, 47–
48, 64–68, 83–85, 102; percentage
frequenting schools, 5–6, 34, 36;
petitions, 61–62, 69–70
girls in the silk-reeling and cotton-
spinning mills, 20, 26; strikes, 26
girls' schools: A-rokuban jogakkō, 84n45,
94; Akita prefecture joshi shihan
gakkō, 45, 54; American Mission
Home/Kyōritsu jogakkō, 53, 62, 73n6,
80, 81, 102, 115, 126n46; Aoyama
jogakuin/Joshi shogakkō/Kaigan
jogakkō, 54, 75, 75n13, 102, 119, 184;
Atomi jogakkō, 47, 102; B-rokuban
jogakkō/Shinsakae jogakkō, 76n18,
84n45; Baika jogakkō, 180, 180n17;
Bara jogakkō, 94; Bishop Poole Girls'
School, 74; Brittain jogakkō/
Yokohama eiwa jogakkō, 94, 94n81;
Chiba joshi shihan gakkō, 44; Chōei
jojuku, 53; Doremus school, 96;
Dōshisha jogakkō/Kyoto Home, 54,
54n69, 76, 76n17, 76n18, 85, 88; Eisei
jogakkō, 82; Ferris jogakkō/Ferris
jogakuin, 60, 73, 73n5, 82n40, 90,
94n81, 95, 101–3, 110n9, 118, 124;
Fujin eigakusha, 153, 153n34;
Hakodate joshi shihan gakkō, 53;
Hara jogakkō, 84n45; Hiroshima eiwa
jogakkō, 55; Iai jogakkō, 94; Jokō
gakkō, 189, 189n51; Jōkō gakusha,
151–53, 152n31; Joshi bijutsu gakkō,
84n45; Joshi dokuritsu gakkō, 79n28,
102; Joshi eigaku juku, 178, 189;
Joshi gakuin, 43n31, 79n28, 83,
84n45, 87–88, 90, 94, 112n14, 124;
Kagoshima joshi shihan gakkō, 56;
Kaitakushi jogakkō, 36, 36n8;
Kazoku jogakkō, 25, 47n44, 52, 109–
10, 184, 189, 189n51, 190; Kirisuto
jogakkō, 119; Kobe eiwa jogakkō/
Kobe jogakuin, 55, 62, 76, 76n16,
80n33, 85, 89, 93, 93n78, 94–96,
96n86, 118; Kobe jogakkō, 61,
153n34; Kōchi eiwa jogakkō, 168n80;
Kōchi jinjō chūgakkō joshibu,
165n68; Kōchi shihan gakkō joshibu,
165, 165n68; Kojo gakuin, 190; Kōtō

joshi jisshū gakkō, 43; Kumamoto
jogakkō, 112n14; Kyōritsu joshi
shokugyō gakkō, 42n26, 56; Kyoto-fu
jogakkō, 186; Kyoto kanbyōfu gakkō,
99; Kyoto jogakkō, 109n5; Kwassui
jogakkō, 79n27; Maebashi eiwa
jogakkō, 94; Meiji jogakkō, 58, 58n81,
59, 59n84, 61, 90, 94n81, 102, 117n23,
119, 181–82, 182n26; Osaka jogakuin,
53, 119; Rikkyō jogakkō, 89, 102,
190; Sakurai jogakkō, 53, 82–83, 87–
88, 90, 115, 119, 126, 131n60; —and
school for nurses, 100–101, 100n102,
112n14; San'yō eiwa jogakkō, 92, 95,
96n86, 153n35, 180, 180n17; Seiritsu
gakusha joshibu, 78, 102; Shinsakae
jogakkō, 56, 84n45, 88, 102, Shizuoka
eiwa jogakkō, 80n33, 112n14, 118,
Shōei jogakkō, 61; Sokkihō joshi
kenkyūkai, 182; Sumisu jogakkō,
127n50; Takada jogakkō, 84n45, 94;
Takebashi jogakkō/Tokyo jogakkō,
41–42, 42n25, 47, 47n44, 54–55, 188;
Tokushima joshi shihan gakkō, 46;
Tokyo jogakukan, 82; Tokyo joi
gakkō, 49, 178; Tokyo joshi senmon
gakkō, 61; Tokyo joshi shihan gakkō,
27, 42, 42n25, 42n28, 45–46, 47n44,
49n52, 50–51, 53, 55, 56, 58, 94, 98,
109n5, 114; Tokyo kōtō jogakkō,
49n52, 51, 51n61, 65–68, 102; Tokyo
kōtō shihan gakkō joshibu, 54–55, 59,
95, 184; Tottori eiwa jogakkō,
120n32, 186; Tottori jogakkō, 120n32;
Tottori joshi shihan gakkō, 120n32;
Tōyō eiwa jogakkō, 76n81, 79, 79n26,
79n28, 80n33, 89, 89n63, 91, 102,
110n8; Ueda jogakkō/Mannenbashi
jogakkō, 41; Yamanashi eiwa
jogakkō, 80n33
Gluck, Carol, 16, 21
Gonda, Caroline, 23, 26
good wives, wise mothers. See *ryōsai
kenbo*
Gotō Shōjirō, 144
Grant, Ulysses S., 188
Griffis, Margaret Clark, 41, 42n24
Gulick, Orramel, 95n84

Habermas, Jürgen, 9–12, 22, 29
Haggis, Jane, 71, 74
hakama, 39, 47, 47n44, 48, 50
Hakuaisha, 98
Hani Motoko, 48, 50–51, 59, 86
Hara Kei, 130
Hara Taneaki, 84n45
Harada Ryōko, 94n81
Harada Yoshiko, 108n4
Hastings, Sally, 2, 28, 177
Hatoyama Haruko, 6n14, 42, 42n26, 45, 56, 177–78
Hayashi Sadako, 90–91
Hayashi Utako, 88
Hegel, Georg Wilhelm Friedrich, 95
Heiminsha, 176–77, 184, 186
Hepburn, Clara, 73
Hepburn, James Curtis, 42, 73–74, 85, 98
Hepburn Juku, 73
Hirano Tō, 97
Hirata Toshiko, 95, 95n84
Hirose Tsuneko, 58n82, 94, 94n81
Hirota Masaki, 3n6
Hirotsu Ryūrō, 162
Hoar, Alice, 81, 84n47
Hōeisha, 53, 53n65
Holbrook, Mariana, 62, 95–96, 96n86
Honda Masuko, 47n44
Honda Yōitsu, 53n66
Hoshino Tenchi, 102
Hutchinson, Lucy, 181

Ienaga Toyokichi, 184
Ignatieff, Michael, 22
Ikuta Minoru, 56
Imperial House Law, 125n43
Inokuchi Aguri, 45, 54
Inoue Nao, 20n52, 61, 63
Inoue Takeko, 98n96
Inoue Tsutomu, 147n16
International Convention of the General Federation of Women's Clubs, 190
Ishiguro Kan'ichirō, 93
Ishiguro Obi, 151
Ishii Fudeko, 26, 57, 109, 110n8, 119, 184, 187–93
Ishii Jūji, 61, 153, 153n35

Ishii Ryōichi, 190–91
Itagaki Taisuke, 143, 144, 151
Itō Hirobumi, 125n43, 133n66
Itō Tetsu, 99
Itō Umeko, 98n96, 133n66
Iwakura mission, 25, 36, 41, 55, 57, 68n108
Iwamoto Yoshiharu, 52n63, 59–60, 65n100, 102, 112–13, 115, 117, 130, 180–81, 183, 185
Izumi Shikibu, 159

Janes, Leroy, 51, 83
Jiaikan, 132, 179
Jinsetsusha, 145
Jishūkai, 103
Jiyū minken undō, 141–42, 145–47, 149–50, 152n31, 154–58, 156n42, 166, 168n80, 176
Jiyūtō, 136, 146, 151–52, 154–56, 162, 164, 181
Joan of Arc, 152
Jogaku enzetsukai, 112, 115, 117
Jogaku enzetsushū, 120, 133
Jogaku zasshisha, 102, 112, 115, 182n26
joken (women's rights), 30, 117, 142–43, 168
Joken shinron, 147n16
Joshi dokuritsu enzetsu hikki, 56, 120
Joshi eigo yomihon, 56
Joshi jiyūkan, 154
Juntendō iin, 98

Kageyama Hideko. *See* Fukuda Hideko
Kageyama Umeko, 153–54
Kaishintō, 161
Kajiro Yoshi, 180, 180n17
Kakumeisha, 147, 154n38
Kaltzoff-Massalsky, Helene, 148
Kameyama Michiko, 98
Kanbyō no kokoroe, 97n91
Kaneko Tō, 155
Kanemori Kohisa, 93, 93n78, 95
Kanezaki Shigeki, 148n20
Kangofu kyōikusho, 98, 98n96
Katō Hiroyuki, 57–58, 102, 110n8
Katō (Takeda) Kinko, 55, 55n73, 57
Kawachiyama Tora, 44

Kawaguchi Kumoi, 181
Kawamoto Sō, 117n23
Kawamura Haruko, 98n96
Keiō gijuku, 81, 98, 133n65, 147
Keizaigaku, 148n20
Keizaigaku kaitei, 148n20
Keizairon mondai shū, 148n20
Kelly, Gary, 25n65
Kelsey, Adaline, 115, 115n21, 133
Kenri teikō, 143, 146
Kidder, Mary, 73, 73n5, 80, 80n33
Kim, Kyu Hyun, 11, 17, 18n45, 21, 143
Kimura Eiko/Akebono, 51–52, 57
Kimura Hideko, 61
Kimura Hisaeko, 61
Kimura Kumaji, 58n81, 59, 117n23
Kimura Matsuko, 61
Kimura Sadako, 109, 110n8
Kimura Seikō, 61
Kimura Tōko, 58n81, 117n23
Kinoshita Misaoko, 185
Kinoshita Naoe, 145, 184–86
Kishida Toshiko, 73, 84n45, 112, 142–43,
    150, 150n26, 151–53, 159, 165, 179,
    181, 193
Kiyoura Keigo, 141
Kobayashi Eiko, 46
Kobayashi Kusuo, 152
Kobayashi Tei, 152
Kōdoku chōsa yūshikai, 185
Kōga Fuji, 55, 95
Kornicki, Peter, 4, 46
Kōsairon, 61, 61n91
Kōsaka Torako, 61
Koware yubiwa, 178
Kozaki Chiyoko, 38
Kozaki Hiromichi, 38
Krummel, John, 79n28, 94n81
Kuki Takayoshi, 80n33
Kuroda Kiyotaka, 36
Kusunose Kita, 24, 144
Kuwabara Nobutake, 56
Kyōgaku taishi, 50
Kyōiku rei, 49–51

Laird, M. A., 78n23
Lanman, Adeline, 98n96
late Mrs. West's teachings, The, 182

Law on Assembly and Political
    Associations/Shūkai oyobi seisha hō,
    31, 136, 136n70, 150
Leavitt, Mary, 64, 112, 114, 116–19,
    117n23, 122–23
Leete, Isabelle, 86, 86n55, 87
Lerner, Gerda, 32n78
Liberal Party. *See* Jiyūtō
London Naval Conference, 118
Longfellow, Henry Wadsworth, 184
Lyon, Mary, 92–93

Mackie, Vera, 12–13, 129–30, 176
magazines. *See* print media
Makino Kiyoko, 109n5
male students' attendance, 6n13
Marsh, Belle, 72n2
Masuda Tsuru, 56
Matsue Tazuko, 56
Matsukata Masako, 98n96
Matsumoto Eiko, 184, 186–87
Matsumoto Man'nen, 45
Matsumoto Ogie, 45, 56
Matsuo Taseko, 8, 39
Matsushima Jū, 146
Matsushima Kō, 147n16
Matsuyama Tōan, 98
McLennan, Ida Augusta, 95–96, 96n86
Meiji Emperor, 123–25, 125n43, 137;
    Empress (Haruko, 1849–1914), 42,
    98–99, 98n96, 123–25, 123n38, 189
Meiji kōsetsuroku, 123n39
Meirin gakusha, 40n19, 50
Meirokusha, 14, 37n10, 125n43, 128, 135
Mihalopoulos, Bill, 179
Mill, John Stuart, 27n68, 144, 146–47,
    157, 161
Milliken, Miss, 87, 89, 103, 124
Mills, Sara, 16
Mineo Eiko, 100, 115, 126, 126n46
Minken jiyūron, 157
Mitani Tamiko, 83, 84n45, 88–89, 91, 103,
    185
Mitsukuri Shūhei, 37n10
Miwada Masako, 40n19, 50, 183, 185
Miyagawa Toshiko, 56
Miyake Kahō, 47n44, 64, 65n99, 82
Miyazaki Nobue, 187

Mizuno Mineko, 110n8
Mochizuki Kōzaburō, 93
Mogi Chieko, 54
Montgomery, Ellen Barrett, 77n19
More, Hannah, 181
Mori Arinori, 33, 37, 58n83, 66, 70, 89,
 103, 128n53
Mori Shizu, 96
Morooka Nobuko, 110n8
Movement for Freedom and Popular
 Rights. *See* Jiyū minken undō
Murakami Komao, 61
Murasaki no hitomoto, 184
Murasaki Shikibu, 159–60
Murasame Nobu, 155–56, 169
Murray, David, 37

Nagai Tsune, 57
Nagamine (Honda) Teiko, 53, 53n66, 113
Nagaoka Chikuko, 189
Nagaoka Moriyoshi, 189
Nagata Kensuke, 148n20
Nagata, Mary Louise, 127n49, 128n51
Nagi, Margit Maria, 130
Najmabadi, Afsaneh, 14
Nakagawa Yokotarō, 153, 180
Nakai Tatsu, 120, 120n32
Nakajima Nobuyuki, 84n45
Nakamura Masanao, 27–28, 37, 41, 46, 50,
 55, 59, 63, 81, 110n49, 181
Nakamura Shizuko, 180, 180n15
Narita Ume, 154, 154n38
Naruse Jinzō, 51n61
newspapers. *See* print media
Nightingale, Florence, 97n90, 181, 187–88
Nihon (Nippon) fujinron, 37n10, 63,
 121n33, 129n53, 134n68
Nihon fujin sanron, 61, 63
Niijima Jō, 54, 54n69, 99
Nishikawa Fumiko, 186
Nishikawa Sato, 155
Nishimaki Sakuya, 149, 150n25
Nishimura Shigeki, 52
Nobejiri Yasuko, 88, 91n72
Noguchi Yūka, 48, 49n52
Nolte, Sharon, 2
novels, 17, 30, 37, 59, 90–91, 132n63, 178,
 184; political, 160–63; —*Bunmei no
 hana: Joken bidan,* 161; —*Joshi*

sansei shinchūrō, 162–63;
 —*Nijūsannen mugen no kane,* 161,
 163, 166; —*Sen'enjō,* 162–63;
 —*Setchūbai,* 162–63

Ōe Sumi, 89, 89n63, 90
Ōe Taku, 80n33
Ogashima Hatasu, 188, 188n46, 189
Ogawa Manako, 179
Ogino Ginko, 45, 58–59, 58n82, 60, 101,
 119, 127, 136, 183
Ōi Kentarō, 164
Okada Masamichi, 151
Okada Yaeko, 151
Okami Keiko, 55
Okumura Ioko, 177
Okumura Kisaburō, 35, 39
Ōnishi Kinu, 93, 180
Onna daigaku, 27, 37, 94, 146
Onna no michi, 109, 114, 174
Onnazaka, 132n63
Onoda Inokichi, 93
Ordinance on Public Assembly/Shūkai
 jōrei, 31, 136n70, 150
Ōshima (Ibuka) Hanako, 43, 43n30, 89,
 89n65, 95, 96n86
Oshioi Kyōko, 153n34
Otis, Carey, 93
Ozaki Kōyō, 127
Ozaki Yukio, 143, 146
Ozawa Saki, 120n32
Ōzawa Toyoko, 180, 182–84
Ōzeki Chikako, 100, 101n104, 181

parity of rights. See *danjo dōken*
Parke, Mary, 84n45
Peiss, Kathy, 8, 48
Penal Code, 128
Pfeiffer, Ida, 181
Pierson, Louise, 80, 86–87
Platt, H. L., 79n26, 79n28
Political Economy for Beginners, 148n20
Prince, Isabella, 66n103
print media: legislations, 11, 18n46,
 114n17, 144; newspapers: —*Chōya
 shinbun,* 47–48, 149, 162; —*Doyō
 shinbun,* 149, 158, 162, 165–67;
 —*Hōchi shinbun,* 165; —*Jiji shinpō,*
 128, 128n53, 134n68, 183; —*Kōeki*

mondō shinbun, 47; —*Kokumin shinbun*, 180, 183; —*Mainichi shinbun*, 184, 186; —*Okayama mainichi shinbun*, 151; —*Shinonome shinbun*, 111; —*Tokyo eiri shinbun*, 162; —*Tokyo Yokohama mainichi shinbun*, 48, 145; —*Yomiuri shinbun*, 52, 56, 65, 184; periodicals: —*Dai nihon fujin kyōikukai zasshi*, 191; —*Fujin eiseikai zasshi*, 101, 183; —*(Tokyo) Fujin kyōfū zasshi/ Fujin shinpō*, 113, 113n16, 114n17, 133n65, 134, 176, 182; —*Fujo shinbun*, 131; —*Haishō*, 119, 132; —*Iratsume*, 49; —*Japan Gazette*, 65; —*Japan Weekly Mail*, 66; —*Jogaku zasshi*, 49, 49n53, 55-61, 64, 91–92, 97n90, 102–3, 111–12, 115–16, 120, 124, 126, 131, 176, 180, 182n26, 190; —*Jogakusei*, 102–3; —*Joken*, 156, 157n45; —*Joken no sakigake*, 165; —*Kosodate no sōshi*, 38; —*Kuni no motoi*, 65–66, 102, 168n82; —*Kyōiku jiron*, 67; —*Meiroku zasshi*, 128; —*Nihon no jogaku*, 113n16; —*Nijūseki no fujin*, 176; —*Sekai fujin*, 157n44, 176; —*Shinbun zasshi*, 47; —*Tokyo keizai zasshi*, 113n16
prosopography, 5–7
prostitution, 25, 128n52, 130, 130n58, 131, 131n61, 133, 133n65, 153–54, 158; *Karayuki-san*, 179; Maria Luz incident, 130n5. *See also* concubines
Pruyn, Mary, 80
Public Peace Police Law/Chian keisatsu hō, 176

Reade, Mary, 98n96
Red Cross, 98
Richards, Ellen, 107
Richards, Linda, 99, 100n99
Rikkyō daigakkō, 190
Risshi gakusha, 144, 147
Risshisha, 144
Roberts, Luke, 70n110
Rokumeikan, 24n63, 26, 26n67, 47n44, 67, 98, 133, 133n66
Roland (Jeanne-Marie Roland de la Platière), 159

Rousseau, Jean-Jacques, 157
Rowbotham, Judith, 77n19
Russell, Bertrand, 144
ryōsai kenbo (good wives, wise mothers), 3n6, 27–30, 33, 64, 69, 102, 108, 136, 155–56, 176

Saigoku fujin risshi hen, 148
Saigoku risshi hen, 41, 181
Saitō Saneaki, 52
Saitō Tsune, 53n65
Sakamoto Naohiro, 164
Sakata Shizuko, 47
Sakatani Shiroshi, 14, 125
Sakuma Shōzan, 60
Sakuragawa Rii, 100
Sakurai Akinori, 52–53
Sakurai Chika, 52–53, 53n66, 118–19
Sakurai Fukiko, 182n23
Sakurai Mineko, 126n46
Sand, George, 115
Sano Tsunetami, 98
Sano Umeko, 88, 88n61, 101
Sasaki Teiko, 98n96
Sasaki Toyoju, 12, 46, 73, 110, 110n9, 113, 115, 131n60, 133–34, 136, 156, 167–68, 179, 183
Satō Takanaka, 98
Satō Tetsuko, 82n40
Scheiner, Irwin, 81
Schoonmaker, Dora, 75, 75n13
Sei Shōnagon, 159
Seiyō jijō, 153–54
Sekiguchi Sumiko, 143, 161
Self Help, 41, 50, 181
Sendai joshi jiyūtō, 154
Shakai heikenron, 147n16
Shakespeare, 95
Shakry, Omnia, 20
Shibuya Zōji, 148n21
Shidachi Taki, 83
Shimada Nobuko, 185
Shimada Saburō, 127, 131, 179, 184–85
shimai (sisters), 30, 93, 160, 166–67, 174, 186, 193
Shimizu Shikin/Toyoko, 127, 136n71, 158, 165, 168, 168n80, 168n82, 178, 180
Shimoda Utako, 57, 181, 183
Sievers, Sharon, 176

Smiles, Samuel, 41, 50, 181
Smith, Linda, 85n50
Social Statics, 143, 146, 147n16, 158–59, 163
Soejima Taneomi, 144
Sōma Kokkō, 163
Somerville, Mary, 159, 181
Spencer, Eliza, 76n18
Spencer, Herbert, 27n68, 143, 146, 147n16, 157–59, 163
Stanton, Theodore, 147
Starkweather, Alice, 76, 76n17, 76n18, 85
Stone, Cora, 96, 96n86
Stone, Lawrence, 5
Subjection of Women, The, 147
Suehiro Tetchō, 162
Sugano Noriko, 35n6
Sugimoto Etsuko, 1n1, 83, 83n42, 90
Sugimoto Kaneko, 98
Sugiyama Tōjirō, 161
Sumida Yorinosuke, 148
Sumiya Koume, 152–53, 153n35, 154, 180
Suzuki Masako, 101, 181, 183
Suzuki Mitsu, 115
Suzuki Yoshimune, 147

Tachi Kaoru, 5
Taguchi Ukichi, 114
Takagi Kanehiro, 98
Takekoshi Takeyo, 113, 114n17, 136, 180–84, 181n21
Takekoshi Yosaburō, 180
Takeuchi Hisako, 151
Takezaki Junko, 112n14
Takinogawa gakuen, 187, 190
Talcott, Eliza, 76, 76n16, 80n33
Tales in political economy, 148n20
Tamura Eiko, 88, 90, 92
Tamura Naoomi, 81, 126–27, 134–35, 186
Tanahashi Ayako, 46, 109
Tanaka Shōzō, 185
Tanioka Teiko, 87
Tapson, Minna, 77, 82n39
Tazawa Shizutarō, 148n20
Telford, Caroline, 92, 96, 96n86
Tennyson, Lord Alfred, 103
Tōa igakkō, 61
Toda Mosui, 184

Togawako Shikako, 61
Tokutomi Hisako, 112n14, 119, 136
Tokutomi Sōhō, 112n14, 115
Tokuza, Akiko, 3
Tokyo Imperial University, 57–58, 61–62, 100–101, 110, 110n8, 133
Tokyo jikei iin, 97–99, 191
Tomida, Hiroko, 3
Tomii Tora, 58n81, 156
Tominaga Raku, 165
Tottori fujinkai enzetsu hikki, 120
Tōyō no fujo, 167–68, 193
Toyoda Fuyuko, 46, 56–57, 57n79, 181
Toyoda Kotarō, 56
Toyoda Tenko, 56
Tristram, Katherine, 74, 82n39
True, Maria, 53n66, 94, 100, 102, 115
Tsuda Mamichi, 14, 130n58
Tsuda Sen, 59, 75n13, 127
Tsuda Umeko, 24, 24n63, 26, 55, 58n81, 98n96, 178, 184, 189, 189n50, 190
Tsuge Kumeko, 151
Tsukamoto Fujiko, 56, 96
Tsukuda Yojirō, 182, 182n26, 183n28
Tsurumi, Patricia, 2, 20, 26

Uchimura Gijo, 161
Ueda Sadako, 41
Ueda Shun, 41
Ueki Emori, 12, 127, 131, 156–60, 164–65, 167–68, 193
Uemori Misao, 151
Uemura Kikuko, 185
Ukita Fuku, 118
Ushioda Chiseko, 131, 131n60, 132n64, 136, 183, 185, 185n35, 186

Vetch, Agnes, 101

Wakakuwa Midori, 52, 125
Wakamatsu Shizuko, 52, 60, 73, 103, 103n107, 113, 118, 124–26, 132, 188, 191n53
Walthall, Anne, 8, 34, 169
Wang, Zheng, 117
Watanabe Junki, 164
Watanabe Kiyoshi, 188
Watanabe Tsuneko, 56, 117n23, 118

Watase Kame, 94, 118
West, Mary Allen, 182
Westlake, Alice, 149
Whitney, Clara, 123, 123n39, 188, 188n46
Wilson, Horace, 53n65
Wollstonecraft, Mary, 14n33
Woman Question in Europe, The, 147
women's groups (ladies' associations):
Aikō fujo kyōkai, 155–56; Aikoku
fujinkai, 42n26, 177, 177n6; Dai
nihon fujin bunshō kairyōkai, 111;
Dai nihon fujin eiseikai, 101, 183; Dai
nihon fujin kyōikukai, 57, 86, 110,
119, 189–90; Echigo Nagaoka joshi
shinbokukai, 109n5; En'yō fujo
jiyūtō, 149; Fujin daikonshinkai, 164;
Fujin jizenkai, 24n63, 98; Fujin
kōdankai, 109; Fujin kōsaikai, 109n6,
164; Fujin shinbokukai, 164; Fujin
shōfūkai, 165, 165n68; Fujin
tokugikai, 156–57; Fukuoka fujin
kyōkai, 109, 114; Jofū kairyōkai,
165n68; Joshi danwakai, 181n21;
Joshi kōsaikai, 109n6; Joshi
kyōfūkai, 165, 165n68; Kangofukai,
101n104; Kochi fujinkai, 164–67;
Kōdokuchi kyūsai fujinkai, 185–87;
Nagaoka fujin kairyōkai, 165;
Okayama joshi konshinkai, 151–52,
154; Ōkikai, 109n5, Osaka fujin
gakushūkai, 111; Seitōsha, 175–76;
Sendai joshi jiyutō, 154; Shukujo
ibunkai, 108n4; Tamamo joshi
konshinkai, 165; Tokyo (Nihon) Fujin
kyōfūkai/ Kyōfūkai, 10, 38, 53,
79n27, 84n45, 87, 89, 95, 101n104,
110, 112–13, 115–19, 117n23, 117n24,
122–26, 131, 131n60, 132, 134–35,
142, 150–51, 165n68, 167–68, 170,
179–80, 180n15, 185, 190; Tokyo
fujin kyōiku danwakai, 109; Tottori

fujinkai, 120; Toyohashi fujo kyōkai,
155–56; Woman's Christian
Temperance Union, 64, 112, 115–16,
182; Zenkoku haishō dōmeikai, 132

Yabu no uguisu, 64, 65n99
Yajima Kajiko, 44n35, 90, 100n102, 105,
112, 112n14, 113n15, 114, 114n17,
117n24, 119, 123–27, 136, 185
Yamada Hisako, 187
Yamaji Taneko, 114n17
Yamakawa Chise, 41
Yamakawa Kikue, 28, 41
Yamakawa Sutematsu, 24, 24n63, 25, 55,
67, 98n96, 99
Yamamoto Kakuma, 54
Yamamoto Ken, 151
Yamamoto Mineko, 54
Yamamoto Uji, 151
Yamamoto Yaeko, 54n69
Yamawaki Fusako, 43, 185
Yamazaki Take, 112, 165–68
Yegashira Hideko, 92
Yokogawa Shūtō, 37
Yokoi Shōnan, 51, 84n45, 112n14
Yokoi Tamako, 84n45, 136
Yokoi Tokiharu, 84n45
Yokoi Tokio, 54
Yokoi Tsuseko, 112n14
Yoshida Shōin, 35
Yoshimatsu Masuko, 167–68, 168n80
Yoshioka Yayoi, 49–50, 58n82, 59, 150,
178
Youngman, Kate, 76n18, 84n45
Yuasa (Tokutomi) Hatsuko, 51, 88, 126,
128n52
Yūshi kyōritsu Tokyo byōin. *See* Tokyo
jikei iin
Yuval-Davis, Nira, 21, 130

Zaeske, Susan, 138

About the Author

MARA PATESSIO is Lecturer in Japanese History at the University of Manchester. In addition to publishing a number of articles in scholarly journals, she has edited (with P. F. Kornicki and G. G. Rowley) *The Female as Subject: Reading and Writing in Early Modern Japan* (Center for Japanese Studies, The University of Michigan, 2010). She is currently working on two separate projects. One deals with late Meiji women's writings and public activities, and the other one concentrates on the novelist, editor, and playwright Hasegawa Shigure's participation in Japanese cultural life during the late Meiji and Taisho periods.

1 Women and Public Life in Early M...   L01-1-13-029-001-1331

Marketplace: AmazonMarketplaceUS
Order Number: 4318112
Ship Method: Standard
Customer Name: asato ikeda
Order Date: 3/18/2020 3:49:31 PM
Marketplace Order #: 113-5266584-4933021
Email: b75g114zzx7xl1n@marketplace.amazon.com

If you have any questions or concerns regarding this order, please contact us at serviceohio@hpb.com